INT
RUSSIA'S
CAULDRON

AN AMERICAN VISION, UNDONE

**THE NEWLY REVEALED CENTURY–OLD
EYEWITNESS JOURNAL OF LEIGHTON W. ROGERS**

STEVEN FISHER

Forest Cat
PRODUCTIONS

Forest Cat Productions

Into Russia's Cauldron: An American Vision, Undone
All annotations and commentary
Copyright © 2021 by Steven Fisher

Photo credits:
The journal of Leighton William Rogers and accompanying photos (other than those specifically mentioned below and the photos of the SS Oscar II; International Women's Day march, Petrograd, 1917; and American soldiers parading in Vladivostok, 1918) are published under a license from Charlotte Roe.

Photo of H. Fessenden Meserve, HUD 313.25. Harvard University Archives. Image courtesy the Hathi Trust Digital Library. Photo of Robie Reed Stevens courtesy of the George J. Mitchell Department of Special Collections and Archives, Bowdoin College Library, Brunswick, Maine.

To contact Steven Fisher:
www.stevenfisherciti.com

ISBNs: 978-1-7377663-0-8 (Hardcover), 978-1-7377663-1-5 (Paperback), 978-1-7377663-2-2 (Ebook)

Library of Congress Cataloging-in-Publication Data

Names: Fisher, Steven A., author.
Title: Into Russia's cauldron : an American vision, undone : the newly revealed century-old eyewitness journal of Leighton W. Rogers / Steven Fisher.
Description: Chicago, IL : Forest Cat Productions, [2021] | Includes bibliography and index. Identifiers: ISBN: 978-1-7377663-0-8 (hardcover) | 978-1-7377663-1-5 (paperback) | 978-1-7377663-2-2 (ebook) | LCCN: 2021918606
Subjects: LCSH: Rogers, Leighton W. (Leighton William), 1893-1962. | Saint Petersburg (Russia)-History--Revolution, 1917-1921--Personal narratives. | Soviet Union--History--Revolution, 1917-1921--Personal narratives. | Bankers--Biography. | National City Bank of New York-History. | Citibank (New York, N.Y.)--History. | Banks and banking--Russia--Saint Petersburg. | Russia--Social life and customs. | Soviet Union--Social life and customs. | United States-Commerce--Russia. | United State--Commerce--Soviet Union.

Classification: LCC: DK268.R64 F57 2021 | DDC: 947.084/2092--dc23

Printed in the United States of America

For everyone with a passionate interest
in a mysterious land called Russia.

CONTENTS

ILLUSTRATIONS

Leighton W. Rogers

Leighton Rogers in the US Army, 1918

Leighton Rogers at the house of English publisher Grant Richards at Marlow-on-the-Thames, 1924

H. Fessenden Meserve

Robie Reed Stevens

The 1916 College Class (National City Bank summer training program)

Frank A. Vanderlip "and his boys." Summer, 1916

The SS *Oscar II* in New York

Babcock, Rogers, Swinnerton, and Stuart at the Grand Hotel, Stockholm, October 13, 1916

National City Bank Petrograd branch staff, 1917

National City Bank Petrograd branch building on Palace Embankment no. 8

Nevsky Prospekt

St. Isaac's Cathedral

International Women's Day march, Petrograd, 1917

American soldiers parading in Vladivostok, 1918

Leighton Rogers' 1916 passport photo introduces each chapter in his journal

AUTHOR'S NOTE

The journal of Leighton W. Rogers comprises over two hundred frail yellowed handwritten pages, safe-kept in the Library of Congress. Rogers started his journal in September 1916 and stopped in April 1918, only to add a short epilogue in April 1919. I meticulously transcribed and annotated Rogers' original work for this book.

The journal's grammar and punctuation, including Rogers' penchant for dashes and semicolons, remain intact except in passages where verbatim transcription served no purpose and might be confusing or simply seem like an error. I kept Rogers' spelling of places and people's names, inside and outside of Russia, and footnoted where Rogers' spelling of a particular name or place differed from accepted modern spellings. I used the spelling "tsar" throughout the book and not Rogers' "tzar." I did not standardize his pell-mell word capitalization or journal dating, which I judged would cause little confusion for the reader. One word in Rogers' journal (of a total 112,796 words) was indecipherable, which I bracketed with a question mark. I corrected and noted the few cases of obvious spelling or contextual errors. When Rogers used words (or slang) in the English language that have passed out of usage, I footnoted the meaning. Rogers' fascinating story contains the names of many places, personages, and notable events of his time that are long gone, forgotten, or otherwise not familiar to the twenty-first-century reader. Historical annotations throughout provide explanatory details. I kept the original text and word capitalization of the secondary sources cited in this book.

Rogers sometimes concealed names with abbreviations (e.g., Mr. S_____) but mentioned the full name in other places in his diary. Where not, I researched the abbreviated name and provided the full name in a footnote.

During his time in Russia, Rogers usually dated his journal entries in both the Russian Julian (old style) calendar, which the West abandoned in the sixteenth century, and the Western Gregorian (new style) calendar. The Julian calendar falls thirteen days behind the latter calendar, i.e., January 1 on the Julian calendar is January 14 on the Gregorian. The Gregorian calendar rules absent of twin dating. The Soviet government adopted the Gregorian calendar on February 14, 1918, and there is no split dating afterward. The timeline in this book uses the Gregorian calendar.

The city of St. Petersburg has experienced several name changes in its history. Originally named Sankt-Peterburg, it became Petrograd, meaning in Russian "Peter's city," in 1914 after World War I broke out so that the city's name did not sound German. The Soviets renamed it Leningrad in 1924, after the death of Lenin in that year. The city's name reverted to St. Petersburg in 1991, after the fall of the Soviet Union.

The National City Bank of New York has also changed its name a few times. It merged with First National Bank in 1955 and became The First National City Bank of New York. In 1962, it shortened its moniker to First National City Bank. In 1976, First National City Bank renamed itself "Citibank." We also know Citibank today as "Citi."

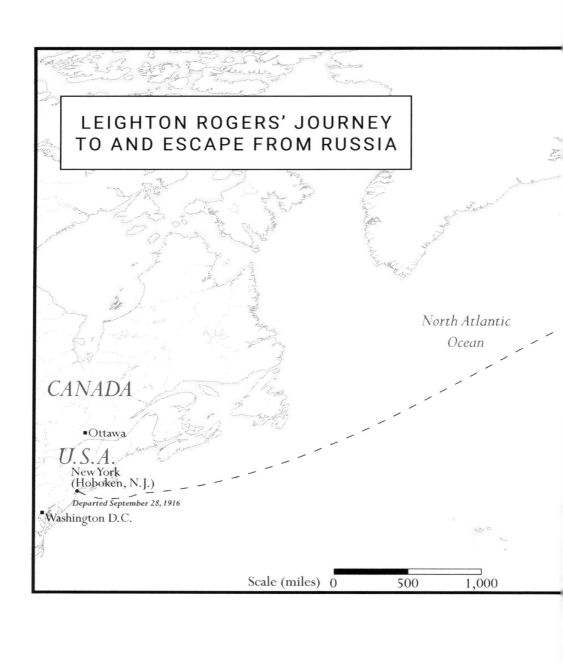

LEIGHTON ROGERS' JOURNEY
TO AND ESCAPE FROM RUSSIA

North Atlantic
Ocean

CANADA

▪Ottawa

U.S.A.
New York
(Hoboken, N.J.)

Departed September 28, 1916

▪Washington D.C.

Scale (miles)　0　　　500　　　1,000

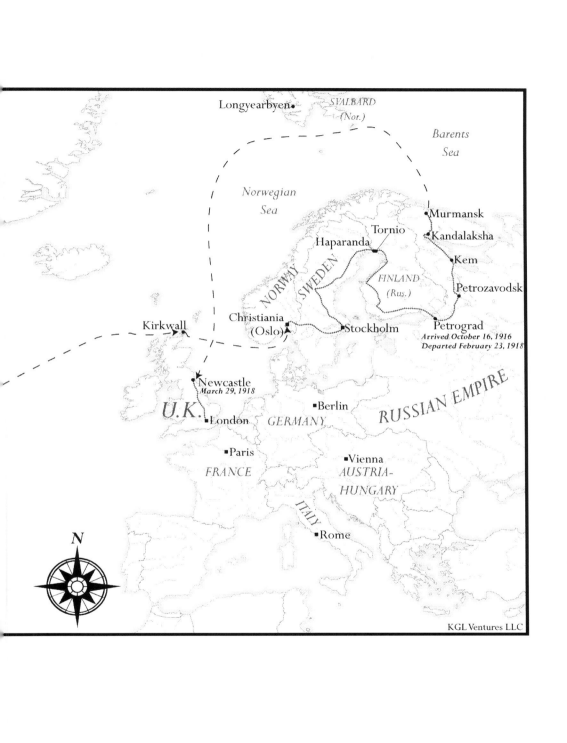

Longyearbyen• *SVALBARD*
                    (Nor.)

                                        Barents
                                          Sea

          Norwegian
            Sea   •Murmansk
                          Tornio   •Kandalaksha
                    Haparanda
                                                •Kem
                                            •Petrozavodsk
                              FINLAND
                               (Rus.)
          Christiania   Petrograd
    Kirkwall (Oslo)   •Stockholm   *Arrived October 16, 1916*
                                          Departed February 23, 1918

          Newcastle
          March 29, 1918
      U.K.•London •Berlin   *RUSSIAN EMPIRE*
                    GERMANY

          •Paris   •Vienna
      FRANCE   *AUSTRIA-*
                      HUNGARY

                      •Rome

    N

1. ADMIRALTY BUILDINGS
2. WINTER PALACE
3. HERMITAGE ART MUSEUM
4. FORTRESS OF PETER AND PAUL
5. CATHEDRAL OF PETER AND PAUL
6. KSCHESSINSKAYA MANSION
7. CIRQUE MODERNE
8. BRITISH EMBASSY
9. MARBLE PALACE
10. NATIONAL CITY BANK OF NEW YORK
11. PEOPLE'S OPERA (NARODNY DOM)
12. FINLANDIA R.R. STATION
13. SMOLNY INSTITUTE (BOLSHEVIK HEADQUARTERS)
14. RESIDENCE OF LEIGHTON ROGERS
15. LAW COURTS BUILDING
16. ARSENAL
17. ALEXANDRINSKY THEATER
18. MIKHAILOVSKY (FRENCH) THEATRE
19. HOTEL EUROPE
20. CATHEDRAL OF KAZAN
21. NICHOLAS R.R STATION
22. KRESTY PRISON
23. MARINSKY OPERA HOUSE (IMPERIAL OPERA)
24. HOTEL ASTORIA
25. TELEGRAPH OFFICE
26. TELEPHONE STATION
27. CATHEDRAL OF ST. ISAAC
28. GERMANY EMBASSY
29. AMERICAN EMBASSY
30. CONTANT'S (KONTAN) RESTAURANT
31. DONON'S RESTAURANT
32. CAFÉ DE LA GRAVE
33. SINGER BUILDING
34. BOLSHAYA KONYUSHENNAYA STREET
35. MILLIONNAYA STREET

PETROGRAD, 1917

KGL VENTURES LLC

VYBORG SIDE

NEVA RIVER

LITEINY
BRIDGE

SHPALERNAYA

TAURIDE
PALACE

FURSHTATSKAYA STREET

KIROCHNAYA STREET

PREOBRAZHENSKY
BARRACKS

TROITSKY
BRIDGE

FRENCH EMBANKMENT

FIELD
OF MARS

PALACE EMBANKMENT

KAMENNOOSTROVSKY PROSPEKT

LITEINY PROSPEKT

PALACE
SQUARE

NEVSKY PROSPEKT

ZNAMENSKY
SQUARE

SADOVAYA STREET

FONTANKA CANAL

N

W — E

S

0   250m   500m   750m   1km

500m

DISTANCE IN METERS

TIMELINE 1914–1920

1914

August 1 – Germany declares war on Russia after Russia refuses to stop its troop mobilization against Austria-Hungary.

August 4 – Britain declares war on Germany; outbreak of World War I.

1915

August 29 – H. Fessenden Meserve, newly appointed National City Bank representative to Russia, leaves New York with his wife and stepdaughter for Petrograd.

September 11 – The Meserve family arrives in Petrograd.

September – Tsar Nicholas II replaces Grand Duke Nicholas as supreme commander of the Russian army after the loss of Warsaw despite Mikhail Rodzianko, president of the Duma, advising the tsar against personally leading his troops at the front.

1916

June 18 – National City Bank syndicates a $50 million, 5 percent loan to Russia.

June 28 – Leighton Rogers joins National City Bank in New York.

July 23 – Newly appointed National City Bank Petrograd branch manager Robie Reed (R.R.) Stevens arrives in Petrograd.

September 28 – Leighton Rogers and his five training class colleagues sail from New York.

October 16 – Leighton Rogers and colleagues arrive in Petrograd and meet Meserve and R.R. Stevens the next day.

November 22 – National City Bank syndicates a $50 million, 5.5 percent Russian government bond.

December 30 – Prince Felix Yusupov and four accomplices murder Rasputin at Yusopov's palace.

1917

January 15 – National City Bank opens its Petrograd branch.

March 8 – International Women's Day march. Start of the February (March) Revolution.

March 13 – The provisional government led by Prince George Lvoff is established. Alexander Kerensky is appointed minister of justice.

March 15 – Abdication of Tsar Nicholas II. Proclamation of provisional government cabinet formation.

March 22 – US government recognizes the provisional government.

April 16 – Vladimir Lenin returns to Petrograd after almost 16 years in exile in Switzerland.

May 17 – Leon Trotsky returns to Petrograd from exile.

May 18 – Kerensky becomes minister of war following the resignations of Pavel Milyukoff and Alexander Guchkov and the formation of a coalition government under Lvoff.

June 13–July 9 – US Root mission, led by Elihu Root, visits Russia. United States Railroad Commission led by John F. Stevens also arrives in Petrograd on June 13.

July 1 – Kerensky orders several new offensives along the Eastern Front in an attempt to boost army morale. The Galician offensive led by General Aleksey Brusilov ends in a humiliating retreat for the Russian army.

July 16–19 – Soldiers and industrial workers mount armed demonstrations against the provisional government in a Bolshevik-inspired uprising. The "July Days" riots are brutally suppressed. Trotsky is arrested and Lenin is forced into hiding.

July 24 – Kerensky becomes prime minister.

August 1 – Kerensky appoints General Lavr Kornilov commander-in-chief of the Russian army.

September 5 – German troops occupy Riga, threatening the security of Petrograd.

September 8–12 – The "Kornilov Affair."

October 23 – Lenin leads the Bolshevik Central Committee to approve an armed uprising.

November 6 – The Bolshevik Revolution begins.

November 7 – Lenin announces the establishment of the Russian Soviet Federative Socialist Republic. Civil war breaks out.

November 26 – National City Bank opens its Moscow branch.

November 27 – Meserve and family leave Petrograd on a trans-Siberian train to Harbin, China, and then by ship to Japan and ultimately the United States.

December 15 – Russia and the Central Powers declare a cease-fire, leading to the commencement of the Brest-Litovsk peace negotiations on December 22.

December 27 – Red Guards occupy the National City Bank Petrograd branch office for five days. Bolsheviks declare nationalization of all private banks in Russia.

1918

January 18–19 – Bolsheviks fail to gain the majority in elections to the Constituent Assembly, which is dissolved by order of the Congress of Soviets on January 19.

February 8 – The Soviet government declares that all debts contracted by the Russian Empire and the Russian provisional government are canceled and expropriates all the assets of foreign nations in Russia including banks, lands, and industries.

February 14 – Russia adopts the Western Gregorian calendar.

February 23 – Leighton Rogers leaves Petrograd by train to Murmansk.

February 25–March 19 – Remaining National City Bank staff leave Petrograd either for Vologda or exit Russia via Siberia.

February 27 – US Ambassador David R. Francis leaves Petrograd for Vologda.

March 3 – Russia and the Central Powers sign the Brest-Litovsk peace treaty.

March 14 – The Brest-Litovsk peace treaty is ratified at the Extraordinary Fourth All-Russia Congress of Soviets.

March 29 – Leighton Rogers arrives in Newcastle upon Tyne, England, and the next morning by train in London.

Night of July 16/17 – Bolsheviks assassinate the tsar and his family in Yekaterinburg.

August 26 – National City Bank branches in Petrograd and Moscow officially close. All remaining foreign nationals of the bank leave Petrograd on September 1 for Finland.

November 11 – The Armistice to World War I is signed.

December 2 – The Soviet government adopts a decree to liquidate foreign banks in Russia.

1919

February 3 – National City Bank opens an agency in Vladivostok.

June 9 – Bolsheviks seize National City Bank's books and files that were safe-kept with the Swedish Consulate General in Moscow.

1920

March 13 – National City Bank closes its agency in Vladivostok

INTRODUCTION

"You fall under a spell. You realize you are in another world, and you feel you must not only understand it: you must get it down on paper."[1]

I nto *Russia's Cauldron* is the story of a young American, Leighton William Rogers, who did exactly that.

This book takes the reader on the dramatic journey of an individual and an institution fighting the inevitable in revolutionary Russia, a story grippingly brought to life in the century-old journal of Leighton Rogers. In 1916, the National City Bank of New York ("National City Bank" or "NCB," the precursor of today's Citibank) sent Rogers to Petrograd, the capital of the Russian Empire, to join a mission hell-bent on achieving American commercial preeminence—a vision set forth by Frank A. Vanderlip, the president of National City Bank, who enthusiastically declared, "Russia's need for capital is like Sahara's thirst for water."

Rogers did not know what would befall him. Fraught with turmoil, wracked by heavy war losses and persistent food shortages, and festering with revolutionary ideas, Russia was a cauldron ready to explode. While not dodging bullets and saber-wielding Cossacks, Rogers, guided by his unique sense of adventure and a protective dose of American humor, sought to understand fact from fiction on Petrograd's anarchic streets. *Into Russia's Cauldron* follows his emotional and philosophical transformation coping with wartime deprivation, processing Russia's churning political machinations while championing National City Bank's ambitions. Rogers diligently recorded his insights into Russia's agonizing transformation from an archaic, oppressive society into an unprecedented social, economic, and political experiment. His story is one of true grit.

At the threshold of a new economic era in the United States, Frank Vanderlip methodically built National City Bank, then America's largest banking institution, into an international financial juggernaut. With its vast undeveloped regions, Russia

---

[1] Arno Dosch-Fleurot, *Through War to Revolution* (London: J. Lane, 1931), 103. Here Dosch-Fleurot, a veteran American newspaperman, is quoting his friend Ludovic Naudeau (1872–1949), the Russia correspondent of France's *Temps of Paris*, who in 1918 was arrested and imprisoned by the Bolsheviks.

beckoned, presenting tremendous opportunities for American capital and technology exports. This book chronicles the bank's foray into Russia by weaving Rogers' journal entries with research drawn from the letters and memoirs of his colleagues and contemporaries, archived correspondence between Frank Vanderlip and bank senior management, newspapers, periodicals, declassified diplomatic dispatches, historical studies, and other primary sources. How did National City Bank achieve seemingly unstoppable growth in assets and profits until the Bolshevik Revolution, and what strategies did the bank employ thereafter to salvage its situation? *Into Russia's Cauldron* explains why National City Bank ultimately lost money and how Rogers and Vanderlip, their fates unexpectedly intertwined, faced the proverbial end of the road in Russia. "Fortune and misfortune live in the same courtyard," an old Russian proverb warns.

The book chronologically integrates Leighton Rogers' journal with concurrent events in Russia and National City Bank's activities. Each chapter contains a brief introduction that puts his journal entries in context with notes and analysis identifying places, people, and historical events in Petrograd, elsewhere in Russia, and abroad, and matters of interest, importance, or amusement to Rogers.

Part I describes Leighton Rogers' background and the events that led up to his employment. It outlines Frank Vanderlip's actions to develop NCB's global outreach and the bank's initial successes in Russia. The reader joins Rogers on an adventurous transatlantic journey and learns of his initial impressions of Petrograd, which alternately awed or dismayed him. Rasputin's murder proved a gruesome harbinger of what was to come. This section conveys a broad sense of Rogers' personality and emerging, as yet unreconciled, thoughts about life and work in Russia. It analyzes why National City Bank, upon opening its first branch in Petrograd in January 1917, immediately attracted unprecedented inflows of customer deposits and highlights the exuberance that blinded the bank's management team.

Part II covers the 1917 February (March) Revolution and its aftershocks. Rogers described his escapades amid the anarchy of Petrograd's innumerable street demonstrations. He made observations about all strata of Russian society, filtered rumors and fake news, and pieced together Russia's turbulent revolutionary politics. Yet Rogers' implicit biases fogged his understanding of Russia's state of affairs. National City Bank's Petrograd branch became profitable within one month of opening and business soon doubled again and again. Rogers worked feverishly. The author analyzes NCB's internal correspondence and actions, which overweighted opportunity and under-weighted risk, including the threat of Bolshevism, as the bank prepared to open a second branch in Moscow and contemplated a third in Vladivostok.

Part III focuses on the October (November) Revolution and the turmoil it wrought. Rogers meticulously described scenes of violence, pillage, and death. He declared his intention to leave the bank to join the US Army. His five-week-long escape from Petrograd is a monumental story of its own. This section studies the thinking and actions behind National City Bank's "wait and see" strategy, which put growth on hold, hoping for the quick demise of the Bolsheviks while averting the specter of large losses in Russia.

The epilogue contains Rogers' prescient advice about Russia, which resonates powerfully today. He foresaw that Russia would be "even more powerful and its potential power for good or evil would be almost beyond conception." He drew attention to questions we face in our contemporary relations with Russia: Does the leadership in Russia care about its people and can we understand what Russians want? This section illustrates how National City Bank aligned with American foreign policy and the ineffectual Allied intervention in Russia. It evaluates the bank's attempts to forestall the inevitable, explores lessons learned from its shortcomings, and finally, reveals the fates of the book's colorful characters who fell *Into Russia's Cauldron*.

Leighton Rogers never published his journal. For this reason, it offers a fresh and valuable perspective because he wrote at the time the events occurred, and not with the benefit of historical hindsight or the detriment of revision, or the muddled memory of years passed. Rogers left us one of the more transfixing, vibrant, and honest accounts of the pandemonium of that time. He balanced fear with hope, tempered excitement with frustration, sifted transient rumors from facts, sought order from chaos, and skirted danger with bravado and humor. Rogers prized human kindness and recoiled against senseless cruelty. He strove to understand Russian culture and the way of the Russians as they struggled to maintain a modicum of normal life. Anarchist street demonstrations, army rebellions, the threat of German occupation of Petrograd, the evolution of World War I, and the continual search for an adequate meal became daily concerns. *Into Russia's Cauldron* renders one person's profound experience under trial. Like sinew, Rogers bound one chapter of Russia's revolutionary maelstrom to another.

The Library of Congress in Washington, DC, holds the Leighton W. Rogers Papers collection. This includes his handwritten journal and a typed, self-edited manuscript titled "Tsar, Revolution, Bolsheviks" that Rogers prepared in 1957 based on his original journal and hoped to publish, but never did. The collection also contains photos, notes, newspaper clippings and letters, and a copy of his novel, *Wine of Fury*, the story of an American financier in Petrograd during the Russian Revolution, published in London and New York in 1924. *Into Russia's Cauldron* refers to passages in Rogers' novel and later typed manuscript when they add valuable perspective to Rogers' original journal.

PART I

The Mission.

September 1916–March 1917

LEIGHTON WILLIAM ROGERS

L eighton William Rogers was born in East Rockaway, Long Island, New York, in 1893. He attended grammar and high school in Orange, Massachusetts, where his father, Lewis L. Rogers, was a director and the advertising manager of the New Home Sewing Machine Company, the second largest producer of sewing machines in the United States after Singer. Orange was the location of New Home's factory, which by 1907 produced approximately 150,000 machines and employed 743 people. Rogers went to Dartmouth College and graduated with a bachelor of science degree in 1916. In March of his senior year, William Samuel Kies, a vice president of National City Bank, visited Dartmouth as part of a tour of fifteen Ivy League and other elite colleges to recruit graduates to join NCB's new international training program. Rogers eagerly attended his presentation. Perusing the bluish cardstock bound pamphlet titled *Opportunities for Young Men in the Foreign Field* that Kies distributed, Rogers learned that:

> our national commercial policy indicates the necessity of our training of a force of young men in this country who shall be willing to devote their lives to the building up of American trade abroad on a firm and substantial basis; young men of character, perseverance, and resourcefulness—men of untiring energy with the tact of diplomats and the broad vision of statesmen. For young men of this type there opens up a career in foreign trade or in banking of almost unlimited possibilities. The National City Bank is the only national bank which has established branches in foreign countries. It needs trained men at the present time.

This was Rogers' calling. Grasping a career opportunity that seemed like a dream come true, he signed on with National City Bank and entered the bank's training program, together with twenty-six other college graduates, on June 28, 1916.[2] He studied international trade, foreign exchange, auditing, bookkeeping, penmanship, and principles of domestic banking, and learned that "the greatest opportunities are looked for in Russia, where the natural resources hardly have been touched. There are

---

[2] "Letter from Leigh Rogers," November 23, 1916, *Class of 1916 of Dartmouth College: First Annual Report, 1917*, 81; *Number Eight*, The National City Bank of New York, September 1916, 112. The latter source mentions July 1, 1916.

railroads to be built and mines to be opened. This means a wonderful opportunity for American capital, and along with this development will go wonderful opportunity for manufactured goods. . . . In time the trade between the two countries might run into unknown figures."[3] Rogers read the bank's June 1916 report titled *Russia and the Imperial Government,* which encouragingly declared, "The Russian Government is gradually making broad and comprehensive plans for utilization of the enormous underdeveloped resources of the Empire" and "Siberia . . . has sufficient resources, if properly developed, to feed and clothe a population equal to that of all Europe."

After three months of training, together with five other freshly minted colleagues, Rogers boarded a transatlantic steamship to travel to his first assignment: Petrograd, the capital of the Russian Empire. His initial salary upon relocating abroad, the bank promised, would be "not less than $100 per month . . . to which will be added an allowance for increased living expenses. . . ."[4] Rogers departed America unprepared for what awaited him in Russia, but surely he understood the meaning of the small print in the recruiting pamphlet he read back in March that prophetically advised a foreign service job "is not meant for the young man who wants a life of ease. . . ."[5]

FRANK A. VANDERLIP

Frank A. Vanderlip was born into a humble farming family in Aurora, Illinois, in 1864. He attended the University of Illinois but did not finish his studies there. After some early farm and machine shop apprentice work, he entered the world of journalism when he took a job at his hometown's *Aurora Evening Post* in 1885. In 1889, he joined the *Chicago Tribune,* where he rose to become a financial editor in 1892. His growing prominence as a financial journalist garnered him an opportunity to join the US Department of Treasury, where he served as assistant secretary from 1897 until March 1901. Upon leaving the Treasury, he traveled four months in Europe. Vanderlip then became fascinated with Russia. He visited St. Petersburg at Easter time and went to Moscow, where he had lengthy discussions with the finance minister, Sergei Yulyevich

[3] *Number Eight,* The National City Bank of New York, January 1916, 12. American exports to Russia grew from $31 million in 1914 to $559 million by 1917. The vast majority of American exports then were war munitions and supplies. "Trade with Russia Grows," *New York Times,* September 11, 1917, 14, quoting a review of international trade prepared by the bank.

[4] William Samuel Kies, *Opportunities for Young Men in the Foreign Field* (New York: The National City Bank of New York, 1916), 13.

[5] Ibid., 16.

Witte.[6] Returning to the United States emboldened, he wrote an influential article for *Scribner's Magazine* in January 1902 titled "The American 'Commercial Invasion' of Europe," where he exclaimed, "That the United States gives promises of reaching a position of industrial supremacy in the world's trade, is acknowledged to-day the world over. . . . We have before us a long campaign of hard work and intelligent prosecution of every advantage which we have, before we reach such a position of industrial supremacy. . . ." Vanderlip asserted that "Russia's need for capital is like Sahara's thirst for water" and cheered that "American locomotives, running on American rails, now whistle past the Pyramids and across the long Siberian steppes."[7]

He was not the first in America to extol Russia's alluring potential. Leading American companies of that era, including Singer, Vacuum Oil, New York Life Insurance, and International Harvester had entered the Russian market before 1900. W. R. Grace & Co., Standard Oil, Armour and Company, and others followed.

Vanderlip enabled the US Treasury's issuance of $200 million in government bonds to finance the Spanish-American War. This brought him to the attention of James J. Stillman, the president of National City Bank, who invited him to join as a vice president in 1902.[8] In 1909, Vanderlip became president of the bank and Stillman became chairman. Having become one of the most prominent bankers in America,[9] Vanderlip set out to transform National City Bank into an international financial institution that could execute the global vision he expounded in 1902. He methodically implemented four strategies to accomplish his goal.

By the time Vanderlip became president, National City Bank was the largest and most powerful bank with the widest branch network in the United States. NCB traced its roots to 1812, when it was chartered in New York after the dissolution of the

---

[6] Frank A. Vanderlip, *From Farm Boy to Financier* (New York: D. Appleton Century, 1935), 121–23.

[7] Frank A. Vanderlip, "The American 'Commercial Invasion' of Europe," *Scribner's Magazine* 31 (January 1902): 16, 6, and 10, and typed manuscript, Box D-3, Frank A. Vanderlip Papers, Columbia University.

[8] Robert Stanley Mayer, *The Influence of Frank A. Vanderlip and the National City Bank on American Commerce and Foreign Policy, 1910–1920* (New York: Garland, 1987), 22.

[9] *Federal Reserve History* "The Meeting at Jekyll Island: November 20, 1910–November 30, 1910," by Gary Richardson and Jessie Romero, Federal Reserve Bank of Richmond, https://www.federalreservehistory.org/essays/jekyll-island-conference.

In November 1910, Vanderlip became part of American financial history when he participated in the "Jekyll Island Group," a gathering of leading American financiers and statesmen on Georgia's Jekyll Island to draft legislation creating a central banking system for the United States. Nelson Aldrich, a Republican senator and chairman of the National Monetary Commission, organized the meeting and invited A. Piatt Andrew (assistant secretary of the Treasury), Paul Warburg (a partner at Kuhn, Loeb & Co.), Henry P. Davison (a senior partner at J. P. Morgan & Co.), Arthur Shelton (Aldrich's private secretary), in addition to Vanderlip. Their work led to the Federal Reserve Act of 1913, which legalized the establishment of American banks abroad. Modifications to the law, including passage of the Edge Act of 1916, greatly assisted the expansion of the American banking system overseas and catalyzed foreign trade expansion and deployment of American capital abroad.

First Bank of the United States created by Alexander Hamilton.[10] The bank was well placed at home but not abroad, and Vanderlip acted to rapidly expand its international branch network. In 1909, he set his sights on obtaining control of the International Banking Corporation. IBC was organized in 1901 by Thomas Hubbard, who had been a general in the Union Army, and Marcellus Hartley, an arms dealer of the Remington Arms Company and a founder of the Continental Bank of New York. IBC conducted commercial trading activities in foreign countries, particularly in Asia. Hubbard was chairman and Hartley president, but when Hartley died in January 1902, Hubbard assumed both roles. By 1909, IBC operated branches in London and in the major commercial centers of Asia: Shanghai, Manila, and Singapore. Although it was not the only American financial institution with an overseas presence before World War I, it was the largest and most successful.[11] Aiming to leapfrog National City Bank into lucrative foreign markets, Vanderlip vainly tried to convince Hubbard to sell National City Bank a controlling interest. Only after Hubbard died in May 1915 did Vanderlip induce the company's shareholders to sell. By October, he wrote James Stillman, "I have just closed the purchase of a controlling interest in the [IBC] and hope to get substantially all the stock in time." A week later Vanderlip added:

> We have now bought 22,000 shares of the 32,500. I have no doubt most of the rest will come in.... With the acquisition of the branches of the International Bank we will have more branches and cover a wider territory than any bank in the world. I can see how it is possible and very probable that within a short time comparatively the City Bank will have a well ordered branch in every import-ant center in the world outside the United States. I think the acquisition of the International Bank has been an extremely fortunate stroke.[12]

A fortunate stroke indeed. Vanderlip had accomplished the first of his four stra-tegic objectives. The acquisition of IBC was not enough, however. Vanderlip wanted to broaden National City's international financial activities into areas such as foreign equity investment, foreign securities trading, and as *The Sun* newspaper reported, "to interest American capital in the development of the natural resources abroad and

---

[10] Mayer, *The Influence of Frank A. Vanderlip,* 32.
[11] Harold van B. Cleveland and Thomas F. Huertas, *Citibank: 1812–1970* (Cambridge, MA: Harvard University Press, 1985), 81.
[12] Vanderlip to Stillman, October 22 and October 29, 1915, 1 and 3, Box B-1-7, Frank A. Vanderlip Papers.

to bring American goods into new fields . . . to engage in almost every sort of a venture."[13] Vanderlip's plan was crystal clear. "Here, then, is the situation:" he outlined in a letter to Stillman:

> We are to have the only available fund of capital for world development. . . . I propose to meet this situation by the formation of a company to be chartered under the laws of some state, probably Delaware, with a capital of $25,000,000. . . . The function of this company is to get together the most expert organization for the examination and eventually for the operation of properties in South America, the Orient and elsewhere. . . . The plan that I propose is to offer the stock for subscription, first, to the stockholders of the City Bank. . . . I should take Chairmanship of the Board and organize the personnel. . . . With the ramifications that such a company will have, there will come very great banking advantages in various parts of the world.

He concluded by asserting, "There is no time to be lost, however, in getting the organization started."[14] Vanderlip lost no time; he had already huddled with powerful American financial circles such as the Rockefellers, W.R. Grace, and Kuhn, Loeb & Co. Their interest exceeded his expectations.[15] American International Corporation formally launched on November 23, 1915, with an initial capital of $50,000,000, double what Vanderlip had envisioned, with National City Bank as the majority shareholder.[16] In blazingly fast time, Vanderlip had accomplished his second strategic goal.

Vanderlip also wanted to beef up bond underwriting and distribution at National City Bank's subsidiary, National City Company. Bond issuance and underwriting activity in the United States grew significantly, particularly during World War I, when the Allied nations issued several billions of dollars of war bonds. National City Bank

---

[13] "New Concern to Make US World Trade Power," *The Sun*, New York, NY, November 24, 1915, 3.

[14] Vanderlip to Stillman, October 8, 1915, 3-5, Box B-1-7, Frank A. Vanderlip Papers.

[15] Mayer, *The Influence of Frank A. Vanderlip*, 140–1. Vanderlip's plan germinated from an idea of Charles Stone and Edwin Webster of the Stone & Webster engineering firm, a corporate client of NCB, who wanted to create an investment trust to support railroad expansion abroad.

[16] The board of directors of American International Corporation was "impressive in its strength," as described in National City Bank's *Number Eight* (January 1916, 5–6.) It included many of America's leading industrialists and financiers of the time: J. Ogden Armour (Armour and Co.), Charles Coffin (General Electric), William Corey (Midvale Steel), Joseph Grace (W.R. Grace & Co.), James Hill (Great Northern Railways), Otto Hermann Kahn (Kuhn, Loeb & Co.), Robert Lovett (Union Pacific Railroad), Ambrose Monell (International Nickel), Henry Pritchett (Carnegie Foundation), Percy Rockefeller (Standard Oil), John Ryan (Anaconda Copper), Chas Sabin (Guaranty Trust), William Saunders (Ingersoll-Rand), Charles Stone and Edwin Webster (Stone & Webster), Theodore Vail (AT&T), Albert Wiggin (Chase National Bank), Beekman Winthrop (Robert Winthrop and Co.), and William Woodward (Hanover National Bank). Frank Vanderlip was chairman and Charles Stone president.

purchased N.W. Halsey Company, which since its founding in 1900 had become the second largest retail securities firm in the United States. It played an important role in the expansion of the American securities market; in 1915 alone, N.W. Halsey placed municipal, public utility, and railroad bonds "to the value of considerably more than $100,000,000."[17] NCB concluded its purchase of N.W. Halsey in August 1916 and became one of the three banks (the others being Morgan and First National) that organized most of the Allied wartime financing, including the Anglo-French Loan of 1915 and three subsequent Allied loans in 1916 and early 1917.[18] By 1929, National City Company reputedly became the largest agency in the world for the distribution of securities.[19] Vanderlip had realized his third strategic priority.

One strategic need remained unaddressed. "Our foreign branches developed faster than we could find trained men to run them," Vanderlip lamented in his 1935 memoir, *From Farm Boy to Financier*.[20] Indeed, NCB's business growth had far outpaced its development of human talent. Vanderlip discussed this at length with Stillman:

> The growth of the Bank in its relation with world affairs has been more, I presume, than you can possibly appreciate. . . . We are really becoming a world bank in a very broad sense, and I am perfectly confident that the way is open to us to become the most powerful, the most serviceable, the most far-reaching world financial institution that there has ever been. The one limitation that I can see, lies in the quality of management. Can men be found who will have the vision, the constructive initiative, the conservatism, and the good judgment to put the institution into the unique position which is awaiting it? I must admit that I have some doubt on that score. The number of American bankers who think in international terms is certainly none too large. The number of men who are willing to give up their home ties and go to strange countries is small.[21]

In October 1915, Vanderlip appointed F.C. Schwedtman vice president to create a one-year college training program for students interested in careers in

---

[17] "N.W. Halsey & Co. Sold to City Bank," *New York Times*, August 20, 1916, 3.

[18] Priscilla Roberts, "Frank A. Vanderlip and the National City Bank During the First World War," *Essays in Economic and Business History* 20, no. 1 (2002): 150.

[19] Thomas F. Huertas and Joan L. Silverman, "Charles E. Mitchell: Scapegoat of the Crash?" *Business History Review* 60, no. 1 (Spring 1986): 85, https://doi.org/10.2307/3115924.

[20] Vanderlip, *Farm Boy to Financier*, 260.

[21] Vanderlip to Stillman, December 31, 1915, 2–3, Box B-1-7, Frank A. Vanderlip Papers.

finance.[22] NCB also instituted a combination recruitment and summer training program with several American universities to train graduating seniors to become a new generation of international bankers. Schwedtman explained, "Commercial education is required . . . and it must be more than college training. . . . We must educate many of our best young men for foreign commercial service. The college and business office must co-operate efficiently. . . . I feel certain that any reasonable effort to that end will have the hearty support of Mr. Vanderlip and his associated officers."[23] National City Bank was the first American bank to establish a training program of such scope and purpose.

Four strategic actions now implemented, Vanderlip proudly assessed National City Bank's position: "With these four organizations, [National City Bank, National City Company, International Banking Corporation, and American International Corporation] we are equipped to do sound financing of any character anywhere in the world."[24] Newly acquired foreign branches, expanded foreign correspondent banking, enhanced bond underwriting and distribution capability, and expertise in international trade finance and foreign exchange made National City Bank a financial colossus. "We have built a foundation upon which is going to be reared a structure of the greatest all-world bank that has yet been seen," Vanderlip assured Stillman.[25] By 1917, NCB had 2,200 employees, nearly 600 of whom worked overseas, plus the employees of its affiliates, the National City Company and IBC. The bank's assets almost tripled between June 1914 and the end of 1917.[26]

The Wilson administration supported National City Bank's rapid international-ization. US economic policy championed foreign commerce in order to reduce cyclical depressions at home and spread prosperity. National City Bank facilitated the growth of American exports and by example showed other financial institutions how to do so. By 1920, American banks had established 180 branches abroad, starting the era of American commercial supremacy Vanderlip prophesied in 1902. National City Bank and affiliate IBC owned 132 of these 180 branches.[27]

---

[22] Cleveland and Huertas, *Citibank: 1812–1970*, 80; *Number Eight*, The National City Bank of New York, October 1915, 4–5.

[23] Address of F.C. Schwedtman at the Southern Commercial Congress at Charleston, SC, December 16, 1915, in *Number Eight*, The National City Bank of New York, January 1916, 16 and 22.

[24] Vanderlip to Stillman, January 7, 1916, 9, Box B-1-7, Frank A. Vanderlip Papers.

[25] Vanderlip to Stillman, April 14, 1916, 4, Box B-1-7, Frank A. Vanderlip Papers.

[26] Cleveland and Huertas, *Citibank: 1812–1970*, 84 and 89.

[27] Mayer, *The Influence of Frank A. Vanderlip*, 128; Roberts, "Frank A. Vanderlip and the National City Bank During the First World War," 153.

MISSION TO RUSSIA

National City Bank scored its first successes in Russia before Leighton Rogers left New York. At the end of 1914, it participated in a $25 million trade credit facility for the Russian government.[28] "Russia undoubtedly offers a field that we ought to occupy at once, considering our close and highly satisfactory relations with the Government there," Vanderlip wrote Stillman. But the need to staff the bank's operations was important and "the difficulty of finding the right man, or men, has seemed to be insurmountable," he added.[29]

Enter H. (Harry) Fessenden Meserve to the National City Bank saga. Vanderlip hired Meserve, who had enjoyed an interesting career before coming to National City Bank, to be the bank's representative to Russia. Born in 1867 in Arlington, Massachusetts, he hailed from an old American family that emigrated in the late 17th century from the Isle of Jersey to settle in New Hampshire. Meserve graduated from Harvard College in 1888 and took a banking job in Seattle, but left in 1897 to spend a year in Yokohama, Japan, working in US–Japanese trade. The next year, he became the general manager of a gold mining concession in Unsan province in northern Korea operated by the Oriental Consolidated Mining Company. He spent twelve years in Korea and in 1910 went to Baltimore to join the banking firm Middendorf, Williams & Company as a partner. Meserve was living in London and Paris in 1914 and 1915 when Vanderlip recruited him. Briefly returning to Baltimore in August 1915 before leaving for Petrograd, Meserve cryptically described his new job: "It is my intention to leave for Russia at once. I am going to engage in important special work in that country, the nature of which I cannot divulge at the present time. My mission will keep me from America for some time; in fact, I don't know just when I will return."[30] Meserve arrived in Petrograd on September 11, 1915, duly established himself, his wife, and stepdaughter in the bel étage suite in the Hotel Europe, and met US Ambassador George Marye within days.[31] Meserve kept a business diary from the time of his arrival in Petrograd until December 1916, which provides rich details of whom he met and how he pursued business. Leighton Rogers later summarized Meserve's role as "steering a clear course through the maze of business and political intrigue."[32]

---

[28] "Russia Places Loan of $25,000,000 Here," *New York Times*, January 14, 1915, 15.
[29] Vanderlip to Stillman, July 30, 1915, 4, Box B-1-7, Frank A. Vanderlip Papers.
[30] "H.F. Meserve Back. Will Leave for Russia Soon," *The Baltimore Sun*, August 11, 1915, 12.
[31] Stanislav Tkachenko, *American Bank Capital in Russia During the First World War* (St. Petersburg, Russia: VIRD Publishing House, 1998), 25.
[32] Leighton Rogers, *Wine of Fury* (New York: Alfred A. Knopf, 1924), 79.

Soon after his arrival, Meserve wrote Vanderlip that National City Bank should open a branch in Petrograd to: [33]

1. Provide US exporters and importers with needed banking services and information about Russia
2. Create a presence to deflect competition and critics of the bank's business strategy
3. Support the bank's existing affiliates, National City Company and American International Corporation
4. Realize the profit potential

The US government actively coordinated with the titans of American industry and finance about Russia. In November 1915, Secretary of Commerce William C. Redfield suggested that National City Bank open a branch in Russia. "Redfield last night [at a Chamber of Commerce dinner in New York] spoke particularly about the desirability of our opening in Russia, saying he had had a number of letters on the subject and that there was really a great demand for us to do that," Vanderlip informed Stillman, also noting that Redfield was "most cordial in his approval of the plan [for the new company, American International Corporation]."[34] President Woodrow Wilson also got involved.[35] While on board the SS *Oscar II*, David C. Francis, who would replace George Marye as the next US ambassador to Russia in April 1916, wrote Wilson "I have also talked with the National City Bank people who thoroughly agree with my plan to promote direct commercial relations between Russia and the United States without the intervention of any other country or influence. . . . Mr. Vanderlip, president of the National City Bank, assured me (I have known him for many years) that he would second any efforts I would make to establish direct commercial relations with Russia."[36] Several weeks after Francis wrote Wilson, Vanderlip and his wife lunched with Russian Ambassador George Petrovich Bakhmeteff and his wife, Mary Beale

---

[33] Meserve to Vanderlip, March 21, 1916 (March 8 on the Julian old calendar), cited in Tkachenko, *American Bank Capital in Russia*, 74–75.

[34] Vanderlip to Stillman, November 19, 1915, 8 and 7, Box B-1-7, Frank A. Vanderlip Papers.

[35] Mayer, *The Influence of Frank A. Vanderlip*, 36–42. Vanderlip and Woodrow Wilson knew each other well before Wilson became president. Over the years, they disagreed on certain matters of policy, e.g., the role of big banks in furthering American foreign trade expansion, although this disagreement ameliorated once World War I broke out and the expansion of American foreign trade became a necessity.

[36] *Special Committee on Investigation of the Munitions Industry, United States Senate*, 74th Cong. (June 1, 1936), 135 (David R. Francis letter to Woodrow Wilson, April 8, 1916).

Bakhmeteff, in Washington, DC. Vanderlip confided that the ambassador was "delighted at our interest in Russia and thinks it was very wise for us to send the vice-presidents over."[37] Samuel McRoberts and Charles Rich, the vice presidents in question, left New York for Petrograd on April 22, 1916, to finish negotiations on the biggest deal National City Bank would achieve in Russia: a $50 million 5.5 percent three-year credit to the Russian government.

Not everyone agreed with National City Bank's strategy in Russia. Fred Morris Dearing, who would become the US assistant secretary of state in 1921, was the US chargé d'affaires in Petrograd. Dearing thought "Sam McRoberts of the City Bank has smelt money and with a beatific vision of a Russia to come (I am not sure that he or any of us analyzes the prospects with sufficient insight) is maneuvering in the offering of a projected fifty million dollar Government Loan. May he not decamp as unceremoniously as he once did in Spain should the outlook lose its promise."[38] Referring to McRoberts as "Smiling Sam," Dearing ruminated:

> The moment our bankers and businessmen get Russia in focus and begin to see the vast potentialities of her resources, they go crazy with dreams. Leaping from the dream to the business, but still a dream, they have no care for the realities, incapable indeed of even realizing their own ignorance, disregard the many intermediate factors between desire and sound business, and with no adequate notions of Russian conditions, Russian history, Russian psychology, Russian politics and Russian realities altogether reach right in to pull the delicious fruit. Smiling Sam is as sure as he once was in Spain that he has something big—it is big all right—all fixed up and that he is going to make a few strikes. The Chief [Ambassador Francis] in his element encourages him. I don't think either are reading the signs very well or indeed even see them.[39]

Dearing's admonitions aside, McRoberts, Rich, and Meserve closed their big deal on June 18. McRoberts gushed about the creditworthiness of the loan: "It is practically incomprehensible that the internal financial system of Russia, with its tremendous resources and its large population, can ever entirely break down, so these bonds, even in case of a default on the foreign debt, could be sold at a moderate discount to those requiring roubles for the purpose of paying customs duties or other

---

[37] Vanderlip to Stillman, April 29, 1916, 5, Box B-1-7, Frank A. Vanderlip Papers.
[38] Fred Morris Dearing, Unpublished papers, April 3, 1916, 119, Folder 503, State Historical Society of Missouri.
[39] Ibid., May 25, 1916, 289, Folder 509.

indebtedness to the Russian Government, or could be used to cover purchases of all forms of Russian property."[40]

Behind the scenes, Charles Rich confided to Vanderlip that "Mr. Meserve is not a man to take on managerial duties, but he is a find for the Bank in the general work of coordinating branches, and perhaps generally keeping things smooth and giving the home office all the current information."[41] Vanderlip acted on this advice and chose Robie Reed ("R.R.") Stevens to become the manager of NCB's future Petrograd branch. Stevens had ten years of banking experience before he joined NCB. Born in Kennebunk, Maine, in 1884, Stevens graduated summa cum laude from Bowdoin College in 1906, where he was, coincidentally, a member of the same national college fraternity as Leighton Rogers, Psi Upsilon. Upon graduation, Stevens joined the International Banking Corporation (before National City Bank acquired it) and worked in Mexico City for two years and in Panama and Colon for two years. He moved to New York in 1909, where he worked with IBC until 1912, and then became general manager of the Chattel Loan Society of New York,[42] a remedial loan association, until Vanderlip hired him. Stevens arrived in Petrograd on July 23, 1916.[43]

Meserve and Stevens would play indelible roles in the future of National City Bank in Russia.

American business and US government policy seamlessly fused in Russia. Meserve met Ambassador Francis the very day of Francis' arrival and the two doyens of Petrograd's American colony closely coordinated with each other thereafter.[44] National City Bank's $50 million deal elicited great excitement in Russia and America. The *New York Times*, in an article titled "Russians Gratified by American Loan; Expect National City Bank Branch in Petrograd to Promote International Transactions," reported:

> The successful conclusion of this loan, which, it is expected, will be the first of a series of financial transactions ultimately putting Russian Government securities on the American market, has been hailed by Russian financial circles

[40] McRoberts to Vanderlip, June 19, 1916, 1, Box A-65, Frank A. Vanderlip Papers.
[41] Rich to Vanderlip, June 19, 1916, 1-2, Box A-81, Frank A. Vanderlip Papers. In the same letter, Rich went on to write, "Meserve is of the unobtrusively persistent type, very well balanced, conservative and with excellent judgement."
[42] *Bulletin of the National Federation of Remedial Loan Associations* 2, no. 1 (August 1913); *General Catalogue of Bowdoin College and the Medical School of Maine, 1794–1912* (Brunswick, ME: published by the college, 1912), xii. https://archive.org/details/bulletinofnation1913nati/page/n15/mode/2up.
[43] Tkachenko, *American Bank Capital in Russia,* 78, and cablegram of Meserve to New York, August 3, 1916.
[44] Harper Barnes, *Standing on a Volcano: The Life and Times of David Rowland Francis* (St. Louis, MO: Missouri Historical Society Press, 2001), 192. They met for the first time on April 28, 1916.

as one of the most important of recent events in the financing of the war. A branch of National City Bank will be opened in Petrograd in the near future.... Americans resident in Russia are much gratified by this news and are looking forward to establishing their interests in such a fashion that they may be able to take advantage of the great opportunities arising at the close of the war.[45]

Francis equally hailed Russia's prospects, writing to his first son, John Dietz Perry Francis, that "the resources of Russia are so enormous and the opportunities for development so numerous and apparent that I now feel inclined to remain here after my official duties are completed for a few years anyway."[46] Heedless of his State Department colleagues' cautions of a potential conflict of interest, the ambassador personally invested $50,000 in the NCB loan, writing to the president of the New York Life Insurance Company, "I think the loan absolutely good and offers promise of good profit; so much was I convinced of this that I made a personal subscription."[47]

National City Bank faced a conundrum. Russia progressively suffered from the war while business opportunities multiplied. By the time Leighton Rogers arrived in Petrograd in October 1916, Russia had suffered war casualties exceeding 5.3 million sick, wounded, missing, killed, and taken prisoner.[48] Soldiers went hungry and lacked shoes, weapons, and munitions. Reports of fraternization with the enemy circulated. The Russian army suffered a morale crisis, as did Russia's urban population, which was constantly short of food. The problem was not one of harvest output but of rampant currency inflation, which destroyed farmers' livelihoods. In addition, transportation networks that brought food and materials into Petrograd became inadequate and overstressed, and the increased mobilization of soldiers for the front created a deficit of labor to distribute what could arrive, leaving much to rot on railway sidings. Industrial output plummeted. Orlando Figes, in his *A People's Tragedy, The Russian Revolution 1891–1924*, concluded that "The First World War was a gigantic test of the modern state, and as the only

[45] Montgomery Schuyler, "Russians Gratified by American Loan," *New York Times*, June 22, 1916, 5.

[46] Barnes, *Standing on a Volcano*, 201. Letter to John Dietz Perry Francis, July 5, 1916.

[47] Ibid., 205. Letter to Darwin Kingsley, July 10, 1916.

[48] L.I. Sazonov, "Poteri russkoj armii v vojnu 1914–1918," [Losses of the Russian army during the 1914–1918 war], in Trudy komissii po obsledovaniju sanitarnyh posledstvij vojny 1914–1920 gg. [Works of the commission of inquiry about the sanitary consequences of the war 1914–1920], eds. M.M Gran, P.I. Kurkina, P.A. Kuvšinnikova, (Moscow: GIZ, 1923), 161 and 163, cited in Alexandre Sumpf, "War Losses (Russian Empire)" in *1914–1918-online. International Encyclopedia of the First World War*, Ute Daniel et al., eds. (Berlin: Freie Universität Berlin, 2018), https://doi.org/10.15463/ie1418.11284.

major European state which had failed to modernize before the war it was a test which tsarist Russia was almost bound to fail."[49]

From 1895 to 1916, the population of Petrograd swelled from one million to almost 2.5 million.[50] Moscow experienced similar growth. Housing became inadequate and sanitary conditions deteriorated. Sharp wartime increases in the cost of living, coupled with longer working hours but unmatched by a commensurate growth in wages, became the sad norm. Figes points out that working women had it tougher, having to queue up to forty hours a week for provisions.[51]

Germany fueled the fires of Russia's woes. German agents secretly funded and spread anti-tsarist propaganda. Domestic socioeconomic pressures and foreign-backed agitation stoked strikes and labor riots, with their omnipresent slogans demanding bread and higher wages. The ultimate German subterfuge delivered Bolshevik revolutionary Vladimir Lenin back to Russia, via a sealed railway car.

Tsar Nicholas II made things worse. He left Petrograd to take personal control of the army in the late summer of 1915, moving 800 kilometers to Mogilev to command at the Stavka (Russian: Ставка), the high command and general headquarters of the armed forces. First, he became far removed from the worsening conditions in Petrograd and, second, relied on Tsarina Alexandra to rule there in his absence. Already severely compromised by her relationship with the degenerate monk Grigori Rasputin, her German provenance, and her penchant for telling Nicholas II what she thought he wanted to hear, Alexandra was the worst possible second-in-command. Russia would suffer dearly.

Diplomats in Petrograd saw the writing on the wall. Ambassador Francis wrote on November 7, 1916, to Frank L. Polk at the State Department in Washington that "There have been manifestations lately of unrest among the workers in the factories and also among the long lines of people waiting to be served small amounts of sugar or meat. . . ."[52] Revolutionary fervor was building. Disputes between the political parties on the left and those on the right continued unresolved in the Duma. Reflecting the frustration and anger on the streets, the language of speeches in the Duma became more provocative and vicious. Historian Richard Pipes tells how Socialist Alexander Kerensky, at the opening session of the Duma on November 1, feverishly accused

---

[49] Orlando Figes, *A People's Tragedy: The Russian Revolution 1891–1924* (New York: Penguin Books, 1997), 810.
[50] И.И Елисеева, Санкт-Петербург: 1703–2003: юбилейный статистический сборник, http://www.demoscope. ru/weekly/2004/0163/tema01.php.
[51] Figes, *A People's Tragedy*, 300.
[52] Barnes, *Standing on a Volcano*, 210.

the tsarist government of conducting a "White Terror" and "filling its prisons with working people," under the orchestration of "Grisha Rasputin." Kerensky warned that "There is no salvation for our country until, with a unanimous and concerted effort, we force the removal of those who ruin, humiliate and insult it."[53] Kerensky would soon assume a leading role in Russia's March Revolution.

Rumors of plots and conspiracies proliferated, and government officials worried about public order. In October 1916, a division of the Okhrana, the secret police, described the deteriorating conditions in Petrograd:

> The gradually increasing disorganization of the rear—in other words, of the entire country—has become chronic and is ever worsening. . . . it has at this moment achieved such an extreme and monstrous stage that it is even now beginning to threaten results achieved at the front and promises in the very near future to plunge the country into the destructive chaos of catastrophic and elemental anarchy.
>
> The systematically growing disorganization of transport; the unrestrained orgy of pillaging and swindling of every kind by shady operators in the most diverse branches of the country's commercial, industrial, and sociopolitical life; the unsystematic and mutually contradictory orders of representatives of state and local administrations; the unconscientiousness of minor and lower agents of the government in the provinces; and, as a result of all the foregoing, the inequitable distribution of food products and essential goods, the incredible rise in prices, and the lack of sources and means of procuring food . . . shows categorically and definitely that a dire crisis is already upon us which must inevitably be resolved in one direction or another.
>
> The above summary may be confirmed by the particularly troubled mood now observable among the masses of the people. . . . The slightest incident is enough to provoke the biggest brawl.[54]

Fruitlessly, the Duma urged the tsar to put in place a constitutional form of government. Nicholas did not appreciate the storm growing around him, but on January

---

[53] Richard Pipes, *The Russian Revolution* (New York: Alfred A. Knopf, 1990), 252–53.

[54] Alpha History, "A police report on deteriorating conditions in Petrograd (1916)," https://alphahistory.com/russianrevolution/police-conditions-in-petrograd-1916/. The Okhrana, officially the Department for Protecting the Public Security and Order [Отделение по Охранению Общественной Безопасности и Порядка], was a secret-police force and part of the Ministry of Internal Affairs.

7, 1917, perhaps acknowledging he did not act correctly, remarked to the chairman of the Duma, Mikhail Rodzianko, "Is it possible that for twenty-two years I tried to work for the best, and that for twenty-two years it was all a mistake?"[55] Pipes summarizes, "As 1916 drew to a close, all the political parties and groupings united in opposition to the monarchy. They agreed on little else."[56] Everyone wanted to act to avoid anarchy, except for the anarchists themselves.

Russia, in its pre-revolutionary throes, thus greeted Leighton Rogers when his train arrived in Petrograd on October 16, 1916. With its long bread lines and omnipresent beggars, Petrograd was a far cry from New York City. The contrast shocked him. On October 17, workers of the New Lessner and Russian Renault factories went on strike. Police charged the strikers with whips and sabers, but soldiers of the 181st Infantry, who were based nearby, defended the workers by hurling projectiles at the police. By October 19, seventy-five thousand workers took to the streets.[57] The tsarist regime received a clear warning signal when military units of the Petrograd garrison not only refused to suppress, but actually supported a street demonstration. Rogers may have referred to this event when he wrote on October 20 of a "vague uneasiness, that feeling of surging unrest?" Only four days in Petrograd, Leighton Rogers had received his first lesson in Russian social discontent.

H. Fessenden Meserve months earlier argued, "A very important factor here is the deep-rooted reverence of the great peasant class toward the head of the Government. . . . The Russian people have never been stirred up and worried like the people of other nations as to the causes and rights and wrongs of this terrible war. . . . They are all following the Government blindly."[58]

The tsar would have loved to agree, but Meserve got it all wrong.

---

[55] Mikhail Vladimirovich Rodzianko, *The Reign of Rasputin: An Empire's Collapse: Memoirs of M. V. Rodzianko* (London: A.M. Philpot Limited, 1927), 253–54, cited in Pipes, *The Russian Revolution*, 269.

[56] Pipes, *The Russian Revolution*, 258.

[57] Figes, *A People's Tragedy*, 302; Tsuyoshi Hasegawa, *The February Revolution, Petrograd, 1917* (Leiden, The Netherlands: Koninklijke Brill NV, 2018), 96–7.

[58] H. Fessenden Meserve report to New York dated April 19, 1916, titled "Will Russia Have a Stable Government After the War?"; Documents from the Russian State Historical Archive, St. Petersburg, RGIA/624/1/5/122–3, cited in Hassan Malik, *Bankers & Bolsheviks: International Finance & the Russia Revolution* (Princeton, NJ: Princeton University Press, 2018), 152.

CHAPTER 1

Transatlantic crossing on the SS *Oscar II*

Rogers sailed on the SS *Oscar II*, owned by the Scandinavian America Line, which was one of the larger steamship lines of the early 20th century and operated passenger and freight service between Scandinavia and New York City until 1935.

The SS *Oscar II* was built at the Alexander Stephen & Sons shipyard on the Clyde in Glasgow, Scotland, and sailed on its maiden voyage from Copenhagen to New York in 1902.[59] The 9,970 gross ton, 519-foot-long steamship offered three classes of accommodation.[60] Rogers shared a cabin with two of his colleagues. He did not specifically mention in which class he sailed, however, John L.H. Fuller, a fellow National City Bank colleague, noted in his diary a year later that he traveled to Europe in first class on the SS *United States* of the same steamship line.[61]

The American economy boomed in the 1910s and 1920s, and a new class of wealthy Americans increasingly wanted to travel in luxury. Steamship companies built larger and more luxurious ships featuring the finest accommodations with these passengers in mind. Famous ships such as the Cunard Line's RMS *Mauretania*, the White Star Line's RMS *Titanic*, and the French Line's SS *France* were unmistakable symbols of high society sailing. However, ships of that era still relied on the immigrant trade as a major source of income well into the 1920s. Only a few decks separated rich society and poor emigrants. Rogers referred to "steerage" on the SS *Oscar II*, but according to the Norway Heritage genealogical research website, the ship featured a formal third class with staterooms offering accommodation for "two, four and six passengers, enabling entire families to stay together."[62] A fifty-page brochure published by the Scandinavian America Line in 1912 proudly promoted the ship's

---

[59] Historical footage of the SS *Oscar II*, with a tugboat by its side, can be viewed at https://www.youtube.com/watch?v=Zz2fdwhhtPI. The SS *Oscar II* was laid up in 1931 and scrapped in 1934 in Blyth, England.
[60] www.Norwayheritage.com is an excellent source for information on steamships of the early 20th century and detailed information on the SS *Oscar II*. See http://www.norwayheritage.com/p_ship.asp?sh=osca2.
[61] *The Journal of John L. H. Fuller*, Indiana Historical Society, TS 1999, MO112, 2.
[62] http://www.norwayheritage.com/p_ship.asp?sh=osca2.

facilities and service for "direct carriage" for Scandinavian emigrants to the United States who would travel in third class.[63] A 1917 brochure trumpeted, "We believe the third-class accommodations of the Scandinavian-America Line are unsurpassed. . . . Passengers in this class are assured of exceptional facilities. . . . Meals are served by uniformed waiters in clean dining rooms at tables set with fresh linen and porcelain tableware; the food is of good quality cooked in the palatable Scandinavian style, and served plentifully and with wide variety in the menus."[64]

Rogers had some complaints about the food served on the SS *Oscar II* and he didn't travel in third class. He amusedly and somewhat unsympathetically commented on the quality of the musical entertainment on board ship as well.

Rogers' travel from New York[65] to Petrograd first entailed sailing to Christiania (which returned to its original name, Oslo, in 1925), Norway, which required spending two days off Kirkwall in the Orkney Islands in Scotland, where British authorities checked the passenger list. Disembarking in Christiania, Rogers entrained to Stockholm, Sweden, and afterward traveled to Haparanda, in northern Sweden, where he transferred on a small ferry boat across the narrow Tornio River to Tornio in Finland (at that time still a part of the Russian Empire). He then took another train from Tornio to Petrograd. Rogers' journey time from New York to Petrograd totaled 18 days.

Ambassador David Francis traveled on the same SS *Oscar II* in April 1916 to assume his assignment in Petrograd. Harper Barnes, in his biography of Francis, points out that University of Chicago professor Samuel Northrup Harper, a Russia specialist and Slavicist, accompanied the ambassador on the journey. The professor recalled that "there were basically three groups on the *Oscar*: American businessmen interested in munitions contracts with Russia who hoped to cultivate the friendship of the new American ambassador; YMCA workers going to Russia to do relief work among German prisoners; and spies."[66] He was correct; munitions were big business. Russia placed foreign orders for artillery shells in 1915–1916 and by then got around twenty percent of its supply from the West. The United States provided over forty percent of the Russian army's machine guns.[67]

---

[63] Gjenvick-Gjonvik Archives, https://www.gjenvick.com/OceanTravel/Brochures/ScanAmLine-1912-ScandinaviaToAmerica.html.

[64] https://www.gjenvick.com/OceanTravel/Brochures/ScanAmLine-1917-DirectServices-NY-Scandinavia.html

[65] The SS *Oscar II* actually departed from the 17th Street dock in nearby Hoboken, NJ.

[66] Barnes, *Standing on a Volcano*, 185.

[67] Pipes, *The Russian Revolution*, 238.

Lenin took the same train route from Stockholm to Petrograd when he secretly returned to Russia on April 16, 1917.

Leighton Rogers put pen to paper the day he boarded the SS *Oscar II*. The first section of his journal spans five months from his departure from New York on September 28, 1916, until the events of the March Revolution and the abdication of Tsar Nicholas II. Rogers enjoyed an entertaining two-week sojourn across the Atlantic Ocean and by train through Scandinavia. His journal entries did not hint at any knowledge or concern about the difficult situation Russia faced. His adventure in Russia, however, was about to begin.

THE JOURNAL OF LEIGHTON W. ROGERS

September 1916

Upon first learning of my assignment to Russia anticipation of future experiences was bright enough to dim reflection on the consequences. So I gave them little thought; and thru the ten day's spent in hurrying from one shop to another, in packing my belongings, in saying "good-bye" to old friends, in hastening home, in the family discussions, in the efforts to dispel the stifled regret in Mother's eyes—during all this there was little thought of what would follow from my going away. But with the preparations over the flood of consequences burst the barrier of anticipation. What would happen during my absence? I was relinquishing opportunity in my own country, I was drawing fine with distance the cord of friendship; family prospects were none too bright, Mother's health was wavering,—all these thoughts had to be combatted. There was no withdrawing, however, for I was bound by a chain of accepted circumstances to execute my assignment, and this chain could not be broken. Not that I wanted to break it, for I could see at its end an improved life, but such is the weight of environment that if given time, it tends to overbalance resolution.

The day wheeled nearer. On the preceding night Father came to New York; I was glad to see him, for even among my friends there was something lacking. It was a pleasant evening; a good meal, enjoyable moments at the moving pictures, and a fine spectacle at the Hippodrome.[68] It must have made him feel quite young again for after the play he wanted to spend a little time and much money at the Biltmore roof garden; but I was compelled to leave him as there was much to do on the next

---

[68] Rebecca Read Shanor, "Hippodrome," in *The Encyclopedia of New York City*, 2nd ed., edited by Kenneth T. Jackson (New Haven, CT: Yale University Press, 2010). ISBN 978-0-300-11465-2, 597–598, cited in Wikipedia, "New York Hippodrome," last modified April 19, 2021, 08:29 (UTC), https://en.wikipedia.org/wiki/New_York_Hippodrome. The New York Hippodrome was a theater in New York City from 1905 to 1939, located on Sixth Avenue between West 43rd and West 44th streets. It was called the world's largest theater by its builders and could seat 5,300 people.

day.[69] It was the first time I had ever been out with Father, and it opened up a new rift in him, through which I could see a bit of tragedy. Someday I shall set it down. It is the tragedy of a man capable of deriving the highest good from pleasure, always anticipating that pleasure, yet forced by circumstances and a courageous adherence to what he considers his duty to forego it that others for whom he hopes much may have the experience. It is sacrifice carried to the extreme, some part of it useless. And what is more tragic than a useless sacrifice?

A bright morning such as only September can produce found me up early, hastening over to the bank, thanks to F.g.S. [Frederick Gilbert Sikes Jr., who was in Rogers' training class and sailed with him to Europe] with his machine, to shake hands with a few artificially interested officers and some sincere fellow-workers; and thence to meet Mother and Father at Altmans.[70] With them was an old friend whom Mother had invited down to the departure in an attempt at lightheartedness as much appreciated as it was a failure. In the taxi cab came two surprises, one from Father in the form of a leather writing case—indispensable—it was just what one would expect him to think of—and one from Mother, a book I remembered having expressed the interest of reading. What few sentences I could conjure up for thanks seemed empty, and as we approached the ferry which was to take us to the dock, words became scarce. Once beside the steamer my time was filled for a space in getting my baggage aboard; this done there was nothing to do but wait. I could see that the noise of the dock, the excitement of those around, and the accumulated feelings of days were battering at Mother's self-control; so knowing that the ship would be late in starting, and that they were planning on an afternoon with the Scarborough's I whispered to Father not to wait; he understood, as he always does, and we turned to take our leave. I refuse to say "goodbye," it was such a hopeless sound; but made no difference; at such a time words were quite unnecessary. In her eyes turned up to mine I could read all that was going on within—but it is best not to attempt to depict such things. I only wanted it known that I understood and may I receive mercy if I fail to attempt to reward her for it. They left and in the hectic mass at the dock I was alone with my thoughts.

---

[69] New York Preservation Archive Project; Preservation History Database; "Biltmore Hotel"; https://www.nypap.org/preservation-history/biltmore-hotel/. The New York Biltmore was designed by the architectural firm of Warren and Wetmore, which also created the adjoining Grand Central Terminal. The hotel had its own arrival station within the terminal. The Biltmore opened on New Year's Eve 1913 and was gutted in 1981.

[70] The Department Store Museum; "B. Altman & Co."; http://www.thedepartmentstoremuseum.org/2010/05/b-altman-co-new-york-city.html. B. Altman & Co. was a luxury department store and chain founded in New York City by Benjamin Altman. Its flagship store was at Fifth Avenue and 34th Street in midtown Manhattan. The company closed the store in 1989.

Not for long, however. A resounding slap on the shoulder and I turned to face three school friends, "Bones," "Roger," and "Pewee." How they came there was beyond me; I did not even know they knew where the boat sailed from. But there they were and welcome. They brought a book for me, a significant book,—"The Idylls of the King" which at once shot up in value many times its price. The call to clamber aboard cut short the subterfuge of repartee between us, and the last handshakes were given.

September 28th. 1916.

Then came the rush to the deck, the creaking of the gangplank, and soon the shore began to move away. Out past the dock, white with waving handkerchiefs, the air filled with good wishes, the two tugs bustled us to mid-stream, and with a last cheer ringing in our ears, and the remembrance of one face in my eyes, we were on our way. Under the shadow of the towering waterfront we slid past the Battery, the Statute of Liberty, to the open harbor. Here we were compelled to anchor for a few hours—for such is the mundanity of fact when we would have romance. However it gave us an opportunity to write letters to be taken off by the pilot, and a last sunset on New York.

Once more on our way we watched the lights twinkle out of sight into the darkness, felt the fresh sea wind and sniffed the salt in it; soon the light ship rocked into view, a tiny boat shot under our bow, the pilot clambered over the side; and with this last connection with the land severed, the ship nodded its approval and headed for the open.

The Oscar II is a small boat and it stands to reason that the cabins are in proportion. This fact brought us up against our first problem—that of packing three young and ambitious men, each with a steamer trunk, into the cabin; before an adjustment came however, it looked as if I was to be compelled to hang from the chandelier by my heels while my two cabin mates performed their evening ablutions. I was thankful to have drawn the crosswise berth as the sea was running length wise, which fact granted me the favor of sleep, for a while. More of which later. However, sleep we all did—leaving the port hole open for air; but unfortunately water comes in port holes as well as air and our cabin was the scene of a young flood in the morning.

With a good breakfast as an inspiration I was on deck early in search of my "sea legs." These came without much trouble and it seemed safe to prophecy a healthy voyage. Lunch time brought the interest of sitting at our table in the corner, seating-plan in hand, engaged in the fascinating sport of connecting names to faces. Next to us are the five track athletes—the best America can produce—on their way to Norway and Sweden for participation in various meets there; all are easily recognized from remembrances of newspaper pictures and previous acquaintance; Simpson, Murray, Ward, Loomis and Meredith.[71] At the table across sits the original little "sunshine girl" a baby of two, unhappily destined to be spoiled by her young mother who seems to take the child more as a toy than a responsibility; near her the young widow, nervous, much like a trembling poplar-leaf; and next to her the cynical, animalic Swedish gentlemen (?) who á la Oscar Wilde "knows the price of everything but the value of nothing." Beside the vivacious German girl we find the moving picture agent, already, homesick and unhappy and across from him "F" the "writer" (that word covers a multitude of sins!). The powerful looking lady next to him—the one wielding the cigarette and the champagne glass with so much dexterity—is Madame C. who some say is making an attempt to return to her native land, Germany, and others that she is a secretary to Dr. Fletcher of mastication fame,[72] that white old gentleman with the vein-laced face who leans so far over his plate and yodels his beer! As for that chubby, slightly bald, little fellow in the pink socks, tan shoes, and wristwatch, gazing with yearning obedience up into Madame's hazel eyes, he—er ah, that is Vladimir; the Russian, an officer in the Tsar's navy and a veteran of the battle of Port Arthur;[73] his appearance, clothes, and efforts to express himself in eight languages, make him out far from what he really is.

The afternoon found me finishing Joseph Conrad's "Nostromo" for the second time. It has become an old friend now, and is as worth having. A novel of avarice, represented by the San Tomé silver mine, it teaches its lesson by depicting the influences of this silver upon two spiritually different people. Charles Gould, interested in results, determined to make the San Tomé mine materialize its wealth if only to retrieve by so doing his father's failure, little appreciates the insidiousness of the power he warms into activity with the fire of his indomitable will. A power for evil which mesmerizes with a silver gleam and absorbs its victim, creeping from one to another, to Gould himself, and on, until, with a shrill of triumph, it owns even Nostromo, "Nostromo the Incorruptible."

---

[71] "Track Stars Go Abroad," *New York Times*, September 29, 1916, 10. The five traveled to compete in Stockholm on October 14–16, in the sprints, hurdles, and shot put. An interesting side note is that Andy Ward barely made it aboard the SS *Oscar II*, as he forgot to bring his passport and was initially not allowed to board. A replacement passport was arranged at the last minute with the aid of Secretary of State Robert Lansing and others.

[72] A.G. Christen and J.A. Christen, "Horace Fletcher (1849-1919): 'The Great Masticator,'" *Journal of the History of Dentistry* 45, no. 3 (November 1997): 95–100, https://pubmed.ncbi.nlm.nih.gov/9693596/. Horace Fletcher was an American food faddist who argued that food should be chewed thoroughly until liquefied before swallowing.

[73] The Battle of Port Arthur (Russian: Нападение на Порт-Артур; Japanese: 旅順口海戦) of February 8–9, 1904, marked the commencement of the Russo-Japanese War.

It is not until it meets Mrs. Gould that avarice fails. Mrs. Gould, who appreciates the fullness of mortality and the emptiness of achievement, who counts her husband's interest more than all the silver on earth, who, by keeping her great principles constantly at work on each day's petty trials, is able to recognize the San Tomé silver as different from these in degree only, who, when having taken her husband it comes for her, meets it with the same serene sympathy that she grants to all life's failures. And from her presence, recognizing its own utter worthlessness when applied to values, it crawls away into the ravine to lose itself forever.

Truly life is worth the living if just to meet such a woman; and in recognizing and depicting her Conrad has shown himself a consummate artist.

At first it is depressing to consider how many beautiful things are dependent upon money for their being.

Our opinions are made up of as many odd rags of thought as is the paper upon which we set them down. (suggested in Carlyle's "French Revolution")

Our greatest principles are most severely tested by the day's petty annoyances.

An artistic genius is often considered different from other people; but it seems to me that a genius is above all things like all people, like other people; he is all people in their mediocrity with the added ability to recognize his own reactions, and the initiative for the most wearing work of transcribing them.

We have a feud on board. It arose over those pesky portholes which are supposed to ventilate our cabins—I knew more would come from this than the water that went in—and it came about in this fashion. The boys in the cabin across the corridor, feeling the need of air in the night, leave their porthole open—and here, by the way, we must wonder with "Count" Swinnerton how there can be a porthole on the starboard side of the ship! But, as I mentioned before in thru this orifice water comes as well as air; to prevent which the powers that be on the Oscar II send a wrench-armed Valkyrie around to lock it up. Arguments and threats are of no avail, even locking the cabin door is in vain, for Brunhilde has a trick key which will unlock any door, save that of beauty, and each morning finds the opening tightly closed. So are the occupants of No. 23 compelled to submit in vociferous rage. But see what happens when Brunhilde invades the field of brains instead of brawn. After the second night of oppression the boys of No. 24, where as I said before dwelt the brains of the party, carefully bruise the threads of the bolt which closes said porthole, and it is impossible to screw it up tightly. Hence, for the time being, en bas[74] Brunhilde and in with salt air and victory!

One certainly cannot complain of the food on this boat, but there are certain phases of it deserving of comment. For instance, it seems to run more to quantity and color than to taste and odor. We sit ourselves down to plates of bronze soup dashed with yellow spots, pink fish half concealed under green mosses dotted with lemon, platters of tan meat garnished with white stripes and a rainbow of vegetables, and last but not least, salads, such salads, cerise, emerald, and ochre containing hidden and unknown things. Truly these gastronomic conceptions do out-Bakst Bakst[75] himself. Such is the mania for color that one can almost hear the salad chef call to the meat chef, "Hey, Mike, what color meat today?" "Auburn, shaded with russet sauce," comes the answer, to meet the counter reply, "All right, I guess a pale lavender salad ought to do this time." So lavender salad it is.

However, these considerations of the eye do not affect us very much, for if one is aesthetic they add a bit to the zest of eating and if not, one can eat with one's eyes closed. So we progressed fairly well up until lunch today, when the pudgy Swedish engineer at the next table asked for some choice breed of cheese. The steward stepped to the door, whistled thru his fingers, and with a rustle, in runs a piece of cheese to hop obediently up on the table and offer itself up for sacrifice! As the actually militant odor billowed out over the room the happy smiles faded to give way to that "we buried Willie yesterday" expression which always betokens inward tragedy. One by one they excused themselves from the table, as did the others of the cabin, until the pudgy engineer and his pet were left alone in possession of the field.

There is a little eighteen-year old girl in the steerage, returning home, no doubt, after some four years in America. Her clothes are not good clothes—the waist too extreme, the dress too short, and the blue and white shoes far too spectacular. There is much that is pretty about her curling brown hair, soft eyes, tip tilted nose, and dainty chin; and this in spite of the crimson on her lips and face. And in this one can almost see the father as she will say to her friends at home, "Yes, America is a wonderful place, but one must have money to be happy there."

His pride vanished in the great democracy of an emotional extreme.

---

[74] Rogers used French to convey "down with" or "to the bottom with."

[75] *Encyclopaedia Britannica Online*, "Léon Bakst," by Kathleen Kuiper, https://www.britannica.com/biography/Leon-Bakst. Kuiper writes that Leon Bakst, a Jewish Russian artist, "revolutionized theatrical design both in scenery and in costume," and that his designs for the Ballets Russes "were opulent, innovative, and extraordinary, and his influence on fashion and interior design was widespread."

I swung around the stern and there, a pencil mark on the slate of the horizon, lay a cruiser. A little bit of England so formed as best to serve her there. Motionless she was, and that restive feeling which betokens scrutiny from some unseen place told me of the powerful glasses leveled at the name on our side. Then with a snort of black smoke, she slid away and down into the deep, as if fleeing from the telltale finger of smudge ever pointing her out.

Eleven o'clock tonight found me still on deck watching the phosphorus. The sky is clouded, there is a dampness in the air, and a surface on the water as of oil. Under this the sea rolls sullenly, refusing to disclose its brilliance. This until our prow cuts the film to disclose the shimmering glow beneath, which dances up the steel sides and falls back with a crash of flame. It is as if all is fire below needing only a slit in the surface to let it out.

There are more lessons in the sea than in all your books and philosophies. It is the primary indisputable fact of physical existence and the great understanding in one. It is the most inflexible in adherence to its rules of conduct and the most flexible in its absorbing powers of all life's creations. Consider what things have gone down beneath it and reflect on the folly of non-adjustment; consider what things are cast at it and acknowledge the futility of aspersion!

We have run into a fairly heavy sea, head on, so that the ship now lifts her head high in air and now plunges deep into the foam. I have been walking the deck all morning to try out my sea legs; they seem to be sound. In vain do I search my system for signs of seasickness but the only signs of uneasiness disclosed are those resulting from the anti-typhoid injection given me by the ship's doctor this morning. One billion typhoid germs let loose in my blood to work as they will; it seems as though these were numbers enough to daunt any foe, but my white corpuscles seem to be bearing up under the strain. I know how a battlefield feels during a conflict.

(Based on the SS Oscar II's record of journey, the next entry can be dated to October 8, 1916)

This morning we passed another steamer at a distance of a quarter of a mile, the "Manchuria," formerly a Pacific mail boat now transferred to the Atlantic service.

We heard by wireless that a German submarine appeared off the coast of Rhode Island and sank seven merchant ships.[76] News variously received by those on board—by the Germans with ill-concealed delight, by the English with consternation, and by the Americans with admiration for the intrepidity of the act.

This has been one of the few sunny days of the voyage. Days of cold winds with slashes of rain have deadened our physical as well as spiritual activities. The sun draws us out today, however, and it is a changed people on board. Strange how much depends upon the mere physical condition of climate. One notices it even among this limited number. Considering individuals for the sake of convenience, there is the Frenchman,—impetuous, effervescent, the German, stolid, objective, the Russian, morose even melancholy, and the American, running the gamut of moods. We are so changeable it is not at all strange that Europeans think us crazy. Today's sun enlivened us into frisking about the deck, standing on our hands, climbing ropes, racing around the stern, and hurdling deck-chair in a joyous debacle of pent up energy. The others looked on curiously for a while, and then trooped below for tobacco and beer. The thought came to me that alcohol was a necessary stimulus to their phlegmatic temperaments, while to Americans it is quite superfluous. They need no such initiative. Only one more argument for prohibition in America.

Art is the representation of a moral idea or a moral fact through a particular physical medium.

In the course of a conversation with Joe Loomis today he remarked, "They told me it was an honor to be sent to Sweden to represent America in athletics, but I think it a damn dirty trick!" Which goes to show just how much he was enjoying the trip.

Of course fourteen days on ship-board are likely to make traveling companions a bit tired of each other, especially when so closely confined as we are; but I thought I had provided against any outward show of such feeling by separating myself from the others for a definite period each morning. But today, before I knew what was coming it burst forth in an argument with _____. This went the way of all such discussions—a

---

[76] Small State Big History, "A German U-Boat in Newport Harbor During World War I," by Brian L. Wallin, http://smallstatebighistory.com/a-german-u-boat-in-newport-harbor-during-world-war-i/. The German submarine *U-53* sailed into Newport, RI, harbor on the morning of October 7, 1916, to the great surprise of US military and civilian authorities there. U-boat captain Hans Rose paid courtesy visits to American Rear Admiral Austin M. Knight, commandant of the US Second Naval District, and Rear Admiral Albert Gleaves, aboard his flagship cruiser, the USS *Birmingham*. Rose was informed he and his submarine had two hours to leave American waters or else be interned. *U-53* promptly left and the next day sank three British, one Norwegian, and one Dutch merchant ship in international waters. All crew and passengers were rescued by US warships dispatched to the scene. After this incident, the British were incensed that German U-boats could operate with impunity near American waters and the Americans were concerned about German naval activities in "their backyard."

contested point, the intrusion of personality, due to a desire to win rather than a desire to arrive at the truth, the step down to dialectics, the slip to innuendo, and the final plunge to personalities. We finally separated with his expressing the wish that he might soon get to Petrograd so that he would not be compelled to see so much of me. And of course my suggestion that he might eliminate that dire necessity by hopping overboard did not help the situation much.

After that my only course it seemed was to bother him as little as possible which I there proceeded to do. The first trial came at dinner. I went all thru the meal trying to act as usual with the exception of being as unaware of _____'s presence as possible under the circumstances. It was laughable at times and I had to repress smiles—as, I wager did he—but there could be no cessation, for pride must be maintained at all costs!—even the cost of friendship!

What makes such a circumstance the more to be regretted is the discovery afterwards that it all grew out of misunderstanding (which would seem to substantiate Carlyle's statement in his "French Revolution"!)

And what a chaos the mind is left in when the final hand fulls [handfuls] of innuendo slime are thrown! Perhaps you were too hasty—No he grew angry first, weren't you a bit sarcastic?—Yes, but he resorted to personalities. Didn't you refuse to admit a point? Perhaps, but so did he. Why didn't you stop the discussion when you saw it falling?—Because it seemed that each new point should win, because he seemed to draw out the evil in me; besides he is selfish, narrowminded, and shallow. But anyway, ought you not make peace?—No for he is just egotistical enough to take such a move as submission. What can you do then?—Nothing but ignore and wait.

Such are the thoughts that course thru the brain and it is not until one sobers down does one realize that two are necessary for a quarrel, that opinions are seldom changed by argument, that experience is necessary.

Today I discovered another Psi U[77] on board, a young doctor from Chicago, on his way to Germany as a member of a special commission. He confided in me, during the course of the discussion, that he was taking numerous rubber gloves and bandages in with him; and as this substance was being confiscated by the English he expected some excitement when we hove[78] into Kirkwall.

---

[77] Wikipedia, "Psi Upsilon," last modified July 3, 2021, 04:06 (UTC), https://en.wikipedia.org/wiki/Psi_Upsilon. Psi Upsilon ΨΥ, commonly known as Psi U, is a North American fraternity founded at Union College in 1833. Rogers was a member of the Zeta chapter of Psi U at Dartmouth College. The chapter, which is still active, has occupied the same wood frame house since 1907.

[78] Past tense of the verb "heave": to pull, raise, or move (a boat or ship) by hauling on a rope or ropes.

This evening a sudden desire for excitement moved us to drag out a grapho-phone[79]—presented to the Captain by Henry Ford—and engage ourselves in the dance. For partners there were the vivacious German girl, the mother of the as yet unspoiled child, Madame in all her silks and jewels, and the shadow-eyed lady of forty-five, as yet unwilling to admit that she was out of the running. Outside, the sea was the heaviest of the trip; the ship swayed, pitched, and rolled; which combination, with the thick carpet, presented difficulties. The sensation of putting out one's foot in a fancy step and finding no floor there to greet it was decidedly unique. Every roll formed a tangled mass of arms and legs heaped up in a corner, making it necessary for one to drag out a partner—not always the same one—and set out again.

This morning we ran into a school of porpoises which broke out on all sides, and followed the ship for miles. The speed with which they swim and the ease with which they curved from the water was astonishing. Someone made the observation that we would soon sight a whale or two; and sure enough, not more than half an hour elapsed before on each bow, hardly more than half mile away, strips of black tipped with a stubby fin rose above the water, now and then to bubble a little like a half clogged fountain. This until they became well aware of our presence, when, with a final spurt of foam, a curving of the broad back, they dived for safety—from us who were only curious. Such is the conceit of fear.

It has been one of those days when everyone wanted to throw restraint to the winds and run and shout for the joy of living; when just to feel solid unmoving ground, under the feet would be a boon and the sight of trees and grass a blessing. But the tilting decks of the "Oscar" are a poor substitute for land, and her stubby masts and soot-covered funnels no trees at all; so there was nothing to do all day long but repeat what we had done so often before—retire to the smoking room and play bridge and drink insipid beer, recline stiffly in the salon and read well-known magazines, or pull up the coat collar and stride about the deck. I did the latter and managed to kill a little additional time by starting the track men in their trials around the deck. Then Simpson wanted some pictures so there was a general lining up on the rear deck for that ordeal.

It is amusing to watch the reactions of the steerage passengers to the sight of these bare legged individuals trolling around the decks, doing their hurdle exercises, and playing with the medicine ball. Some stared in open-mouthed amazement,

---

[79] Wikipedia, "Graphophone," last modified May 24, 2021, 05:43 (UTC), https://en.wikipedia.org/wiki/Graphophone. Graphophone was the name and trademark of an improved version of the phonograph. It was invented at the Volta Laboratory by Alexander Graham Bell and his colleagues in the 1880s.

others in admiration—there last mostly from the fairer sex whose action elicited disgruntled comments from their men—at the bronzed, shapely leg muscles and the swaying shoulders, while still others regarded them with that amused wonder, so often shown before the monkey cages at the zoo. "Ted" Meredith said he felt like a prize colt on a horse ship.

This over there was little left to do. Of course it is only natural that we should be bored at this time, but it must also be admitted that ours is a peculiar group of passengers. Everyone is intent upon business, and serious business, there is no pleasure seeking element in it, and the result is that each keeps more or less to himself. The only "live wire" in the whole party is our friend Vladimir. It seems that Vladimir is an officer in the Russian Navy—wherever that is—and a veteran of the Japanese–Russian war besides, being aboard one of the cruisers that went down before Togo's[80] fleet. He is a most interesting person. With the European weakness for femininity he follows "Madame" about like a little terrier, if one can imagine a terrier decked out in red socks, and tie, wristwatch, abdomen supporter and shining forehead! He also possesses a smattering knowledge of some eight languages; so that a conversation with him is like listening at the chimney of a Berlitz School. His habit of saying "Pos-i-tively" to every other sentence has fastened that word to him as a cognomen. So "Positively," we call him. Tonight he informed us that in the morning we would meet the English patrol boat, and be taken in hand, to be conducted to Kirkwall by an English prize crew.[81]

As weather goes it has been another gray day—just like all the others, damp, chilly, and windy; but for incident it has been by far the best of the voyage. Against the days grayness its particular facet of experience shines out brilliantly. For, early in the afternoon, from far down on the—let me see, we must be nautical here—starboard side, the black bulk of an English cruiser slid towards us as if pushed along by its streak of smoke. We all gathered at the rail to comment on her size, number of guns, and such, and to listen for the shot signaling us to stop. But instead of this, suddenly, as if changing her mind womanlike, she turned and hastened back to the horizon. We could not fathom it, until, on our port side, a discerning eye sighted another patrol boat—this time a plain freight and passenger steamer, stripped, painted, and fitted with a few guns. She trudged steadily along straight towards us, signaled with a puff

---

[80] Marshal-Admiral the Marquis Tōgō Heihachirō (東郷 平八郎, 1848–1934) served as admiral of the fleet in the Imperial Japanese Navy and became one of Japan's greatest naval heroes by winning a decisive victory over the Russian fleet at Tsushima in May 1905.

[81] A prize crew are the members of a ship chosen to take over the operations of a captured ship.

of white and a sharp report, and crossed our bow to wait as we shut down and came to a stop. We could see the men flocking to the side, far too many it seemed for such a small ship, and the officers on the bridge, glasses in hands. Soon a small boat, with its contingent of men, oars in hand, swung out over the side, caught, tilted dangerously, suddenly righted, and shot downward to hit the water with a resounding smack. With the tackle loose, the oars clutched the water, and the boat came on, crawling up and down the waves, slowly but surely, until only a few feet from our side. Down went our ladder and tackle, in shot the small boat, to cling fast to our ropes. The men were of all types, old and hardened, young and anxious, middle aged and uninteresting, but all sitting their places with the easy assurance of the sailor. An officer clambered up our side, then another, followed by an electrician; they smiled at our welcome and hastened to the bridge. Meanwhile, our passengers pressed to the rail, some to shout greetings to the upturned faces below, others to eye them curiously, commenting on the effrontery of England so stopping us and taking possession; while still others, and I am glad to say the majority, saw these men, not through partisan eyes, but as men, and brought to the side to drop to the eager hands, apples, oranges, cigars, cigarettes, papers, and magazines. Then, from the bridge over our heads came a call, "All right, prize crew aboard!" Six men, each with a carriage bag and armed with a heavy caliber revolver mounted to our deck where they promptly scattered; our ladder came battering up and the small-boat, struggling like a wounded bug, crept back to his ship. The shouted goodbye lost themselves in the wind, our propellers took up their task, and we drew away from the patrol boat with her insistent guns. She too, after rescuing her infant, snorted smoke from her nostrils and strode away. And with an English officer on the bridge, and English guard on board, and our wireless in the hands of an English operator, we were no longer on Swedish territory headed for Sweden, but a part of England bound for England.

Sailors have a peculiar fascination for the landlubber, a fascination which weaves in the latter's mind all sorts of fanciful pictures and leaves him in chagrin at the discovery that he is only a human being after all, through intimate acquaintance with himself, perhaps a little more human than the rest of us. This afternoon a curious group surrounded each sailor, plying question after question. The particular one I selected for the Inquisition was a young chap, possibly twenty years old, with smooth pink skin, and round blue eyes set in star-like eyelashes. He had little to say for himself and confined most of his talking to answering our questions. Someone asked about the patrol boat and it turned out to be an interesting subject. Its interior was completely cleaned out, cabins, partitions and all, leaving one ship-length room which accommodated the four hundred men aboard. These men were divided into groups of six or eight or ten, each in turn going into Kirkwall with some ship such as ours. After a few days ashore to stock up with supplies, visit friends, and enjoy the feel of solid ground, a mail packet brings the crew out again to the patrol boat, on which it waits its next turn. Thus the patrol boat is enabled to stay out for months at a time,—for as long as she can carry provisions for her crew, while her men have a trip ashore once or twice a month.

Our friend happened to ask the name of our ship, not having noticed it when he came on board, and when someone replied with a half contemptuous snort—as most Americans would have done—"Huh, the "Oscar II" the peace ship, Henry Ford's Peace Ship," we all stood around abashedly, wishing to apologize for the incident, and preparing ourselves gracefully to accept the expected innuendo. But there was no laugh, no joke, only quite seriously, the sailor said "Enery Ford's a big man an' did the best 'e could in a good cause, but this war's a 'eap too bitter to be settled like that."[82]

This afternoon we sighted land. At first it appeared far off on the horizon, a long low strip of purple, creeping nearer as the afternoon wore on, until we could see the cliffs, the green, and the lighthouse; and finally the out-lying reef with its white fringe, and the rollers breaking on the yellow sand beyond. Although only an outlying strip, just the sight of its solidity, its living greenness, put a new joy in life. For man is not a sailor by nature, and after fourteen days, this was a return to the nature. What lighthouse it was or where it was we do not know, for there seems to be some doubt as to our route. Some say we are bound for Kirkwall by the regular way between the islands, and others state that owing to extensive submarine operations—a sample of which Newport saw some ten days ago—we are being taken around the islands. But no matter what our route the trip has taken on a new interest. That the ship has changed its course was plainly seen by the white arc of our wake as we swung around the headland and headed up the coast. The opinion seems to be that we shall arrive in Kirkwall during the night. With this conclusion, when darkness came and there

---

[82] Steven Watts, *The People's Tycoon: Henry Ford and the American Century* (New York: Alfred A. Knopf, 2005) 229; David Traxel, *Crusader Nation: The United States in Peace and the Great War 1898–1920* (New York: Knopf Doubleday, 2006) 206, cited in Wikipedia, "Peace Ship," last modified June 28, 2021, 01:39 (UTC), https://en.wikipedia.org/wiki/Peace_Ship.
The SS *Oscar II* was also known as The Peace Ship, https://www.gettyimages.com/detail/video/the-ss-oscar-ii-chartered-by-henry-ford-for-a-peace-news-footage/497732244. American industrialist Henry Ford organized an amateur peace mission to Europe in 1915 by chartering the SS *Oscar II* and inviting a large group of pacifists, writers, socialists, and workers for various causes to join him with the objective of promoting a peace conference among the belligerents of WWI. The press ridiculed Ford and referred to the SS *Oscar II* as the "Ship of Fools" as well as the "Peace Ship." Ford fell ill when he arrived in Norway and five days later abandoned the mission and returned to the United States.

was no more good in remaining at the rail we went below to the smoking room to play cards, smoke, gossip, drink light beer, out. We seem to be in the center of the circle of ships—ships of all nations, and ships of all kinds, French, Dutch, Norwegian, Swedish, and one American, schooners, tramps, liners and motor driven freighters. Squalls come tearing over the slopes, the flags stiffen, the ships swing at their anchor chains, the lighters scream louder, the water foams, and the gulls sweep and swirl in derision. It's no fun on deck, so we go below. How long here, what happens here no one seems to know.

For purposes of journal writing this has been a great day. But such is the type of events that one must needs be a Thackeray with a fine eye for small things sans pettishness to set them down properly.

In the first place the guard, or squad of inspectors sent aboard by the customs authorities last night has evidently been quite busy, as this morning we found that one of our number had been locked inside his cabin and a guard stationed outside his door, under suspicion as a German. This particular person suspected to be guilty of such a heinous crime is a man named Fox, said by some of our smoking room gossips, or perhaps by confession, a writer. A writer—whew! What terrible implications that word carries! It amused me secretly because I never liked Fox; he was always too damned comfortable. One of these colorless blondes, with his jelly-roll body draped in a colorless blonde knit jacket, he was always sitting at his ease in the smoking room, sipping colorless beer and giggling at colorless stories. I don't think he's positive enough to be a German although undoubtedly he is pig-headed enough. But anyway he was locked in his cabin three fourths of the day, sputtering and storming through the keyhole, until they let him out.

He immediately ducked for his corner in the card room, where like an enraged and wet hen he gathered his brood about him and sputtered to his heart's content.

There too "Alkali Ike" is quite peevish this evening. "Ike" is an Alaskan explorer, or miner, or an Alaskan something, for he has an outfit, anyway. An outfit which he took great pain that everyone on ship board should see, hanging his blankets, shirts, buckskin jackets, moccasins etc. up on a wire on deck to dry out—though Lord knows it has been damp as the devil all the way over. "Ike"—I call him that for lack of his real name, was wont to sit with Fox and others in the smoking room and swap stories à la Robert W. Service.[83] It seems the British—the blighters—took a liking to

---

[83] Wikipedia, "Robert W. Service," last modified July 8, 2021, 14:41 (UTC), https://en.wikipedia.org/wiki/Robert_W._Service.
Robert W. Service (1874–1958). A British-Canadian poet and writer, often called the "Bard of the Yukon."

his outfit and inspected it very carefully, appropriating some of his rubber articles. And so it has been a sorry day for "Ike" too. He wants America to declare war on England today.

And then of course there's the big scandal of the voyage concerning Mrs. Schmidt, Dr. Martin and the Dane. Everyone on ship-board knows by this time and has whispered to someone else how Frau Schmidt—a young German wife returning to Germany without her husband—how she, speaking only German naturally liked being with Dr. Martin, who also spoke German; how they were together all the time, how, of course he was old enough to be her father and all that, but how it wasn't quite right for them to see so much of each other; how the Dane, old and large enough to know better, said as much, how his saying reached the ears of Dr. Martin, how he stormed into the smoking room and called the Dane many things, how there was nearly a fight, how the matter was taken to the Captain of the ship he being judge, jury and all the court on his own ship, how that worthy deemed that the Dane should apologize, how the latter did so quite ungracefully, and how the affair is over save for the whisperings which still fly about the decks. "Is that so?" "Yes, and—" "Well, who would have thought it"? "I know, that's what makes it so—?" "Why, she's young enough to be his daughter." "Certainly, only—" "But it mustn't be talked about," "Oh no, I wouldn't mention it to a soul, only you—" "It's disgraceful." If this is the way it goes with the higher order of animals on one little ship, what must have poor Mr. and Mrs. Noah put up with, with all the orders.

To add to all this, all during the day we have been undergoing the throes of inspection. It began this morning when the rattle and screech of the steam winches awakened me. The mail was being hoisted out of the hold in great sacks and lowered over the side to the deck of a lighter, presided over by a young officer, standing on the pilot house, notebook in hand. This over, and the lighter steaming away with our mail to be censored, the winches commenced on the piles of trunks in the hold. One after another, up they came, to be piled on the deck at random. Steamer trunks, old leather trunks, boxes bound with rope and wire, and the costliest of compartment trunks stood side-by-side, rubbing buckles on the slippery deck; old trunks, new and shining ones, trunks covered with labels, and some devoid—all awaiting their turn. This went on all day, and as a matter of fact still is going on, for I can hear the rattle of the winch, the clank of chain, and the thud of the trunks as they hit the deck.

But only our cabin baggage was inspected today. Early in the afternoon an officer made the rounds of the cabins, marking a chalk number on each door; thus when, the inspection squads came a'board they found their fields of operations all laid out for them. Two sailors came to our cabin; one an old bearded Irish man with a bared chest weathered like the side of a barn and the other a young chap with a smile in his eye. The old fellow was all for business, wishing to look through all our luggage and be on to the next cabin. But our young friend was all for talking; evidently the work didn't appeal to him. "Hit's too much like a' pryin into people's private affairs," he remarked. "What's the use, Bill, these 'ere chappies aint got nothin we want; can't yu see that?" But Bill was bent on carrying out his duty so we opened up our trunks for his benefit. They pawed the things over a little, Bill in silence, and a bit gingerly as he saw the contrast of his hardened hands and the white smoothness of our clothes. "You chaps 'ave a bunch of clothes, you must be goin away for a long stay," remarked our friend. "For three years!" he ejaculated, at my reply, "whew" and he whistled softly. "That's a long time, a long time to be away from yer girls; eh, wot'll yer girls think o'that? They don't like it, you know, these women folk, they don't. I've got a girl in Monmouth and the last time I was there, she asked me to stay an marry 'er; and Jaysus!, but I wanted to," said he with a slap of his fist on the top of my trunk, "but, I couldn't, I couldn't, no sir, I ad to come back 'ere."

Across the hallway the boys had made the fatal mistake of promising the sailors half of what they found. Under this incentive it was not long before one of them unearthed Fred's bottle of brandy brought along for medicinal purposes; holding the boys to their promise, the sailor soon drained half the bottle, and a good half too, and the inspection was over. The inspection cost us nothing save a toothbrush and a tube of paste which my friend requested in his naïve fashion. "I'd like one of those" said he simply, espying my store of brushes. I gave him one. "Now this 'ere aint exactly much use without some 'o that,"—pointing to my boxes of paste tubes. So a tube of paste became his also. "Thanks," he said, sincerely, "it'll 'elp 'em a lot,"—smiling to show a gleaming and perfect set of teeth.

I finished out the day with Dr. Rowen, my Psi U friend, in the smoking room. He smiled broadly to himself over his beer and finally consented to let me in on the secret. "I had all I could do to contain myself," he said, "when I went into the cabin to have my passport inspected, because the officer was seated on the exact cushion that concealed numerous dozen pairs of rubber gloves I am taking into Germany with me!"

While Sunday is supposed to be a day of rest a great deal depends upon what is meant by rest. If rest means a change of action then today has been a restful one. A change for I am quite sure none of us have ever felt or acted so foolishly before. We gave a benefit for the band. If I have not mentioned the band before it is not because they have been forgotten, nor is it because I have been charmed into silence. Better let it go with saying it is because I have tried to ignore it. But on ship board it is difficult to ignore anything, let alone that which is both visible, to be heard, and may I say nasal? But our band is quite wonderful in its way. All the way across, each morning and each afternoon it has assembled on the rear upper deck, its several units gathered around the permanent music stand built there, to wheeze out a program composed of Strauss waltzes, here and there Grieg, and quite frequently bits of ragtime not more than a year old. After having thus combated the elements for an allotted time it methodically troops below once more, to prepare for the evening concert. In the evening, at dinner, our band lays down its sounding brass, takes up the wood and string and becomes an orchestra. So while we sup we must also hear the same tunes droned out in the salon above our heads. Their souls are really in the brass though, for I think they cling to the band music even when they are an orchestra.

But for some unknown reason it became known that for them money was necessary,—perhaps to bribe them to quit for the remainder of the voyage—I still think it was for this worthy purpose that so many contributed—anyway the uniform and instruments were borrowed and soon a new band, far out doing the original in bizarreness of sound, was parading the decks in bedlam. Through the cabins, down in the steerage, up on the upper deck, everywhere filed the bleating and stumping line, with the yawning cup in the leader's hand ever growing fuller. Sailors on passing lighters regarded us with awe, while passengers crowded to the side of the newly arrived "Frederick VIII," [84] anchored not far away, and wondered, no doubt, whether all of Henry Ford's party had been led off the "Oscar II," after his notable trip. But much money was forthcoming and the band promised to give an extra concert for our pains!

All day long we have watched the trunks come up out of the hold. The winches hiss, chain rattle and up comes a bundle of trunks, to thump to the deck and be ranged into line by the burly deckhands. All kinds of trunks, wardrobe, old leather, strapped wooden trunks, square trunks, oblong, long, and short, all rubbing shoulders in the democracy of submission. Each one must be opened by its owner and its contents inspected before we can go our own way. Much of the work will be over today.

Far beyond the town of Kirkwall lies a military observation post part of whose equipment is a captive balloon. Practically all day long it hangs in the air struggling at its rope, a huge sausage-shaped affair with a swelling at one end, for all the world like one of those misshapen floaters you used to carry away from the county fair. Once in

[84] Norway-Heritage; "SS *Frederik VIII,* Scandinavian America Line," http://www.norwayheritage.com/p_ship.asp?sh=fredv. Launched in 1913 and scrapped in 1936.

a while it goes reluctantly earthwards, and an aeroplane soars in its place, but not for long, the clumsy thing clamors skyward again and resumes its watch.

Today has been a dull one in spite of the fifty mile an hour gale which tore up the surface of the harbor and ripped through the rigging of the ships. With such a gale there was little to do outside and as usual nothing below save the inevitable bridge, smoke, and beer. I clung to the deck for a while watch the ships veer and tug at their buoys, the snubby lighters struggle around with their screaming sirens, and the seagulls defying the gale. It seems to bother them little; with but the slighted tilting of the wings they are able to slide forward against the wind, remain absolutely motionless, or hurtle through the air before it. Not so the man made bird-machines. In spite of the gale the military observation balloon went up and remained there tugging at its mooring line; suddenly this snapped and through the mist we could see the misshapen bag bobbing in the clutches of the wind, disappear into the mist. It being an offshore wind it was hardly a pleasant prospect for the two observers therein, tearing out to sea in such a craft. I wonder what became of them.

It is rumored that tomorrow we leave Kirkwall; and if so I shall not be sorry. I shall always remember it à la Sir Walter Scott with its towering castle on the moor, naked, misty and melancholy.

We left Kirkwall early in the morning so I missed catching a glimpse of the entrance of that excellent harbor. We are now setting out across the North Sea and true to its reputation it is a most choppy and interesting body of water. The weather has been a little cold, but clear, and the night has been wonderful with the wind, the gleaming moon and the hurrying clouds. Andy Ward and I have been up on the rear deck hanging over the rail, fascinated by the rise and fall of the water, talking over all the topics of the day. They are of course many and varied, ranging all the way from Andy's many girls to the poor quality of the beer served on board ship.

It is still choppy and windy outside. There is very little to do save wrap oneself up in a steamer rug and read the time away. Everyone is tired of talking to the same people about the war, and about the petty scandals on board, so that for the most part, a dignified silence reigns. We are all anticipating the arrival at Christiania. It will seem good to feel solid, unmoving land, underfoot once more. They say that tomorrow we shall be steaming up the fjords, to arrive at Christiania either late at night or on the morning of day after tomorrow.

CHAPTER 2

Grand hotels and Swedish baths

The SS *Oscar II* arrived in Christiania on the evening of October 11, 1916, after a voyage of fourteen days. A local Norwegian paper wrote the next morning that the ship carried onboard (besides Rogers, his five NCB colleagues, and the five American track men) eight hundred barrels of Baldwin apples.[85]

Rogers described his four-day train journey through Scandinavia. His activities included searching for a good meal, some sightseeing, and a swim. He did not comment on the precarious geopolitical situation of Norway or Sweden, nor did he seem overly concerned about German submarines, despite his attention to the wire news about a U-53 attack.

Norway and Sweden had declared their neutrality upon the outbreak of World War I and pursued uneasy balancing acts among the Allied, or Entente, Powers (the coalition led by France, Great Britain, Russia, Italy, Japan, and, starting in April 1917, the United States), and the Central Powers (Germany, Austria-Hungary, the Ottoman Empire, and Bulgaria). Although Norway and Sweden had similar needs and concerns, they approached neutrality differently.

At the outset of the war, Norway had one of the largest merchant fleets in the world, along with plenty of experienced merchant seamen. Stig Tenold of the Norwegian School of Economics points out that "The high demand for seaborne transport during the First World War, combined with Norwegian neutrality, created a boom for Norwegian shipping."[86] The British blockade forced Germany to restructure its trade, and Norway benefited greatly: Exports to Germany more than tripled between 1913 and 1916.[87] But Norway had to balance a tenuous neutrality between Germany and Great Britain. Great Britain, its supply chain threatened by the German navy, struck

---

[85] The author thanks Jan Peter Wiborg and Tore Langholm, researchers from NorwayHeritage.com, for unearthing newspaper articles and shipping and train schedules from September and October 1916 that confirmed the dates and times recorded in Rogers' journal.

[86] Stig Tenold, "The First World War: The Neutral Ally," *Norwegian Shipping in the 20th Century*, Palgrave Studies in Maritime Economics (Palgrave Macmillan, Cham, 2019), https://doi.org/10.1007/978-3-319-95639-8_3.

[87] Ibid.

a deal with Norway to use Norway's excess shipping tonnage in exchange for Great Britain supporting Norway's economic interests, including coal supply. A "tonnage agreement" formalized this arrangement in the spring of 1917. "Norway had become the neutral ally," concludes Karl Erik Haug of the Norwegian University of Science and Technology.[88] Neutrality, though, exacted a heavy cost. Indiscriminate surface attacks by the German navy, mines, and torpedoes all took their toll. Norway lost more than 2,000 sailors and more than 500 ships—half its merchant fleet—during the war.[89]

Sweden pursued a different strategy: "benevolent neutrality." Sofi Qvarnström of Lund University explains that for Sweden, "because of its non-interventionist policy, its trade dependence on the belligerents, and its status as a small state, neutrality was a natural choice."[90] But neutrality proved complicated. Swedish Foreign Minister Knut Wallenberg (1853–1938) advocated a "benevolent" nonalignment with Germany. Qvarnström points out:

> Some argue this was a concession made of fear of a German ultimatum that would force Sweden to side with Germany. Sweden would benevolently agree—sometimes after an initial refusal—to German demands and requirements: Swedish lighthouses were blacked out, the Sound between Denmark and Sweden was mined, and a transit ban on military equipment across Sweden was adopted to hinder British and French shipments to Russia. Sweden was the only neutral country which defended violent German acts including the violation of Belgian neutrality, the deportation of civilians in Belgium, submarine warfare and the sinking of the *Lusitania* in May 1915.[91]

Ultimately, neutrality became unbenevolent for Sweden. Henric Häggqvist of Uppsala University explains how the interdiction in foreign trade, which started later in the war, cast Sweden into a recession and resulted in "sharp price increases, food shortages, rationing, and food riots and protests all across the country."[92]

[88] Karl Erik Haug, "Norway" in *1914–1918–online. International Encyclopedia of the First World War,* Ute Daniel et al., eds. (Berlin: Freie Universität Berlin, 2016), https://doi.org/10.15463/ie1418.10809.

[89] Asbjorn Lysgard and Ole Christian Tenden, "The Norwegian Merchant Fleet–The Small State's Multi Tool for Future Crisis," *Arts and Social Sciences Journal* 10, 3 (July 3, 2019), https://www.hilarispublisher.com/open-access/the-norwegian-merchant-fleet--the-small-states-multi-tool-for-future-crisis.pdf.

[90] Sofi Qvarnström, "Sweden" in *1914–1918–online. International Encyclopedia of the First World War,* Ute Daniel et al., eds. (Berlin: Freie Universität Berlin, 2016), https://doi.org/10.15463/ie1418.10150.

[91] Ibid.

[92] Henric Häggqvist, "Wartime and Post-war Economies (Sweden)" in *1914–1918–online. International Encyclopedia of the First World War,* Ute Daniel et al., eds. (Berlin: Freie Universität Berlin, 2019), https://doi.org/10.15463/ie1418.11402.

When World War I commenced, Great Britain blockaded Germany's access to the North Sea and English Channel. Germany retaliated by introducing unrestricted submarine warfare. The waters surrounding the British Isles became a war zone and all merchant ships, flying a neutral flag or not, would be fair game. On May 7, 1915, a German U-boat sank the British ship RMS *Lusitania*. The *Lusitania* was transporting a supply of munitions, but was principally a passenger ship. Nearly twelve hundred passengers and crew, including 124 Americans, perished in the tragedy.[93] President Woodrow Wilson immediately demanded the German government cease attacks on unarmed merchant ships. By September 1915, Germany acceded and suspended U-boat warfare altogether, although German navy commanders pushed to resume unrestricted submarine warfare. Increasingly concerned about Germany's prospects in the war, Kaiser Wilhelm relented in February 1917. The resumption of submarine attacks on passenger and merchant ships provided a key impetus for Wilson to declare war on Germany two months later.

In 1916, ocean liners such as the SS *Oscar II* sailed north of Scotland to avoid English ports. The SS *Oscar II* flew the flag of neutral Denmark.

After one of the least appetizing breakfasts of his life in Haparanda, Sweden, (worse prospects awaited in Petrograd) Leighton Rogers boarded his final train to Petrograd, and arrived at Finlandia Station at 10:30 p.m. on October 16, where Enevold Detlefsen, National City Bank's accountant, awaited. Rogers remained in the environs of Petrograd until February 23, 1918. He spent 495 days in Russia.[94]

---

[93] The Lusitania Resource "Passenger and Crew Statistics" 2003–2021, https://www.rmslusitania.info/people/statistics/.

[94] "Letter from Leigh Rogers," November 23, 1916, *Class of 1916 of Dartmouth College: First Annual Report, 1917*, 84; photos of Rogers' passport stamps dated October 2/15 showing entry in Tornio and October 3/16 entry in Petrograd, Leighton W. Rogers Papers, Scrapbooks Folder, Library of Congress. Rogers wrote he "arrived about eleven o'clock on the night of October 16th, very tired, but happy in having had a great time." He met with Meserve and Stevens the next day.

It has been a long time since I have written and a great deal has happened. Moreover the facilities for writing are not of the best. We are on our way to Petrograd from Stockholm, and although the train moves slowly, it has such an oriental twist to its progress that it is difficult to write.

I shall never forget the approach to Christiania. All during the day we steamed along a rugged, irregular coast, turbulent with rocks, with frothing waves at their base and struggling pines above; now and then a light house broke the scene of loneliness, always perched on a bare space of rocks, and almost surrounded by foaming surf, angry at man's tentative venture into its domain. Later in the day we found ourselves winding thru the fjords. At half-speed we crept along, turning and twisting, thru narrow defiles between sheer walls of solid rock, so near as to be almost within touch and opening out into placid caves and bays,—and from there again into the narrow ways—the rocks studded with little colored roofed houses, clinging amidst the pines like postage stamps, now in clusters of villages and now singly. Of roads and pathways there seemed to be none, the only means of communication being the little boats anchored to buoys or fastened to the rocks. As the night came on these little villages became clusters of twinkling lights to which blinked in answer to our own as we crept past. Not a great distance from Christiania we came to the narrowest pass in all the navigable fjords and the most heavily fortified,—although as far as we could make out it was not fortified at all. On each side the rocks loomed up seemingly within reach, and although we could feel that we were under surveillance, not a light or a sound betrayed our watchers. We were told by Norwegians on board that here the rocks are honey combed with heavy guns, and below the water line torpedo tubes are drilled in the solid rock. In one of the curving harbors we came to a stop and a boat put out from shore, where we would dimly see a crowd of people gathered at the dock; but it was not long before we went on our way again.

And then suddenly, as we swung around a corner of rock, unexpectedly, as one comes upon a wild animal, we came upon Christiania. There it was, a blaze of light rambling over the whole hillside, from top, to the water's edge, and even beyond, in the lights of many anchored ships. We viewed it with the same delighted surprise, with which one greets the first glimpse of New York, or Dreamland Park[95]

---

[95] David Goldfield, *Encyclopedia of American Urban History*, (Thousand Oaks, CA: SAGE, 2006) 185, cited in Wikipedia, "Dreamland (Coney Island, 1904)," last modified August 5, 2021, 11:19 (UTC),

from afar, and like children, could hardly contain ourselves till we came to our pier. This we did in due time, warping easily into the stone lined wharf, covered with rambling sheds, towering cranes, and the crowd of silent, expectant people. As our gangplank lowered, the silence was broken by cries of family names, as people too anxious to await the passing of the crowd recognized or sought to recognize each other. We said goodbye to our friends Loomis, Meredith, Ward, Simpson and Murray, as we did not expect to see them again and crowded for the gangplank. I gave our steward my few last pieces of American money and directed him to bring our trunks to a designated corner of the ramshackle customs house, which we could make out dimly lighted on the pier. Then with suitcase and coat in hand I crept down the steep plank to solid ground once more. I had expected to feel it rock, so accustomed was I to the movement of the ship—and had been told it would seem to do so—but it had the same old firm feeling.

The crowd bustled and surged about us, shouting, gesticulating, embracing and ordering; already the winches creaked and rattled and our trunks began to bump onto the wharf. We stood together in the indicated corner and soon our steward had all our trunks and hand baggage in a heap beside us. He was a nice chap—that steward—and we rewarded him again for his good work.

As many people seemed to be leaving immediately and others seemed to be having their custom inspection then and there, we hardly knew what to do. Finally, we decided to get it all over with, and as luck would have, in the dark of the shed, I managed to haul an inspector over to our heaps of baggage. With the aid of one of my pocket lights he watched us open our trunks, pawed gingerly at the white goods on top which seemed to frighten him, closed them, and pasted his label on the outside. Someone engaged him in conversation as the rest of us scattered around to find our large trunks which had been stored in the hold. As discovered we dragged them over for inspection (?). About this time our party received an addition in the person of a husky individual in the uniform—consisting of a cap—of a licensed dock man. For lack of another we shall know him by the name of Jake. Jake it seemed had labored around the docks in New York for a few years and besides a strong back and a mighty fist had acquired a few words of English. He was a great help in finding our trunks. I finally located mine, forming one of the corner stones of a huge pile of miscellaneous baggage topped by the largest and flimsiest looking piece of baggage I have ever seen.

---

https://en.wikipedia.org/wiki/Dreamland_(Coney_Island,_1904)#cite_note-1. Dreamland was an amusement park at Coney Island, Brooklyn, New York City, that operated from 1904 to 1911. It was the last of the three original large parks built on Coney Island, along with Steeplechase Park and Luna Park.

How to rescue mine was the problem. Jake, however, easily solved it by jerking my trunk out from under the pile, which tottered for a moment and then crashed to the pavement, the great flimsy top piece alighting squarely on one corner and splitting open in a leisurely manner. I looked on in fear and awe, but Jake only grinned and pulled my piece and me away from the carnage. After the inspector had completed his labor of pasting the labels on these trunks we gathered round and drove a bargain with Jake whereby he was to have all our luggage at the proper station at four o'clock the following day. With his nonchalant assurances that we should find it all safely there, we gathered up our suit cases and set out. I turned and respectfully nodded goodbye to the ship with its name "Oscar II" painted on the side in great white letters.

It was pitch dark and the waterfront was deserted save for our party, and one other—Vladimir; who came puffing out of the corner of the Customs House laden with bags, coats, rugs, and canes. We joined forces—Vladimir was a valuable find because of his linguistic prowess, and made our way out of the docks building to the street. That too, was deserted, and no cars seemed to be coming our way. We deposited our baggage on the cobbles and set to whistling and shouting for a cab. We must have been a strange sight,—a noisy mass of humanity and luggage floating in the emptiness of the street. Soon two vehicles answered our signals of distress,—a small and somewhat dilapidated cab and a taxi. Loading all our baggage and as many of our party as possible into the taxi, the remainder clung to the cab and we thus made our triumphal entry into Christiania. Vladimir enlivened our advance on the unsuspecting city with tales of the nice things to eat and the pretty girls it contained. But alas, hotel after hotel turned us away; the city was overcrowded, and it looked as if we would have to be content with the sky as a cover. But finally a one horse pension was discovered not far from the center of things and here we managed to rent one room for the six of us for the sum of thirty kroner for the night. It was evidently the pride of the landlord's heart with its two beds, heavy blue curtains, piano, and two three-foot pictures of Grieg and Ibsen. We deposited our baggage, and, after extracting a promise from his Majesty that our return would be greeted with the sight of more beds, set out to scour the town for something to eat. But it was very late. We just managed to squeeze our way into the café of the Grand Hotel[96] and snatch a sip of Swedish punch at which my hair stood up in deference; but not for long, they soon evicted us and we wandered thus unwelcome from hotel to hotel, and from café to café. Too late. With

---

[96] The Grand Hotel in Christiania (Oslo) opened in 1874 and continues to operate. The hotel's website (https://www.grandcafeoslo.no/english) boasts that Henrik Ibsen enjoyed his daily lunch in the hotel's Grand Café. There too, the artist Edvard Munch once offered to swap his painting *The Sick Girl* in return for 100 steak dinners.

no thought of evil intent we finally found ourselves down around the docks once more. Here sustenance was found in the shape of tiny hot dogs with vicious mustard, served out by an angel of mercy, a bit tipsy, but an angel of mercy, for all that, who had established herself under an arc light in the dirty square. We surrounded her cart and soon drew quite a crowd of tipsy dock hands and others. Amongst these "others" was a dilapidated "child of pleasure" who insisted on dancing an interpretation of Grieg's "Butterfly" in the circle of the arc light, and who was quite put out we did not stay to applaud with the inebriated dock hands. We were now in need of sleep, however, and we betook our weary way back to our haven of rest. Three more beds were made on the floor and by packing three into the two already mentioned, the six of us could find accommodation. After many muffled exclamations and creeping about on creaking floors, the silence of slumber set in. For me, however, only the silence, for I could not sleep. It was cold, the bed clothes were gradually drawn off me, someone snored chromatically, and the mice played The Pursuit of Villa in the partitions.

Morning finally came and with it rain. This made little difference, however, as we had determined to spend most of the time indoors stocking up with food,—so sick were we of the rations on board ship. After an unforgettable breakfast in the Grand Hotel we engaged a taxi and instructed the driver to show us Christiania. This he did in a thorough manner, enlivening the trip by applying New York names to the different places of interest. "Bronx Park," "Polo Grounds,"[97] "Fifth Avenue" etc. all brought down thru the somewhat twisted medium of the driver's brother's description in letters from America. Our sightseeing trip over and paid for with a ridiculously small sum of money, we split up and went our various ways, with the provision that we meet at the station at five o'clock. The train left at six. I walked about a bit in the rain, purchased me a respectable walking stick, and finally landed in a movie house. Here I watched the doings of our former fistic hero, Jim Corbett,[98] in a thrilling detective "dramer,"—watched it for as long as I could stand the melancholy music, and then bolted for the welcome rain. I never listened to such a collection of gloom as was that music before in my life. Train time soon came around and found us all at the station and engaged in a general argument with the baggage force over

---

[97] Society for American Baseball Research, "Polo Grounds (New York)," by Stew Thornley, https://sabr.org/bioproj/park/polo-grounds-new-york/. The Polo Grounds was the name of three stadiums in Upper Manhattan, New York City, used mainly for professional baseball and American football from 1880 through 1963.

[98] Wikipedia, "James J. Corbett," last modified January 30, 2021, 16:26 (UTC), https://en.wikipedia.org/wiki/James_J._Corbett.
James J. Corbett (1866–1933), American professional boxer and a world heavyweight champion. After retiring from boxing, Corbett appeared in many motion pictures in the 1910s–1920s.

our baggage. We had too much; it was by far too heavy; an extra car must be put on the train for it, we must pay heavily. Yes, of course. Americans=Pay Heavily, is a common theorem in Europe. But alongside the cute little cars our pile of trunks did look formidable; so after much expostulation and argument over the scales we paid our excess baggage, saw our trunks loaded aboard a special car and sought out our compartments. We had two. In one of them we found an occupant, a harmless look-ing little chap guarded by an excitable little chap with a big badge and a red cap. We claimed that the entire compartment was ours. The red capped dignitary, whom we took for the conductor, admitted it, but pointed to the next compartment which was really the stranger's but was somehow or other at present piled high with bedclothes. He stated that his care would remain in our compartment. We answered by saying "not if we know it," and assembled such a show of force that the red capped individual who was none other than a Bennett's Tourist Agent[99] withdrew his ward from our clutches and went out to debate the question of clearing out the compartment with the conductor. We rolled down our sleeves and installed ourselves in our rightful possession. Some people do not understand the fact that although Americans are willing to pay high, they demand what they pay for.

Soon the bells rang, the guards blew their whistles, the engine gave a frightened shriek, as if someone had trod on its tail and we were off for Stockholm. There was no dining car with us, but the food question was effectively solved by girls boarding the train and selling baskets of food; neatly packed lunches of sandwiches, cheese, cakes, & milk or beer. Later on, a stroll through the creaking train, disclosed the fact that our fine other companions of the voyage, the track men, were also aboard, bound for Stockholm, so we joined forces again and talked away the time. It went slowly as the train's progress was laborious, accompanied by much rattling and bum[p]ing. When a little chap, I once had a toy steam train which puffed and rattled its way about a circular track sprinkled with bridges and tunnels. I always wanted to ride in it, and now I felt that I was having that experience.

The remainder of this tale will, I hope, be told from Petrograd. After a somewhat frigid night spent in the attempt to cling to the narrow berths in the train we arrived at Stockholm about eight in the morning. It had snowed during the night so that the country as we approached the city glistened in the bright sunlight. I remember I got that impression early,—everything seemed to glisten about Stockholm. When

---

[99] Bennett's Tourist Office, founded by Thomas Bennett (1814–1898) of Oslo, Norway, made arrangements for travelers to Europe.

our train pulled into the station it was met by a great crowd which murmured about the "Amerikan, the Amerikans." We puffed out a bit and thought, "Well this is great stuff; probably a delegation of Sweden's prominent bankers come to meet us." But we only had to pull our chests in again as the crowd was not composed of bankers at all, but sporting and camera men come to meet the fine athletes who we for the moment had forgot were on the train.

The boys had to line up in front of the station and face the battery of pocket cameras, reporters—cameras, and moving pictures cameras. We jealous ones of small mind stood by and made would–be humorous comments on the operation in a some-what successful attempt to make the boys smile. Joe Loomis did put on an expansive grin once. With the operation over our two groups split up, bade goodbye and good luck one to the other, and went our various ways,—they to a lodging provided by the athletic authorities and we to the Grand Hotel.[100] There must be a Grand Hotel in every city of size in Europe; if ever you land in a strange foreign metropolis it's always safe to ask to be taken to the Grand Hotel. The one in Stockholm is a very comfort-able affair, finely situated on one of the larger canals facing the parliament buildings on an island across the way. The first thing of course was breakfast and believe me we did both ourselves and the chef of the Grand Hotel justice! Grapefruit, cereal, bacon and eggs, coffee and rolls just about hit the spot and we rose from the table feeling fit. On the boat I had been told that Stockholm was famous for its baths and swimming pools, so, as we were bound for Russia where I had heard baths were considered more of a luxury than a necessity, I determined to give the Swedish baths a trial and myself one last swim before hibernating in the land of ice and snow.

I approached the be-medaled general behind the desk in the lobby and in my best Swedish inquired the way to the best bath; this dignitary answered me in English as English as my own and told me the way to the "Mälerbadet."[101] Although

[100] Arthur Brown Ruhl, *White Nights and Other Russian Impressions* (New York: C. Scribner's, 1917), 11. The Grand Hôtel in Stockholm opened in 1874 and continues to operate. It was the preferred meeting place over "anywhere else in Europe" during World War I to share talk of international politics, according to Arthur Ruhl of *Collier's Weekly*. "There were said to be forty thousand foreigners in Stockholm, and about thirty-nine thousand of them went crisscrossing in and out of the Grand Hôtel lobby," Ruhl wrote. The first Nobel banquet took place at the Grand Hôtel in 1901.

[101] Wikipedia, "Mälarbadet," last modified June 8, 2021, 15:19 (UTC), https://sv.wikipedia.org/wiki/M%C3%A4larbadet.
The correct spelling is Mälarbadet. Mälarbadet operated in Stockholm from 1906 until 1918. It was located on Norr Mälarstrand 12, which was two kilometers from the Grand Hôtel. When the bath opened in 1906, it featured Scandinavia's largest and most exclusive indoor swimming pool, which included eighty-four cabins and two club cab-ins with room for fifty people. The bathing palace was fronted by a five-story plastered Art Nouveau façade designed by the architects Victor Bodin and Bror Almquist, which featured decorative wrought-iron balconies, and portals and details in carved sandstone. The original Art Nouveau entrance of the building still exists.

not all wished to swim everyone wanted some kind of bath so we hired a fleet of taxis, told the pilots where we wished to go and set out. It was not long before we arrived and found our way into the office of a huge plaster and cement building. In spite of the linguistic difficulties we each bought the kind of ticket we wanted, or rather bought some kind of ticket and then did as we durned[102]pleased. "Bob" and I wanted to swim so we were entitled to a private dressing room apiece, I entered mine and got my clothes off; investigation didn't reveal anything that could be construed into a bathing suit so I put my head through the curtains and beckoned to one of the two female attendants I saw loitering in the big room outside. In vain did I try a smattering of French, German, English and the two words I knew of Swedish,—meaning "thank you" when I came to think of it,—for not a sign of enlightenment swept across their moon-like faces. Just in time however to save me from abandoning the whole project a Swedish gentleman with a knowledge of English entered and he explained to us that in Sweden people went swimming without the impediment of the suit. That struck me as all right,—we always did it that way in the "good old college" days, but he left us with the problem of the two ladies standing in the corridor. How was I, a respectable young son of America, to get from my dressing room to the pool, past two ladies when I didn't even possess the proverbial fig-leaf of our old friends Adam and Eve? Ah, my little black rain-coat! I threw it over my shoulders and set out down the hallway. At my approach the two ladies snickered, pointed at the coat and began to gargle out a lot of words which of course fell on uncomprehending ears. Our hero tried to push right past them as they blocked the way; he might just as well try to run the blockade of the British Navy. The two Amazons emitted their war cry, hopped aboard his neck, and began to claw at the coat. Our hero was completely surprised at the suddenness of the attack and despite the fact that he resisted strenuously was at somewhat of a dis-advantage, having only one hand to fight with,—the other being busily engaged in holding the coat about his person. The struggle waxed fierce with no attention paid to the rules of war—there being much submarining and aerial work on both sides, while hellish cries of "Lay off" "What the devil" and "Whose bath is this?" brought his comrades to the arena thereby adding their shrieks of glee to the terrible noise of combat. It was almost an even fight, however, until the two Valkyries introduced cooperation of resources into the conflict along with a couple of forty-two cen-timeters in the form of one knee placed firmly in our hero's stomach, another in

---

[102] Dialect form of "damned."

his back, and a concerted yank at the coat. This stroke of strategic genius brought victory, for the coat fell and our hero with a despairing yell fled down the corridor to the pool, leaving both the coat and his modesty in the hands of the victors. So ended a great moral disaster! Reports after the battle had it that the Amazons figured I was planning to hop into the pool still inside the coat and their efforts were solely in its behalf. It seems that it is the custom in Sweden to have female attendants at these baths. I was so fussed after this incident that I went away from the place leaving my watch and pocket book in my dressing room, necessitating a long walk back from the hotel for them.

With the bathing over we walked around the city for a while sightseeing. Some of the boys visited various banks to change their money for roubles, others took a turn through the museum on the island, but I just walked. Stockholm is the cleanest place imaginable; it looks as if someone had just scrubbed every inch of it with a brush and soapy water. In some parts of it the buildings are quaint old affairs, swollen out at the top, and overhanging, but the newer parts of the city are of spick-and-span concrete.

After lunch we pursued our usual course of hiring taxis and going for a sight-seeing tour of the city. There is one magnificent park in Stockholm worthy of the best attention; while the stadium where the Olympic Games[103] were held is also interesting. We spent so much time riding around that only a few moments remained to us to surround a last good Swedish meal before our train left. With great argument and much tipping we finally got the waiter to hurry out the food and we dived into it. At that half of us left early and let Count stay to devour our desserts, in order to make sure of the train. When we did board this it was with a great load of periodicals and edibles; Bob had a huge box of chocolates which cost him somewhere around eleven kroner.

The trip from Stockholm to Happaranda[104] is a cramped tiresome one, even though we did enliven it with conversation, argument, and reading. I read Oscar Wilde's "De Profundis," which, it seems to me, is the greatest insincerity this gentleman ever wrote. We also made new acquaintances on the train, one Mrs. Hansen,

---

[103] The 1912 Summer Olympics were held in Stockholm from May 5 to July 22, 1912.

[104] Haparanda stad; Haparanda's History, https://www.haparanda.se/kommun-och-politik/haparandas-historia.html.

Haparanda is a small municipality in northern Sweden adjacent to the town of Tornio, Finland. It was the only open railway crossing at the border to Russia during World War I. The International Red Cross exchanged about 75,000 badly wounded Austro-Hungarian, German, and Turkish prisoners of war back to their home armies via Tornio and Haparanda from 1914 to 1918. Two hundred nineteen of them died during transit and were buried in Haparanda.

and her son, residents of Moscow, where the boy works in the American Consulate. They told us they were making a second attempt to return to Russia after having been sent back to Stockholm from Tornio because of irregularities in their passports. Passports! We all examined ours furtively, now that we were approaching the mysterious Russian border.

Throughout all this I've forgot to mention our friend Bovcock, the engineer from the Baldwin Locomotive Works[105] going to Russia to superintend the setting up of a consignment of engines manufactured for and shipped to Russia by that concern. He is a funny little chap, older than we are, but full of the devil. A self-made man, one who has worked hard from childhood, he refreshes us all along with the practical view of the current situation. He has been quite lost in the foreign exchange transactions so we have appointed ourselves financial advisors to him and affairs have so far gone along smoothly.

We got off the train to stretch our legs a couple of times, indulging in snowball fights much to the consternation of the other passengers. The train meals bothered us; there was so much fish in them. Few of us like fish and "Chuck" Stuart despises it. But that staple has conferred upon him a new nickname; he learned the Swedish or Norwegian or Finnish word for "no" which was "ikke" and not a time that fish was handed to him did he fail to lift his hand and say "ikke fisch." So we call him Ikke now. "Count" is sore at the fish too; the first time we had it he thought it was all we were going to get so he dived in and cleaned up on it, only to be deeply chagrined afterwards to find out that it was only a preliminary dish.

After a ride through country abrupt with rounded hills and rocky gorges,— as if someone had spilled a huge market basket full of packages, we pulled in at Happaranda. This was the most god-forsaken looking place any of us had ever seen. Set away up on top of the globe close to the Arctic Circle where the sun shone weak from distance it was cold and bleak even at this time of year. The town consists of a few low, scattered, log buildings, some few more elaborate ones of clap-boards and a brick hotel.[106] The river bank is lined with ambling docks at which were

[105] American-Rails.com; "Baldwin Locomotive Works (BLW), 1825—1956"; https://www.american-rails.com/baldwin.html. The Baldwin Locomotive Works, founded in 1825, was one of the "Big Three" American manufacturers of railroad locomotives. Originally located in Philadelphia, it moved to nearby Eddystone, PA, in the 1920s. It exited the market in 1956.

[106] Swedish Lapland; "Haparanda Stadshotell; A Stay in History" by Hakan Stenlund, https://www.swedishlapland.com/stories/haparanda-stadshotell/. Rogers refers to the Haparanda Stadshotell. The hotel still operates and the 21st-century reader would have a decidedly more positive impression. According to the hotel's website (https://www.haparandastadshotell.se/en/about-us/), it "was opened amidst pomp and solemnity on December 5, 1900. The building was designed by the architects Fritz Ullrich and Eduard Hallqvist from Stockholm in the classical

huge barges piled high with thousands upon thousands of boxes sewn up in white cloth,—presents in route to the soldiers. Across the river we could see Finland and the town of Tornio, the low rail road station and the stark white domed church. After a breakfast of rare old eggs and coffee at the hotel—by the way one of the dirtiest places of its kind I've seen—we returned to the station and had our baggage inspected. I forgot to mention that before we could get out of the station we were examined and had to walk through false doors and blind alleys in a system that would do justice to a Coney Island "pit." The inspectors found nothing of interest on us or in our baggage and we were therefore passed for transmission to Tornio. Two little tug-boats puffed up to the wharf and our baggage was loaded aboard. Bovcock's was placed on the other boat from ours, so he followed it. His boat gave signs of setting out first and Bovcock stood out on deck waving good-bye and giving us the laugh. The tug backed away from the dock, breaking the ice which had already begun to form, as she went and then, with her bow clear and "Bov" kidding us at his loudest the worthy captain gave "full speed ahead," forgot to turn the wheel and with remarkable dexterity ran her plumb ashore! Soon our boat pulled out in fine style and we bid "bye-bye" to "Bov." Our captain was clever too and effected a magnificent landing by running head on into the dock at full speed; but finally after maneuvering about and missing it cleanly a couple of times we managed to make connections. Bovcock followed along about an hour later.

Here at Tornio we had to undergo inspection again and got our first glimpse at the Russian system so bound up in red tape that it is all red tape and no system. After our passports were stamped at a little coop on the dock we were herded with some hundred-odd others into a small room in the dirty low-roofed station. Here we had to exhibit our hand luggage to the inspectorial eye, fill out numerous blanks, deliver all printed matter in our possession over to be censored and later mailed to us; walk through another labyrinth, which emitted us into a combination waiting and dining room where we were to wait some five-odd hours for the train to Petrograd. I've never seen so much fish served up for human consumption in my life; fish everywhere, every kind of fish prepared in every possible manner. It began to snow outside and what with the smell of food, the darkness, the crying of children and the pungent odors the wait was not a pleasant one.

---

style. . . ." On April 15, 1917, Lenin passed through Haparanda on his secret journey back to Petrograd. That month, the Russian newspaper *Novoye Vremya* wrote that at least 217 spies and agents lived in Haparanda—"not bad for a town with fewer than 1,500 inhabitants," Stenlund writes.

Finally our train pulled in, we clambered aboard and slid out on the last leg of our journey. Before reaching Petrograd we had yet again to get out at a lonely station and fill out blanks and have our passports inspected.

CHAPTER 3

"Petrograd must be the weather waste heap of the world"

"What if, when the fog dissipates and lifts, this decayed and slimy city lifts with it, rises with the fog and disappears like smoke, and what remains is the previous Finnish swamp, and in the middle of it, for the sake of decoration, the Bronze Horseman on his steaming, exhausted horse?"
Fyodor Dostoevsky, *The Adolescent*

L eighton Rogers circuitously admitted that he "could not speak three consecutive words" of Russian when he arrived in Petrograd.[107] He may not have read any works by Dostoevsky, but he called the weather correctly. Meteorological records attested to the winter of 1916–1917 in Petrograd being a particularly cold one. J. Butler Wright, the new chargé d'affaires in the US Embassy who replaced Fred Dearing, wrote, "The climate at this period of the year is certainly depressing. Slush, fine rains, and moderate wind conspire to make it sloppy in the streets and, I imagine, impossible in the country."[108] Maxim Gorky considered the weather that winter "as cold here as in Lapland."[109]

Staying warm was not the only challenge Rogers faced when he arrived in Petrograd. Suffering from food and fuel shortages, downtrodden by the war, and

---

[107] Rogers, *Wine of Fury*, 72; Dosch-Fleurot, *Through War to Revolution*, 101. Rogers allegorically referred to himself when he described the lives of several foreign bankers in Petrograd in his novel. "Six young men, the nucleus of the clerical force of his branch, arrived from the United States. They were inexperienced. They could not speak three consecutive words of the language." Arno Dosch-Fleurot approached the matter differently. Upon arriving in Petrograd in early 1917, he remarked, "I was not only in a new country, I pondered, but one for which I was not prepared. I checked up on my notions about Russia and found I had a sordid one from reading Dostoievsky's 'Crime and Punishment,' a tragic one from seeing Tolstoy's 'Resurrection,' a terrible one from reading George Kennan's 'Darkest Siberia.' "
[108] J. Butler Wright diary entry, November 24, 1916, cited in Allison, *Witness to Revolution: The Russian Revolution Diary and Letters of J. Butler Wright* (Westport, CT: Praeger, 2002), 5.
[109] Figes, A *People's Tragedy*, 307.

discontent over mounting, unresolved social and economic problems, the populace of Petrograd was a petri dish for revolution.

H. Fessenden Meserve and R. R. Stevens didn't seem to notice. They worked at breakneck speed to implement the next phase of National City Bank's strategy in Russia. Basking in the appreciation of the Russian Finance Ministry following the close of the much-acclaimed $50 million credit to the imperial government, National City Bank applied to Finance Minister Pyotr Lvovich Bark for a banking charter to open its first branch in Petrograd.[110] Meserve and Stevens hoped to open the branch by October 14 and in late July, began scouting out locations for the new branch office. They located an opulent edifice, the former Ottoman Embassy, on No. 8 Palace Embankment, which they deemed most suitable. On September 16, Meserve and Stevens signed a three-year lease, effective September 1, 1916, for 45,000 rubles in annual rent (approximately $13,000).[111] Leighton Rogers and his colleagues excitedly described their new sumptuously appointed offices.

Bark informed Meserve on November 13 that the ministry approved the charter "with some modifications."[112] NCB was concurrently completing the syndication of a new $50 million 5.5 percent, five-year Russian imperial government treasury bond issue[113] and increasing its purchases of Russian government treasury bills and acceptances. In New York, Frank Vanderlip applauded National City Bank's success. "I feel today that of all the foreign countries, there is none that offers a more promising outlook than Russia,"[114] he told a gathering of representatives of underwriters of the new imperial Russian government credit at the Biltmore Hotel on November 16. F.C. Schwedtman repeated the mantra in a *New York Times* article earlier the same week, titled "Predicts New Era for United States": "Russia is eager to learn American business methods. It is a fertile market, as yet practically ignored by our

[110] Social Networks and Archival Context; "Bark, Petr L'vovich, 1869-1937 [Russian: Пётр Львович Барк]" https://snaccooperative.org/ark:/99166/w6003gd4. In 1911, Bark became assistant minister of trade and industry. Beginning in 1914, he served as minister of finance until the abdication of Nicholas II. After the 1917 revolution, he lived in England, where he became managing director of the Anglo-International Bank and was knighted in 1935.
[111] Tkachenko, *American Bank Capital in Russia*, 79; The National City Bank of New York, *History of the operations of the Petrograd and Moscow Branches*, 3, Box RG12, Folder 1/2.
[112] "Russian Charter to Bank," *New York Times*, November 14, 1916, 16.
[113] "Russia has $60,000,000," *New York Times,* November 22, 1916, 18. The $50 million 5.5 percent Russian government bond was priced at 94 ¾ to yield 6.75 percent. The bonds were dated December 1. The public offering of the bonds was made under the names of National City Company; J.P. Morgan & Co.; The Guaranty Trust Company; Lee, Higginson and Co.; and Harris, Forbes & Co.
[114] Cleveland and Huertas, *Citibank: 1812–1970*, 100.

manufacturers. . . . Russia's banking system offers great promise, but it is as yet only meagrely developed . . ."[115]

Meserve had plenty of reasons to celebrate at year end. He oversaw the conclusion of two precedent-setting capital market transactions for the Russian Empire, received a charter to open the bank's first branch in Petrograd, secured a lease on a beautiful, superbly located palace to house said branch, bolstered his staff with Leighton Rogers and many more Americans, increased purchases of attractively yielding short-term Russian government securities, and enjoyed the unquestionable support of his home office and the Russian Ministry of Finance. On December 6, he hosted a party at the Café Demon, inviting J. Butler Wright[116] and other diplomats and notable members of the American colony in Petrograd, including Countess Nostitz.[117] Wright and Nostitz became customers of National City Bank in the new year.

Leighton Rogers gradually acclimatized to life in Petrograd. He learned about the omnipresence of the police and the hesitance of Russians to discuss politics in public. Despite frequent gloomy winter clouds, he appreciated, as he described in his journal, the city's "broad, bleak squares, the wide streets ending in columns and arches, the worn color of the buildings like old masters, the glittering colored domes and spires against the tinted clouds." The Russian church fascinated him with its elaborate rites and magnificent bejeweled appointments. His daily routine, including a less than straightforward ride on a city tram, provided daily adventure.

Importantly, the prospects for National City Bank looked good.

---

[115] "Predicts New Era for United States; F.C. Schwedtman of National City Bank Sees Big Foreign Trade for Nation," *New York Times*, November 12, 1916, 4.

[116] J. Butler Wright diary entry, December 6, 1916, cited in Allison, *Witness to Revolution,* 9.

[117] Countess Nostitz (Lilie de Fernandez-Azabal) (1875–1967). A French-American socialite. She wrote her memoir in 1936 titled *The Countess from Iowa.*

(This following entry dated to October 16, 1916)

We arrived at Petrograd at night about ten-thirty and as we stepped from the train were met by a deep voice booming, "Citybank, Citybank." We followed it up and found the owner of it to be Mr. Detlefsen[118], the bank's accountant who had come to meet us.

He engaged queer little carriages just big enough for two for us, gave the necessary directions to the drivers and we set out. It was very dark, the streets were slimy with mud, feeble lights glimmered and we plodded along the empty roads. All around us searchlights fanned the horizon and I divined that the street lights were dimmed on account of Zeppelin[119] attacks. There was no one else around us, we jogged along alone and in silence and I half expected this burly pirate in the huge hat up on the driver's seat to lead us down a side alley where we might be attacked at any moment. Finally we turned down a broad side street of cobbles which sloped towards the center where the gutter ran full of mud and water, avoided a telegraph pole which lay aslant across it, and stopped in front of one of the many dark, plaster buildings.

Soon the rest of the party came up, the drivers were paid after what seemed much superfluous argument and we climbed the stairs; we were split up into two groups of three and as it was late taken to the two rooms reserved for us at once. We were tired, depressed, even disappointed, after our long trip, but all this disappeared when we found in our room a table set for tea with rolls & jelly. It was a God-send. I saw a woman's hand in that and Mr. Detlefsen said his wife had insisted that tea be waiting for us. We said good night and sat down to it with great relish, and after a preliminary examination of the room, which is only to be temporary quarters for us, we went to bed to dream of journey's end.

(This following entry dated to October 17, 1916)

Got up rather early today in order to look the place over; had a good sleep, and after dressing, enjoyed my chocolate and rolls. Our room is a large one with clothes closet, chiffonier, writing desk, two beds and a convertible sofa,—we flipped up

---

[118] Enevold O. Detlefsen (1881–1954), accountant of National City Bank.
[119] A Zeppelin is a type of rigid airship named after the German inventor Count Ferdinand von Zeppelin, who pioneered rigid airship development at the beginning of the 20th century.

for that last night and Bob lost out and now has to sleep on it for a time. I guess it won't be for long though, as these quarters are only temporary; Mr. Detlefsen did mention though, that the city is crowded with refugees from Poland, making it very difficult to get rooms. But to resume,—the funniest thing about the place is the huge porcelain stove in the corner; it reaches almost to the ceiling and from the tiny door at the bottom, looks as if it would take a week to get the stove heated, let alone expect it to heat the room.

This morning Mr. Detlefsen took us over to the Hotel Europe[120] to meet Mr. Meserve and Mr. Stevens,—the Representative and the Manager in Russia respectively. Our way led down the quay alongside the Neva to a river ferry which took us across to a landing in front of the Cathedral of St. Isaacs,—a huge affair—from whence we walked through a park, out on the Nevsky Prospect, the big street of Petrograd, and up to the hotel. Here we met Mr. Jenkinson, a secretary,—I can't remember whose, and later were ushered into a room to the august presence of the above-mentioned Representative and Manager. Mr. Meserve, a slender, blonde man of some fifty years, soft-voiced, polished,—the only striking thing about him at first being his red tie, smoked a cigar; Mr. Stevens, also slender but dark and much younger, without a voice it seems because he didn't say anything, smoked a cigarette. They welcomed us to Russia cordially enough and then sat across from each other in our charmed circle wordless,—each waiting for the other to say something. Neither of them did. They both smoked. Mr. Meserve smoked his cigar better than Mr. Stevens did his cigarette. Mr. Meserve looked as if he was pleased to see us but didn't know just what to say, while Mr. Stevens looked as if he didn't give a damn and didn't want to say anything. After a while we shook hands and went out.

It was even colder outside than in the hotel so Mr. Detlefsen suggested that we walk over to the bank and look it over. It is in the building occupied up to the outbreak of the war by the Turkish Embassy. The location is magnificent; on the same quay as the Winter Palace, and directly across the Neva from the old fortress of the city. The windows of our future offices command a wonderful view. Such an interior I have never seen before. A marble staircase with be-mirrored walls leads up to the second floor. It seems that all banks in Russia are on the second floor—to the rooms the bank

---

[120] Historic Hotels of the World Then & Now; "1875 Belmond Grand Hotel Europe" https://www.historichotels-thenandnow.com/grandeuropestpetersburg.html. The Grand Hotel Europe opened its doors in 1875. During World War II, it served as a hospital and orphanage. The hotel was luxuriously renovated and reopened in 1991; Barnes, *Standing on a Volcano*, 195. H. Fessenden Meserve lived in the Hotel Europe and worked there as well until National City Bank opened its Petrograd branch. The hotel was a favorite dining locale of Ambassador Francis.

will occupy. These consist of a huge gold and white salon, gorgeous with Victorian gilded chairs and divans, cupids, roses, doves and the like; with huge windows hung in gold curtains, long mirrors at every side, balconies and mural paintings of typical Victorian scenes up above. At the end of this monstrosity are two rooms which are to be the offices of Mr. Meserve and Mr. Stevens. Off the office of the latter is a little room all decked out á la Turkey, with plush furniture, curiously painted oriental walls and ceiling, which is to be a waiting room. Past this is what was once the state dining room of the embassy, now all torn up and undergoing a carpenterial operation to make it a bank; behind this are two small rooms which will be used for stenographers and the like. This completes it; but I've never seen so much gilt and silk and glittering gloss. It will hardly be a workman like atmosphere.

I was about ready to pass out when we got home and what the walking didn't do the lunch did. A couple of small rolls, a thin pat of butter, a concoction of ham and cabbage—durn little of it too—and no dessert! And they consider this a dinner for a full grown man! If they keep that pace up I'll last about two weeks, like the farmer's cows down to one straw a day that up and died and ruined the experiment. But the worst was yet to come; some of the boys wanted to buy fur coats so Mr. and Mrs. Detlefsen took us out to some pawn shops—this being the best place to buy them. It was miserable weather when we went out,—a heavy sticky snow,—the wettest one I've ever encountered made everything slimy underfoot. God only knows where we walked and how far, up and down, and back again; lost once when Mr. Detlefsen got separated from us. If what we saw of Petrograd today is a sample I'd say it is the dirtiest city in the world. Cracked plaster buildings, slimy cobblestoned streets, and hosts of the great unwashed did not fill the mind with beauty. Finally some of the boys got what they wanted or what the few hock shop dealers wanted them to have, and we came home. Never again!

We visited the station again today to get our baggage thru the custom. With us went one Roberts, one of our employees, who saved much time and trouble by slipping the inspector the high sign so that not all our trunks were examined and we consequently got them in short order. I spotted him as being good at that stuff as soon as I saw him,—those sly, fox-like, near-set eyes.

We've managed to get our clothes stored away in various closets and dressers, and although it is rather crowded with three in a room, I guess we can get along. All except the meals is comfortable enough; but they are so sparing that had we but the appetites of canary-birds what we get would not be sufficient. Breakfast isn't so bad, nor the tea at night, but through the day,—if it keeps up we'll starve. However, it is planned to have meals served at the bank, and this will simplify matters.

These people are uniform-crazy. Uniform, uniform, uniform, everyone wears a uniform. Soldiers, sailors, students, newsboys, nurses,—even the little kids attending school;—made old men before their time by the long trousers, long-belted coat, cap, and hair-covered knapsack for the books.

(This following entry dated to October 20, 1916)

From the way things look now we shall not be able to get down to work for a month or so yet and we are therefore to have a fine opportunity to observe and to get a start on our study of Russian. Difficulties in connection with the signing of the charter will delay the opening of the bank. Nevertheless, we are to have a Russian teacher who will give us daily lessons, and we are also to report for work and study each day just as if we were in full operation. And from the appearance, sound, and smell of this language we shall need all the spare time we can get to master it.

We created a tremendous disturbance on our floor last night by ordering three baths. Had we understood the preparation taking a bath involved perhaps we might not have done it. First the maid has to see that the tank in the bath–room is full of water, there she has to bring in wood and build a fire in the stove under it, and finally she has to feed and tend this fire through the course of an hour until the water is hot and the bath is ready. Of course this isn't so bad for one bath but when three are ordered and the process has to be repeated three times it is rather hard on the maid. Besides some of us had sponge baths in our room when we first arrived and I think the maids can't figure us out for taking so many baths. They don't know whether we are very clean for taking so many or whether we are very dirty and have to take them!

I have never encountered funerals as often as here. They are of all kinds from those of high military or naval officers carried out with great pomp to the meagre ceremony of the poorest peasant. I saw two today and they presented the most vivid contrast. The first was the final tribute to a ranking officer of the army. Ahead came two men dressed in a white uniform peculiarly like our dress suit, wearing white silk hats similar to our opera hat, carrying each a silver lantern burning dimly, and leading a white horse draped in a silver net, which extended from his back to a two-wheeled white and silver cart laden with greens. Behind this walked a priest in gorgeous silver robes, who now and then took greens from the cart and scattered them in the roadway. Not far behind him came more white-clad lantern carriers leading the be-plumed horses of the hearse; and this a brilliant affair of white and silver contained the coffin, set in between four pillars which towered high supporting a roof studded with twinkling lights and hung with tasseled curtains. The coffin itself was of beautiful natural wood, and bore on its top the cap and sword of the deceased. In the rear of the towering hearse, which rolled along like a huge car of juggernaut, walked the immediate relatives, the widow clinging to a rail on the hearse for support. Following them came priests in their brilliant robes and hats, jewels glittering, carrying the decorations awarded to the dead hero on velvet cushions; surrounding the priests were assistants bearing ikons and banners, as well as choir boys. The procession ended in a military band intoning the death march and a battalion of soldiers, their bayonets standing out against the leaden sky like limbs in the forest. As this imposing, senseless tribute filed down the street the passersby removed their hats, crossed themselves, and then lined the way to watch. The second procession was not much,—only a peasant and his wife, rags fluttering in the breeze striding down the middle of the street unnoticed, bearing between them a tiny little coffin bearing pitiful attempts at decoration, unheeding, going grimly to dispose of it.

The sun is among the things I miss most here. We seem to be away up on top of the world shrouded in white mists which swallow up even the sun's bright light. It hangs there, low in the sky, ever buffeted by the drifting clouds and only once in a while, when a break comes by chance, is it allowed to flash its radiance from the spot of blue, the paint plastered walls with reddish-gold, and leap like flame from gilded cross to spangled dome. Then suddenly the low clouds close the gap and the splendor is but a memory to be clung to through more lonely weeks of shadow.

I watched the Russian carpenters at work on our counters today. The old whiskered, mat-haired, tattered moujik[121] in his flowing shirt and high boots, working with the most ancient of hand constructed tools, with his apprentice working round him, faded in the dim light, and carried me with him away from the sound of trams, electric lights, and all modernity into the dusky ages of the feudal lord, the artisan and the slave three hundred years ago. Three hundred years.

Impressions are superficial and do not usually merit deep consideration, but occasionally one flits through the mind and leaves behind a vague idea which clings in spite of reason. Coming across the Nicholas Bridge I experienced such a one. A sky of curdled clouds hurrying nowhere out of nowhere, now and then rimmed with dying sunlight which burned blood red in the west; a wild wind moaning up the river,

---

[121] *Moujik* or *Muzhik*. A Russian peasant.

blowing far and wide the fountains of sparks from the fleeing tugs and whistling derision at the clumsy jackdaws;[122] an hairy peasant dragging his laden sledge painfully over the slimy stones, the hiss of the flying silt as a luxurious motor flies past blazing with lights and heavy with ease,—what strange psychological alchemy brought out from all this that vague uneasiness, that feeling of surging unrest?

In Russia it is impossible to avoid the people's religion. Churches are in every square, usually plaster towering edifices with fine domes spangled or gilded and topped with the glittering Slavic cross; in the squares are shrines for public worship, not without the collection boxes which cluster on their walls in myriads; and in every room in every building, public or private in the land is the ikon, the picture of the saint or the Savior, some plain on painted wood, others gorgeous with gold and brilliants, with a flickering lamp swung before it, the guardian spirit of the household and the constant reminder to the Russian that God is ever watching, everywhere.

It seems to be much the same with the pictures of the emperor and empress also. Their pictures hang in every public building, store, and home. But this I am told is a matter of law. Foreign concerns are not exempt and if the foreign merchant wishes to open his place for business in Russia he must have the pictures of their majesties conspicuously displayed; while if he wants the notice of the Russian people he must have the ikon in its place.

Beggars everywhere. Of all kinds they are, old men and women in rags and tatters, blind, deformed, little children hideously misshapen, pitiful young girls with children, soldiers, mutilated in war,—these are the sort one meets. Of course some are real and worthy; the majority are not, and the last are the easiest to distinguish. They put on such exhibitions of deformity and misery as would do credit to P.T. Barnum[123] himself. The soldiers are as a rule the worthy ones. My blood boiled when I heard how as a reward for being dragged from their homes, sent to fight half trained, and mutilated as they are, they receive the privilege of begging. That is all, turned out on the streets, and to the generosity of the passersby. This is great, for everyone seems to give, everyone from the poorest, oldest lady to the youngest school child. To be sure their contributions may be only kopeks but it is the spirit that counts. I like to think they do it from the generosity of their hearts and not because they think it gets them nearer heaven as some cynic has said.

---

[122] Jackdaw. A small gray-headed crow.
[123] Wikipedia, "P.T. Barnum," last modified July 8, 2021, 10:02 (UTC), https://en.wikipedia.org/wiki/P._T._Barnum. Phineas Taylor Barnum (1810–1891) was an American showman, politician, and businessman, remembered for promoting celebrated hoaxes and for founding the Barnum & Bailey Circus (1871–2017).

Oct. 26, 1916.

Today being Sunday and a big day here we are going to visit the art museum known as "The Hermitage," built by Catherine the Great. This morning most of the other boys have gone off to church after trying to inveigle me into going; but I went last Sunday—this is an American church—and I must confess that the mentality of the speaker was so shallow that I couldn't even get my feet wet. I did my best to be tolerant but it seems to me that it is an insult to the good Lord to send shallowness out to represent Him.

This is a city of open spaces of many colors and an indefiniteness that suggest much with little—which is the essence of art. The transition from the positive, abrupt, mechanical brightness of New York to Petrograd's haze and distance was at first forbidding, but I am beginning to like the broad, bleak squares, the wide streets ending in columns and arches, the worn color of the buildings like old masters, the glittering colored domes and spires against the tinted clouds; and the Neva with the haze arising from its surface, muddy, inpatient, lined with giant wood barges all alike in shape and size, spanned by bridges which become strings of light-beads at night; and the noises, the clatter of iron-shod carts and trucks over the cobbles, the swish of the wind, and the tinkling of many, many bells of all sizes and tones, forming a background for the compelling boom of the great bell of St. Isaacs which seems to sound from nowhere and envelope everything.

It is election day at home and we are wondering who the four years' joke is on this time, Wilson or Hughes; "the elocutionary ostrich or the bearded lady" as Roosevelt labels them. Now Theodore, you stop!

Having made arrangements with a very agreeable Belgian gentleman living here in the house to converse for an hour or so each evening after dinner in order to get practice on the respective languages we are trying to learn, he English, and myself Russian, we begin this evening. He asked me whether I had read any of the speeches that were being made in the Duma, which of course I have not, because I cannot read this gibberish yet. He promised to obtain a copy of the last few, those which have caused so much discussion, and to tell me about them. He started to do this tonight but at the beginning someone came into the room and he shut up like a clam. Afraid of someone overhearing him, I suppose. Everyone seems to be afraid here. When they mention politics people naturally fall into a whisper. All I could gather about this Rasputin is that he is a degenerate monk who has somehow or other got a position of influence over the royal family through the Empress. Although no one dares mention his name outright, he is being denounced indirectly in the Duma by various of the liberal and socialist members, a Paul Milyoukoff and a rabid socialist whom they seem unable to silence, named Kerensky.

It is maddening the way you are watched here. The police have an organization which extends all over the country and it is said that more than three people cannot get together in a room in any building in the city without its being known to the police. By far the great majority of those in Petrograd live in apartment houses, and on the ground floor of each of these buildings is an apartment for the janitor and his family. This man is in charge of the building, like the concierge in France, so they tell me, and in addition he watches the door. In the door of his apartment leading to the entrance hall is a small round window and no one can enter the building without their [there] being a face at that window to see who it is. Never have I come in without being watched thus, and the times it so gets on my nerves that I'm tempted to enter some night with a brick and put the window out of commission. All these janitors or "dvorniks"[124] as they are called are agents of the police and must report anything out of the ordinary in their building to the nearest police station.

Nov. 12, 1916.

We visited the Cathedral of St. Isaacs today. This is the mother church of the Russian religion.

We came through the little side door into the nave, dark, smelling of incense, and seemingly boundless. As our eyes became accustomed to the light we could see more, the huge pillars of vari-colored marbles with their brass bases and capitals, the golden and be-jeweled ikons which glittered in the light of numberless candles burning before them, the mural paintings so high up and so far away as to be almost invisible; and the gold doors, now tightly closed, leading to the Holy of Holies, flanked by pillars of alabaster and lapis lazuli.

Before one gorgeous ikon a priest in a robe of gold thread conducted a service for the hundreds of kneeling worshippers, who remained motionless on the hard marble floor during his long intonation of the service. Newcomers entered the cathedral, bought their candles at the desk at the door, tiptoed over to place them in a socket before the ikon, joined the kneeling flock and the service. In the midst of it the priest

---

[124] Russian: дворник (dvornik, concierge; one who takes care of the pavement and yard in front of a house), from двор (dvor, courtyard).

stopped his chant, and while his congregation continued in worship he took from his pocket a small mirror and a comb, carefully combed his long hair, and his beard, and after a prolonged inspection of his features, put the implements back whence they came, and continued the service! If I ever catch one of these priests out alone on a dark night in full ceremonial regalia of gold robe and jeweled crown my fortune is made!

Nov. 19, 1916.

Petrograd is heated by wood-burning stove and these require a great amount of wood. There is very little coal in this part of the Empire and transportation problems make it exceedingly difficult to ship it here from the mines. Moreover, what we know as central heating, that is, one furnace in a large building which heats the rooms by means of radiators, is also comparatively unknown except in the most modern buildings. The great dependence is upon the huge china stove with the tiny firebox, and wood. This is carried down the river from the timber lands in huge barges as much as two hundred feet long, each of which carries a young forest in itself in cut wood. These are brought down with the current to the city, ushered under the numerous bridges by tugs and tied up, sometimes three rows of them, to the stone waterfront of the quays which are the main avenues of the city. Here they are unloaded, the wood is carted away and the barges are towed reluctantly back upstream. When the river freezes the traffic in wood is over; Hence the first few cakes of ice send the tugs and barges into hysterics; one sees them looming around in the night anxious to move before the ice locks them in, and hears the sirens of the tugs shrieking like some great animal whose tail has been stepped on.

Thanksgiving.

It has been a good day. This afternoon we attended a reception for Americans at the embassy where, "a good time was had by all." The Ambassador did the thing up in fine style with a dance, after the reception, serving with the refreshments a regular southern punch which was a knockout. Our gang nearly wore a circle in the carpet around the bowl.

Then, this evening Mr. M————[125] gave a Thanksgiving Dinner for the bank staff, a dinner which was a huge success. Altogether, in spite of the fact that we are strangers in a strange land, it has been an enjoyable day.

---

[125] H. Fessenden Meserve.

Dec. 1ˢᵗ.

Petrograd must be the weather waste heap of the world. In the month and a half we have been here, the sun has only been visible twice. All the rest of the time the sky has been low with rolling clouds. The one short time the sun did shine it worked wonders with the city, bringing smiles to the people's otherwise serious faces, and dancing always in one's eyes when reflected from some gilded dome. We saw it again Sunday, a huge crimson shield resting on the horizon, easy to look at through the haze, but moody and sullen, soon dropping down out of sight.

There is always a haze, and it softens all definite outlines and makes the city a place of indistinct and therefore impressive masses and shapes; and a rain or snow falls always, burdening the lungs and bringing a layer of silt to the surface of the streets. These are of cobbles set in dirt only about three feet above the water level, and the slightest moisture seems to coat them all with an inch deep layer of mud.

The sun only describes a very low arc on the horizon so that at this time of the year, three o'clock in the afternoon finds night begun with all the lights glimmering through the fog.

Dec. 10th, 1916.

A New York subway rush is mild compared to riding on the Petrograd trams. One comes down the street with people fairly hanging out of the windows and clustered about the steps like flies. Do you wait for it to stop and for the people to get off? You certainly do not. While still in motion you dive for the brass rail at the step, land with both feet on someone else's feet and then the fight begins to make your way into the car. Old women hop gracefully aboard likewise and kick and claw with the best of them; men elbow women and women pull men off by the collar and everyone shouts for everyone else to move up further in the car,—an impossible feat. Once on the platform you are safe, for there you stay in the open air but for the others whose ambition it is to get inside the car, the fight has just begun. They push and squirm and kick until the very sides of the car bulge; and if anyone leaves the door open more than long enough to slide inside that one has committed a cardinal sin; hence added to the din of combat are the imprecations of those within heaped upon the heads of those without. I have yet to find a car so crowded that I couldn't board it, in fact the other night Fred and I made the twenty-seventh and twenty-eighth persons on a platform of a car meant to hold ten. Getting off is quite a different matter; you just dive from the platform into the crowd, usually pulling two or three with you who hadn't the slightest idea of coming and knocking down any number of others whose aim it was to get on. At first all this roughhouse wasn't fun but now it has got to be a point of honor never to let a tram pass by simply because it is too crowded; and there is a great admiration at the technique displayed by some old lady with a crutch and bundle who hops lightly aboard the speeding tram and within a minute's time has fought her way into the center aisle, from whence she calls down the wrath of heaven upon some unfortunate who has left the door an inch open.

Dec. 17, 1916.

Here it is the middle of December and until today we have barely had enough snow to cover the streets. Moreover the Neva is not frozen over yet,—something almost unheard of for this time of the year. However, today the snow is coming as if in earnest and it looks as though winter had come. If so, we can bid farewell to wheels and welcome runners. Then we can ride in the sleighs instead of these wheeled vehicles they call "ishvostiks."[126] They are four wheeled affairs with a box for the driver high up in front, and a narrow box without a back, perched behind, for the passengers. For support there are only two small handles, one on each side to hang hold of. But the idea is, of course, that no Russian ever goes anywhere without a girl, and hence they are supposed to cling to each other! The driver wraps himself up in heavy robes until he is rounded out to gigantic proportions and wears an abbreviated top hat which looks as if it had been brought up under a bureau. The rig is very light and when hitched to one of these little Siberian ponies, goes like the devil. The idea of the heavy wrappings around the driver is that the bigger he makes himself, the more prosperous he is supposed to be; and vice versa. Races between competing drivers are quite the thing and these make for many accidents in the streets, but it is only considered a good joke if one is run down; there is no recourse. Moreover the passenger is in as much danger as the pedestrian, because he must maintain his balance on the perch with only the two handles to cling to, and this is quite a feat when taking corners on one wheel.

Part of the process of engaging one of these rigs is the preliminary argument over price. Before the war there were once forty thousand of them in the city and one could ride almost any distance for a rouble, but now they are greatly diminished in

---

[126] Rogers meant *izvozchik*, Russian: извозчик, the driver of a small horse-drawn carriage for hire, not the carriage itself. Rogers also incorrectly used *ishvestik* in his journal.

number and more imperious in their demands. In spite of it, however, they can usually be beaten down to one half of what they ask. Their use is almost universal. When one moves one piles in as much as possible and rides on top of the heap; when one takes goods to market one loads it in one of these carriages; in fact the other day I saw one bearing a farmer and two dead pigs to market. Perhaps as a result of all this the little carriages transmit insects quite effectively. Of insects there are all kinds here; every house seems to harbor them and many people; the only efforts at their obliteration being to try to drown them in perfume. One bit me on the arm in a tram the other day, but was quite invisible thereafter, so I suppose the poor thing died of lockjaw or the hoof and mouth disease.

The other evening, all of us feeling energetic, we took our skates and hied[127] us to a skating rink on one of the canals. They lay them out on the larger canals every winter, huge affairs with warm dressing rooms, buffet lunches, lounging rooms, and of course the rink itself fitted with slides, tracks for the fast skaters, a grand stand, and an orchestra. The ice is brilliantly lighted by arc lights and presents a gay scene, even from the street. None of us were any match for the skaters we found there. Even the girls made our efforts look feeble, and we soon grew tired and withdrew to watch the fancy skaters cutting figures, and the couples dancing to the music.

My Belgian friend has moved. Where to I, don't know. He never even said farewell, just folded his tent like the Arabs and as silently stole away, as the poet has it. I shall not hear all the gossip he had to tell me. I don't think I'll miss much of that; I never can give much attention to the tales one always hears about royalty, and people in the public eye.

---

[127] To hie (verb). To go quickly, hasten.

CHAPTER 4

"Before all the ikons blazed hundreds of candles"

The Russian Orthodox Church underwrote Russia's autocratic system, and on top of this construct sat Nicholas II, the divinely appointed tsar. The tsarist state bureaucracy continually supervised and subordinated the church. Exigencies of early twentieth-century Russia, however, led to a growing contradiction and antagonism between church and state. This contradiction became a significant challenge for the church when revolution broke out in 1917 and new thinking challenged long-standing social norms.

When Rogers arrived in Russia, the church was undergoing critical reform, spurred by the All-Russian Church Council. This movement, influenced by the ideals of the anti-monarchist 1905 Revolution, originated a decade earlier. The tsarist government had blocked the council, but after the March Revolution, it finally met in August 1917. The meeting adopted the key decision to restore the patriarchy in the Russian church, ending a period of some 300 years when the tsar directly governed the Russian church through the Most Holy Synod. But cataclysm overtook the church's reform agenda when the Bolsheviks, upon taking power, declared a separation of church and state. Lenin saw no place for the church in his vision of a classless revolutionary society, and brutal repression ensued.

Leighton Rogers wrestled with contradictory feelings about the role of the Orthodox Church in Russian society. On the one hand, he duly detailed his visits to Petrograd's splendid cathedrals, and their grandeur filled him with wonderment. Opulent church ceremonies led by richly adorned, chanting priests; towering colorful frescoes; the omnipresence of icons and crosses; the heavy fragrance of incense; and the liturgic chanting of choirmen overwhelmed his senses. Less than eighteen months later, however, Rogers wrote, "It seemed to me that a church organized for political control of its people, as this one is, embracing such a huge and ignorant mass, and placing so much emphasis on the symbolic in its worship . . . was bound to lead its patrons into mistaking the symbol for the idea, the idols for the spirit and thus provide only a glorified sort of idol worship."

Dec. 24, 1916.

The day before Christmas, and I intended to write at length about things. But there's been too much to do. I received my first Christmas present this morning when two letters came, one from the family and one from my old partner in crime, Dick R – – –. The last time we exchanged letters he was in Minneapolis and I was in New York; now he is on the Mexican border kicking about the heat and I am in Petrograd kicking about the cold; he wishes he were over here, and I wish I were down there. So there you are.

Intent upon being a good correspondent I set out this morning for the bank with all my unanswered letters and the avowed purpose of cornering a typewriter and paying off all scores. Planning to make it an all day affair I took with me my lunch,—three Russian rolls, and two cakes of chocolate. But I had no more than finished the second letter than Mr. S – – – –,[128] the manager entered and, after rustling through a few papers came into the room where I was and invited me to lunch with him at the Hotel Europe. Did I go? There[Three?]—and—one half guesses and "this beyouuuutiful gilded fire shovel to the winner."

Christmas Eve we attended a service at the cathedral. It was very impressive. The vast cathedral was crowded, the people standing solid over the great expanse of floor. In the center a battalion of soldiers was drawn up for the service,—I suppose they were soon to depart for the front. Before all the ikons blazed hundreds of candles and these with the huge chandeliers aglow, made the interior glitter and gleam with mosaics and paintings. In the center of the cathedral on a dais stood two priests clad in gold robes and supporting huge candles, waiting. From behind the great studded gates to the inner chapel came the music of the choir of men's voices strangely beautiful in chords and cadence, seemingly based upon a different harmonic scale than our music. Before the gates a priest chanted the service in a magnificent bass voice, chorused by the choir and the people present. Suddenly the gates swung open, and the procession, headed by a priest in blazing gold and silver robe studded with jewels, wearing a dome-shaped hat literally encrusted with them, and carrying a jeweled censer came out to the dais in the center. From here the procession went slowly around the church blessing all the ikons, after which it passed back through the gates again;

---

[128] R.R. Stevens.

these swung slowly shut to blot out the light from the great colored window with its representation of the Crucifixion, the candles over the altar, and to dim the chorus as it disappeared in the depths of the cathedral. As we made our way outside we found the great square massed with people, following the service as best they could, and gazing in awe at the cross outlined in flame at one end of the structure and the four great blazing torches at the four corners of the roof.

But all these nice things have their difficult side and this one is that I did not accomplish what I set out to accomplish, hence I have decided to stay here this evening in spite of the Christmas dinner at the house. I don't care very much anyway about sitting down to the festive board with a bunch of knife swallowing "furriners;" it is decidedly unromantic. Of course the Russians do not celebrate our Christmas, because we, according to their way of thinking, are all wrong in our reckoning. Christmas for them comes on our sixth of January when they have a great hullabaloo about it for almost a week; bells ringing steadily, priests reciting their little pieces in the churches and great gastronomic onslaughts on the denizens of the finny[129] tribes. But for "aw that" we win both ways because we have our own Christmas and theirs too. That is a great thing about the Russians, they observe so many holidays. Every time a member of the royal family has a birthday or a saint day, or on the day of the death of a relative, and even on the anniversary of a miraculous escape from a train wreck or the like, there is a holiday. On these days no one works, except the bell rings and on some of them it is a crime to work. No chance of any of us getting arrested! The more important holidays are accompanied by special services in the churches and salutes of sixty and one hundred guns from the fortress across the river. We get all the benefit of these, because the fortress is just opposite us.

January 1st.1917.

There's much to put down about the holidays. I meant to keep away from the Christmas party at the house last week but Fate seemed to have it otherwise. When I arrived home at nine o'clock it was just after the dinner. At my entrance, Pasha, our waitress, whose night it was out, but who had stayed in order that she might wait on us at the festivities dragged me into a side room to a little table covered with a complete dinner she had saved out for me from the debris of the early evening. It was so long since I had seen such a repast that I declared all rules off and sailed in with

---

[129] Relating to or resembling a fish.

such a burst of "wim, wigor, and witality" that the table was soon as clean as a bone. In the lounging rooms were more "eats" and the inevitable tea; people were dancing; there was much conversation and piano playing; and someone, in the form of a special treat, had just served some vodka. I thought I'd tasted all forms of intoxicating liquors, but this stuff was liquid dynamite. I felt as if I'd swallowed a young blast furnace. It's no wonder they abolished the stuff here. Even the little bit I'd taken had its effect because when I sat down to play my three pieces on the piano there were too many black keys and the effort had to be abandoned.

Arising early Christmas morning we got into old clothes, hied over to the Finland station and took a train for a small town about forty versts[130] away, called Pargolova.[131] Here, we engaged in argument a flock of sleigh drivers over the price of a couple of rigs for the afternoon and after ranging them up against each other and introducing a little American competition all we had to do was sit down and let them bid until the price came down within our reach. We finally hired two for seven roubles apiece for the afternoon. They were curious little affairs with a high, curving set of runners, high dash board, and narrow little seat in front for the driver, and a low seat in back for two passengers, and the whole affair stuffed with hay, whether for feeding the horse or to keep our feet warm we couldn't make out. We clambered in, waved farewell to the drivers who no doubt thought it was the last of their horses if one could judge by the touching farewell they took of the animals once they were in the hands of these "crazy Americans." It fell to my lot to drive ours, to me, who does not know a check rein from a manger; but being ready to try most anything once, I took up the reins and we were ready to start. Not knowing whether this particular horse was equipped with a self-starter or had to be cranked there was some doubt as how to begin. However, he looked quite old and decrepit as he stood there half asleep so I landed him a good one with the leather whip. The experiment was highly successful and before I could extricate myself from the other two of the party in the hay we were off, halfway around the curve and streaking for the open prairie. The others were not far behind and a lively race ensued. Our horse had a longer wheel base, however, and opened up with a few fancy steps which soon put the other sleigh in the rear and

---

[130] A Russian measure of length equaling approximately 1.1 kilometer or 0.66 mile.

[131] Иппо Б. Б. Парголово и его окрестности. Л., 1954; St. Petersburg Encyclopaedia "Shuvalovsky Park"; Wikipedia, "Pargolovo," last modified September 4, 2020, 22:11 (UTC). Pargolovo (Russian: Парголово) was a family seat of the junior line of the counts Shuvalov, starting with Peter Ivanovich Shuvalov who received the Pargolovo manor from Empress Elizabeth in 1746. The Shuvalov Park contains a network of old ponds; the Yellow Dacha, a wooden lodge designed by Maximilian Messmacher; the Parnassus hill, which used to offer views of the capital's downtown; and the Church of Sts. Peter and Paul, built in the 1840s to a Gothic Revival design by Alexander Brullov.

almost had me flying out horizontal at the end of the reins. Not to be defeated without a struggle those behind began to snatch up lumps of snow, make snow balls and heave them at us; but in response to a bit of strategic genius we only ducked allowing them to land on the old horse, which opened up another notch with each one. This gave us a fine lead. We were thankful that Russia was such a large land, because had we been in England we would have run off the island. The horse seemed to know where he was going, and as we didn't, we left it all to him. It was a great day, snowing a little, the country beautiful with rolling hills; and we tore along mid a cloud of snow. All that was needed to complete the picture and make it what most people think Russia to be was a pack of wolves hiking after us.

We finally arrived at a place called Uke, a winter sport haven where there were toboggan slides, ski jumps and the like, but as yet not in operation. Here, after a little refreshment at a shop, we turned around and headed station-ward. With still quite a way to go who should we meet but the drivers out on a hunt for their outfits. They greeted us like long lost brothers with many "Thank Gods," and seemed in great relief to find that their horses were still as made, with four legs and tails and everything. After waiting an hour a train pulled in, and carried us back to Petrograd.

It was not our last ride of the day however, because on our way through the city to a reception given for us we paid our *ishvestiks* well and had a mad race down the Nevsky—the main thoroughfare. A boy of twelve drove ours no doubt taking his father's place when he went off to the front, and he treated us to a wild ride, swerving around corners on one runner, missing lampposts and pedestrians by inches only, and even giving the burly police at the crossings a thrill as we swept past. When we tore under the great arch and out into the Winter Palace Square, swerving fully twenty feet across the frozen surface, I thought we were gone, but no, the sleigh righted itself and we skimmed on, beating the others to our destination by inches.

CHAPTER 5

"Rasputin is dead"

C harge d'affaires Fred Dearing foresaw trouble. Referring to the machinations Rasputin instigated with the Empress to set her against Foreign
Minister Sergey Sazonov, Dearing wrote, "The air is thick with talk
of catastrophe."[132] On November 1 came a warning from Grand Duke Nicholas
Mikhailovich,[133] a first cousin to the previous tsar, Alexander III, who wrote to
Nicholas II to stop the empress from bringing the monarchy into further disrepute
by meddling in the affairs of the government. "You stand on the eve of an era of new
troubles," the grand duke counseled. The tsar did not bother to read his letter.[134]

Rasputin was born the son of a Siberian peasant in 1871. "Rasputin" in Russian
means "debauched one." Wandering itinerantly and obscurely across Russia,
Rasputin experienced a religious conversion after taking a pilgrimage to a monas-
tery in 1897 and then developed a reputation as a "Mad Monk" as he journeyed
from town to town. He finally landed in St. Petersburg in late 1903. His perverted
religious fervor, combined with a mesmerizing, hypnotic glance, facilitated his
astonishing entry into social circles in Petrograd, including the Russian Orthodox
clergy and the imperial family. He was introduced to the tsar and empress in 1905
and in 1908 "stopped" the bleeding of their hemophiliac son, Alexei. Capitalizing
on this "feat," he began his gradual ascent to the pinnacle of evil influence he exerted
on the ruling family of Russia. Rasputin infuriated nobles, church orthodoxy, and
commoners alike. He manipulated the empress, and through her, fouled many of
the Russian Empire's most critical affairs.

Something had to be done. Prince Felix Yusupov, the husband of the tsar's niece,
decided Rasputin had to die. Yusupov invited Rasputin to dine, on a false pretense,

---

[132] Fred Morris Dearing, Unpublished papers, March 27, 1916, 87, Folder 502.
[133] Wikia; Military; "Grand Duke Nicholas Mikhailovich of Russia," https://military.wikia.org/wiki/Grand_Duke_Nicholas_Mikhailovich_of_Russia. Grand Duke Nicholas Mikhailovich fell from favor due to Empress Alexandra's dislike of him. The Bolsheviks executed him along with several of his royal relatives on January 28, 1919, in the Peter and Paul Fortress in Petrograd.
[134] Pipes, *The Russian Revolution*, 256.

at his palace on the night of December 29, 1916. There, Yusupov and his co-conspirators, Grand Duke Dmitri Pavlovich, Vladimir Puriskevich, a monarchist, anti-Semitic, right-wing politician, and two others, murdered him. The majority of Russia's aristocracy welcomed the news of Rasputin's demise. Grand Duke Dmitri even received a standing ovation when he appeared in the Mikhailovsky Theatre the following evening.[135] At the New Year's Eve party at the American Embassy, Rasputin's murder was the hot topic for discussion among the sixty guests who attended.[136]

The tsar officially granted National City Bank's charter on December 31, 1916,[137] and the Petrograd branch opened for business on January 15, 1917. National City Bank then employed sixteen expatriate staff in Petrograd, in addition to several Russian staff and a Russian language teacher.[138]

Rogers plowed into work, which unsurprisingly demanded an increasing amount of his time. Thoughts on Rasputin's death, America's impending entry into the war, the German threat, and Russia's next move rose to the forefront of his mind.

The events of March would rearrange his thinking.

---

[135] Figes, *A People's Tragedy*, 290.
[136] Barnes, *Standing on a Volcano*, 213.
[137] Tkachenko, *American Bank Capital in Russia*, 80.
[138] *Number Eight*, The National City Bank of New York, February 1917, 29–30.

3'd Jan. 1917.

Rasputin is dead. His body was found under the ice in the Neva after a disappearance of five or six days. It seems the Empress had the secret police searching for him and they discovered what was left caught in the ice just below a hole therein which had been chopped with an axe. The city fairly buzzes with talk about it, but subdued talk at that; the police still have these people frightened. But everyone seems happy about it. The newspapers refer to it slyly and the doing away with the dirty monk seems to be regarded as a great feat. I didn't realize he was so important, and I refused to believe the stories they whispered about him and the royal family. They seemed incredible, but they must have been true. It takes one straight back to medieval times, the Middle Ages, to hear them and reflect that they are true. It shows, however, the ignorance and superstition that abounds in the circle of autocrats which dominates the lives of two hundred million people.

Rasputin was a degenerate monk, who, after being thrown out of the Russian Church for his behavior and his conflicts with the powers that be in that institution, became a wanderer about the country, making his way from town to town, remaining in some for various lengths of time and being ejected out of others, where his escapades in immorality made him unwelcome. He is said to have worn a monk costume made of cloth akin to our burlap, with a piece of rope fastened about his waist, tattered shoes, making altogether, with his huge powerful frame, matted hair and beard, a striking figure in his wanderings. He at last came to Petrograd, and took his place in the dives of the city, where the small hypnotic power he possessed and his somewhat unique doctrine created something of a sensation. His was the doctrine of sin. "You cannot go to heaven until you have repented of your sins," he preached "and the more you repent the better off you will be in heaven: therefore sin mightily in order that your repentance may be great and your entrance into heaven the more certain." Not so bad, at that!

To those seeking a moral excuse to let loose and abandon themselves to the fabled "wine, women, and song" this was the opportunity and it is little wonder that this man and this doctrine became the rage in the under world. But they were soon destined to have their place in the ranks of those highest up.

When the Tsarevitch, the dearly beloved son and heir of the Tsar and Tsarina, was born, Fate burdened him with a constitutional trouble of some sort which made him subject to bleeding at the nose and mouth when over-excited or nervous. There was no remedy for these attacks save that of quiet and rest. As the boy grew older the attacks seemed to be more frequent and his future appeared anything but bright. On the occasion of a particularly severe attack, when the royal family was fearful of the boy's life, a lady-in-waiting to the Empress informed her that there was in Petrograd at the time a monk named Rasputin, who had the power to quiet afflicted people. In her agitation and love for her son the Empress had the monk sent for to be brought to the palace. Here, with his slight mesmeric powers, Rasputin succeeded in quieting the boy and eventually stopping the hemorrhage. Whereupon he left. This performance was repeated many times, until Gregory—this being the monk's given name, diminuated into Grisha—realized the importance of the hold he had upon the imperial family. He began to make use of it, asking favor after favor, and meeting refusals with the statement that if his demands were not granted, he would never attend the sick Alexei, the Tsarevitch again. This frightened Her Majesty to such an extent that she saw to it that Grisha got what he asked for.

His demands grew and grew until he was practically taken into the family, became one of the court circle, with a place at its functions, his reception being commanded by the Empress who feared for the life of her son were he displeased. Rasputin was finally appointed guardian to the royal children and his position became secure. He spread his doctrine around his new circle and gained many followers; the meetings at which he preached it became infamous all over Russia in the whispered gossip of the disgusted people. The details, running the gamut of immorality, make our old friend Balzac read like John Bunyan;[139] and Rasputin is said to have originated a few new wrinkles of his own in the sin line which would make the antics of the cities of Sodom and Gomorrah look like a Quaker village in comparison.

In spite of the fact that the people were horrified and disgusted at the stories of this monk who came to dine with royalty clad in his old uncleansed habit of a wanderer, with unwashed face and hands and matted hair, who at the table ate with his fingers, disdaining knives and forks, and who at times even did without fingers, bearing his face in the food like a pig, in spite of their disgust, they could do nothing. Because Rasputin was clever, and he saw to it that the Empress, through her spiritualism and her love for her son, never got out of his power.

[139] *Britannica,* "John Bunyan," by Roger Sharrock, https://www.britannica.com/biography/John-Bunyan. John Bunyan (1628–1688) was an English writer and Puritan preacher best remembered as the author of the Christian allegory *The Pilgrim's Progress.*

He accomplished whatever pleased him. He removed leaders in the church as well as leaders in the army; and it was said that he under the German influence, was the prime mover of the separate peace idea. It was he, so it is said, who influenced the Tsar to remove the Grand Duke Nicholas, called the ablest strategist in Europe by no less an authority than Hindenburg, from command of the Russian armies and appointed himself, Nicholas the Emperor, instead. The jokers have it that the Tsar did this because he thought it the speediest way to end the war, as Hindenburg would die laughing!

But anyway, Rasputin is dead. No one seems to know who killed him. Some say that young Prince Yousippoff and a band of friends did it, but no one is certain. Nothing seems to have happened to that young man anyway, and meanwhile everyone has it that it is the best thing that could have happened for the good of Russia, and the conduct of the war in general.

The Empress is supposed to be completely upset by the event. She has had the body taken to Tsarsky Selo and placed in a mausoleum there, to await a state funeral, with silver coffin and much ceremony; she is said to have announced her intention of having dear Grisha canonized,—made a saint in the Russian Church!

We found that before we could open our bank it had to be provided with ikons,—one for each room—and with the regulation pictures of the Tsar and Tsarina. These pictures have to be hung in a conspicuous place in the entrance hall. Then, having the ikons, they must be blessed. Hence, today when we opened, there was quite a ceremony. Priests and a choir came over and officiated at the opening service which lasted about an hour. Each of our ikons was blessed as were all those of us who will work in the bank under them. This done, we were officially a bank and could proceed with our business.

(Rogers dated a similar passage in his later manuscript to January 10, 1917)

A Swedish doctor has just come in and occupied the rooms next to ours. In a talk with him last night he told of coming through Germany a month or so ago from the front where he had been working, and of having seen them extracting the grease and fats from the bodies of the dead by some chemical process, not far behind the lines, sending the casks to the interior to be made into grease for greasing shells. He added that on his trip to the interior he saw these same casks come rolling into an oleomargarine plant for the manufacture of imitation butter! It is difficult to imagine some German family sitting down to dinner and someone spreading his brot with oleo saying, "Well, here goes young Franz Sauerkraut."[140]

Petrograd—the city of Peter—was built by the herculean efforts of Peter the Great. That monarch was determined that Russia should have an outlet on the sea and with this end in view compelled more than forty thousand slaves to work for years constructing the city. At best it is but a poor seaport, opening as it does, only upon the Gulf of Finland and cut off from the outside world as it can be at any time by the whim of Denmark or of Germany. But it was the best that could be done for a location. Peter traveled through-out Europe getting ideas for his capital which he attempted to incorporate into it. Of all European cities he liked Venice for its beauty and resolved that his city should be something similar to Venice. Hence, when the plans were drawn, they included a canal system which is one of the metropolis's chief features. These canals were easy to dig because of the marsh land which makes up this section of the country, extending for miles on all sides. The canals of course aid greatly the drainage of the place, and furnish much relief for transportation, much of the heavier carrying being done by barges and tugs. But this same marshland which made possible his dream of a canal city also made imperative a tremendous amount of labor to provide a foundation for it. Hundreds of thousands of piles had to be sunk in the marshes before heavy buildings could be constructed, and the labor demand was tremendous. But labor was cheap in those days and his forty thousand slaves worked almost without recompense. It is said that news of a strike or an outbreak of some kind among his laborers brought Peter back from Western Europe in a hurry to settle the affair, which he did by ordering some four thousand of them to be massacred.

But the foundations were driven, the city was built, and Peter got his seaport. There was, of course, great protest when Mother Moscow was abandoned as the capital of the empire and the government removed to Petrograd, but protest made little headway with the great tyrant and Petrograd became the capital. It is hardly a brilliant one, however, although it has a sort of eerie beauty with its haze and color.

Constant repairs are necessary in the wet climate. There is no building stone to be quarried within reasonable distance, hence practically all buildings are of brick and plaster, which are quick victims for the moisture. Also in many sections the founda-tions are sinking, and this threatens the most magnificent edifice in the empire and

---

[140] Stephen Pope and Elizabeth-Anne Wheal, " 'Kadaver' Rumour," in *The Dictionary of The First World War* (New York: St. Martin's Press, 1995), 263. Anglo-French propaganda that the German army was boiling down dead troops for their fats was based on a mistranslation of the word *Kadaver,* meaning "animal corpse," in a German newspaper report on the use of dead horses.

one of the greatest in Europe the Cathedral of St. Isaacs, one entire corner of which has already sunk a foot or so below the remainder, which is liable to crack at any moment and send the tons of red Finnish granite in shattered heaps to the ground. As this is one of the few solid, granite structures in the city its loss will be doubly mournful.

Directly across the river from the bank is the Fortress of Peter and Paul, built by Peter the Great to guard his city. It is now obsolete, of course, and the space within its granite walls devoted to parks, the Cathedral of Peter and Paul where the Tsars and Tsarinas are buried, and various small public buildings. The old guns still line the walls, and one of these is used to announce the noon hour each day. All clocks are set by its report, which can be heard for miles around the city. This gun points our way and the racket is terrific, while were it loaded the shell would shatter into the Winter Palace which is a little way down the quay to our left.

It is said that a revolutionist did load the gun one day some twenty years ago, much to the Tsar's surprise, who at noon, had the pleasure of feeling the shot tear a great gap in the Winter Palace. It is this attempt, so the story goes, that led their majesties to make the palace at Tsarsky Selo their Petrograd home. Anyway, they no longer live in Petrograd.

The Winter Palace Guards who drill in the square before the palace every morning are the finest looking troops I have ever seen. They are all young fellows, but selected for height and weight so that each one, when in full uniform is as nearly like his fellow as human care can make him. Six footers every one of them, and weighing from one hundred seventy to two hundred and over, they are a formidable looking body of men. Their drilling is perfect and as they go through their maneuvers with uncanny speed and precision, every arm moves in unison, every foot lifts and lowers in time, every belt buckle is at the same height so that their line is straight edged, every cap is at the identical tilt, and every great coat cut to the same length. They are as near machine made as possible. That the discipline which accomplished this must be rigid is illustrated by an incident which happened not long ago:—it was very cold and one young soldier, in the course of the snappy manual at arms, dropped his rifle to the snow before his clutching fingers could grasp it again, thereby marring the unity of the performance. The officer in command strode up to him, shot out a few Russian expletives and struck the boy squarely in the face with his clenched fist. There was not a sound, not a movement in the whole company, not even a head turned to see what had been done. The soldier picked up his rifle, spat blood out upon the snow, and the drill went on.

Cockroaches everywhere! Today, while calling at the residence of a very well to do family, we saw them on the wall in the living room. It is no disgrace here; it is actually impossible to keep them out. This is partly due, the lady told us, to the fact that the servants have a good many legends and superstitions about them, and if they moved to work in a house that has not its quota of roaches, they bring some of them in order to make sure of good luck.

Although my knowledge of opera is very limited, having only heard it in Boston and New York, the opera is produced here far better than at either of those cities. German opera is taboo here now, but the standard works given everywhere are all presented in addition to the many purely Russian operas which one rarely hears in other countries. With all these, and the four opera houses in the city in operation, there is a bewildering choice for the music lover.

The four houses are the Imperial Opera which is given in the Marinsky Theatre, also the home of the ballet; the Music–Drama or the Conservatory,—opera, run by the Conservatory of Music, produced in the theater attached to the school, and cast from the students with the assistance of some outside singers; the People's Opera, a huge house, charging popular prices, mostly attended by the soldiers and middle class music lovers, which in the field of having the great artists surpasses them all. This is because many of the big singers have broken with the Imperial Opera and prefer to scatter their talents before the less wealthy and aristocratic of Petrograd society. Here are performances given by Shaliapine,[141] called the greatest singing actor in the world; Smirnoff the famous tenor,[142] and Madame Lipkowskaya the soprano,[143] none of whom I have yet heard. And lastly we have the opera given at the Alexandrinsky Theatre which is the poorest of the lot.

But the performances themselves are put on with more care than is exercised at home; all parts are consigned to the hands of good singers who are in addition good actors, and this combined with effective scenery, splendid orchestration, and fiery leading, gives a keen effect of unity and realism which is decidedly lacking at home.

---

[141] *Britannica,* "Feodor Chaliapin," by Gregory Freidin, https://www.britannica.com/biography/Feodor-Chaliapin. Feodor Chaliapin, also spelled Fyodor Ivanovich Shalyapin, (Russian: Фёдор Иванович Шаляпин) (1873–1938) was one of Russia's most famous opera singers. He was a "Russian operatic *basso profundo* whose vivid declamation, great resonance, and dynamic acting made him the best-known singer-actor of his time."

[142] Wikipedia, "Dmitri Smirnov (tenor)," last modified November 14, 2020, 12:50 (UTC), https://en.wikipedia.org/wiki/Dmitri_Smirnov_(tenor). Dimitri Alexeyevich Smirnov (Russian: Дмитрий Алексеевич Смирнов) (1882–1944) was a leading Russian operatic tenor with a lyric voice and a bravura singing technique.

[143] Wikipedia, "Lydia Yakolevna Lipkowska," last modified July 11, 2021, 14:24 (UTC), https://en.wikipedia.org/wiki/Lydia_Lipkowska. Lydia Yakolevna Lipkowska (Russian: Лидия Яковлевна Липковская) (1882-1958) was a Russian operatic soprano of Ukrainian origin.

It is the care in casting the roles which has much to do with preserving the illusion, so often neglected with us. The Russian artistic sense would not tolerate the sight of a three hundred-pound soprano singing Cho-Cho-San in Madame Butterfly. No matter how perfect her voice she would be booed from the stage. Rather sacrifice a little voice to preserving the illusion and have the part in the hands of a soprano of reasonable size, acting ability, and beauty, possessed of no mean voice in addition. We have much to learn from them.

There is still much talk about the Rasputin affair, but no one seems to know just who did it or just how it was done, although nearly all references are to Yousippoff. There are said to have been strange doings going on at his house on the Moika Canal the night before the disappearance.

The newspapers continue their hints at the Rasputin affair and one of them has even been closed down for its audacity.

Rasputin may be gone but there seem to be others ready to play the same game. Mr. S – – – told me today about hearing from a good Russian friend of his how Protopoppoff, the most reactionary of all the Tsar's ministers, now goes to the Empress saying that the spirit of Grisha has descended from heaven into him and is acting through him. Whenever he wants anything he visits her, makes a few funny faces, waves his hands in the air, makes known his request and ends it with "The Spirit of Grisha demands it." He gets it! Can you beat it? In a country that is supposed to be modern. The pity of it is that two hundred million people must submit to it. At first I couldn't believe it but Mr. S – – – is the soul of honor and states that it is true.

It was supposed to be Petrograd's gayest café. Walls of poorly imitated marble, dusty carpets, crowded tables, struggling palms, a gaudy stage, glaring lights and an air of hollow gaiety. At a circle of tables running under the balconies sat the habituées of the place, and above and behind them were the stalls or private dining rooms, with their double windows opening out into the main floor, showing the table set for dinner, and in the corner the canopied bed. Soon the last mannikin made its bow, the orchestra squirmed through its last selection, the lights dimmed and we hastened to the doors in company with those others who sat on the main floor. The locks clicked behind us as the cold night air struck us in the face; the place was officially "closed," but it yawned all too wide for those locked within.

It is strange that one doesn't go to the theater much here. It may be because the field of opera and ballet is so broad, but there are few theatres in Petrograd where straight drama is presented. One of the few is the French Theatre where a French company gives French plays and farces. But after my first attempt at that I gave it up.

A typical unmoral farce of the French kind, replete with banging doors, whirling exits and entrances, broad French humor and broader jokes, based on quite unnatural situations, without even the consolation of being well done. The only American plays known here are "Romance" and "Potash and Perlmutter."[144] Of these the latter is a great favorite!

Went to the movies the other night and saw an antique Charlie Chaplin picture, or a "Charlot" as they call him here. I laughed even as much as when I first saw it because the action ensued in a bank, and with some experience with that same atmosphere, I could appreciate how perfectly the world's greatest comedian simulated it,—also how great an artist he is. But my mild laughter was completely lost in the uproars of the theatre full of soldiers, who demonstrated their delight like children.

It's quite a while since I wrote here, but I suppose the flurry of moving has had something to do with it. Fred and I got pretty tired of the old place, being so crowded, and we sought new quarters. Although I was enthusiastic about this place when I saw it, and listened to the heavy line of the landlady, I'm beginning to think now that we are stung. There's no more room than in the last place, the bathing facilities are almost nil, and the old girl has already begun to re-nig on the breakfast she promised to serve. Perhaps we can stick it out until May or June and then find a good place, which ought not to be difficult because so many families leave the city for the country during the short summer. But at this domestic stuff we certainly are the Babes in the Woods. When you can't speak the language, you're easy meat for a conspiring landlady.

(This entry was likely on Feb. 3, 1917)

We heard today about the rupture of diplomatic relations between America and Germany. The news came as a great surprise after Wilson's speech to the senate in which he said that "peace without victory" was the solution.

I cannot understand Germany's attitude. Her people must be insane. They have alienated their last friend. But I must say that they wore out my patience long ago,

---

[144] Internet Broadway Database, "Romance," https://www.ibdb.com/broadway-production/romance-7598. *Romance*, written by Edward Sheldon, ran for 160 performances at Maxine Elliott's Theatre in New York from 1910 to 1913; Wikipedia, "Potash and Perlmutter," last modified April 20, 2021, 22:53 (UTC), https://en.wikipedia.org/wiki/Potash_and_Perlmutter. *Potash and Perlmutter*, written by Montague Glass and Charles Klein, opened at the George M. Cohan Theatre on August 16, 1913. The play was a comedy featuring the characters Abe Potash and Mawruss Perlmutter, who are business partners in the garment industry. The play was a hit and ran for 441 performances on Broadway.

and I feel that the break is a good thing. Neutrality begets no friends and at least now we have friends in the Allies, where before we did not. No one can accuse us of entering into the war, if we eventually do as I think we shall, for selfish reasons, because we shall have been dragged into it in spite of ourselves. We have been very patient, itself a great virtue, but there is a limit to all patience. And those people who mistake patience for weakness, as many do, must learn their error from the exhibition of fighting we shall put up, when we get into it.

I forgot to mention our expedition to a Russian bath. We'd heard much about them and at last decided to give the experiment a try. Upon entering the building we walked through long corridors heavily carpeted trimmed with palms, and much nude statuary, purchased our tickets at the desk, and were ushered to a private dressing room. Before leaving, the attendant inquired as to whether we would have our massage and soap bath in our room and desired the female masseurs or whether we would observe that ceremony in the large public room. We declined the invitation for the ladies, and elected to bathe in the open. We disrobed and stepped into the steam room, which was fitted with tiers of seats like a baseball bleacher, and a brick stove wherein rested a heap of hot stones. Steam was produced by throwing buckets full of water upon these stones. It filled the room in an instant and we retired to the bleachers to await developments. The higher up one sat the hotter it was in the rising steam, and it wasn't long before those of us at the top had to descend. For some minutes we sat there and almost melted—I could feel myself wasting away like butter on a griddle, and it was with a real effort that I slid from the seat and walked out into the massage room. Here we were laid out like corpses on long slabs and pummeled for a half hour by a masseur who used in this process various kinds of soap and some sort of sweet smelling herb. With this done and covered with soap so that we looked like snowmen we either hopped in the small pool or stepped under the showers. We then took huge towels and retired to our room to rest in luxury on the couches there. After generating enough energy we dressed and crawled home. Although tired that night, in the morning I felt like a million dollars and could have taken on the whole Petrograd police force at once.

It is striking how feeling for the United States has changed since our severance of diplomatic relations with Germany. Not so much with the Russians but with the English and French. Englishmen here don't seem to have much use for the French, and the French shrug their shoulders most expressively when you speak of Great Britain. But both of them looked scorn itself when the United States is mentioned. They have had little use for us. I remember that day in the tram when our gang, assembled on the rear platform, discussed the war in general, when something was said about our getting into it, an Englishman who had been listening in, gave us the contemptuous leer. Whereupon we switched the conversation to Great Britain, and Bab delivered the knockout by repeating that old one, "England will fight to the last Russian" which caused the gentleman to get off the car in his ire.

But now the feeling has changed and we get the glad hand and the smile everywhere.

All save the Russians. They never did seem to hold it against us because we were out of it; rather did they hope we kept out. Not because they didn't want help, but because their humanitarian sense got the better of their political feelings. When our coming in was mentioned a Russian looked at you a bit sadly and said, "Don't. It is too awful. Why join in the terrible business? You will lose thousands of your best young men. It is not worth it." This even now, when they feel that our intervention is inevitable and they are glad to have it, they still feel sorry for the sacrifices it will entail. They are a great people.

This language! I'm beginning to think I shall never learn it. Of course it's the alphabet which contributes more to the difficulty than anything else. There are in the tongue many foreign words, of German, French, and English origin which would be readily recognizable to anyone with a smattering of those three languages, but this outlandish alphabet disguises them to look like strange words. In addition, the language is very highly inflected, the meaning being shown by changes in endings of words. Then too, it is characterized by an entirely different way of thought. That is the heart of the difficulty,—these people do not use the same thinking processes that we do and hence they express their thoughts in different form. But in spite of all this, we are making some progress and perhaps the day will come when we can talk with some degree of fluency. It is fascinating to the ear, being very forceful and expressive, and when well spoken is beautiful in a sinuous, powerful way.

I think I mentioned once about our moving and getting the worst of it. We certainly have stepped from the frying pan into the fire. The new landlady is changing the rules on us already. Our most energetic kick comes from the fact that she refuses to allow us to sleep with the windows open. And before we came in we made that an express condition, having in mind the arguments our mania for fresh air got us into at the other place. Every night she tells us not to leave the window open, and every night we open it, so that every morning there is an argument. She, of course should win, because she can talk faster, louder, and longer than we can, but it doesn't get her much because we can't understand and just wave her off in silence. She gets back at us though by serving up terrible breakfast of coffee made of acorns and shellac, and bread with straw in it. It looks as though we would move again just as soon as we can find a new place.

It's been quite a while since I wrote last; but we are very busy at the bank now and by the time I get home at night I'm so tired I can hardly keep awake. Thus do my good intentions of writing in this journal every little while go astray.

PART II

The February (March) Revolution, the July Days, and the Kornilov Affair.

March 1917–October 1917

Historians debate when to mark the beginning of the March Revolution. Some designate Thursday, February 23/March 8, International Women's Day, when more than 100,000 workers went on strike to protest food shortages, but historian Richard Pipes argues "that date has to be February 27/March 12, 1917, when 'worker demonstrations turned into a soldier mutiny,' and the tsarist authorities lost control of the capital."[145]

The March Revolution was spontaneous and exploded like a volcano. No particular leadership claimed responsibility. The tumultuous events between International Women's Day, the announcement of the new provisional government, and the tsar's abdication two days afterward surprised local radicals; Lenin was still in exile, writing and eating Swiss chocolate in Zurich, and Leon Trotsky was editing a Russian socialist newspaper in New York. Few diplomats stationed in Petrograd expected a revolution. Professor U.V. Lomonossoff, speaking at a dinner for the Russian Mission in New York several months later, opined that "The Russian people did not start the revolution; the Czar and Rasputin started it."[146] Eyes and feet on street level, Leighton Rogers sensed turmoil and wrote several days before the beginning of the March Revolution that "there was something in the air."

What was "in the air" reflected what the Russian masses felt on the ground. Ineffectual political representation and a Duma constrained by an anachronistic and corrupt imperial administration kindled a bonfire of revolutionary ideas exhorting the peasant and industrial workers' classes to action. Richard Pipes points out that widespread inflation and food shortages caused by the war and government mismanagement "produced tension between town and country which Russia had not experienced before. The city accused the village of hoarding and profiteering . . ."[147] According to Pipes, "the urban population, which had expanded considerably from the influx of industrial workers and war refugees and the billeting of troops," bore the brunt of the suffering.[148] No commensurate increase in housing and transportation infrastructure ameliorated these pains. By late 1916, Pipes summarizes, "Petrograd could obtain only half of the fuel it needed, which meant that even when bakeries got flour they could not bake."[149]

---

[145] Pipes, *The Russian Revolution*, 279–80.
[146] "Asks for Patience with New Russia; Socialist Leader, at Dinner to Mission, Predicts Disappearance of Anarchy," *New York Times*, July 9, 1917, 3.
[147] Pipes, *The Russian Revolution*, 242.
[148] Ibid., 237.
[149] Ibid., 245.

International Women's Day brought unseasonable springlike weather to Petrograd, and everyone went outdoors. By noon, tens of thousands of women flocked to the Nevsky Prospekt, Petrograd's major boulevard, carrying patriotic banners demanding change. Before the end of the day, "100,000 workers had come out on strike," protesting food shortages, and shouting, "Bread!" and "Down with the tsar!"[150] The next day, the number of striking workers doubled, and the day after further increased to nearly 300,000. On March 10, the tsar, at his military headquarters in Mogilev, sent a telegram to General Sergey Khabalov, the military commander of Petrograd, ordering him to suppress the demonstrations. Petrograd awoke to see fully armed military units posted across the city. Incidents of shootings and killings occurred in various parts of the city, the bloodiest of which occurred on Znamensky Square on March 11. On March 12, military units in the city, composed mainly of young recruits, in particular, the Pavlovsky Regiment, mutinied against authority. Tsarist authorities lost control as mutinying soldiers joined the demonstrating workers and Petrograd convulsed in all-out insurrection. The Duma, defying the tsar's orders not to meet, reconvened and after several days of frenetic discussions and arguments, forged an agreement among various political parties and appointed a provisional committee, soon renamed the provisional government, and announced a new cabinet on March 15 led by Prince George Lvoff with Alexander Kerensky as minister of justice.

Nicholas II abdicated the same day, and the Russian Empire ceased to exist. Orlando Figes relates that the March Revolution's cost, according to the official figures of the provisional government, in Petrograd alone was 1,443 killed or wounded, although a friend of Prince Lvoff told the French journalist Claude Anet that the true figure was five times higher.[151]

Endorsing the revolution, Rogers cheered when the United States acted first to recognize the provisional government, just one week after its announcement: "We must bow to Russia for the finest spectacle in [the] history of the governed exerting its God-given right to govern." Most Americans, including President Wilson, held the same view. Russia had accomplished a transcendent achievement of overthrowing an anachronistic, incompetent, and repressive regime, and this outcome was a victory for democracy. The expectation was that, now freed from alleged pro-German sentiments held within the tsarist government, Russia would continue to fight Germany and support the Allies. Rogers applauded the United States' declaration

[150] Figes, *A People's Tragedy*, 308.
[151] Ibid., 321.

of war on Germany on April 6 and hoped America's involvement would shorten the course of the war.

Even so, Rogers harbored uncertainty about the revolution. Presciently, he wrote in his journal, "What will come of it, no one knows." He realized that the revolutionary movement in Russia was complex, its path convoluted, and that the Russian masses might view democracy differently.

Vladimir Lenin returned to Petrograd on April 16. Arriving to a tumultuous crowd at Finlandia station, he climbed atop an armored train car to address the gathered throng of his followers, calling for the Bolshevik Party to use armed force to seize control from the provisional government. Societal contradictions increased over the summer months, as did military and political havoc. Kerensky, who within months had become minister of war, believed that a Russian military victory would restore the soldiers' and people's morale, and hence gain popular favor for the weak provisional government. He thus ordered a massive military offensive. On July 1, after a two-day artillery barrage, the Russian army, led by General Aleksey Brusilov,[152] attacked to capture Lvov, the capital of Galicia, the largest, most populous province in the Austro-Hungarian Empire. For several days, the Russian army advanced, cheered on by the Russian people, and Rogers, writing in his journal. But the German army came to the help of its ally and counter-attacked, throwing the Russians back into a headlong humiliating retreat. It was the Russian army's last offensive in the war. Kerensky, having staked his reputation on a military success, instead faced political disaster.

The failed "Kerensky Offensive" led to the "July Days." Ignominious reversal on the battlefield kindled a new insurrection in Petrograd. In early July, the provisional government ordered certain units of the Petrograd garrison suspected of Bolshevik sympathies to the front. Ongoing Bolshevik agitation exacerbated dissent mounting on the streets. On July 15, four Constitutional Democratic Party ("Kadet") ministers in the provisional government resigned and Prime Minister Lvoff threatened to resign days later. Certain military units in Petrograd mutinied on July 16, notably the 1st Machine Gun Regiment, which at more than 10,000 men was the largest military unit in the capital and possibly the most radicalized. Leftist-leaning sailors and factory workers joined them in armed demonstrations. Chaos engulfed Petrograd's streets during July 16–19, as if the March Revolution days had returned. Lenin and his colleagues debated within

---

[152] Pope and Wheal, "Brusilov, General Alexei" and "Brusilov Offensive," in *The Dictionary of the First World War*, 87–89. Aleksey Alekseyevich Brusilov (Russian: Алексе́й Алексе́евич Бруси́лов) (1853–1926), has been called the most successful Russian general of World War I. Brusilov's July offensive, however, resulted in almost one million Russian casualties. He later joined with the Bolsheviks in the Russian Civil War.

their ranks whether to conduct a putsch against the provisional government, but when the provisional government released detailed information to the public about Lenin's German connections, the elite Preobrazhensky, Semenovsky, and Izmailovsky guard regiments, which had not mutinied, became enraged. In the evening of July 17, they dispersed the Bolshevik mobs besieging the Tauride Palace, the headquarters of the Soviet. The provisional government asserted further control on July 18–19. After three days of riotous street fighting, more than 700 people had been killed and wounded.[153] Ultimately, the bloody "July Days" were missed opportunities for both sides. Lenin hesitated but probably could have taken power. Kerensky and the provisional government, politically hamstrung, could have followed through with their initial decision to arrest Lenin (he fled in disguise) and put him on trial for high treason, but didn't. Lenin and his Bolshevik cabal would live for another day.

Next came the "Kornilov Affair." Kerensky became prime minister of the provisional government after the conclusion of the July Days. The propertied classes in Russia called for order. Unifying the government and re-instilling discipline and control in the armed forces became Kerensky's critical task. Kerensky tried to forge a consensus among the conservative, liberal, and leftist factions of the government to enact promised military reforms. On August 1, he offered Cossack General Lavr Kornilov,[154] a fierce military disciplinarian, the position of commander-in-chief of the Russian army. Kornilov and Kerensky, however, had conflicting views on politics and military matters. Immediately upon his appointment, Kornilov set his own terms, some of which were tantamount to dictatorial. Knowing that the Germans would soon attack Riga, which would bring them much closer to Petrograd, Kornilov saw great disorder. He declared that Russia "has no authority and that such authority must be created. Perhaps I shall have to exert such pressure on the government. It is possible that if disorders break out in Petrograd, after they have been suppressed I will have to enter the government and participate in the formation of a new, strong authority."[155] Kornilov feared a Bolshevik uprising and sent troops toward Petrograd to be ready to suppress it. Kerensky, however, construed Kornilov's action as an attempted

---

[153] John Pinfold, *Petrograd 1917: Witnesses to the Russian Revolution* (Oxford, UK: Bodleian Library, 2017), 164.

[154] Wikipedia, "Lavr Kornilov," last modified May 9, 2021, 03:44 (UTC), https://en.wikipedia.org/wiki/Lavr_Kornilov. Lavr Georgiyevich Kornilov (Russian: Лавр Георгиевич Корнилов) (1870–1918) was a general of Siberian Cossack origin in the Russian army during World War I and the ensuing Russian Civil War. After his unsuccessful endeavor in August–September 1917 and his arrest, he escaped from jail and took charge of anti-Bolshevik opposition in the south of Russia. He did not fare well in battle and was killed by a shell on April 13, 1918, while laying siege to Ekaterinodar.

[155] Pipes, *The Russian Revolution*, 446.

military coup d'état. He dismissed him on September 9 and summoned him to Petrograd. Kornilov refused. Kerensky then brokered a deal with the Petrograd Soviet for its support against Kornilov and armed the workers of Petrograd. As Kornilov marched toward Petrograd, his troops deserted, and the government arrested him on September 13 without a fight. But Kerensky had made perhaps the biggest mistake of his revolutionary career. He secured the support of the Petrograd Soviet at the cost of agreeing to pass arms to the Bolshevik military organization and releasing Bolshevik political prisoners, including Trotsky. The weapons given to the Soviet were never used but the Bolsheviks kept and utilized them two months later when they launched their own coup d'état. The provisional government had thus surrendered valuable power and arms to the Soviet, which it did not regain. The Bolshevik Party gained from the Kornilov Affair and Kerensky and the provisional government lost.

The foreign community in Petrograd viewed Kornilov favorably, if not as indispensable. J. Butler Wright wrote on August 2, "The shadow of a military dictator grows larger and larger—and I am not disinclined to believe that it is the solution of the question."[156] Jack Pincott, an Australian attached to the Armored Car Division of the Royal Navy's Flying Corp, described Kornilov as "the one man who may save Russia." Rogers exclaimed on September 10: "The people are so sick of this gibbering of the socialists, their crass inability to deal with facts, and the posing and speech making, that they will welcome any resolute, active, power. And Korniloff is certainly that." After Kornilov's arrest, British insider Albert "Bertie" Stopford, in his letter of September 13, wrote, "As the Kornilov attempt to bring order has failed, I will tell you what I foresee now, for the cards are shuffled again. . . . the Bolsheviks will become more daring and try to turn out the Government; then would come anarchy, with 70,000 workmen fully armed. The failure of Kornilov has completely knocked me over, and yesterday I could not walk. I still foresee an ocean of blood before order comes."[157]

Rogers summed it up: "It is unfortunate that the government finds itself in Petrograd. This is the center of all the various forms of agitation to which it is subject. Stability is next to impossible." Ambassador Francis, however, declared, "I have not yet lost all hope for Russia, as the Provisional Government can still save the situation if it takes prompt and decisive steps to restore the discipline of the army and navy."[158]

The ambassador's hopes did not materialize.

---

[156] J. Butler Wright diary entry, August 2, 1917, cited in Allison, *Witness to Revolution*, 106.
[157] Pinfold, *Petrograd 1917: Witnesses to the Russian Revolution*, 191 and 204–5.
[158] David R. Francis, *Russia from the American Embassy: April 1916–November 1918* (New York: Charles Scribner's Sons, 1921), 161.

CHAPTER 6

"Late in the night, the new Russia made itself known"

Rogers did not foresee the revolution breaking out as it did. His taste for adventure soon gave way to concern for his personal safety. On International Women's Day, he wrote that people could not buy bread on the streets. The next day, he noticed the doubling of guards on street corners and machine gun placements on building roofs, and reported the imposition of a night curfew, exclaiming the city was "taught like a strained wire." Rampaging Cossacks threatened his dinner rendezvous at a favorite French café. On Saturday, March 10, Rogers, still undeterred, ambled on a familiar mission in the neighborhood of the National City Bank office to deliver 9 million rubles' worth of Russian bonds to the Volga-Kama Bank. Summoned to return, he received a sharp admonishment from his colleague, Charles "Chuck" Stuart: "Don't you know that a revolution has started?" To which Rogers calmly rejoined, "This was news to me."

That evening, French Ambassador Maurice Paléologue invited the Vicomtesse du Halgouët, his secretary's wife, to enjoy a symphony at the Marinsky Theatre. Upon exiting the theater, they experienced a similar epiphany. The ambassador wrote in his memoir: "The square of the Marie Theatre, usually so gay, looked utterly desolate; my car was the only vehicle there. The Moika bridge was guarded by a picket of gendarmes and troops were massed in front of the Lithuania Prison. Madame du Halgouët shared my astonishment at the sight and remarked: 'Are we witnessing the last night of the *régime*?'"[159]

Rogers saw widespread indiscriminate street shooting and one violent scene at the Pekars café/bakery shop next to the Hotel Europe.[160] Danger on the streets forced

---

[159] Maurice Paléologue, *An Ambassador's Memoirs, Vol. 3*, 3rd ed. (New York: George H. Doran Company, 1924), Saturday, March 10, 1917, memoir entry, 216. Paléologue referred to the Marinsky as the Marie.

[160] Lascelle Meserve de Basily, *Memoirs of a Lost World* (Stanford, CA: Hoover Institution Press, 1975), 82. Lascelle, H. Fessenden Meserve's stepdaughter, also wrote about the Pekars café incident in her memoir, but mistakenly dated

him to spend several nights despondently sleeping on a couch in the bank's office. Stressed and anxious, he mis-calendared dates of his journal entries.

Rogers understood he was witnessing history being made. On Sunday night, as the mutiny of the Petrograd garrison began, he wrote, "Late in the night, the new Russia made itself known." Not everyone made that call. Newspaperman Arno Dosch-Fleurot and friends watched a French farce at the Mikhailovsky Theatre the same evening, and noted "Between the acts the Russian officers present, and all other men present as well, stood up, according to custom, facing the empty imperial loge." Dosch-Fleurot doubted "if there was one of us who believed he was performing that act of empty homage for the last time."[161]

While not working long hours at National City Bank or dodging bullets on the streets, Rogers tried to enjoy life in Petrograd. He recounted his frequent visits to the opera and ballet, where Russia's finest artists performed, jaunts to the countryside, tennis, swimming and boating activities, pleasant dinners in riverside and garden restaurants, trading tales with friends and colleagues, and sharing fortuitously found food supplies. Rogers stayed on mission, but the revolution's virulence always lingered close-by. The tone in his journal vacillated between insecure optimism and encroaching despair.

National City Bank's Petrograd branch enjoyed success from the day it opened. Meserve proudly wrote to Vanderlip on February 23, 1917: "I am sure it will please you to hear that today, only a little over a month since we opened our Petrograd Branch, we have passed the point which is always so eagerly striven for by all new banks; viz., the interest we are today receiving from our investments, practically all in Russian Government 5% Treasury Bills, (exclusive of the interest on our Rs. 5,000,000 Guarantee Fund Bonds) is more than paying all our running expenses, including all our interest charges. In addition to this, we have also already signed up additional business which should double our present earnings within three months. We are working hard, and I think the position of our Petrograd Branch at the end of this year will be a most pleasant surprise. . . . I am especially anxious to start another branch in Moscow as soon as possible..."[162]

Unsurprisingly, the March Revolution in Petrograd surprised National City Bank in New York. A month earlier, Samuel McRoberts had paternalistically written in the bank's internal employee magazine:

---

it to Thursday, March 8.

[161] Dosch-Fleurot, *Through War to Revolution*, 124–25. Dosch-Fleurot referred to the Mikhailovsky as the Theatre Michel.

[162] Meserve to Vanderlip, February 10/23, 1917, Box A-67, Frank A Vanderlip Papers.

It has been the fashion in America to condemn the form of the Russian Government, and to confidently predict its immediate overthrow. Again, the study of the development of the Russian nation and the ethnological conditions incident to that development discloses the imperative necessity of some unusual form of centralized, and even despotic power. . . . and however critical we may be of a despotic form of Government, we cannot avoid recognizing its usefulness in the development of the Russian nation. . . . It is well understood in Russia that a constitutional government must be evolved out of the situation and cannot be obtained by revolution...

McRoberts finished his article optimistically proffering that Russia could "not only give a profitable outlet to American capital, but will lead to the establishment of an extensive commercial trade between the two countries."[163]

Meserve assured Vanderlip that the bank's investment in Russia was sound: "Russia itself will come out in the end stronger than ever. I still consider all foreign investment here advisable and safe, and I sincerely hope that the United States will now be willing to help Russia more in every way."[164] Undeterred, Vanderlip wrote James Stillman, the NCB chairman, that "The Russia revolution, no inkling of which reached us until yesterday afternoon, seems to be received with apathy by people whose appetites are jaded by sensations. The stock market remains firm in the face of it all."[165]

Meserve's and Vanderlip's comments reflected the supportive sentiments of the US government and the American people for Russia's revolution. On March 22, the United States became the first country to recognize the provisional government of Russia. The next day, an editorial in Washington, DC's *Evening Star* summarized the goodwill of America: "It was appropriate that from the world's greatest representative republic should come the official greeting to the Russia of popular liberty. . . . A free people naturally wants all the other peoples of the world to be free. It is the American hope that Russia will hold its new freedom, develop it and through it work out a great national destiny."[166]

---

[163] McRoberts, "Russia," *Number Eight*, The National City Bank of New York, February 1917, 10–11 and 13. McRoberts delivered the same message in an address to the American Institute of Banking, Boston Chapter, on January 16, 1917, which was one day after the opening of NCB's Petrograd branch.

[164] Documents from the Russian State Historical Archive, St. Petersburg, RGIA/624/1/5/202, cited in Malik, *Bankers & Bolsheviks*, 137, Meserve to Vanderlip, March 29, 1917.

[165] Vanderlip to Stillman, March 16, 1917, 2, Box B-1-7, Frank A. Vanderlip Papers.

[166] "The New Russia Recognized," *The Evening Star,* Washington, DC, March 23, 1917, 6.

At present there's not much to write about, save for the political squabbles of which there seem to be many. But I can't make much out of them except for the fact that the people through the Duma, which is their parliament, want a change in the government. They want the old reactionary bureaucrats ousted and their places filled by new men who will be responsible to them, to the Duma, and not to the whims of the Tsar. That seems to be the way it is now,—the Duma, although made up of representatives from all over the empire, can do nothing but talk. It has no executive power. The Tsar has all of that, and it is he who puts into execution what the Duma suggests,—that is if he approves. If he does not approve, he does as he pleases, and whenever things get too hot in the Duma he closes it. There has been much talk of the Imperialists making a separate peace with Germany, and the people are protesting vigorously. Of course the death of Rasputin put a quietus on much of the separate peace talk, but it is still strong and the Duma is excited. There are many fiery speeches against the Tsar, the Empress and the whole system,—they don't dare speak that sentiment out but that is the intimation; there are demands for a different system, one which will give the people more influence in governmental affairs, a constitutional form of some kind; and there are all kinds of threats if these demands are not granted,—strikes, riots and the like.

But from what I am told not much will come of it; this thing goes on all the time, although they are bolder now, but the attempts are always put down. They say that when the war broke out in 1914 the streets were barricaded against the labor uprising which threatened; but the wave of war patriotism blotted out this demonstration.

It is rumored that someone took four shots at the Empress the other day,—an officer of her own personal guard. Four shots without hitting. Pretty poor. They say he has been hung, but the whisperers in the cafés will tell you that it is not known whether the boy was hung because he shot at the Empress or because he missed her!

There is much talk about a general strike in the near future. Some big plant here has been closed by order of the government, for what reason I did not hear, but in sympathy with the workmen of it, the labor groups are threatening to call a strike of all industries throughout the city. In that case everything will stop, even the munitions works, and as these are vitally important, a decision of some sort in whatever the muddle is, would come soon. This general strike was the same thing threatened in 1914 when the war broke out; and it would no doubt be serious business,—at least to the already undersupplied soldiers at the front, who would be the ones to suffer eventually.

The Chief of Police of the city has replied to the threat of the general strike to the effect that all men not working would be arrested and impressed into the army for front line duty as soon as they could be got ready. This is a wallop to the high and mighty laborers who thought they were so free and exempt from military service. I wonder what they'll do about that. If it were in normal times I should say go ahead and let them strike and fight it out; but in these times with the welfare of millions in the line dependent on the supplies those in the rear send them, it seems criminal to stop making the supplies. It seems to me, though, that the government has called the strikers' bluff. None of them want to fight very badly.

A general strike has been declared for next Saturday, and it looks as though it would occur. What can be done to stop it I don't know. The strikers don't seem to worry much about the threat of being sent to the trenches, and they have openly defied the powers that be. What's going to happen no one knows. In addition, as our landlady told us in the course of our morning argument with her over the open window, the supply of bread is short, and food of all kinds has mounted in price. She said there would be trouble unless something was done before the strike began, but others seem to be of the opinion that such clashes are common here and that this one will be settled as others have been settled. The Duma is sitting in a late session arguing over the matter and trying to reach some conclusion. But the members of that body seem to be divided too, with a small majority demanding a change in the imperial policy and a change in the ministry and the remainder clamoring for things as they are. They say it's a hectic session with deputies leaving the hall in rage, others talking themselves blue in the face, and others threatening all kinds of things to the opposition.

Thursday

The general strike is not as yet called off, and the strikers seem intent upon trouble. They say that this morning there was hardly any bread at all, many shops being closed entirely and notices posted on the doors to the effect that there would be no bread for days. For once then in many months the long lines did not form at various shops about the city. They had got to be a familiar sight, these rows of patient women, with baskets on their arms, shawls over their heads, standing there from five o'clock in the morning until nearly noon. Sometimes their lines extended for blocks. This morning in a poor way, must have been a vacation for them. This evening, on the way home from the bank, we noticed that at the important corners, where before there had been but one policeman, there were two.

Friday 25/10 March, 1917.
(February 25 on the Julian old calendar/March 10 on the Gregorian calendar fell on a Saturday. However, the Duma met on Friday, therefore, the day/date for this entry should be Friday, February 24/March 9)

Although we had bread today at the bank, it was only because the cook was fore-sighted and had laid in a supply. They say it was practically impossible to get it in the city today. This really is serious because the majority of the populace, the poor, have only their bread, cabbage, grain, and tea for their meals, and the larger part of their frugal fare is the bread. So what are they doing these days? It can't go on like this forever. Even this morning it was reported that Cossacks had been seen in various parts of the city, but we didn't see any then. The guards of police have been doubled almost everywhere, however, and it is plain to see that the authorities are getting ready for trouble of some kind. We heard in the bank that there had been trouble at a couple of bread shops this morning but the police had broken it up and closed them. The Duma is supposed to have been in session today but no one seems to know what the outcome of it is. We also heard that on the roofs of buildings around the square near the Nicholas Station, which is supposed to be a trouble center, machine guns have been placed. This is supposed to be the first time such a precaution has been taken since the Revolution of 1905. It does look as though something were going to happen. Especially as the police issued an order today warning all people to be inside their houses by eleven o'clock tonight, and adding that all found outside after that hour would be arrested and if not arrested they ran danger of being shot. People are all excited. There is much talk about it. Some are afraid and some laugh but it is plain that there is something in the air. There are many mounted police out, galloping up and down the streets.

Friday.

Well, I've seen the Cossacks about whom I've heard so much,—and believe me, they fully come up to expectations.

Some of us boys have been in the habit of going to a little café called the Café de la Grave,[167] kept by a Frenchman, and located in the basement corner of the building on the Nevsky and the Bolshoi Kanushnaya,—meaning Great Stable Street. The food is very good there, cooked splendidly, and it's not expensive, hence our habit. We have made an appointment with Wilse R———[168] to meet him there at seven o'clock and have dinner with him. Fred and I came over to the room after work at the bank was done, and about six thirty set out for the café. It was very dark then, of course, and difficult to see far ahead. We came down the Sadovia, turned a couple of times and were headed for the Nevsky when, just as we were nearing the corner, there came a terrible racket ahead of us, and around the corner, out of the darkness, galloping at full tilt down the sidewalk came a troop of Cossacks, shouting like mad, carbines bouncing across their backs, sabres flopping at the horses' sides, and flourishing mean looking steel spears long enough to spit six men on at once. Although I have been wanting to see the Cossacks and this was the realization of my wish, I took no time to look. We both jumped and ran and when I stopped running I found that Fred was no longer with me. In a few minutes I got my breath, sneaked cautiously down side streets, and finally slipped into the café where I found Wilse waiting for the remainder of the party. In a little while Fred came in very much out of breath, claiming that he had established new records for all distances up to half a mile. He'd been chased almost over to the Field of Mars, before he left them behind and had spent some time looking for me. We ate our little meal and set out for home up the Nevsky. The sidewalks of this thoroughfare were lined with troops of Cossacks mounted, their lances couched, compelling the pedestrians to walk up the middle of the street, between a double row of horses and in steel points. It was hardly a pleasant sensation. The horses were skittish and all the way I could feel myself wriggling on one of those lances like a fishworm on a hook. I'll never fish with live bait again.

Meanwhile, with the atmosphere of the city taut like a strained wire, things go on. People say the Duma will find some solution, that the strike will be called off at the last moment, and others that it will not be called off by the workers, that they mean business this time, that they are angered by the mishandling of the food supplies, and that to avoid trouble the government will back down. It doesn't look as if they would, though, from the appearance of all the police and guards in the streets. If anything is

---

[167] A restaurant in the guise of an Irish pub called "O'Hooligans" operates in this location today. The address is Bolshaya Konyushennaya Street 14.

[168] Rogers refers to Wilson "Wils" Fiske Reynolds (1894–1982), Princeton class of 1915. Reynolds left Russia and returned to the United States several months later and joined the US Navy in August 1917.

going to be done about it, it will have to be done in a hurry, because tomorrow is the day set for the strike to begin. We shall see.

Saturday 26/11 March 1917. *(The date is incorrect. Saturday fell on 25 February/10 March)*

Good night! What a day. The general strike is on all right, and the trouble is begun. This morning when we went down to work we found the streets thick with police, both mounted and unmounted; none of the factories were working, and the Nevsky was a long line of closed shops with here and there a boarded up door or window, which certainly looked prophetic of trouble. It was rumored that last night the first death occurred when a workman was shot trying to break into a bread shop door—"Les Miserables" stuff—but no one was sure of it. The streets were crowded with people even at the time we went to the bank, none of them seeming to have anything to do except walk around on the lookout for something to happen. Curiosity. They didn't seem to be particularly angry but seemed to be enjoying themselves, looking here and there "guying"[169] the police guards at the corners, and laughing at the mounted police as they galloped up and down the street,—all like a crowd at a great country fair. But I hated to think of what one shot would do in it. There certainly would have been a panic.

But to tell things in their proper order, right here is where I made my debut. It still strikes me as being very amusing but I can imagine what a scare it threw into the others, chiefly Mr. S – – –[170], for which I am sorry because he has enough to worry about. It is one of my tasks in the bank to have charge of the security department, which includes those of the bank as well as of those of our customers. Our own investments in Russian Short-Term Treasury notes we keep in a vault at the Volga-Kama Bank. This morning we had some nine million roubles worth of these securities on hand and in order to get them safely stowed away before Sunday, I had the telephone girl phone up the Volga-Kama, and inform them that I would be up there and would want to get into our vault, giving the particular hour of my arrival. This met with the approval of Mr. S – – – and I put the nine million in my pocket and started out. It may sound a foolish thing to do, but on the contrary it is quite the custom. The banks are nearly all in one small section of the city, and there are so many police that

[169] To guy (verb). To make fun of; to ridicule.
[170] R.R. Stevens.

it would be very difficult for a robbery to occur anywhere around that district. So with the RS 9,000,000 in my pocket,—at the current rate of exchange it amounted to about three million dollars cash, I set out. As it happened, this morning, there being so many people in the streets, I took a slightly shorter route than usually, cutting in back of the bank, and crossing the square before the French Theatre, I stopped for a few seconds to glance at the poster containing the announcement of their program for the coming week. I had been a bit early in my start so that when I left the square and headed down the Michaelowskaya for the Nevsky and the Volga-Kama bank, who should I hear shouting my name from across the way but one of the boys from the bank, I turned, and up came Chuck S – – – [171] from out the crowd, breathless and with a funny look on his face. "Where the hell have you been?" he demanded, gasping. "Been?" I replied, "I've just started ten minutes ago: I'm going to the Volga-Kama to put this nine million away." "Why, what's the trouble?"

"We've been phoning all over the city for you, but couldn't get hold of you anywhere; the Volga-Kama said you hadn't been there; and we thought something had happened. They sent me out to look for you. Don't you know that a revolution has started?

This was news to me: I hadn't heard anything about it, in fact, didn't see much out of the ordinary save what I have described. "Yes," said Chuck, "they've started fighting in two or three sections of the city and it's likely to break out here anytime. Mr. S.– – – wants you to get back to the bank as soon as you can. So we hustled back and tucked the nine million away in the safe. And although there has been a little dirty work which I'll set down, there wasn't any revolution and personally I saw little to be worried about. Had I thought a revolution was going to start then and there I might have skipped with the nine million and had nothing to do but push buttons all the rest of my life!

But to resume. The Cossacks galloped up and down the streets and even along the sidewalks as they did last night when Fred and I got our first thrill. We went out in the afternoon, and joined the crowds but didn't see much. There would be a clatter of horses hooves and up the sidewalk a troop of Cossacks would go, lances waving, great coats flying, shouting at the top of their voices, and from them the crowds surged to the street, only to flow back again when the hated ones were gone. Some few bread shops were open this morning and there was a little bread, but the supply gave out in the afternoon, and all were closed. At this time soldiers made their appearance as

---

[171] Charles "Chuck" Moore Stuart.

patrols and the friendly way they handled the crowds contrasted with the manner of the Cossacks and the police.

But the big happening of the day occurred at the little café and cake shop in the corner of the Hotel Europe—Pekars is the name. It's an attractive place with white tables, chairs, bright lights, and a rash display for these hard times of cakes and cookies in the window. Here, in the afternoon, the crowd gathered thickly, some I suppose, to look at the food they could not have; it grew so heavy that someone was pushed up against the window, which cracked and fell with a crash in splinters. The tinkle of glass drew more of a crowd to see what had happened, the crowd drew the police, and in the police arose a desire to show authority; shots rang out. Two workmen were hit,—innocent bystanders—and fell to crumpled heaps on the snow before the eyes of the frightened spectators, who, fascinated by the trickling pools of red on the white walk, remained rooted to the spot, almost to be run down by the crashing hoof of the Cossacks attracted to the place like animals by the smell of blood. The corner was cleared; the bodies carried away and window boarded up.

But I imagine they can never clear away the story of what happened there. It will certainly add fuel to the fire of these people's thoughts.

Tuesday 1/14 March 1917. *(Tuesday fell on 28 February/13 March)*

It's been impossible to write since Saturday because after we got down to the bank on Sunday morning as we have been in the habit of doing for the purpose of writing letters, hell began to pop outside and kept popping for two days and two nights, making it impossible for us to get back here to our rooms. So we slept there on the gold couches, or tried to, ate meals of dry black bread, cabbage soup, and tea, played cards, worked a little, dashed out once in a great while to see if there was anything to be seen, and upon discovering that there was,—far too much for comfort, in fact,—dashed back again. It was only this morning that we could venture out for a look around. The first thing noticeable was the fact that the city is completely in the hands of the rioters. They have captured the capital of the empire from the forces of the Tsar. Everyone is now waiting breathlessly,—from their own efforts and from surprise that it is done,—to learn what he will do. The next move is his. Will he advance on the capital? No one knows.

But to get the thing down with some semblance of order. In the first place it is absurd to attempt to write it all here; there has been far too much, with all I have gathered from experience, description, and rumor. But we can at least attempt it.

Sunday was a magnificent day, clear, cool and snappy, and golden from a huge gold sun, low down on the horizon. When we went out in the morning a quiet, reserved throng filled the streets, a throng without the good humored curiosity of the day before, but still orderly and very much intent upon affairs more its own than anyone else. A knot gathers on a corner in conversation, perhaps in derision of the police sweeping ridiculously up and down the street, seemingly trying to stir up trouble; a group of Cossacks descended, the knot unraveled itself, some of its units scattered, others remained firm and laughed in the horses' hoofs. They were arrested and marched away up the Nevsky under a laughably heavy guard, to the shouts of derision and sarcasm from the sidewalk. We proceeded to the bank and there met the others, told our stories and listened to theirs. We remained there throughout the day and when it did come time to go to our quarters it was impossible. But throughout the afternoon and evening we heard now and then from new arrivals what was happening.

The order came to clear the Nevsky. From side streets and alleys rushed squads of mounted police and Cossacks, swirling down upon the now frightened populace with glittering lances, sweeping them before their horses into the side streets, at each corner heavy guards took up their places, and for the remainder of the day, orders had it that walking on the Nevsky was prohibited. It remained clear until late in the afternoon, when at one corner a venturesome group, perhaps under the excuse of crossing, made its way to the forbidden path and set boldly out. At the next corner a squad of soldiers, afterwards found to be police in army uniforms, dropped to the snow in a long line stretching from curb to curb. The venturesome ones stopped, turned, some to flee and some to huddle to the walls, but too late, the call of a bugle soared out on the crisp air, drowned in a ripping crash of guns and the swish of lead. Here and there a shrinking figure or a strangely broken heap; some struggled to the wall, others lay still. Thus it began and thus it continued all through the afternoon, a bugle blast, a rip of lead, and here and there over the city the crumpled splotches of black in the streets.

At the Nicholas Station the crowd grew bolder,—perhaps because there were more women in it, and rushed the soldiers,—real ones this time because they refuse to fire on their own people and gave way before them. The police took up the assault and answered with machine guns from the surrounding roofs, and unarmed, the people were obliged to flee, not however, without leaving their mark behind and their toll as well. Further downtown at the Ekaterinskaya Canal, the police fired into an apparently peaceful group, not even attempting to enter but simply talking with the soldiers stationed at the corner; and two men and three women fell as a result of this volley. But enraged at this wantonness, a group of soldiers fired on the police with some damage,—which was quite immaterial beside the great fact that it was the opening of hostilities between the two groups of guards. At night no one ventured on the Nevsky, which stretched in a broad streak of ghastly white under the glare of a naval searchlight we could see perched in the tower of the Admiralty building.

We sat there in the bank all afternoon and evening, listening to the crackling rifles, the rippling of the machine guns, and wondering what it all meant. To us it sounded much worse than it really was, I suppose. When it became so dark that we could not see more, we had to give up even the games of bridge which had taken up some of our time. It was not feasible to have the lights going because someone was certain to take a shot at them just for luck if not for anything else, so we sat in the darkness and talked it over. In the evening someone went upstairs and obtained sandwiches from the cook and we all sat around in the little waiting room to Mr. S – – – office, and ate these, our dinner. When finished, after sitting in silence for a while, one of the number, "Count" S – – – got leisurely to his feet and delivered himself of the following. "Well, we've a great bunch of Americans, afraid of a little musketry. What's the use of sitting here all night; a bullet can just as well come in through the window and pick you off as it can in the street. I'm not going to stay; I'm going to walk all the way home, the firing be damned, and sleep in a good bed tonight. So good night." Whereupon he walked out, took his hat, coat and rubbers, and we heard the door slam behind him.

He'd been gone about five minutes when a terrific outburst of all kinds of firing, rifle, machine gun, and some kind of heavier piece, came from the direction of his house, and not more than thirty seconds had elapsed before he came dashing in again, to sit down in the circle once more saying, "Well, I guess I won't go home after all, it's pretty cold there, and it's warm here." Of course we gave him the laugh and the incident was enjoyed by all of us. He said that when the firing started he was just making the turn of the corner into the street where the shooters were. He also claims distance records. After a while, when there seemed to be no sign of the battle stopping, we got our heavy coats and made beds as best we could on the divans in the reception room, and tried our best to sleep.

Late in the night, the new Russia made itself known. What particular barracks it was is not certain; but the residing company found itself called out for guard duty, and the members well knew that it meant to fire upon their own people. It is not certain just what happened to start it, but this company killed most of its officers and rushed out to other barracks to enlist aid against the punishment they thought would be meted out to them. The news of this event spread quickly from barracks to barracks and it was not long before all others had done likewise, although in many cases the officers were themselves willing to mutiny with the men, if not, death. One troop of lancers rode through the streets with the body of a hated officer wavering on their pikes. They all joined forces by marching from one barrack to the other, and the battle with the hated police began.

In the morning the fighting was progressing fiercely. From corner to corner, wall-to-wall, tree to tree, and even from house top to house top, it took its bloody way. On the roofs were bulwarked the police machine guns which rained their hail of lead upon the heads below.

Under the fighting color of scarlet the rebels fought their way from street to street, here and there relieving bands of workers and joining them. Garages were thrown open, cars confiscated, to circle around the city under fluttering pennants of red in search of enemies. Rumbling motor trucks, glistening limousines, and bullet-bodied runabouts crowded to capacity, bristling with arms, men stretched at full length behind their bayoneted running boards, a snapping red flag in front, swept the streets, now halting to engage in a fight, now speeding away to reinforce some needy group. Here and there an armored car lumbered down the street, machine guns spitting lead from its veering turrets and the enemy bullets dropping to the ground like so many peas.

The struggle swung to the Litania Prospect and clustered around the Arsenal there. The government guards, strongly entrenched, with plenty of food, and a wealth of guns and ammunition, put up a stubborn battle. Guns spat from the doors, and windows shattered to the pavement under the fire from the besiegers from the surrounding housetops; bullets crashed into the heavy wooden doors while from inside and all around came the yells of the fighters and the wounded. Slowly the guards retreated to the rear of the building, the besiegers advanced, beat down the doors and glass and with shouts of glee rushed inside. The defenders were still dangerous, however; they sped out through the side doors and around the long block, intending to take the victors in the rear; but these last were not to be so surprised; with the speed of inspiration they dragged the three four-inch howitzers stored there to the street, and in an instant, from behind a barricade of boxes and doors, and from under the defiant red banner the three ugly mouths leered in the faces of the arsenal guards.

The Litania is the street of our residence and in the afternoon, not hearing much noise from that direction Fred and I started for our room. We made good progress until we turned the corner of the side street and the Litania and saw there, almost directly in front of our house, the barricade and the three howitzers pointed past our door. We discreetly turned around and went back to the bank for the night.

The fight was over at the Arsenal, however, and in possession, the mob felt free to vent its rage. Across the street from the Arsenal stands the Law Courts building grim in its solidity as the symbol of justice in Russia. And hated as the symbol of tyranny which for long has held its clutching fingers at the throats of the populace. In went the windows, down came the doors, and scattered before the cyclone of a pent up rage the records of years of oppression flew in clouds of white from the gaping windows down to the street, where fire wiped them out forever. This spread to the building itself and as is ever the way with tyranny it consumed itself in the flames of its own instigation.

The fire drew crowds, and with them from other districts, came the news of victory over the forces of the government. With the city in the hands of the people it was not long before other fires sprang up, each one a nest of the hated police. Soon all these marvelously accurate records which had enabled the police to seize at will any living person in the empire,—all vanished in the fires and under the heels of the spectators. Thus the Law Courts conflagration became one of victory. Far into the night it flamed red against the sky, dancing, leaping, tossing sheaves of white to the air to the music of the cheering, rejoicing populace.

This morning the weather was again beautiful, as if set out to order with the sun doing yeoman duty to brighten up the city for the occasion. Fred and I arose from our gilded couches early and walked out for a look around. We headed for our rooms and at the Litania found plenty of activity. The street was crowded with people, mostly soldiers at this early hour, standing in groups talking over the doings of the night before, comparing souvenirs of police swords, revolvers, buttons, and dividing the spoils of bags of sugar and stores of meat found in the Arsenal. This building was now garrisoned by the rebels, and across from it stood what remained of the Law Courts building, a huge plaster shell, smoking and smoldering yet. In the street heaps of soiled and charred records testified to the completeness of the night's work. As we walked along, there were smiles from everyone. Happiness seemed the order of the day, and this, coupled with the brilliant showing of scarlet everywhere, brightened up what might have been a desolate scene. We walked around the barricade and the three howitzers, which showed signs of service and felt fortunate that we had not had to spend the night with them belching under our windows as we might have done. Up the street came a parade of soldiers,—the members of the first regiment to revolt, bystanders said, and a great cheer went up at their appearance, a cheer which quite drowned out the song of the marchers. Nearly every one fell in step behind them and away they went to other parts of the city, singing on their way. As we stood there watching, and being congratulated and congratulating everyone else, a motor flew past with a student in the tonneau[172] scattering printed announcements therefrom; there was a mad scramble for these which almost broke up the parade. We scrambled also, and finally managed to share one with some soldiers, who asked us to read it for them. This was a poser,[173] but we could read the Russian even if we couldn't translate. The sense was as follows:

> The evil forces of the old regime have been overcome, but there is much left to do. Order must be restored and the remainder of the common enemy destroyed. Soldiers, remember that you are soldiers; your duty is to keep order. Do not shoot promiscuously in the streets; save your ammunition; the time is coming when it will be needed. Meanwhile be assured that the Committee is laboring at the Duma to bring strength to the new Russia.

That looks as though they hoped to make a revolution out of it.

Notices were posted as to stations where food and arms could be obtained, and before the morning was over, every citizen appeared under arms. Soldiers with army rifles, bodies crisscrossed with strips of bullets, laborers with shot guns, clumsy hunting rifles, boys with rusted swords and ancient pistols, women strutting through the streets with knives and bayonets, and everywhere, all of them, wearing the scarlet symbol of revolution. Hat bands, arm-bands, knots, and badges; on wagons and automobiles, in the form of banners made from any handy bit of red cloth.

They were still searching for the police, and still are tonight. In motor cars the fighters speed from street to street; stopping suddenly, its occupants swarming to the pavements, to the shelter of corners, lampposts, and doorways, to fire at some house-top from which streams an answering hail of machine gun fire. Then a dash across the open street, followed by the shivering of a door, and the eager ones climb to the roof to continue the fight. Here, outnumbered, the hated police cannot hold out long, and with an exultant shout, one by one, forced to the edge at the bayonet point they crash to the street below to be spit upon and reviled by the gathering crowd. The iron heel is on the other foot now. A people who for years have bended their necks under

---

[172] A tonneau is an area of a car or truck open at the top. It can be for passengers or cargo.
[173] Poser. A puzzling or baffling question.

the oppression of these same police are now throwing off the burden and, actuated by the long years of pent up hate and desire for revenge, the process cannot very well be a pleasant one.

But it is not without its humorous side. With some bent on fighting and some intent upon their ordinary business, others not knowing what is going on, and still others just curious, it is not strange that with the whining bullets, the pops, and volleys of rifles and the ripping of machine guns that there should be hurried retreats to shelter, timid peerings about each corner, huddling behind lampposts, scurrying for any kind of shelter, and even jumps at far away unexpected reports. In spite of the danger these incidents are highly amusing. Through it all there are few signs of terror or hysteria. There is a skirmish in a square, people waiting to pass are gathered in a knot just around the corner; the firing ceases, and the knot breaks up. People walk through the square looking curiously around at the changes in scenery, but quite unconcerned as to any possible danger. It may be that they are used to it, although I doubt that anything just like this has happened for years; or it may be that they are naturally so stolid as not to become excited about it.

We walked over to the Hotel Astoria, where a young battle was reported to be in progress. We arrived in the great square as the last shots were being fired; the rebels had just rushed the hotel and gained possession. We waited behind the pillars of the cathedral for a few minutes and then walked around the hotel. This, the finest hotel in the city, was under German control, and was used by the government to house inactive officers and their women on the luxury of the land. Police were discovered on the roof and the battle started. From behind the huge columns of the cathedral, from the roof of the massive German Embassy, and from the shelter of the statue of Nicholas I, the people swept this last strong hold of the enemy. The arrival of some armored cars finished it. Under the protection of machine gun fire, the soldiers rushed the building. Every plate glass window gaped open, and the building swarmed with soldiers. As we went by the lobby was crowded with them, eating such food as they had never before tasted, and shouting the Marseillaise—long a forbidden tune in Russia,—to the accompaniment of a piano played by one of their number. With the food there was much liquor and the affair might have been dangerous had not the officer in command asserted himself and ordered every bottle to be smashed in the street. It was done. We stood by and watched them obey the order implicitly. To be sure the wine cellar was comparatively small, but it's the spirit of the thing that is remarkable. Without such discipline, this business could be very ugly. Meanwhile the Duma has not been idle. Messages have been dispatched to the Tsar informing him of his last opportunity to save his Russia by agreeing to the changes made; to the Tsar's uncle, the Grand Duke Nicholas, the strongman of the Empire, at the Roumanian Front, seeking his support, and to all other generals of the army. The Tsar has made no reply. The city is wild with rumors. Some have it that Nicholas has been captured; others that he is marching on Petrograd with two Army Corps to crush the rebellion; and still others that he is withdrawing troops from the front, allowing the German army free access to Russia in the hope of crushing it under Hun control. Some say that the Tsar will run for his life; but others claim he will come to Petrograd alone. The fact is, that there is no telling what he will do. From what I can gather out of it all, he never knows what he is going to do himself, least of all anyone else. I suppose a great deal depends on who reaches him first with advice. Anyway it's an exciting moment for Russia.

The Duma has formed three committees, one of safety to organize the defenses and bring order to Petrograd, one of supply to furnish provision to the city, and an executive committee to over-see the whole business. They seem to be getting results, with a promptness that is amazing. Trains have resumed their schedules, food has begun to come into the city, and the most welcome news of all, the deputation from Moscow arrived with the information that their city, the heart of Russia, is completely and quietly in the hands of the rebels.

Although the city is completely in the hands of the revolutionists there is still fighting between the few remaining members of the police and the soldiers. The police have to fight; there is no mercy for them, even if they do surrender. In spite of the danger from stray shots and the likelihood of encountering a spirited battle on a small scale at every turn of a corner we all went out for a look around. On all sides lies splintered glass, and where not wholly broken, windows stand pierced neatly with round holes. Doors are smashed in and spotted with bullet holes; the sides of buildings are flecked with the marks of flying lead—wherever a bullet strikes on these plaster buildings out comes a chunk as big as a plate—the huge clock on the end of the Singer building—the only modern American office building in Petrograd,— though still brightly lighted, stopped running a day or so ago in deference to three holes through its vitals. Here and there in the streets lies a horse, or an abandoned motor car put out of commission by flying bullets or a collision.

From house to house the search still goes on; every suspicious character is immediately arrested. The door of the apartment below us has been beaten with rifle bullets, until the frightened residents finally opened it to allow the search party to go through in quest of police or machine guns. They came in here a short time ago, and looked around our small quarters. Fred's Princeton and my Dartmouth banner on the walls excited great curiosity, and after learning that we were Americans they beamed and bowed in thanks to our congratulations and politely withdrew. But now and then, the search yields its reward, and another fight on the housetops ensues, always ending below in the street in the same way.

Wednesday.

Order seems to be coming out of chaos. This morning new announcements came from the Executive Committee with more instructions for the eager people. The most important was a plea for order and emphasis on the necessity for co-operation between the people and the temporary governing body in order not to interrupt the connections binding Petrograd to the armies at the front. A new police body, called the State Militia, and composed mostly of students and members of the Cadet schools here has been formed. Distinguished by the white arm band they are busy about the city with full police authority disarming all civilians, stopping rioting and looting and restoring the normal order. Their success is remarkable. Orders are out that all confiscated automobiles are to be reported to a committee which is to care for them, with the provision made for repaying the owner for any damage done to his machine; moreover unnecessary use of automobiles is prohibited, and at all important streets and exits of the city guards stop every car, demanding papers showing its purpose in running.

It was rumored that two sets of troops had been sent against the city by the Tsar, one detachment of Cossacks and one guard regiment. There was great excitement, but no demoralization.

Forming on the Field of Mars and swelling as it marched, a huge body of troops and civilians marched to the Nicholas station to give the troops a warm welcome. Another gang formed at the corner of the Nevsky and Sadovia. Here we watched it grow. Everyone was armed, and many had no idea how to use their arms. Beside us a rifle went off in the air as a civilian attempted to show a clumsy soldier how to load and fire it. It certainly was not a formidable crowd, militarily speaking, but it was an enthusiastic and determined one. But the wisdom of leaders asserted itself and diplomacy won another victory. A deputation is said to have met both bodies of troops outside the city and brought them over with but little argument, to the side of the revolutionists. Late in the afternoon a rumor spread that the Tsar had been cornered and that his answer to the demands of the Duma is on its way. In addition, telegrams began to come in from the generals at the front assuring the people of the army's complete support of the movement.

Arrests were made all through the day of important personages, the military commander of the city, to a great degree responsible for the conduct of the police and the Cossacks, the commander of the Fortress of Peter and Paul, and many members of the old government.

Late in the afternoon, to a member of the new militia at the Duma, came a bent figure muffled almost from view in a heavy overcoat. "Are you a member of the guard," it questioned. "Yes," replied the student. "Then take me," came the answer, "but keep me from the soldiers. I am Protopopoff, the Minister of the Interior." The guard conducted his prisoner inside to the committee sitting in session and it was not until transferred to the guard house in the Fortress that the former Minister of the Interior, pale and shaking, rested secure from the crowd which would have torn him into shreds had it known of his presence. Such has been the procedure all through the day, the arrest of men of former prominence, ministers, generals, and under officers, the judgment before the Committee, and their disposition either to the guard house or the Fortress, or, if willing to swear allegiance to the government, whatever that is, sent back to their troops. Few have resisted. It is foolishness to do so, as is shown by the case of a general who lived in the building just down the quay from the bank. It seems that he was suspected of having a machine gun on the roof of his house, and it was most likely true, because we noticed holes cut for some such use, but when the soldiers came to make a search the door man fired upon them; enraged they rushed through the house, whereupon the general fired and ran out through a side door and down the street to the quay. We heard the hullabaloo from the bank and got to the windows just as the general, in the act of climbing the stone wall and jumping down to the ice, got a well aimed bullet in the top of the head. He fell back in the street, dead, and still lies there as an object lesson of what it means to resist the new order of things. When we came home tonight the body was there, but mostly stripped of its uniform, for souvenirs.[174]

[174] Memories of Russia 1916–1919 by Princess Paley; "Chapter 9 My Sorrows Begin," https://www.alexanderpalace.org/memoriesrussia/chapter_IX.html; Albert Henry Stopford, *The Russian Diary of an Englishman Petrograd 1915–1917* (London: William Heinemann, 1919), 113 and 118; C.T. Swinnerton, letter, March 12, 1917, 9, File XX073-10.V. Hoover Institution Archives, Stanford University. The unfortunate general was General Count Gustave Stackelberg, otherwise Gustav, Baron von Stakelberg (1853–March 15, 1917). Several accounts describe his demise. According to Princess Paley, some revolutionary soldiers forced their way into his house on the Millionaya and made the general follow them to the Duma, but they had scarcely left his residence when a gunshot rang out. The frightened soldiers imagined they were being pursued and began to fire. Count Stackelberg began running down the street, and the soldiers shot him down a few yards from his own home. Stopford wrote that he heard from

This afternoon we walked out to the Duma. The surrounding streets were a sight never to be forgotten. A shifting, wavering sea of faces now parting and billowing up against the walls, as a new arrest borne in an open truck picked its way to the gates, now washing over the swathe again in eager restlessness. Now silent when some important personage mounted the gate to speak, now bursting into a mighty roar as some popular hero sifted through on his way to the halls. On each side of the heavy iron gateway stands a lamppost. On one of these a tattered battle flag, a relic of Napoleon's disastrous attempt to subdue Russia had been hung, the other bore a battered breastplate, another relic of these times. Between these two symbols of the past the prisoners were marched, through the gates, between the long lines of infantrymen up into the hall to stand before the Committee with the shouts of the crowd ringing in their ears and the voice of what Russia might have been had they done their duty, whispering its condemnation. Whatever their guilt or innocence, in this final and perhaps too lenient court they at last met justice face to face.

Leighton Rogers and his colleagues about the incident and recounted Rogers' description of the event in his memoir. Chester Swinnerton wrote, unsympathetically, "Yesterday, while the excitement coincident with the killing of Count Stockelburg [sic] was at its height, about a hundred yards away a soldier and his sweetheart were sitting on the parapet and chinning away as if they hadn't a care in the world."

CHAPTER 7

"We must bow to Russia
for the finest spectacle in history"

The March Revolution ended almost as quickly as it began. Rogers' journal entries exuded excitement and relief. He admitted it was "inconceivable to think of a complete overthrow being accomplished with so little disorder." Rogers assessed the immediate political actions of the new provisional government following the abdication of the tsar. He admired Russians as a "generous people" and "notoriously patient" but sensed a dangerous undercurrent flowing in Russian society. "What will come of it, no one knows," he prophetically contemplated. "The result is only to be known from the perspective of years, we are far too near the rush of events now to see anything but surfaces, and they rarely represent the truth."

Exciting times and pivotal events commanded his attention and pride. "It's great that we, the foremost Republic of the world have taken the lead in recognizing this new Russia," he wrote, "It has placed us in the best light possible with these people; they already regard us as their best friend." On April 2, President Wilson, addressing a joint session of Congress, requested a declaration of war against Germany, prompting Rogers to exclaim, "A revolution in the largest empire on the globe, and a few weeks after that, a declaration of war by the world's greatest Republic. Whoever is directing the show on this heated world of ours is having a hectic time of it."

Rogers optimistically judged National City Bank's prospects, noting, "The Revolution seems to have caused many people here to place their money and securities in our care, and in consequence we are literally swamped with work."[175] This phenomenon accelerated in the months to follow, requiring him to work longer and longer hours.

Reveling in the bank's success, he missed one important reason for it.

---

[175] Rogers, *Wine of Fury*, 190. Rogers described his excess workload: "All this came not without its price—a price demanded and paid in human effort. The young men . . . extended their already over-long working hours in an endeavour to keep up with the inrush of new business."

Thursday. *(The date is March 2/15, 1917)*

Order was almost complete today. People have given up their arms, and are returning to work. Guards are stationed at all buildings to watch for marauders or looters; every intoxicated person is arrested on sight. And I must add that I haven't seen more than two or three, in the whole business, which is a marvel. I cannot conceive of this happening in New York and that being the case. In the streets we see once more the sledges loaded with food coming from the outlying villages and the stations. Everyone seems happy and the whole city smiles.

It is almost inconceivable to think of such a complete overthrow being accomplished with so little disorder. Considering that it is the consummation of years of desire, that time after time its attempts have been crushed with retaliation, that at last in the face of tyranny, oppression and deceit which taxed the very life blood of the people they have risen, and overthrown all without venting their revenge in looting or useless slaughter. With any other people less patient and generous than the Russians I fear the result would have been far different. Of course the great factor in all this has been the absence of vodka. Whoever was responsible for its abolition two years ago accomplished far more for the good of his country than he ever dreamed of.

This evening the Duma sent out another proclamation, which runs as follows:

THE NEW GOVERNMENT

The Executive Committee of the National Duma announces the following:

Citizens;

The Temporary Committee of Members of the National Duma, with the co-operation of the troops and the population, has now attained such a degree of success over the dark forces of the old regime as permits it to proceed to a more solid structure of the executive authority.

For this purpose the temporary Committee of the National Duma appoints as Ministers of the first public cabinet the following persons, the confidence of the country in whom is assured by their past public and political activity,

Prince G.E. Lvoff	President of Council of Ministers
P.N. Milyoukoff	Minister of Foreign Affairs
A.F. Kerensky	Minister of Justice
N.V. Nekrassof	Minister of Ways and Communications
A.I. Khovaloff (*corrected: Konovalov*)	Minister of Trade and Industry
Prof. A.A. Manuiloff	Minister of Education
A.I. Gutenkoff (*corrected: Guchkov*)	Minister of War
A.I. Shingareff	Minister of Agriculture
M.I. Tereschenko	Minister of Finance
V.N. Lvoff	Chief Procurator of Holy Synod
I.V. Godneff	National Comptroller
F.F. Rodicheff	Minister for Finnish Affairs

(Rogers corrected the two misspelled names in his later typed manuscript, "Tsar, Revolution, Bolsheviks")

In their present activities the Council will be guided by the following principles:—

1. Full and immediate amnesty in all political and religious affairs, including terroristic attempts, military insurrections, and agrarian crimes, and so forth.
2. Liberty of word, press, assembly, union and strike; the extension of political liberties to those in military service within the confines permissible by all military-technical conditions.
3. Abolition of all class, religious, and national limitations.
4. Immediate preparations to convoke, on the principles of universal, direct, and secret suffrage, a Constituent Assembly which shall establish the form of administration and constitution.
5. Substitution of National Militia in place of the police, with elected leaders, and subject to the local administration.
6. Election to local administration on the basis of universal suffrage.

7. The troops taking part in the revolution are not to be disarmed and removed from Petrograd.

8. While retaining strict military discipline in the ranks and in military service, all limitations for soldiers in the enjoyment of public life, as enjoyed by all other citizens, are abolished.

The temporary government considers its duty to add that it in no way intends to take advantage of the circumstances of the war to cause any delay in carrying out the above reforms and measures.

Signed:
The President of the Duma
Prime Minister
Ministers

It is done. The new government has established itself without even awaiting the answer of the old. There is much speculation as to the actions of the Tsar. No one seems to have heard much about him. What will he do? All day long and even late tonight this question has been asked and there is no answer. But it doesn't stop speculation over what form the government eventually will take. Some want a Constitutional Monarchy, others insist upon a Republic. Speakers in motor trucks hurry from one center to another advocating and expounding this and that doctrine. Parades wind through the streets shouting their beliefs, unhampered, stopping here and there to listen to some speaker, grow larger and move on their way. It is a new experience for them and they are making the most of it.

Friday.

This morning the Tsar's message was published:—

MANIFESTO OF NICHOLAS II

In the days of the great struggle with the outer enemy, who for nearly three years has been striving to enslave our country God has pleased to send down upon Russia a fresh affliction. The troubles which have begun among the people threaten to effect unhappily the further conduct of the stubborn war. The fate of Russia, the honor of the heroic army, the welfare of the people,—the whole future of our dear country demands the carrying on of the war at any cost to a victorious end.

The fierce enemy has exerted his last forces and the hour is already near when our valiant army, together with our brave allies can finally break the enemy. In these decisive days in the life of Russia we have considered it a duty of conscience to facilitate to our people close unity and the rallying of all the forces of the people for the earliest possible attainment of victory, and, in accord with the Imperial Duma, we have considered it well to abdicate the throne of the Russian Empire, and to renounce the supreme authority. Not wishing to part with our beloved son, we transfer our inheritance to our brother, the Grand Duke Michail Alexandrovitch and bless him on his ascending the throne of the Russian Empire.

We enjoin upon our brother to administer the state affairs in complete accord and unbroken unity with the representatives of the people in the legislative establishments on those principles which they establish, taking an inviolable oath upon this in the name of the ardently loved country.

We call upon all true sons of the fatherland to fulfill their sacred duty towards him—submission to the Tsar in the severe time of universal national affliction—and to aid him, together with the representatives of the people to lead the Russian Empire on the way to victory, prosperity, and glory.

May God bless Russia.

NICHOLAS

March 2/15, 1917, the 15th, hour in the city of Pskoff.

(There are slightly different English translations of Nicholas II's message. For example, see Richard Pipes, The Russian Revolution, 315-6)

So the century-long dream of these people is at last come true.

Their feelings are varied. Some greeted the Tsar's message of abdication with regret, a few with florescent ravings, but the greater part of the people expressed satisfaction—but all with a tinge of sorrow for the overthrown. "He wasn't so bad after all." This is the attribute of a generous people.

I forgot to explain the other day, how it was that the new government was announced before the Tsar's abdication came.

When presented with the speech of abdication the grand duke, in a declaration acknowledging the tribute paid him, held it to be a matter, not for decision by the

Tsar, by himself, nor by any single individual, but a decision resting with the great body of the people. If they willed it he would give Russia his best as Emperor. If not he would continue to do all in his power as a citizen. This decision met with approval and it no doubt gave a strong argument to the constitutional monarchists. But it could not silence the debate everywhere carried on over the vital question. In vain the Duma tried to arrive at a conclusion; the two parties could not agree. It was at last decided to form the new ministry. The Provisional Government, which should govern until the Committee on Organization could construct an Assembly from representatives sent by the people from all over the country to cast their vote on the future government of Russia. This is how the new government, a remarkable group of Russia's ablest men, came to direct the course of the country. Effort is being made to carry on the war with renewed ardor, and the people seem once more to have settled back into their normal life.

What will come of it, no one knows. The result is only to be known from the perspective of years, we are far too near the rush of events now to see anything but surfaces, and they rarely represent the truth.

But whatever the outcome is, we must bow to Russia for the finest spectacle in [the] history of the governed exerting its God-given right to govern.

It goes to show how many varied influences there are at work in this business when you contemplate the poster, I tore from a wall on the Sadovia, on the 2/15th Wednesday [Thursday] last. This was a call to all good Anarchists and Maximalists to assemble at that corner on a certain date for a grand meeting of protest against the passing of the government from the hands of the tyrants of the old regime into the hands of the tyrants of capitalism as represented by the Provisional Government. It was signed by the Anarchists. And the city was plastered with them.

10/23 March.

Today the United States of America officially recognized the new Russian government. Ambassador Francis and his staff proceeded to the Marinsky Palace where he was received by the Council of Ministers, and delivered the following speech:—

"As the duly authorized Representative Ambassador of the United States of America I have the privilege to give you notification of the fact that the United States has officially recognized the Provisional Government of the whole of Russia. For me it will be a great pleasure to continue our good relations, both official and personal with Russia with the new formed government at its head. I feel quite certain that the friendly relations between our two countries will continue to develop to the mutual benefit and satisfaction of both."

It's great that we, the foremost Republic of the world have taken the lead in recognizing this new Russia. It has placed us in the best light possible with these people; they already regard us as their best friend.

Among all the radical elements of the country it seems to be held as a wonderful thing that the Minister of Justice of the new government is an active socialist, Kerensky is his name. He is the hero of all the "dvorniks" and maids in the city. They all speak of him. A young chap he seems to be also. He has also already announced that those members of the old regime guilty of neglect and crime will be punished, after a public trial. He has, however, come out empathetically against any prosecution of the Tsar or any members of the royal family. He is for exiling them and leaving them alone.

Unfortunately, just at this time when there is so much that I might write about, I have very little time in which to do it. The Revolution seems to have caused many people here to place their money and securities in our care, and in consequence we are literally swamped with work. From eight in the morning until ten or eleven at night are our hours, and by the time I do get home after such a day I am ready to go to bed at once.

Looking backward from what has happened it seems strange that people did not know it would happen, didn't prepare for it more. Because the effort was quite spontaneous, although the desire which instigated it has of course been burning in these people for centuries.

The primary indication of the immediate trouble might be found in the records of the Duma of last November, in the vehement speeches of the liberal "Left" directed at Rasputin. More indications can be seen in the audacious killing of Rasputin, which never could have happened in former times. And the approach to the climax might have been discerned in the attempt to murder the Empress, which came nearly upon the dissolution of the Duma at its last session. This dissolution of the representative body of the people was great fuel for the flames.

Then it got to be a question of how long a people would tolerate a government which looked with favor upon the common enemy and supported the war only as a sham. A government, which as the Revolutionary poster said, fed its enemies bread and its people lead.

The Russians are notoriously patient, whether from understanding or from igno-rance, matters little; the point was the duration of this patience. The government seemed to have its fingers upon the pulse, seemed able to sense just how far its masses could be driven, seemed gifted with the ability to compensate them at the point of outbreak with some trivial concession. Consequently, no one knew but that this crisis would be tided over in the same manner. But a great change has appeared in the Russian people since the beginning of the war, I am told. A change which has awakened them, has served as an educator, has set them thinking and working, as they never thought and worked before. An instance of this is the fact that when the industrial organization of the country and the supply departments of the army broke down under the strain of the tremendous Russian armies on the front, the people themselves, through the Zemstvos,[176] a net of local organizations something similar to our grange,[177] only more broadly developed, undertook to help keep the army sup-plied, particularly in the matter of red cross materials, and actually did more than the government organizations. The leader of this vast movement and its chief organizer was Prince Lvoff, the present President of the Council of Ministers.

In consequence of this change in the attitude of the people, changes in the gov-ernment have been more than ever, during the last two years, the common subject of thought. General opinion seemed to favor restraint until the end of the war when the situation could be remedied without danger to the country: but as things went on, from bad to worse, and the pro-German tendencies of the government came to the fore, and began to have their effects in failures by the Russian armies, it was seen clearly enough that if Russia hoped to win the war she must effect some changes in her con-duct of it. These changes could only come through changes in the Ministry, and the voice of the Duma had been raised in efforts for them since the beginning. The great demand was for a Ministry responsible to the people, the Duma, and not simply to the vacillations of the Tsar. Changes were made, time and again, with the resignation of one minister and the appointment of another,—and usually one of a more reactionary type,—witness the appointment of Steurmer, the pro-German premier.[178]

---

[176] Wikipedia, "Zemstvo," last modified January 3, 2021, 13:49 (UTC), https://en.wikipedia.org/wiki/Zemstvo. A *zemstvo* (Russian: земство) was a local or district institution set up during Emperor Alexander II's great eman-cipation reform of 1861. It consisted of locally elected representatives who supported efforts for self-government. After the November Revolution, the Bolsheviks replaced the *zemstvo* system with a multilevel system of workers' and peasants' councils, or soviets.

[177] An American farmers' association organized in 1867. The Grange sponsored social activities and community service, politically lobbied to support farmers, and aided in farming equipment and infrastructure purchasing.

[178] Wikipedia, "Boris Stürmer," last modified July 17, 2021, 20:40 (UTC), https://en.wikipedia.org/wiki/Boris_St%C3%BCrmer. Boris Vladimirovich Stürmer (Russian: Борис Владимирович Штюрмер) (1848–1917) served

But that they were not the proper ones is shown by the fact that the last Ministry endured only a month. These practices of back sliding on the part of the Tsar have of course enraged the people; but they were helpless. Because, when their representatives in the Duma had worked themselves up to the point of taking some drastic step, they have found the Duma dissolved and forbidden to meet by an imperial edict. They were unable to accomplish more by argument.

Moreover, it was clear, judging from the antics of Rasputin and the Empress at least, that there was much influence being exerted at Court for a separate peace with Germany. And this the people feared most of all. More than any other one thing, the Revolution just completed was directed against that. It has been essentially a patriotic movement.

Not the least topic of conversation which has arisen out of this business is that of how easy it all was. People do not seem to be able to realize it even yet, nearly a month after. It's because royalty does not follow the thoughts of its people, it is far too removed to see them clearly. It builds for itself a towering dais of power, constructed from the lathes and plaster of artificiality and convention, surrounds itself with mirrors for counselors, and perches a-top in serene self-satisfaction, quite blind to the spectacle of the people petitioning their desires. This mighty framework, with the glittering crown above is an awesome sight,—until some venturesome one makes a tentative thrust and down comes the structure in a cloud of splinters and plaster, nothing but empty framework, disclosing its weakness to the public view, its splinters and dust exciting only wonder as to why it had not been done before.

There are some amusing complications arising out of the fact that the Tsar meant so much to these people. Being the head of the Church he was the "Little Father" to them, the direct representative of God on earth, and I think by the more ignorant he was worshipped, without there giving much thought to the Deity. He was also the symbol of the State, the Country, and their patriotism was not for the land that gave them birth, but for the Tsar. He it was who asked them to fight, not the country. Hence, we hear that as he is no more, to many of the peasants in the wilder regions, there is no more God, no more religion, and they refuse to go to church. Also some of the soldiers see no more reason for fighting, there is no Tsar, hence no need to fight for him, say they. Just what explanation can be given to these poor, ignorants is difficult to figure out.

---

as prime minister, minister of internal affairs, and foreign minister of the Russian Empire in 1916. The provisional government arrested him after the March Revolution. He died of uremia in September 1917 at the hospital of the Peter and Paul Fortress.

America in the war! Three hundred cheers,—and a very solemn prayer.

Coming on top of their Revolution and our official recognition of it, it certainly stacks us up ace high with these people. Some of them in the beautiful simplicity of their minds attribute our step to the energetic influence of the Russian Revolution! Can you beat it? The Revolution is of course the greatest event in the world's history for them. They will date time from it.

But if our getting into the war means that we shall send an army to France, it also means that I must be in it in some way eventually. Or else I'll get in the Russian army. There's no time like the present for that, though, because the way we stand with the Russians now, I could draw down a general's rank! I don't see why I couldn't putter around in a pair of red striped trousers and heavy rubbers as well as the rest of 'em!

But seriously, it is staggering the way things are happening now a days. A revolution in the largest empire on the globe, and a few weeks after that, a declaration of war by the world's greatest Republic. Whoever is directing the show on this heated world of ours is having a hectic time of it.

24/6 April 1917.

The most wonderful event since the Revolution was the funeral of those killed in it, which occurred yesterday. There are many conflicting rumors as to the number of Revolutionists fallen, but the number must have been nearly five hundred; and no one knows the number of the Tsarists, which must have been far greater. But they of course weren't buried in the great grave with the others.

Behind the bank is an immense tract of land, a parade ground, called the Field of Mars. It is in the center of the city, and with the barracks along one side, the British Embassy, the Marble Palace, and a government building at one end, and the Summer Garden along the other side, it is a center of a great deal of the life of the city. Hence a very fitting place for the burial ground of those who died for the new freedom. In the center of this field a huge grave was dug by soldiers, and lined with cement; at its corners and sides banners of scarlet and black and white were hung and the whole area festooned with wreaths and flowers. The fifth of April was declared a national holiday and the city prepared for the funeral. Considering the complete overthrow of one government and the substitution of another, the complete reorganization of the police force, and the small number of police in the volunteer force, which has shrunk considerably in size, and considering the great opportunity there has been and still is for disorder, one could have expected such trouble with the huge procession planned. But people were put on their honor to be orderly and each person seemed to guard his honor well.

The procession formed in sections in different parts of the city, all to meet at the Field of Mars and file past the open grave where those who bore coffins could step out of line and deposit their burden and those who had flowers could cast them in.

During the night previous, the weather was terrible, rain and snow, so that the streets were ankle deep in slush; more over a constant drizzle of rain fell all through the day. But the sections formed, early in the morning, the procession started, and all day long and well into the night it filed down the streets, sixteen abreast, a mighty wave of humanity, old women, children, workmen, servants, sailors, soldiers, priests, people from every walk of life to the number of a million, marched in perfect order throughout the day. So constant was the movement and so solid the line that people found it impossible through the day even to cross the Nevsky. There were thousands of banners, banners of all descriptions,—some picturing Russia's freedom, others bearing golden mottoes,—among them many reading "War until Victory." Hundreds of bands played the funeral dirges, now remained silent while the marchers sang the new national melody of triumph, or the stirring Marseillaise. Perfectly the sections joined each with the one ahead at the entrance to the Field of Mars, across which the line moved to the open grave where the farewell glimpses were taken before moving sadly onward. It was not like any other procession I have ever seen—with people taking part merely because they think it the thing to do,—these people were part of it because it in some way expressed their new national feeling. It was a serious thing. And the order and unenforced discipline were nothing short of marvelous.

I saw them late at night, when the field and the grave were bright with the light of huge military searchlights whose rays, sweeping over the heads of the marchers, caught on the waving banners as they came across the open their bearers singing their mournful dirge, quite oblivious of the mud and slush, to plod on, out of the light and disappear from view in the darkness of the street beyond. It was something never to be forgotten; and whenever the old government is recalled the picture of that grave will rise and impress once more upon the minds of these people the price they paid for their freedom.

We are now having the Russian spring, and such a spring as cannot be anywhere else. One does not realize how much snow falls in its steady way throughout the year until it begins to melt, and then it is seen to be a foot-thick layer of ice over all the city. The drainage system is not of the best and consequently the streets are a young swamp, impossible to cross in many places. I have never seen so much mud in my life. An American political campaign is but a feeble comparison.

From what we can gather of it, all America is wild with excitement over the war. I would give much to be in it. I am proud of the deliberate way we have come into the thing; and unless mistaken, I think that many of the President's critics are just now beginning to realize the caliber of the man. In the light of fifty years his work in this crisis will be a source of pride to every American. Meanwhile, let's hope our participation will be as active and as ardent as our avoidance, because we can certainly do much to shorten the whole terrible business.

The Easter holidays have begun. Easter in Russia is the greatest time of all the year, all work is stopped for a week, and the cities are in gala attire. Great services are held in the churches, parades in the streets, and feasts in the homes. There are many little customs which are quaint and pleasing. The best of these is the lighting of the ikons in the home again from the great ikon in the cathedral. Practically every room in the country has its ikon in a conspicuous corner; these are usually painted pictures of the saint under whose period of the year the father of the home was born. And they vary in finish from the simple painted board of the very, very poor, to the platinum and jeweled images of the great ikons of the cathedrals some of which are worth hundreds of thousands of roubles. Before each ikon hangs a small oil lamp, the flame of which is never supposed to be extinguished. At Easter time it is the custom for some member of the family to go to the cathedral where the great miraculous ikons are, light a candle at the flame before one of these, guard this flame carefully with a hand or a paper cornucopia, and carry it home,—there to re-light the lamp before the house ikon with the holy flame. On the night of this ceremony the streets are a pretty sight, with the tiny lights hurrying to and fro, now and then the glow escaping from the guarded flame to light up the shining face of the carrier.

The holidays are nearly over. Considerable time is spent in cleaning both the person and the dwelling, and in preparing good things for the feast which always accompanies Easter,—bread and cakes decorated with flowers to be taken to the Church and blessed by the priests, and all sorts of candies, cookies, and easter eggs; there is much receiving and sending of presents, which include bonuses from the employer of the head of the house. It is an expensive time for the employer; he is compelled by custom to give his workmen not only ten days holidays but a bonus of one or two months' pay as well, which amounts to something when it is considered that the men receive three or four times as much as they did before the war.

The blessing of the bread and cakes is another quaint custom. The streets are thronged with hurrying people laden with their sweets gaily decorated with flowers and wrapped in colored cloths and many times bearing candles, these are placed before the priests who bless them with holy water, the candles are lighted and the good things taken back home.

It is Easter Sunday and there's a spirit in the air. The streets are filled with people crowding to the sun; old men still in furs bending over their walking sticks, nurses happy in the care of bubbling babies, while down the way come soldiers, free without their great coats, herculean boys, thumping along in lock-armed camaraderie, laughing and singing. On the corner in the sun sits a beggar basking and bowing, while around him play the children. Over it all floats the sound of bells, those of the smaller churches dancing in oriental jangle against the compelling boom of that of the great cathedral. Smiles and music and people warmed to a new life by the spirit in the air.

On the Saturday night before Easter Sunday the churches are crowded with people, and each person carries a small candle. The Corpus Christi is placed on a platform before the door of the Holy of Holies, and surrounded with a rail before which the people file to do their homage. At half-past eleven this is moved away, an aisle is made through the crowd to the entrance of the church, along which is stretched a carpet. Shortly before twelve the choir, unseen behind the great doors, begins the singing and on the first stroke of twelve the doors swing open, the choir bursts into the anthem, "Christ is risen" and the procession consisting of priests in their golden robes and crowns, pages bearing banners, lamps, and ikons and other holy treasures, files slowly through to proceed out the door and around the church. Those inside remain to join in the chorus upon the return of the procession. The square outside is crowded too, and sparkling with candles, and these people also join in the service as the procession passes. The procession re-enters the church, returns to the Holy of Holies, the great doors swing shut, the singing dies away, and the good people walk slowly homeward.

Yes, it is the gala season, and fitting it is, when the spring is coming, their short spring, and the summer. This year, the cup of joy is overfilled for are they not free at last after centuries of oppression? The feeling permeates the whole atmosphere of the happy city.

15/28 April 1917.

Tonight our gang won the basketball championship of Russia! Sounds like a lot, but there are only two teams in the country, both of them at the Y.M.C.A. we have been attending, one composed of Russian boys and our team composed of five demon Americans; both are coached by "Doc" Long the director. As part of the athletic exhibition put on tonight, he scheduled a game between our team and the Russian organization. Neither of us know much about the game, but we have a collection of roughnecks, so we managed to upset the smooth functioning of the Slavs with a little rough work, put over a few baskets while they got their breath, and won by a comfortable margin. A good team could have made monkeys out of us. The Russians play no better than we, but they are too polite to be rough.

16 [18]/1 May 1917.

It's been a bad day for us. We didn't prepare last night, and in consequence of our neglect had to get through the whole day on one meal. When they have a holiday over here, they have a regular one; no one does a stroke of work, motor men, restaurant keepers, or any one, and the poor unsuspecting public is thrown back upon what it has in the larder. We had ours full over the Christmas and Easter holidays, but we didn't think this would be a regular one. But it was, and the amount of food to be found in the city wouldn't have kept a humming bird through five minutes of its glittering life.

Upon rising this morning we found it snowing and as cold as midwinter; after a hearty (#%()"??) breakfast of tea and bread, Fred and I set out for a stroll, not because we wanted to, but because we had to in order to keep from freezing in our damp room. We managed to kill time until the noon hour when we landed at the bank and had our one good meal. After this, the place was closed and I went to the Hermitage Gallery to kill the afternoon. When it came time to eat again there was no place to go. Every restaurant was closed, every trolley line dead, not a store open, and we searched for hours without seeing a sign of food. We walked until actually faint from hunger, and were about to give up in despair and "pass out" in the street, when I suddenly, without any warning, gave birth to the brilliant scheme of going to the opera, lining up at the buffet there, and eating to our heart's content. We crawled over to the opera house, on the other side of the city, miles away, and upon arriving there found it surrounded with crowds waiting to get in listening to speeches of labor leaders from the platforms built out in front, and in general so completely crowded that we saw our chances of even getting inside the lobby door fade. We gave up and crawled back to our rooms, begged the maid to give us more tea and bread and went to bed in order to keep warm. A glorious holiday!

We managed to get down to the bank this morning without fainting and there we got food, which put us in form again. This evening Mr. S – – – – invited us to attend the opera with him, and it was a wonderful performance,—Boris Godunoff with Shaliapine singing the title role. One of the greatest things of its kind I have ever seen or heard. His work is magnificent. I have heard "Boris" without him and it nearly put me to sleep; but Shaliapine energizes the piece,—he is Boris Godunoff, and he literally holds you on the edge of your seat with the singing tragedy of the character. I never want to hear it again without him. The performance given in "The People's Theatre" packed the house with soldiers and people of the working class,—as they say here—and their demonstrations at the close of each act have rarely been equaled for wild enthusiasm,—even our best baseball and football games do not elicit so much. To these artists, I suppose, it is something far more worth having than great sums of money.

CHAPTER 8

"The growth of our bank is unprecedented in banking history"

National City Bank continued its meteoric rise. "The growth of our bank is unprecedented in banking history," Rogers wrote in awe on May 20, and on June 14, added, "Our balance sheet has again doubled itself and shows no signs of pausing in its flight skyward."

Frank Vanderlip was most pleased. In an April letter, he congratulated Meserve on a job well done:

> To make satisfactory progress with a new branch in the extremely unsettled conditions that are now current is reason for sincere congratulation. . . . I believe there is reason to expect that enormous interest will be shown in the development of closer financial relations with Russia when the times become more composed. I do not need to tell you that my own view has been for many years that we should see the time when Russia would offer perhaps the most attractive field in all the world outside of the United States for the employment of some of our surplus resources. The present tremendous current of events is undoubtedly hastening that time. I think you are in the center of one of the most significant developments in international relationship in the world, and I congratulate you on the progress that the Petrograd branch is making. I am also in accord with your views in regard to Moscow.[179]

Vanderlip shared his thoughts with his French business confidant, Prince Andre Poniatowski:[180] "The Russian situation, of course, continues to be one of great dynamic

---

[179] Vanderlip to Meserve, April 28, 1917, Box B-2-4, Frank A. Vanderlip Papers.
[180] Prince Andre Poniatowski (1864–1954), a French economist, financier, and industrialist based in Paris, was considered in France an authority on American finance.

possibilities. It presents what seems to me to be one of the greatest opportunities in history for great leadership if the right leader or leaders can be found."[181]

Meserve immediately wrote back and pleaded for haste: "Almost every day I am faced with the need to have a branch in Moscow."[182] The March Revolution, and the crescendo of unrest that followed, boosted National City Bank's business. Rogers described in *Wine of Fury* that "nearly everyone of means in Russia . . . [wanted] to transfer the responsibility for their fortunes to this new American institution of apparently unshakable stability."[183] This pattern followed each episode of turbulence in Russia. Rogers' colleague Boies Hart observed the same after the Bolshevik Revolution and the opening of the Moscow branch in late November, remarking, "Business came in droves. If we can only stick it out we will probably be in solid here forever."[184] Bullish as he was, Meserve myopically underestimated the risk side of the equation. NCB's management never glimpsed the double-edged sword of the "flight to quality" syndrome hanging over their heads. "Flight to quality" denotes a herd mentality to move away from riskier assets and institutions to safer ones. In National City Bank's case, this meant moving one's savings from a local Russian institution (or even from "under the mattress") to a highly capitalized international bank with headquarters in the United States. Mesmerized by the Petrograd branch's rapid acquisition of clients and assets, Meserve and team failed to appreciate that their clients' rush to National City Bank also reflected their underlying concerns about Russia's instability. This implied significant risk to the bank itself. But no alarm bell sounded.

Ambassador Francis did not share Meserve's unbridled optimism. In a May 16 letter to home, he cautiously foreboded: "There is a feeling of uneasiness generally prevalent because the Provisional Government . . . is not looked upon as sufficiently strong or stable. . . . A test of the powers of these forces must be made very soon. . . . I trust it will not result in bloodshed but such an outcome would not surprise me."[185]

Another risk Vanderlip and Meserve didn't take stock of was Vladimir Lenin and the Bolsheviks. No one in National City Bank commented on Lenin's return

---

[181] Vanderlip to Prince Poniatowski, May 17, 1917, 3, Box B-1-8, Frank A. Vanderlip Papers. The reference to leadership indicates that Vanderlip had concerns about the quality of the provisional government's leadership similar to those Ambassador Francis expressed in his May 16 correspondence. McRoberts' February 1917 article and Vanderlip's comments in his letter to Poniatowski, in addition to later comments he made on Russia after the Bolshevik Revolution, showed Vanderlip's sympathy for the idea of a dictator saving Russia from anarchy.

[182] Meserve memorandum, May 1, 1917, from Tkachenko, *American Bank Capital in Russia*, 98.

[183] Rogers, *Wine of Fury*, 189.

[184] Boies C. Hart, *Petrograd, Rio, Peking and Points Between* (New York: Citi Heritage Collection, 1946(?)), entry dated November 18, 1917, Chapter 4, 63.

[185] Barnes, *Standing on a Volcano*, 244.

to Russia on April 16. Did they not know what Lenin and his party stood for? "Export of capital is parasitism raised to a high pitch," Lenin wrote and published in December 1916,[186] words rather inimical to Frank Vanderlip's global vision. J. Butler Wright of the US Embassy did take notice. On April 21, he wrote about "A socialist named Lenine (sic), who . . . has been making the most incendiary harangues in public, stating that all the property owners should be killed and their land taken from them." Yet, in a subsequent diary entry three days later, Wright downgraded the danger, writing, "It seems that the anarchistic demonstrations are decidedly against public sentiment—and are defeating their own ends"[187]

Close communication and policy coordination between the US government and National City Bank continued. On April 19, Secretary of State Robert Lansing sent a telegram to Ambassador Francis asking him to relay a message to Meserve that Lansing had received from NCB's Samuel McRoberts about protecting Russia's reputation in the United States and keeping Russia in the war:

> Congress has voted seven billions war loan, three billions to be advanced to Russia and Allied Governments. There has been great enthusiasm here over Russian governmental reforms but recent reports widely circulated in public press indicating new government in control of Radical Socialists who are seeking to bring about separate peace with Germany seriously affecting Russian interests here, and if continued may prevent Russia's participation in loan to the Allies. At your discretion communicate this widely to Russian leaders and urge that every endeavor be made to correct this unfortunate and growing impression upon American people. If new Government can maintain order and successfully prosecute the war it is impossible to overestimate the enthusiastic friendship that will be engendered in this country opening up tremendous possibilities for Russian development after the war. A separate peace will be fatal to American cooperation. McRoberts.[188]

Just before the July Days revolt, Vanderlip wrote to Stillman that "Our assets in Petrograd now foot one hundred million rubles. We are under obligation to pay

---

[186] Vladimir Lenin, "Imperialism and the Split in Socialism," *Sbornik Sotsial-Demokrata* 2 (December 1916).
[187] J. Butler Wright diary entries, April 21 and 24, 1917, cited in Allison, *Witness to Revolution*, 68–9.
[188] US State Department, Office of the Historian, Papers Relating to the Foreign Relations of the United States, 1917, Supplement 2, The World War, Volume 1, "The Secretary of State to the Ambassador in Russia (Francis)," File No. 763.72119/566a,
https://history.state.gov/historicaldocuments/frus1917Supp02v01/d43.

nothing better than paper rubles, and our investments are practically all in government obligations or loans secured by government obligations, so that I do not see how we can be very seriously affected even if political conditions should continue unsatisfactory. Of course there is always danger of mob violence and sooner or later we will probably have some unpleasant experience of that or some other kind, but we are doing very profitable business in the meantime."[189]

Vanderlip never imagined the scale of the unpleasant experience that would come National City Bank's way.

---

[189] Vanderlip to Stillman, July 6, 1917, 5, Box B-1-8, Frank A. Vanderlip Papers.

7/20 May 1917.

The growth of our bank is unprecedented in banking history; in one short month we have tripled in size. As all this additional work has been taken on without any increase in the size of the staff it follows that we are, to say the least, busy. The days go by in clockwork fashion. Up at eight, bank open at nine, work unceasingly and at a terrible pace until one, lunch, and more work again until time for dinner at six o'clock, and after that still more labor until half past ten or eleven, until no more is possible with any degree of accuracy; then back to our rooms, for bed and a repetition of the performance the next day. There is even no rest at night, because my dreams are peopled by strange beings gaily colored like Russian bonds, with coupons for tails pursuing promissory notes at breathless speed through a maze of vaults.

Speaking of our work, a few days ago my department handled one million dollars' worth of gold in bars, which kicked around my room all the afternoon. I had the distinct pleasure of using a pile of them to rest my feet on. Cheap, yellow, stuff. I looked at the fussy, aged, bearded, and bent employee of another bank who superintended its transportation,—he could have it—I'd rather have my youth and health.

Sunday again, and for many, church. But for me churches are damp, dull, dead places, and there is no joy in them. They turn thought inward and make for self-consciousness. Feeling thus, it is easy for the magnet of the sunshine to draw me to the street. Here is life,—workers strolling in their freedom, girls selling flowers, shining carriages with the beaming faces of children, powdered women with pampered dogs, beggars, happy for the sun despite their attempts at misery, soldiers strolling hand in hand, no older in joy than the children playing on the green within the outstretched arms of the Kazan Church; old men dozing on the benches, women feeding doves, a group of soldiers intent upon a little Mongolian juggler, nurses leading the wounded and the blind,—people everywhere, sending praises to the highest in the unconscious joy of living.

Just at the busiest time the other night when six o'clock found me confronting a desk piled high with papers of all kinds Mr. S – – – came out and placed a foot high pile of bonds on my desk, saying, "I've promised Mr. Sazonov, the former Prime Minister of the Empire and now the newly appointed Russian Ambassador to Great Britain, who says he is starting for London tomorrow morning, that he could have his receipt for these papers tonight at six o'clock, or anyway sometime tonight." My expression must have been a peculiar one, because he smiled and asked, "Is that a large order?" He might just as well have promised to place the Fortress of Peter and Paul on the Prime Minister's front porch by 6 o'clock; but I replied that we would try. "Count" volunteered to help me, said he'd try to run the Russian typewriter, because, according to the Russian banking rules, these receipts must contain a detailed description of every security, number, date, series, name, etc. Even with a Russian typist it is a tremendous task, and for us who could only hobble on the machine it was more than that. Hercules' little job of dusting out the Augean stables, was trifling beside it. However, we plugged along and finally finished it at quarter to eleven. It was duly signed by Mr. S – – – – and "Count" and I walked up to Mr. Sazonov's house to deliver it. He met us in the waiting room with the following, delivered in a most forced English accent, "But I thought I was to have it earlier, why are you so late?" "Count" growled behind me and crunched the tops off a couple of teeth, and I came nearly handing the old boy one on the chin, but we managed to restrain ourselves and get out of the house without committing any violence. But the air was blue all the way home. And the gentleman probably doesn't know that he had the narrowest escape of his diplomatic life. A few days later, who should walk into the bank but Mr. Sazonov himself, and when I observed that he had postponed his trip to London, he replied, "London? Most absurd. I have never had the slightest intention of going to London."

No wonder there are wars here when fingers of men like this pull the diplomatic strings.

We have moved again and this time have struck it right. Two rooms, a bath, light and airy, with a balcony overlooking a pretty garden across the street, comfortable furniture, and a maid to keep things in shape.

To get this we had to compete with representatives from Mitsui and Co.,—the richest financial and trading organization in Japan. But strategy won and the Japs had to retire in confusion. At our last interview with the landlady who was undecided to whom to rent the place before she left for the country, Fred observed, "About these Japs. You'll remember the first time they called to look the place over there were two of them; you said that yesterday three came. And I tell you that if you let them have the rooms, you'll return from the country in the fall to find the whole Japanese colony of Petrograd encamped here; they'll be hanging from the chandeliers like bats." This won the day, and the rooms.

We have joined the English tennis club on the Vassily Ostroff,[190] and expect to get a great deal of enjoyment from it when the warm weather comes. We went out yesterday in spite of the coolness and tried it out. The courts are very good, and fast; there is a neat but not gaudy club house where refreshments are served in the warm weather, and a dressing room with lockers and bathing facilities.

It really ought to be warm now, according to the talk of some of the "oldest residents." I was quite discouraged this morning when I got up to find it snowing, and in the merry month of May! But nothing seems to be going in accordance with the rules now-a-days, least of all the weather. It's a long, long trail back from this to the golden sunshine of college days and college work, when the greatest problem was figuring out how to "buffalo"[191] the "profs" the next day.

We've had an attack of acute "operaitis." Four nights this week have found us either at the opera or the ballet. They've been having some big performances at the Narodny Dom—"The People's Opera"—and we couldn't miss the chance to hear three of Russia's greatest singers all at once. And one night at the ballet we had the opportunity of seeing the two greatest dancers in the world on the same stage.

The Revolution seems to have given the opera even added impetus. The audiences are more cosmopolitan, perhaps because it is easier to obtain tickets, and the performances seem to have a certain spontaneity about them which is engaging. The only thing lacking is of course the splendor of the audiences and the patronage of royalty which somehow spurred the singers and dancers to put forth their best efforts.

1/14 June 1917.

Our balance sheet has again doubled itself and shows no signs of pausing in its flight skyward. Everything and everyone is going at breakneck speed and things have now about reached the limit of physical endurance. It is physically impossible to work more, or faster. We are at it until late at night and have now to start earlier in the morning in order to begin with the day's custom. I have ceased taking Russian lessons, in fact have stopped most of those things which take time and energy, for the simple

---

[190] Wikipedia, "Vasilyevsky Island," last modified June 21, 2021, 22:39 (UTC), https://en.wikipedia.org/wiki/Vasilyevsky_Island. Vasilyevsky Island (Russian: Василье́вский о́стров) is an island in St. Petersburg bordered by the Bolshaya Neva and Malaya Neva rivers (in the delta of the Neva River) and by the Gulf of Finland. Among the museums on the island is the Old St. Petersburg Stock Exchange (bourse). Many 18th century edifices line the Universitetskaya Embankment, including the Kunstkamera, Twelve Collegia, Menshikov Palace, Imperial Academy of Sciences, and St. Andrew's Cathedral.

[191] To buffalo (verb). Informal, North American. To overawe or intimidate (someone).

reason that when I get through at night I am too tired to think or to indulge in any exertion; my only desire is to get to sleep as quickly as possible.

Summer is here now. She came in quietly one night not long ago and has been behaving beautifully ever since. The nights are cool and the days are warm, and of such great length that it is possible to do much. While I am writing this it is eleven o'clock at night, but still as light as noon-day out of doors. The trees seem to have burst into leaves overnight, and the parks and gardens are beautiful. After the long winter, nearly nine months, it seemed as though the sun had been extinguished, but now it is working over-time.

Sunday being a beautiful day some of us took a trip out to one of the beaches not far from Petrograd. At least, not far when distance is reckoned, but a good distance when figured in time. The little train which took us out to the place couldn't make more than fifteen miles an hour and nearly two hours were needed for the twenty-five mile trip. Two hours of standing up on the platforms between the cars, with a foot on one car and the other foot on the second car,—which was all very well until we rounded curves when one was either pushed together or pulled almost apart and two hours with cinders from the wood-burning locomotive flying down between the cars and eating holes in flannels.

The engineer had a pet fox terrier puppy which disdained to ride with us, but ran alongside the train all the way out, and through the sand at that!

It was a pretty place, with a pine grove, pavilions, concert halls, and dance floor, a terrace restaurant and an orchestra,—and last but not least a bathing beach. We were there early, and at once got into our bathing suits and went in. The water was very cold and also very shallow, making a walk of about half a mile out into the gulf necessary before it became deep enough for a good swim. When we looked back, there seemed to be other people on the beach sans costume; curiosity drew us in shore to watch the arrest that must surely follow. But no, these men were soon joined by women bathers also minus costume! And that seemed to be the vogue. When we came out, our suits elicited a bit of curiosity, so much so that we took them off and went in with the rest. It was quite a shock at first to see the couples and family groups playing around on the sand like Adam and Eve, and it was some time before we got over it. This at one of the best beaches in Russia too.

We had dinner at the terrace, listened to the concert, watched the people, saw the glorious sunset over the Gulf of Finland at nearly midnight, and came home completely tired out but completely rested.

It's tea, tea, tea. I've never drunk so much tea in my whole life as I have in the few months we've been here. It's everywhere; and I believe it's tea that flows in the gutters.

We have it in the morning, served in a glass always, with a holder like our soda glass holders, to keep it from burning the hands; at ten-thirty in the morning all business stops, while tea is served to the workers,—even in the banks, everything is dropped, a boy carries huge trays laden with glasses of tea and each employee sips it for a half hour or so while business waits at the door. At lunch time the meal ends with a glass or two of tea and one more is forthcoming at about three-thirty in the afternoon when again business must needs halt while all Russia has its tea; of course, that dinner brings a couple of glasses in addition is a foregone conclusion, and the tea debauch ends in a blaze of glory at ten o'clock at night when all good Russians gather around the samovar to discuss the days doings and consume at least two or three glasses of the national beverage. So there you are,—if you do as the Russians do, you put away ten glasses of the stuff a day. The maid has just appeared at the door and asked, "Do you wish your tea now, Baron." And I, resignedly, have answered, "Yes, Sasha, bring it in." She insists upon giving us a title. Nearly all the servants do; even if you come from a country where titles are not, if they think you ought to have a title, a title you get. Instead of being just plain, ordinary John Citizen Mister, to them you become a Baron, just like that.

Yesterday, Art Ruhl, who is over here for Colliers,[192] and I, with one of the gang from the bank, went for a stroll in the residential and suburban section of the city,— the Kameniostroffsky[193] immortalized by Rubinstein's music under the same name. After strolling around and looking over the beautiful summer residences and the parks we hired a rowboat and set out down the river. A beautiful ride, past summer homes set in trees and gardens, palaces belonging to former ministers and royalty, past the yacht club where the boats are being overhauled for the coming season, and finally out into the Gulf. Here, at the mouth of the river, we came to a small island which we had all to ourselves, and we straightway made the most of the opportunity for a swim. Suits, of course are not used here, and we had a good time of it.

On the way in we stopped at one of the pleasant river restaurants where the orchestra played such modern American tunes as "Every Little Movement" and "The

---

[192] Arthur Ruhl was a popular member of the American colony in Petrograd. "A most interesting person whom we enjoyed greatly," wrote J. Butler Wright, who lunched with Ruhl several days after Ruhl's evening stroll with Leighton Rogers. J. Butler Wright diary entry, June 16, 1917, cited in Allison, *Witness to Revolution*, 91.

[193] "Why Rubinstein wrote *Kamennoi Ostrow*," *The Etude Magazine*, April 1912. One of Rubinstein's most popular pieces is his *Kamennoi Ostrow*, Opus 10, No. 22. "Rubinstein, the dreamy-eyed, wandered here, happy and enchanted with the bells. Their music so haunted his ears that on his return to the chalet of the Grand Duchess Helene, whose honored guest he was, he wrote his famous composition, *Kamennoi Ostrow*, in which the soft chimes of the bells ring as sweetly as they do on the island."

Pink Lady,"[194] and enjoyed a very good but very expensive dinner. There was more music, and at the close we trailed home to pull down the black curtains which keep the sun and light out during these bright nights, and retired.

This morning we arose early in order to make sure of getting a place on the river boat for Schlussellburg.[195] This town, a four hours trip up the Neva, is on the shore of Lake Ladoga, supposed to be the largest fresh water lake in Europe, and it is as the outlet for this great body of water into the Gulf of Finland that the Neva functions as a river, although barely over forty miles in length. We had planned to take the eight o'clock boat and thus avoid the crowd, but it seemed as though everyone else in Petrograd had the same idea because they all seemed to be waiting there at the quay when we arrived. We formed in flying wedge formation, however, and in spite of the efforts of numerous members of the new police force who didn't seem to want us to take the trip, we fought our way to a place on the upper deck. Imagine a policeman wearing bone glasses, having any authority! After leaving the factory district of the city the trip became interesting, although there is nothing striking about the scenery,—the landscape being typical of this section of the vast country,—low flat stretches of plain with now and then a forest of spruce trees, each one straight and conventional like the toy trees that come with children's sets,—country villages, always centering around the white church with its many domes and bells, and little wharves to which the peasants clad in their vari-colored costumes come to clamber aboard, meet friends, or only to see and wonder.

Schlussellburg is a small town, all cathedral and fortress; the houses are constructed from hand hewn logs caulked with okum[196] like a ship, and the church is built of whitewashed boards. These set in the unbending spruce trees on the shore of the immeasurable and very blue lake, formed a picture of broad flat color and of unutterable loneliness.

---

[194] Wikipedia, "Every Little Movement (Has a Meaning All Its Own)," last modified January 8, 2021, 00:13 (UTC), https://en.wikipedia.org/wiki/Every_Little_Movement_(Has_a_Meaning_All_Its_Own). *Every Little Movement (Has a Meaning All Its Own)* was a popular song. Its music was written by Karl Hoschna and its lyrics by Otto Harbach for their musical, *Madame Sherry*, which opened on Broadway in 1910; Wikipedia, "The Pink Lady," last modified December 17, 2021, 03:21 (UTC), https://en.wikipedia.org/wiki/The_Pink_Lady_(musical). *The Pink Lady* was a musical comedy with lyrics by C. M. S. McLellan and music by Ivan Caryll that opened at the New Amsterdam Theatre in New York in 1911, where it ran for 312 performances.
[195] Wikipedia, "Shlisselburg Fortress," last modified June 15, 2021, 02:55 (UTC), https://en.wikipedia.org/wiki/Shlisselburg_Fortress. Shlisselburg (Schlüsselburg) was an important medieval fortress in northwest Russia, first built in 1323. It was the scene of many conflicts between Russia and Sweden. Today the fortress and the city center are UNESCO World Heritage sites.
[196] Okum or oakum. Loose fiber obtained by untwisting old rope, used especially in caulking wooden ships.

CHAPTER 9

"Whether Russia can get herself together in time"

The Allies worried about Russia's ability and willingness to continue to prosecute the war. The United States sent three missions in the summer of 1917 to shore up the provisional government and its resolve to fight: the Root mission, the Railroad Commission, and the American Red Cross mission. Everyone had something critical to say about these undertakings, including Rogers.

The Root mission, led by former Secretary of State Elihu Root, arrived in Petrograd on June 13. Quoted in the *New York Times* on July 2, 1917, the mission detailed what it saw in Russia:

> The industrial disorganization of the country and the obstacles in the path of reconstruction introduced by anarchistic and reactionary elements, irresponsible persons, and fanatics of all kinds working with the direct purpose of assisting the enemy or the equally malign desire to cause the downfall of the Russian democracy are much more serious than America has been led to believe. The Provisional Government has been successful in enlisting the support of the great majority of the people, but until it is able with a strong hand to demonstrate its complete authority and exercise his authority in punishing all irresponsible persons and cliques, which by the creation of dissension in the country are attempting to prevent Russia from consolidating the benefits gained from the triumph of the revolution, there can be no real stability or security. . . . [197]

---

[197] "Find Russia Improving But Still in Straits; Root Commission Sees Obstacles to Reconstruction, but Signs Are Encouraging," *New York Times,* July 2, 1917, 3.

Another member of the mission, Charles Edward Russell, watered down Root's warning in a public appeal several days later "to my fellow democrats in the United States and Great Britain for a more sympathetic attitude toward the struggling democracy of Russia. I appeal to editors not to print wild-eyed stories of impending ruin and chaos and to newspaper readers not to believe such stories if printed. There is no anarchy here. There is only a limited amount of disorder."[198] Root changed his tone a week later to optimistically claim, "The mission has accomplished what it came here to do, and we are greatly encouraged. We found no organic or incurable malady in the Russian democracy. . . . The solid, admirable traits in the Russian character will pull the nation through the present crisis. Natural love of law and order and capacity for local self-government have been demonstrated every day since the revolution. The country's most serious lack is money and adequate transportation. We shall do what we can to help Russia in both."[199] Americans may have wanted to hear this message, but Root underestimated, or worse, ignored, the problems the provisional government faced and the threat from the increasingly vociferous Bolsheviks.

Rogers viewed the Root mission as a farce: "We met some of the members . . . and when we asked them what they hoped to do, they replied that they didn't know; but that they had six hundred thousand dollars to spend and were going to do it. There is no place or time here for that kind of man." Rogers added, "What it has accomplished, no one knows. Even important members of it do not speak with enthusiasm of its work." Journalist Arno Dosch-Fleurot bellowed, "It was so absurd it made me angry. . . . a useless formal performance, when the whole of Russia was on the loose. . . . Mr. Root knew but could not admit, that Russia was through with this war."[200] DeWitt Clinton Poole, the vice consul in the US Consulate in Moscow, had nothing better to say and concluded that "They had simply gotten nowhere."[201]

The Railroad Commission arrived in Petrograd on the same day as the Root mission. President Wilson promised the provisional government that the United States would help rebuild Russia's transportation systems. He selected John F. Stevens, the former chief engineer of the Panama Canal, to chair a board of prominent US railroad experts to "give assurances to the Russian national authorities that this country stands ready to furnish all the rolling stock and other material that may be needed to increase

[198] "Russell Would Stop Criticism of Russia," *New York Times,* July 6, 1917, 3.
[199] "Root Now Certain of Russia's Success," *New York Times*, July 11, 1917, 1.
[200] Dosch-Fleurot, *Through War to Revolution*, 163–64.
[201] Lorraine M. Lees and William S. Rodner, eds. *An American Diplomat in Bolshevik Russia: DeWitt Clinton Poole* (Madison: University of Wisconsin Press, 2014), 12.

the capacity and efficiency of the Russian and Siberian railroads."[202] Upon arriving in Petrograd, Stevens stated that "the commission's aim was to assist the Russian people . . . Its primary object is to help the Allies in the war against Germany."[203]

As with the Root mission, observers on the ground remained skeptical. "The railroad commission is having a typically 'Russian' time of it—finding that these people are long on talk and very short on *practical* ideas," wrote J. Butler Wright.[204] Rogers concurred: "In the Russian laborer the Commission lines up against a force stubborn, ignorant, and misled."

The American Red Cross mission, led by William B. Thompson, a copper magnate and Wall Street financier, and Frank Billings, a well-known physician from Chicago, showed up in July. They were "sent to Russia as the first step of the plan . . . to do something immediately to hearten that country."[205] Leonid Strakhovsky, in his *American Opinion About Russia*, concluded that the mission's activities did "inestimable damage to Russia and the United States at that time by misleading both. . . . from the outset the Commission had a purely political aim and had nothing (or very little) to do with Red Cross functions."[206] Rogers, during his railway escape from Russia in February the next year, sarcastically criticized the American Red Cross when he saw "Some members . . . riding luxuriously in the rolling palaces from the Tsar's royal train. I stopped in to see them one afternoon, but even though . . . I was the only American besides their own party in the place, I got no offer of help from them. I must have looked like a roughneck. Or else, maybe they are not supposed to help stray and distressed Americans."

The July Days riots left no doubt in Rogers' mind that Russia's future was at stake. Not to mention his own future in Russia. Street fighting came too close for comfort. Rogers was almost shot trying to get home on July 17, though that did not stop him from animatedly writing about his harrowing adventure hours later. The same evening, fearless Philip Jordan, the devoted valet of Ambassador Francis, witnessed a fire fight between horse-mounted Cossacks and radical soldiers just one block from the US Embassy. "It was one grand Sight," he wrote. "The sky was full of the prettiest fireworks you Ever saw. . . . I was laying flat behind the man that was pumping the

---

[202] "Railroad Commission Starts for Petrograd," *New York Times,* May 10, 1917, 9.

[203] "Root and Stevens Reach Petrograd," *New York Times,* June 14, 1917, 1.

[204] J. Butler Wright diary entry, June 22, 1917, cited in Allison, *Witness to Revolution,* 93.

[205] "Red Cross Experts Will Go to Russia," *New York Times,* July 2, 1917, 8.

[206] Leonid Ivan Strakhovsky, *American Opinion About Russia 1917-1920* (Toronto, ON: University of Toronto Press, 1961), 20–21.

machine gun."[207] Francis complained about the provisional government not acting forcefully enough and recorded that he warned the Russian foreign minister, Mikhail Tereshchenko, that he would "recommend no further assistance until stable government formed which would prosecute war and suppress lawlessness."[208]

Rogers' confidence in the provisional government waned, as did that of most foreigners in the capital. The possibility of Russia seeking a separate peace with Germany, which would endanger the position of the Allies, was abhorrent. Rogers feared the effectiveness of German propaganda and the looming threat of German forces approaching Petrograd. His frustration with the Russian people increased. Whereas in March, he praised the Russians for the success of their revolution, he wrote three months later, "What do these people hope to accomplish by their shooting one another? What good can it do? Can't they see that in all this Germany rejoices, and her agents progress?"

Russian and Western definitions of democracy differed. Dosch-Fleurot perceptively pointed out that the intelligentsia and middle and upper classes of Russian society (and no doubt most of Petrograd's foreigners) felt the revolution was over and that Russia should set up a constitutional assembly to legitimize it. The working class and poor viewed their newfound "freedom" and democracy from a different perspective. Councils of soldiers' and workers' delegates appeared everywhere. A social and economic revolution needed to happen as well.[209] By September, Rogers comprehended, "There are those who strive to make it social" and "the people are sick of having liberty, freedom, revolution and the like shouted at them. . . . Just what form this demand will take is hard to for-tell but it will make itself heeded."

Like most of his contemporaries, Rogers viewed Russia through foreign lenses, which often led him to paternalistic, if not erroneous, conclusions. In fairness, these were turbulent, unclear times, and sorting facts from rumors proved challenging. Rogers even complained of the "fake news" that some American correspondents produced for consumption back home. Discouragement dashed hope and vice versa, as life in Petrograd deteriorated. "I do not appreciate the possibility of being dragged from my perch of an interested spectator down to becoming an excited participant," Rogers wrote. He no longer gushed about NCB's asset and profit growth. Instead, he dissected the diverging political opinions among classes, complaining that the

---

[207] Barnes, *Standing on a Volcano*, 247.
[208] David S. Foglesong, *America's Secret War Against Bolshevism: US Intervention in the Russian Civil War, 1917–1920* (Chapel Hill: The University of North Carolina Press, 1995), 53.
[209] Dosch-Fleurot, *Through War to Revolution*, 137.

"pitifully ignorant moujiks" had been led astray, and that "hairbrained laborers can appear . . . and change the course of the Government."

Still, foreign investors wanted to see past the war and domestic turmoil. Russia represented great opportunity for profit. "Flight to quality" continued, and so did National City Bank's plans to expand. In short time, the bank had attracted an impressive list of clients that included the leading investors in Russia, including Singer Sewing Machine, Otis Elevator, Babcock & Wilcox, Vacuum Oil Co., Eastman Kodak, Okura and Co., W. R. Grace & Co., New York Life Insurance, Studebaker Corporation of America, American Express Co., and Irving National Bank, among many other companies. NCB banked the private accounts of many American, Dutch, Danish, and British diplomats, Frank Billings and William Boyce Thompson of the American Red Cross, Archibald Hart of the YMCA, and several members of Russian nobility, including Grand Duke Boris Vladimirovich. Some particularly interesting clients included Queen Olga Konstantinovna of Greece,[210] who kept 1.5 million rubles' worth of jewelry in a safe-deposit box, and the British author Somerset Maugham, who was spying for the British rather than writing his next novel.[211]

Meserve needed more staff to bolster the Petrograd operations and open a branch in Moscow. Between May and October 1917, NCB sent an additional thirty-one men to Petrograd.[212] Upon their arrival, Rogers sized them up, and, forlornly, himself. "How fresh and healthy they looked, and what strength and enthusiasm. They made me look at myself and consider how far I had fallen in my year here. I feel like a shell of my former self. But I hate to think about it," he wrote.

---

[210] "Bank Here is Sued Over a Queen's Estate," *New York Times*, April 18, 1931, 14. Queen Olga Konstantinovna died in Rome on June 19, 1926, and her estate sued National City Bank for $192,475, alleged to be the value of cash and securities deposited in NCB's Petrograd branch (there was no mention of jewels). The bank argued that the suit had been brought too late, both under the Russian ten-year statute of limitations and the American statute of six years.

[211] Tkachenko, *American Bank Capital in Russia*, 84–88. Ted Morgan, in his biography of Somerset Maugham, stated that Maugham used his spying experiences as the basis for *Ashenden: Or the British Agent* (1927), a collection of short stories about a gentlemanly, sophisticated, aloof spy. This character was considered to have influenced Ian Fleming's later series of James Bond novels.

[212] *Number Eight*, The National City Bank of New York, May 1917, 50; June 1917, 47–49; July 1917, 39; August 1917, 37; October 1917, 38; *The Journal of John L. H. Fuller*, 1; Hart, *Petrograd, Rio, Peking and Points Between*, entry dated in July 1917, Chapter 2, 17; Tkachenko, *American Bank Capital in Russia*, 98.

17/30 June 1917.

Energy seems to have deserted me. I suppose this is due to the fact that a box of baseball equipment arrived for us and we at once went out to the field and let loose in a game of ball. It was my first in a year and my last for another year, from the way I feel,—like Old Man Rome himself,—just about to fall. Of course the Russians think we are just plain crazy, chasing that little ball around, or else they must regard it as a Convention and Clambake of the Bomb Throwers Union.

We're going to teach a bunch of 'em the game and then play for the championship of Russia; and when our Moscow Branch opens we shall start a league.

Tomorrow is a holiday and it has been announced that on the Field of Mars, there will be a huge demonstration in favor of peace and also one at the same time in favor of continuing the war. Anything may happen and we're all wondering what the outcome will be.

Fred and I have been trying to lay in a stock of food for the event, having in mind our harrowing experience on the last holiday, and it is amazing to note how prices have jumped. We managed to find some canned stuff and a few eggs, although these will probably fly away before morning.

Both meetings were held, and at each of them, speakers raved and tore their hair all afternoon, but nothing came of it. The crowds walked around from one meeting to the other, seemed to agree with which ever speaker they heard last and went on about their business. That's the way with these people, you never can tell what they'll do. When trouble is expected and every preparation is made for it, they are as quiet as mummies, but when everything looks rosy and peaceful, they're liable to go up like rockets. I think, though that having got over this day, without a great deal of excitement, they will settle down, and the general trend of affairs will improve. But we must wait and watch.

Of course, had Russia carried out her end of the agreement and advanced as everyone expected her to advance, the war would have been over by Christmas; but she was too busy with her Revolution and it will probably be better for the world in the end that she completed it when she did. But this same Revolution cancelled a great many of the Allies' best efforts. Whether Russia can get herself together in time to carry out her part remains to be seen. Just at present things seem to be dragging, along as they have done for the past few months with no one interested in work, and every one thinking about play and their freedom. Having acquired it they do not know how to use it. There exists such a diversity of ideas as to just how the affairs of the country should be conducted that all the effort spends itself in argument and loses its motive force. The intelligent are for continuing the fight and are upholding the Provisional Government; but the poorer and more ignorant as well as the extremists are for a cessation of the fighting.

We get little news of what is going on in the outside world and what little does filter through only whets the appetite for more. I suppose all my friends will be in the army soon. A letter from Dick came today in which he said he had been resting up for a month after returning from the Mexican border, but supposes that in a few weeks he would have to slip on the flannel shirt again and start out to war; seemed to think it a great life with a new war every spring!

It's good to know that they are preparing for a long war at home and let us hope those determined preparations will make their impression upon the Germans. I think they will. Although the Germans are a wonderfully disciplined race, and although their military organization is splendid, it is becoming a little worn, and internal troubles among the people are causing the government to stir uneasily. I should not be surprised if the strain of winter made them offer tempting peace terms by Christmas. But no matter how satisfying the terms are I don't see how we can accept them, as long as they are made by the present German government; they are valueless, for has not this government openly declared its agreements to be scraps of paper? There is no way out until the German government is overthrown either by its own subjects or by force of Allied arms.

The Root Mission to Russia arrived from the United States a few days ago. It seems to be made up of big men all right, but just why it is headed by Root is causing much speculation. Russia never heard of him. There is just one man in America who should have been at the head of this Mission and that's Roosevelt. He's the only man they know over here. I say this not because I'm a Roosevelt fanatic but because it is a fact.

The entrance of the Mission into the city was strange. One would think that its arrival in the capital of the country would be made the occasion of some ceremony and liveliness. But there was hardly any of it. A few under Ministers met it at the station and conducted it to the Winter Palace where quarters had been prepared. No bands, no decorations,—save perhaps a few at the station. There are no flags in the city, at least American flags, not even one hanging over the Winter Palace, the American headquarters, or at the Hotel Europe, where many members of the Mission live. But few know that the American Mission is here. One of the papers has got out an American Number with a few pictures of the Mint and the Ford factory in it, but otherwise there's not much out of the ordinary. Strange.

We met some of the members at the Hotel Europe and talked with them a while. They were secretaries to somebody or other, and when we asked them what they hoped to do, they replied that they didn't know; but that they had six hundred thousand dollars to spend and were going to do it. There is no place or time here for that kind of man.

Speaking of Roosevelt the papers have it that he has been obliged to call off his proposed expedition to France. It is good. I cannot see how a man of this perspicacity could have thought of it in the first place. Surely he must know that this war is like no other, that it is a business of fighting with the old romance left out, that however fine it would have been to lead an army of volunteers to France, such an army would be of little use, untrained, as it would be, against the trained German forces. In these days, as someone has so aptly said, the army at the front is only half the offensive weapon,—the polished spearhead of which the organized nation is the shaft. Roosevelt must realize that he can do his part, the part for which he is fitted, and a great part, by helping to fashion this shaft so that there will be as few knots and crooks in it as possible and that others, who know far more about it than he, will polish up the point.

The favorite topic for the Germans now is of the reported colossal failure of the American War Loan; of the weakness of the American army; of the delay in building American ships; and their failure to get across the ocean. They are spreading this all over Russia. It is preached by her agents from every street corner. I know now why the Russians have been so friendly to us,—it's due more to absence of German propaganda against us than to any superiority over the others of the Allies.

That baseball equipment is proving a life saver. We had a great set-to on the Field of Mars today. Our gyrations drew an enormous crowd of soldiers and civilians and they soon waxed enthusiastic over the game, drawing in so close behind me encased in the catcher's mask, protector, and mitt that a foul tip caught one of them squarely between the eyes; he blinked and laughed, thinking it part of the game I suppose. At a hot moment a voice from out the circle near the plate shouted, "say, where are youse guys from?" It belonged to a Russian who lived in Boston for some years and became an ardent follower of the Braves.[213]

---

[213] WorldAtlas; "The Oldest MLB Teams," https://www.worldatlas.com/articles/mlb-teams-by-date.html. The Boston Braves were a Major League Baseball franchise from 1871 to 1952. The Braves moved to Milwaukee in 1953 and then to Atlanta in 1966. They are one of the oldest continuous baseball franchises in the United States.

(This following entry can be dated to July 8, 1917)

The Root Mission leaves tomorrow. What it has accomplished, no one knows. Even important members of it do not speak with enthusiasm of its work. Perhaps there's not much it could do; but that should have been thought of before. Mr. Root made a few speeches in English which a very, very few understood here; and replies were made politely in Russian which I'm sure hardly one of the Mission understood. Cordial reserve has been prominent on both sides; and as far as the Mission being American in spirit goes, it might just as well have come from Abyssinia. Mr. Root's reputation as a brilliant lawyer for some of the world's greatest corporations preceded him and made the socialists, who are the majority here, shy; as did the names of several others of the Mission, known here only for their connections with trust or vast financial interests. I don't know what the officials who received it, think, but I do know that the vast majority of Russians who were aware of the Mission's presence, regarded it as a body of businessmen here to get information about Russia to aid in her exploitation. And I don't think that is the American spirit.

Parades, parades, parades. When this is over I shall never want to see another. The streets are blocked with them every afternoon. Work seems to have been given up and parading entered into as a profession. Yesterday it was a procession of housemaids which blocked what little traffic there was[,]thousands of them, plodding along through the slush, intoning the mournful Hymn of Freedom. The day before that, it was a parade for students demonstrating for some privilege they wanted and had not had. And previous to that, not more than a week ago I saw one of children parading with their banners for the right to select their own parents! Sounds a bit startling, but it is very true. These were illegitimate children of which are far too many in Russia, and they wished to be allowed to attach themselves to a family of their own selection.

Kerensky's swift rise from a humble socialist lawyer to the Premier of the world's largest nation is already being capitalized. When you walk in the parks and on the main streets you are confronted by hawkers selling his photograph, or a lithograph, or a clay bust poorly done. Pictures of him are put up at auctions whose purpose is to raise money for the Red Cross and the like, and short histories of his short life are sold at a rouble a volume on the corners. What a trick of fate it is that puts him in the position where this is the order of things. I wonder that he has the courage to face it, to accept the stupendous responsibility of it all.

"Count" and Chuck speak of strange doings around their house. They say they are watched, not that they've seen any one keeping track of them, but that the feeling that they are under surveillance now and then arises. Also that various times they have been followed when going from or returning to the house. It can't be that anyone is watching them, because it would be a simple matter to get all the information about them at the bank. This leaves their landlady up for consideration. She's so good to look at that there's bound to be trouble near where she is. She has a very charming manner and is brilliant and educated,—too much so, it would seem for one in her position. She speaks all the languages in Europe from what I can gather.

Some of these members of the Ministry under the Tsar must be worrying a little now. They are to be tried by a public court. Of course the worst of the lot is Soukhomlinoff,[214] the Minister of War under the Tsar, whose incompetence, neglect, or deliberate treachery have been the death of thousands of Russia's best soldiery. Many of the great army scandals are laid at his door,—huge supply trains mysteriously falling into the hands of the Germans, vast stocks of rifles being burned or destroyed by explosion so that, even as late as 1916, Russian regiments have gone to the front with half their number without rifles, sent into attack thus lacking in equipment knowing that they must follow along unarmed until those ahead fell and they could pick up the rifles and continue, and the shell order placed in Japan which was delivered and the shells found to be made to fit German field pieces instead of Russian. In the popular belief he is held for them all.

The correspondents of American newspapers over here are sending much that is not true back to their papers, if one can judge from the copies we get from home. I couldn't understand it until I reflected that snappy editors demand news from them, and in spite of the fact that there are days even in Revolutionary Russia when there is no news, they manufacture some and give the snappy editor what he wants. The poor public, four and five thousand miles away doesn't know the difference. I cut a picture from one of the leading New York papers a few days ago, which I am told on the best of authority is a fake. It depicts graphically a street fight in Petrograd at the moment when the revolutionists have fired upon the peaceful crowd with machine guns. And I am told that the correspondent, having been censored by his paper for not sending

---

[214] Pope and Wheal, "Sukhomlinov, General Vladimir," in *The Dictionary of The First World War*, 457–58; William C. Fuller, *The Foe Within: Fantasies of Treason and the End of Imperial Russia* (Ithaca, NY: Cornell University Press, 2006), 256. ISBN 0801444268. Vladimir Aleksandrovich Sukhomlinov (Russian: Владимир Александрович Сухомлинов) (1848–1926), a general of the Imperial Russian Army, served as the chief of the general staff from 1908 to 1909 and as the minister of war from 1909 to 1915. Nicholas II, who held him responsible for military defeats, dismissed him in June 1915 and placed him under house arrest in early 1916. Released during the March Revolution, he was rearrested in September 1917 and released on May Day 1918. He fled Russia and ended up in Weimar Germany. He lived the remainder of his life in extreme poverty in Berlin, where he was found dead of exposure on a park bench on the morning of February 2, 1926.

good stuff across, paid two soldiers one hundred roubles apiece one fine day to fire a machine gun into the air from the roof of a building on the Nevsky, while he clicked the photograph from the window across the way.

It is pleasant on these "white nights" to walk in the Summer Garden, around the winding paths, through the trees and shrubbery and the statuary. It seems as though all of Russia is there, from the aristocrat down to the lowest Mongolian juggler or beggar. All taking this opportunity to breathe in the warm air, feel the glow of sunshine; the young to play at love and the old to regret that the game is over. For there is lovers walk, and on these magic nights it is a procession of couples, rich man, poor man, student, merchant, officer, and soldier,—the last with his shining faced companion, making short work of a ten kopek cornucopia of sunflower seeds, which they chew incessantly, spitting the husks steadily as they talk. For there is freedom in the air, this is a midsummer night, and they are having their dream.

A gentleman doing business with us today had an interesting explanation of the "why" of the Revolution. In his opinion it was forced by the Tsar's government to afford an excuse for making a separate peace with Germany. In the secret treaties negotiated at the beginning of the war between England, France, and Russia, he claimed there was a clause to the effect that although the Allied countries bound themselves not to make peace without the concurrence of the others, they were released from this obligation if any internal condition arose which threatened the established government. The powers that were, planned to force rioting, disorder, and an attempt at revolution in Petrograd—an attempt which they could put down at will, and make use of this to put in operation that special clause in order that they might negotiate for a separate peace with Germany. He is quite convinced of it. The only flaw in the scheme was the inability of the Tsar's forces to cope with the uprising they had incited. It proved to be their Frankenstein.

It is plausible. Moreover, it explains many of the regulations, economic, and financial enforced as it was said, to safeguard the stability of the country, but which even at the time, were directly contrary to the best established principles of economics and finance. Witness the regulations governing the purchase of exchange, which shackled the import and export trade of the country. And witness the strange shortage of bread at the most critical time before the outbreak, when just before and soon after, there was plenty. The theory has given rise to much discussion in our little group, anyway.

Ever since the rascal's death there have been so many stories of how it occurred that we are at last relieved to know just how Rasputin died. We were told today by a great friend of one of the party that killed him. A few members of the younger set of the nobility decided that Rasputin must be put out of the way for the good of the country. They therefore formed a group of some eight men and worked out a plan. It was decided to poison the villainous monk at a dinner which they would tender him at the house of one of the members. The dinner was prepared, Rasputin invited, and his acceptance received. They obtained the poison, cyanide, and enough of it to kill ten men. Not being familiar with its use, before putting it in the wine, meat and fruit prepared for the dinner, it was tried on a dog belonging to one member of the party,— they being assembled for the affair in his house on the Moika Canal. The animal ate the poisoned meat and almost immediately died. Throwing the body out in the garden to be buried later they place equal quantities of the cyanide in the wine, meat, and fruit, marking the pieces and the bottle so that no member of their little league would be mistaken. At the last minute Rasputin telephoned saying that he could not come. Whether he had become suspicious or not they never knew. Hastily they dispatched a messenger to him with the information that a certain dancer from Moscow of whom he was very fond, would be at the dinner especially to see him. The bait attracted, Rasputin came, and was informed to his great disappointment that the young lady's train had been delayed en route and that she could not attend. He was persuaded to sit down with them and eat. This he did. He first drank a glass of the deadly wine. The others watched in suspense. Nothing happened; it had no effect. The monk then ate a bit of the poisoned meat. Still they watched, furtively and breathlessly. Still no effect. Here, some of the party, and pressed to some degree by the reputation for unworldliness which the monk had, became afraid lest he really should be possessed of spiritual power of some high nature and they be guilty of the attempt to kill a holy man. They were almost ready to give way to their terror, and it was with difficulty that their leader, the young prince restrained them. The education he had received in all the capitals of Europe would not permit him to think this man as being superhuman. Good sense had its reward. It was only delay in the poison taking effect, due, no doubt, to the massive physique of the victim and his tremendous vitality and strength. Rasputin suddenly complained of feeling ill; he arose from the table and staggered to the stairs, fell, and rolled down their length to the floor below, where his great body lay still. The plan was to dispose of the body in the river. Two of them bent down to roll what was left of Rasputin in a blanket when the monk sprang to his feet, and fought them desperately, roaring out their treachery at the top of his mighty voice. The Prince drew a revolver and shot the monk twice; he fell again and lay still. They wrapped the corpse in the blankets and were about to carry it out to the limousine when agents of the police, having heard the shots, came to the house, asking what the shooting had been.

The Prince showed the body of the dead dog in the garden, saying that his pet had gone mad, making it imperative to shoot it. This explanation satisfied the police and they disappeared. The party, with the body in its midst entered the limousine and were driven across the bridge to a concealed spot on the river's edge; not without some disturbance, however, as the victim in the wrappings, again began to struggle, and had to be beaten still with the pistol butt, until there was no more sign of life. At the river edge they clambered out, chopped a hole in the ice, and deposited their burden therein, so that the current swirling below would carry it far out into the Gulf and all that was left of Rasputin would disappear forever.

In the morning, when it was discovered that the monk was missing and it became known to the Empress, she, after recovering from her prostration, immediately ordered all the police out on the search. Days passed before the trail in the snow along the river was found, then the hole in the ice, and finally the frozen corpse itself with stiffen fingers clutched over the edge of the ice, in a last struggle, after two doses of cyanide, two bullets in the chest, and a beating over the head, to prevent being washed out into the gulf. Her Majesty had the body brought to Tsarsky Selo, her residence about twelve miles outside Petrograd, and there interred in a mausoleum awaiting burial after a great state funeral and canonization in the Russian Church. She intended to make a saint of him! Realizing that it would never do to have the degenerate monk transformed into a martyr by royal command, the party again assembled on a night a few weeks later, rumbled out to Tsarsky Selo in a truck, over-powered the guard at the tomb, stole the body, fled to a faraway park and burned it, thus putting an end for good and all to the influence of Rasputin on this earthly sphere. Such is the story we get from divergent sources, and such is the one we are compelled to believe, strange and bizarre as it does seem.

July 3/16. 1917.

I have come to the system of dating the pages of this journal in order that each date may frighten me into writing the next day's events therein. At present I am so far behind that I doubt if I shall ever catch up. Each day I have said to myself; "Now I must take time out and catch up with my journal," but always it has been put off another day. And so it has gone, until today it seems that the only remedy is to start in anew at once and to maintain above all others the firm resolve to write my bit each night.

Today offers much of interest. Week before last I was discouraged with the outlook, due to the activity and unrepressed audacity of the anarchists; last week's news of the initial advance of the Russian army was cheering and things began to lighten a bit. But tonight, the night before the "Loan of Freedom" celebration, the dissensionists are at it once more and the streets are crowded with people, some curious, some for and some against the Provisional Government. This last-mentioned body, although it has lost four of its members by resignation during the day, has assumed a strong hand in affairs and as immediately following the Revolution, one sees machines crowded with armed soldiers, and armed with machine guns touring the streets. Bands of Cossacks are patrolling the streets,—like old time up to now two shots have been heard from the direction of the Nevsky,—what they mean I do not know.

It seems that today has been a bad day for the food suppliers. The shops were said to be bare all day and food of any kind scarce,—a situation similar to that existent just previous to the outbreak of last February. It only shows what an important part food plays in the political peregrinations of man's desire. That government which can ensure the bread supply has man's confidence and support. The worst part of this situation is that the lack of food is blamed to the Provisional Government when in reality it is due to the people's refusal to work to produce food ever since the birth of their so called freedom.

There has just been a great outburst of rifle and machine gun fire from Nevsky-way, accompanied by the usual scurrying of people, automobiles, and barking of dogs. All lights have gone out and there is a great shouting and yelling in the streets. At first Fred and I retired to the sofa but the firing only lasted a few minutes so we again ventured forth to our balcony, making most excellent targets in our white pajamas—but one never thinks of those things in Russia. What is it all about? What do these people really want? Does anyone know; do they know? Some say the soldiers want this government replaced with another,—a Socialistic one; others that the Capitalists—wherever they are must go; others that a printing of all Russia's treaties and agreements will satisfy the mob. But we must wait and see. I'm afraid there will be scant patriotic celebration tomorrow.

July 4/17, 1917.

The shooting last night was serious. It seems that as a sort of counter movement against the "Loan of Freedom" celebration scheduled to begin today, a large body of soldiers from one of the barracks, mostly older men—started a parade. Bearing banners stating their wish to return to the country, their need for bread, and here and there a more radical one reading "Down with the P. G." they made the tour of the streets. Their appearance caused approval amongst the anarchists and Maximalists,— eager to join any group against the present government, and disapproval amongst the more intelligent supporters of the new regime. In addition to this there was the split in the ministry which came about as follows: Dissension grew in the southern province of Ukeraina[215] until that section declared its independence and broke away from Russia proper. To patch up the matter two of the ministers were dispatched post haste with full powers to settle. To do this they had to sign an agreement with the governing body in Ukeraina one clause of which gave the latter the right to secede from Russia if they saw fit. Upon their return to Petrograd the two emissaries found their action very much in disfavor and themselves in a critical position. Other members of the Cabinet stated that if any part of Russia received the right to secede they would resign at once. It was demanded that the action of the two ministers be annulled. The knowledge of this split, with the increasing agitation of the anarchists filled the streets with curious people. Speeches were made, and as usual amongst these people all fully armed, the inevitable extremist fired his gun. Instantly the shooting began. One group of soldiers met another and hostile group on the Nevsky near the City Duma and immediately the attack opened, the assembled crowd getting the full benefit of the bullets. Machine guns ripped from the Duma, and answered from the Admiralty Building, rifles cracked, and people ran, screamed, huddled, and fell.

This morning at the bank reports were conflicting. Only a few had been injured; more had been killed than all through the Revolution of Feb. and March. All the ministry had resigned, including Kerensky, only six ministers had resigned and Kerensky was still in office. Kerensky had returned to Petrograd from the front; he had left Petrograd fifteen minutes ahead of a deputation sent to arrest him. And so forth. At present we do not know; we must wait.

But these things we do know. All through the day parades filed across the Troitsky Bridge bearing white, red, and black flags, soldiers, and anarchists armed, and sailors from Kronstadt, drawn up here by the report of counter-revolution. Desultory shooting has also been the order of the day, and the city has had a really Fourth of July air. Only far more serious. On the main streets shops were smashed and the supplies distributed to those who would take; those things which could not be taken were

---

[215] Serhy Yekelchyk, *Ukraine: Birth of a Modern Nation* (PDF) (New York: Oxford University Press, 2007), Chapter 4. ISBN 978-0-19-530545-6. Rogers refers to Ukraine. The Ukrainian Central Rada declared Ukraine's autonomy on June 23, 1917, and formed a Ukrainian cabinet of ministers. It initially formed part of a federation with the Russian Republic but proclaimed its (short-lived) independence from the Russian Soviet Republic on January 25, 1918.

smashed, automobiles were confiscated, streetcars stopped, and filled with joy riding soldiers. Banks were closed and all business suspended. Every now and then bands of Cossacks were seen making the rounds of the city, walking their horses, with rifles and spears ready for use. They were very quiet, however. On the Millionaya—the street back of the bank, in the garden of P. d. Bark—the Minister of Finance under the Tsar, were laid out the bodies of eight soldiers, victims of the street fighting. In a side street an armored car was stalled, having been deliberately run into by an anarchist motor truck. In the streets lay dead horses, while concealed in courtyards and alleys were the numerous victims of the whole asinine business. Ignorance! What can you do with it. There are only two ways to fight an ignorant mob, beat it with the mailed fist or educate it.

After a scanty dinner at the bank some of us remained there to work as usual on the so-called "night-shift." It was fairly quiet, save for the occasional pop, pop, of rifles in different parts of the city, when suddenly we heard this terrific yelling and thundering of horses' hoofs down the Millionaya. We rushed to the balcony just in time to see a troop of some three hundred Cossacks dash down the street, young officers in the lead, all shouting, brandishing their swords, and hurtling along went their three field guns of three inch calibre. It was a thrilling sight, much like the pictures one sees of the cavalry charge of Napoleon's time. It did not take long for us to decide that if we intended going home at all that night we had better go while the going was good. So we poor dusty bookworms hastily tucked away our cares, locking them in the safe, and set out homeward. Like the political situation the weather too was dark and gloomy and 'twas plain that in a short time, old man "Jupe" Pluvius[216] would have his hand in the mess. This disturbed Fred and me the more because at dinner we had purchased from the cook five pounds of sugar which she happened to get hold of,—purchased it for two roubles a pound and considered ourselves lucky at that. Consider paying fifty cents a pound for sugar! If the rain came and found us out our investment would be ruined, and on our hands we would have only "watered" stock. However we set out up the quay and progressed in good order and undisturbed as far as the Troitsky Bridge and here we found a guard of soldiers. Having just seen the Cossacks fly up the Millionaya and out and on up the quay past the Summer Garden, I figured that I had much rather cut across the Field of Mars (now the Field of Freedom) in the full open space where I could see what was nearby than take a chance on going through the Summer Garden with all its trees and unknowns. So we set out across said field.

---

[216] Jupiter Pluvius, an epithet for the supreme god of the ancient Romans, Jupiter.

Hardly had we traversed more than fifty yards, however,—just enough to get fully out into the open—than rifles began to pop and spit over near the Summer Garden, presumably at the corner of the Fontanka and the quay. A few at first and then a volley. "Whin-n-ne"! went a bullet over our heads, and then volleys of them, like angry bees, buzzed past. On the street we had left people ducked for any kind of cover, doorways, windows, lamp posts, trolley poles, anything that might afford some sort of protection. The huge crowd of interested soldiers gathered out in front of the Pavlovsky barracks broke up like a swarm of ants and scurried for cover within the barracks or behind its great pillars. But Fred and I—alone in the seemingly endless field with our precious bag of sugar! Behind us in the streets all the available shelters were already occupied, and in front nothing but a vast open field—save for one shelter—the temporary shed built beside the great grave of the Revolutionary Victims. A hail of bullets whined over our heads—we ducked and dashed for the Grave—to keep out of the Grave! We must have been a great sight—alone on that vast field sprinting for cover, me with the bag of sugar held out before me as if it were something to run for. The comparatively short distance seemed miles and our time hours,—tho I swear we established new records for the distance. A short distance from our goal and "Crash!" went one of the field guns we had seen hurtle down the Millionaya which sound of course made us let out another notch. We finally landed behind our shelter, finding it already being utilized by a couple of soldiers but there was still plenty of room. Hardly had we arrived there, then across the end of the field we had just vacated we saw a group of horses tear past down the street, so rapidly that I could not see plainly but it seemed as though the riders were leaning low on the horses' backs. Soon the bullets ceased and we crept along behind the wood piles and out into the streets for home. From the other side of the Summer Garden came shots, straggling, around the corner an armored car, its turrets veering and its machine guns ready, a huge red banner streaming from an opening in the front. We hurried down the Panteleymonskaya [Panteleymonovskaya] towards home, quickening our pace with each report. There came heavier cries, Jupiter Pluvius as if scornful of these puny sounds of mankind here below—let loose his heavy artillery and massed his battalions. Just as Fred and I came opposite the residence of our friends "Count" and "Ikke," "Jupe" turned on the shrapnel and the rain came down in a volley,—a regular "curtain of fire" as the war reports say. We took refuge with the two above-mentioned gentlemen, their friend Easterly and their charming—dangerous, landlady until the storm was over, when we betook ourselves home in peace. The rain quite put a stop to all the hostility, and the streets seem all very quiet. No one likes to fight when wet anyway, and I sometimes wonder if a high pressure hose or two as they have in New York wouldn't do more to stop the street fights than all the lead in the country.

July 5/18.

The morning when we emerged from the iron gate at the exit from the Summer Garden a file of motor trucks thundered past—each laden with armed soldiers, then two armored cars with their red banners. "What, at it again" we echoed and hastened our steps. The trucks stopped and the soldiers dismounted at the Troitsky Bridge, and it was plain to see that trouble was expected there.

At the bank we learned from the Russians that as most of the opposition live across the river, all the bridges were to be opened to prevent anyone crossing in an effort to stir up trouble,—hence the guards. We also learned that the horses we had seen returning across the Field of Mars, whose riders we thought were riding low over the horses' necks, to escape the bullets, really bore no riders at all, they being stretched out in the quay after the volley of greeting from the Maximalists barricaded at the corner of the quay and the Litania; also that this barricade had been blown to smithereens by a shot from one of the field pieces as we had surmised. The Cossacks lost ten of their men and some thirty of their horses, and the latter loss angered them more than the first. "We can always get more men, but such horses—never" they say; and grimly resolve to avenge the loss. Later in the morning the bridges swung open and no one could cross from one side to the other; nor were boats allowed to go through them up the river. Rumors were many and varied. The Government was falling, all the ministers had resigned—even Kerensky; the Government was not tottering, it was assuming a firm hand. The police across the bridge—the headquarters of the Leninists and Maximalists—was to be bombarded and cleaned out, soldiers were coming from the front to clean up the city, many soldiers in the city garrisons were going over to the Maximalists and tomorrow would see civil war.

Of course all the shops were closed today save those broken open during the night by the demonstrators, and these were cleaned out at the time—and in consequence we had little or nothing to eat. Our noonday meal consisted of thin soup, a chunk of black bread apiece and a glass of tea—without sugar. For dinner this evening more was in order and in addition to this we had some sort of bird, roast duck, Bill Welsh claimed, but it had the resisting powers of ostrich. After dinner we sneaked home while the sneaking was good.

6/19 July.

We got up bright and early this morning in order to make sure of getting to the bank, only to find our way thru the Summer Garden blocked by guards at the fence corner where we usually climb over for the sake of the shortcut and at the gate. Inside, parked around amongst the trees we could see troops of Cossacks and their horses. That meant that trouble was expected nearby. We tried the Field of Mars, only to find that too guarded by the Cossack with his pistol, sword, rifle and spear; beyond at the entrance to the bridge we could see a machine gun squad. It was to be an interesting day. We managed to make our way around the field and finally arrived at the bank. Jacob, our doorman, had been conversing with some of the Cossack guards and he fairly bubbled over with news. The city was under martial law. The Provisional Government, the Council of Soldiers and Workmen's Deputies, and the third group in the fuss, whatever they are, agreed to turn the affair over to the military commander of the city, who is to have complete author-ity to do as he sees fit to quell disturbances in the streets. The loyal troops have taken the Lenin palace [Kschessinskaya Mansion] and all eyes are now on the Fortress of Peter and Paul. Thither the Maximalists retreated and were holding out. The place was surrounded by troops and covered by the troop's field gun, on the other hand the Maximalists had complete control of the guns of the Fortress and threatened to bombard back were they attacked. Moreover, at the mouth of the river some distance out from the city lay one of the gunboats manned by the sailors from Kronstadt who threaten to bombard also as soon as the Government troops start. But the Government says that being the case, it has aeroplanes with which it will in turn bombard the gunboat. So there you are.

Guards were at all the corners of the quay warning people from that section, and the bridges were all closed to permit the movement of troops and armored cars to the other side. From the fortress came not a sound or sign of life, save the stirring now and then of the ragged faded flag on its staff at the corners—there since the Revolution. We had not been long at work,—no customers of course, with all the streets blocked—when a troop of soldiers on portable bicycles came silently by. We went out on the balcony to watch them, and their number seemed endless. They were from the front and had come to Petrograd to help put down what they heard was a counter-revolution. That they were seasoned troops was plain from their thin bronzed faces, the worn look of their equipment,—and the very completeness of this last, all there and ready down to the camp kitchens already steaming and the oxcarts with hay for the horses. Slowly and in magnificent order, keeping the front wheels of their cycles in line, they rolled across the bridge and in a methodical business-like way, made ready for the siege. Their arrival must have made some impression on those within the fortress for after lunch we heard that they had met the mediating committee sent by the Provisional Government and had given in. And so the remainder of the day went quietly. We heard that these soldiers were good and sore and really meant business, as upon their arrival in the city, at the station where they should have been met by bands and a cheering populace they were greeted by the rip of machine guns concealed by the Leninists on the roofs of neighboring buildings. Many of their number were wounded and killed.

7/20 July.

This afternoon I went out for a little stroll before dinner and upon trying to go through the Winter Palace Square found the place a veritable arsenal. Here are armored cars, motor trucks lined up and thousands of troops to fill them, Cossacks, machine guns, artillery, and every sort of war apparatus imaginable. It is the headquarters of the military commander. All the telephones have been confiscated and only military messages are transmitted. As soon as any trouble starts in one part of the city, the guards of that district phone into headquarters. Immediately an armored car, motor trucks full of soldiers, and the troop of Cossacks set out for the spot of irritation. So it goes. The system seemed to be working splendidly in the city once more going about its way.

After dinner some of us stayed down to put the books in shape and about ten o'clock Mr. Stevens came up and invited us down to his apartment to celebrate the victory of the P. G. by testing some Russian wine from the Crimea, which he had been fortunate enough to obtain. Of course we all accepted and the wine proved so good that the affair turned out to be more than a test and more than the test bottle was opened. We sat around and talked until about twelve when the movement started to go home. Hardly had we got our coats and hats however then, from across the river came the telltale crack! Crack, then R-rrip! of the machine guns and they were at it again. For quite a while we peered out of the windows trying to make out where it was, but found our decision was quite a mistake when we went outside and crept along the side of the building to the corner. It came from down the quay, seemingly from the Palace Bridge and the Bourse. The firing was the heaviest and most sustained I have ever heard and the steadiness with which the machine guns spit showed that experienced hands were manipulating them. All the lights went out in that section and from round the corner we could see the spurts of flame break out in the darkness. To our little group were added a couple of students and girls, one young chap who knew all about the situation and insisted upon explaining it to us. Our "hot dope" expert G----[217] was with us—in the country a month—but nevertheless an authority on the social and political life of Russia (!)—and he and the Russian had a great time expounding their conflicting theories in English and Russian respectively. We received reinforcements in the way of some curious soldiers from the barracks behind us, and an old fellow on a bicycle who came tearing out of the night, hopped off to mop his face and tell us there was fighting going on, hopped on again to go pedaling away muttering "Thank gods" over something. A motor truck came lumbering through the darkness and having in mind the truckloads of soldiers that rode around the city to disperse crowds during the day someone suggested that they might let fly a volley at us to disperse our little group. The suggestion was as good as the volley and some sped down the street, our expert on Russia in the lead. When the empty truck trundled by and nothing happened G came back saying that he only went after his coat which he had left in Mr. Stevens' apartment. Someone remarked that the coat must have been made of gold plate the way he went after it.

The steady firing kept up for a few minutes more and then died down to a few stray pops; so we bid each other a "calm night"[218] as the Russians say and went our respective ways.

I wonder what it all means, I thought the affair was over. What do these people hope to accomplish by their shooting one another? What good can it do? Can't they see that in all this Germany rejoices, and her agents progress?

8/21 July 1917.

Well, this morning we found out what all the firing was about. The first machine gun squad of the Petrograd garrison, known to be in majority of "Bolshevists" tendency, was ordered to disband. This it refused to do and in the night opened fire on the Government troops stationed in the Palace Square. After a brilliant but somewhat futile exchange of shots they had been forced to flee and some of their guns were taken. This morning, the Cossacks visited the barracks en masse and it

---

[217] *Number Eight*, The National City Bank of New York, May 1917, 50. Possibly J.A. Gregoor, a sub-accountant, who set sail for Petrograd on May 12, 1917.
[218] Russian: Спокойной ночи.

was not long before a parade came past our building—a strange parade. It consisted of the Cossacks and a band, followed by the First Machine Gun regiment sans shoulder straps, guns, swords, and honor. Behind them, trundled carts laden with their arms, machine guns and all! During the day two or three other regiments were broken up in the same manner—the men sent away, either to the front, other regiments, or back to the country.

All day long they have been arresting Leninites, bringing [them] before the authorities in some cases imprisoning them and in others releasing them, or sending them out of the country. It is said that the regular soldiers have difficulty in restraining the Cossacks who are fuming over the loss of their men and horses. They say that for every one of their number lost, and they count the horses as men, twenty "Bolsheviki" must hang! Many of the latter's meeting places have been broken up, with the discovery of all kinds of guns, knives, poisons and bombs. The Council of Soldiers and Workmen's Deputies is agreeing to these arrests and has even formed a committee to investigate Lenin, to find out whether or not he is a German agent! Naïve!

This evening I walked up the Nevsky and found the inevitable groups in the streets arguing over this and that. At the newspaper offices excited groups were reading the bulletins which told of the valiant Russian soldiers evacuating their trenches without firing a shot and permitting the Germans to occupy them. The German agents are busy there too. Oh these pitifully ignorant moujiks, they are so inherently good, but so misled. Although he has but returned Kerensky with his indomitable energy is off for the front again. He seems to be the only man in Russia able to cope with the situation; and he goes on his iron will, as it is well known that he is affected with a dangerous constitutional disease. He certainly is to be admired.

9/22 July

Sunday again. I walked through the Summer Garden in the morning and on my way was surprised to see an American flag hung in the trees over a pathway. It gave a thrill, which was not even dimmed by the sordid fact that the Russians were using it merely to advertise an "Americansky Auction" to be held there during the afternoon! During the day I paid my Rs. 25 for two meals at the "Europe," scanty ones at that, with soup, meat and potatoes and a dessert. Before the war such would have cost five at the most. The papers confirmed the Russians abandoned their trenches, saying that these things were done wholly against the orders of the leaders. When these last orders were issued to fight the soldiers called a mutiny to decide whether the orders should be carried out or not. The final decision was not. These things would be ridiculous, even funny, were it not that they prolong this terrible struggle.

10/23 July.

We were greeted this morning with the news that the Russians are retreating all along the line, and rapidly. Galitch,[219] captured by the troops of the 18th of June [July 1 on the Gregorian calendar] with 40,000 prisoners and eighty guns, has been recaptured by the Germans with more prisoners and over a hundred guns. There is of course much talk about it. The agitators are already blaming Kerensky saying that the advance never should have been made in the first place. It's now reported that Germany, now that Russia has turned down her peace offers intends to get her out of the way by force of arms and plans a great offensive. If true they will no doubt win a lot, also they will lose for I think nothing better could be done to awaken these dolts than a good scare of defeat and the prospect of years of work of 24 hours per day in a German mine. With that prospect in view, they might fight.

The Committee of the Council of Soldiers and Workmen's Deputies now admits that it is forced to believe that Lenin is a German agitator. Important documents were found at his residence and it was disclosed that he has an account of some two million roubles in one of the Russian banks! They passed the resolution to permit the P.G. to arrest him, but of course, when the squad arrived, he had flown to Finland. And they say that two days ago he was captured and released because this Council had no evidence that he was pro-German!

July 11/24, 1917.

Very little news today. The newspapers were late in coming out and when they did I failed to hear what has happened. No doubt the army is still in retreat.

I had a bad day today. Got in wrong twice with the manager; once this morning when he called me down for writing a "perfectly silly letter"—it was as usual a letter evading some law and I didn't do it very artistically—and again when I went out to attend a meeting at the American Hospital and he suddenly happened to want some letters I was keeping in my files. The funny part of it all is that it does not bother me

---

[219] Galitch, or Halych (Russian and Ukrainian: Га́лич) is a historic city on the Dniester River in western Ukraine. The city gave its name to the Principality of Halych, the historic province of Galicia. Rogers' reference is to the Russian army offensive in Galicia.

in the least. Nothing does now, except this war and the thoughts of it. Beside the consideration of the gigantic evil striding across the world's horizon everything else is too mundane to bother about.

At the American Hospital I received two different bits of advice to leave Russia. One from a comparative newcomer who prophesied no food during the winter and difficult times ahead, and the second from an inhabitant of some eighteen odd years who remarked that one is soon "flattened out" here by the great steamroller of materialism. Cheerful!

12/25 July.

Nothing much of interest or importance today. At the bank the same old round of mundane affairs; and in Russia the same circle of hopes and fears. The news from the army is about the same, some parts of it willfully retreating without any pressure from the enemy, and other parts starting on the offensive. It is said that all the advantage gained by the victory of the 18th of June has been re-gained by the enemy because of the refusal of the Russians to fight.

13/26 July.

It is said that on Saturday there will be a big funeral in honor of the Cossacks killed in the last street fighting. If so there will be trouble as sure as the devil. Why do these people openly invite trouble? They might know that to hold such a parade will either draw the fire of the "Bolsheviks" or bring from them the demand that they be allowed to have a parade in honor of their dead; and if this is granted, there surely will be trouble.

14/27.

I forgot to mention in Tuesday's notes that three new men arrived from the States to take up their work in the bank. About the first remark made when we saw them was, "How healthy they look!" They certainly were refreshing to look at, with their clear faces, and new clothes, refreshing 'till I considered my own appearance, with shoes worn over, trousers in need of press, frayed collar, and tired expression. I looked myself over and thought—well, what did I think?

There's no more news about the parade tomorrow except that it is sure to be. There is the rumor also that the "Bolsheviks" say they will start another uprising on the 18th because the last one didn't come out the way they wanted it to.

The funeral procession is to start from the square before St. Isaacs Cathedral, to proceed down the Morskaya and up the Nevsky. I have an appointment with a dentist on the Morskaya so I shall arrange to see the procession also.

15/28 July.

The funeral procession was to start at ten in the morning but by twenty minutes past one—the time the dentist finished with me—preparations were still going on around the cathedral. I lingered down the Morskaya interested in the art shop windows until the affair started. An enormous crowd filled the street and pressed back by the militia men it became a solid mass on the sidewalks. From every window in the enfilading buildings hung curious faces, and amidst a strange silence the people awaited the procession. It came. First a squad of Cossacks, black pennants fluttering at their pikes, stepping their horses slowly down the street, alert, restless, an advance guard for those that followed; then the floral offerings, magnificent in their variety, and gorgeous in their color, each piece borne by other Cossacks on foot, nurses, or soldiers; after them the standard bearers from the cathedral, with their silken and gold banners, golden and silver crosses, bejeweled and glittering ikons, then the choir—of little boys, about two hundred of them followed by the bass voices,—all in heavy blue robes.—Here an incident happened that well shows what a tension the crowd was under. Far down the street the crowd suddenly surged up against the buildings, a woman screamed piercingly and pandemonium broke loose. Around me the people struggled for the shelter of a door, a window, the corner,—anything that would give shelter, shrieking, fighting and trampling. I struggled too, but it was useless—impossible to move. An old lady next to me had her market basket torn from her arm and its contents smashed on the sidewalk. In trying to reach the corner I thought to myself, "Good night, some madman has thrown a bomb." Then as nothing happened, good sense returned and brought the people back with it. The choirboys had completely disappeared, vanished, blue robes and all, like a bursting soap bubble. Gradually, the choir masters collected them again; from windowsills, doorways, poles and every conceivable kind of shelter they came running back, blue satin robe held high in hand, to rejoin the flock. The men's voices took up the song once more, and the boys joined in. The procession reformed itself, and continued on its way. There came the dignitaries of the church, with robes of gold and silver thread, crowns of jewels, and staffs of ebony, and after them the eight coffins, on separate carriages—the customary silver hearse used in Russia; behind each coffin alone and unguided, walked the dead Cossack's horse, carrying all the equipment, a part of the saddened group of family and friends that followed to the grave!

Then came the ministers of the Provisional Government, Kerensky foremost and alone in a plain uniform, walking slowly; he seemed years older than his pictures, and after him the others of the ministry. People wanted to cheer, some did wave their hats, at this man carrying the fate of Russia on his shoulders, walking there so fearless of having it snatched away with his life by some extremist's folly. After came troop upon troop of Cossacks, the horses stepping proudly to the many bands, each at the head of another troop, or a squad of marines, or soldiers. As far as the eye could see down the Morskaya and out across the square were soldiers and bayonets, pennons and banners. I watched it for an hour and then came away, a bit mystified as to why such a show should be. And then it dawned upon me that the government had shown both its nerve and strength to the people. It was a test which seems to have been well passed.

16/29.

While walking down the Nevsky for my usual twelve rouble Sunday lunch at the Hotel Europe today the many dilapidated decorations put up around the banks caught my eye. Originally intended to advertise the Russian Freedom Loan they now advertise only the attempt at counter-revolution or the uprising of the "Bolsheviks." On the 3rd, 4th, & 5th of July instead of machines loaded with people touring the city selling Freedom Loan Bonds we had machines-loads of soldiers and Maximalists shooting at each other. Instead of the booths and platforms being used as sales centers for the Bonds they were used as refuges and shelters from the bullets of armed bands. And so they stand yet, faded, bedraggled, and torn, roughly used by the rush of events.

17/30 July.

This morning on our way to work we were confounded by the sight of the squad of women soldiers drilling in the enclosure around their barracks. Imagine a dinosaur striding up the street to meet you in the early morning and you will evince some of the surprise we did at the sight of these women. All in uniform, with hair closely clipped, and handling the rifles like veterans they went through all the evolutions of the soldier. A half amused, half chagrined crowd of men soldiers hung around the iron fence watching. They were evidently perplexed. If this were only intended as a demonstration to shame the men deserters then it would have been done in the open streets; and the soldiers would have teased and laughed the women away; but to see them going at it in the seclusion of their own barracks yard in such quiet sincerity, did lance silent ridicule at the men, and it was evidently felt from their sheepish grins. It is said that there is already one battalion of women at the front which has given a good account of itself under fire. "Sic transit gloria mascula."[220]

18/31 July.

When it comes to recording the daily events I seem to fail completely for I rarely learn what has really happened until three or four days after. A week or so ago the whole ministry resigned—leaving Kerensky standing in office alone, by common consent endowed with the power to select a new Cabinet, his Cabinet. Thus does the stern eye of necessity glance over the rank and file of seekers for a place in the sun, weigh them, and pick the true from the dross. Worth will be recognized. And Kerensky, who before the war was at best only prominent within his own party as an energetic and forceful lawyer now finds himself alone in the fierce light of history speaking and acting for Russia, as Ribot, Lloyd George, and Wilson[221] speak and act for France, England and America.

As in the others the outstanding characteristic in Kerensky is courage, a dominating, magnetic courage, which converts all dissension.

It is an absolute lack of fear, both physical and moral, including absence of that most destructive form—selfishness. Here is a man who strides into the midst of mutinying soldiers, and by sheer courage and will dominates them, throws their cowardice in their faces and comes away with their applause ringing in his ears; who walks in the full view and alone in a procession thru the streets where only a week before assassins had sworn to kill him. Surely it is evident that the force behind this personality is courage. To see one's way, and follow it unflinchingly is the secret of life. So have done all great men.

[220] "Thus passes masculine (or male) glory," a word play on the famous Latin phrase "sic transit gloria mundi" (thus passes worldly glory).
[221] Alexandre-Felix-Joseph Ribot, four-time French prime minister; David Lloyd George, prime minister of Great Britain; Woodrow Wilson, president of the United States. All were in office in 1917.

19/1 August.

Things seem better today. News from the front has it that although the Russian troops are still falling back in many places, they are doing so in good order and to selected positions. The death penalty has been reestablished in the army and deserters are to be shot. The Roumanians seem to be advancing in great style and it may be that their success will pique the Russians. It is already being felt here now—this feeling that the Allies think Russia has failed them in a critical period, and it may elicit a determination where other incentives failed.

The last week has been filled with discouraging reports,—the entire Russian army in demoralized retreat, the Germans massing before Riga, the treachery of Finland, the scarcity of food, and epidemics; but I think all these are more to frighten the people into united action than anything else. Little is heard from the Government; but I have a feeling that it is strengthening its hand quietly. It is announced that the borders will be closed to new arrivals and to departures,—which will enable the Government to stop undesirables from entering and to capture undesirables upon their attempting to leave. We are also informed that the population of the city is to be decreased by about 600,000 persons in an effort to alleviate the food situation. Many factories will be moved and regiments which are not needed for the protection of the city. In this way too, the authorities can remove many agitators.

We read today that our friend Lenin has left Stockholm for Germany with some of his Stockholm friends. His Russian friends are strangely silent.

20/2 August

And now the Duma, or a small part of it, steps forward claiming that it has entered the political field in order to save Russia. That is the cry of all parties today—to save Russia. And each new party that steps into the imbroglio on that plea is too blind to see that it only augments the confusion and so does its part towards ruining Russia. But it must be admitted that the Duma has authority to act as it does. A fairly representative body gathered together from all parts of Russia by popular election, its words should carry more weight than those of a wholly unrepresentative, self-elected body such as the Council of Soldiers and Workmen's Deputies. It is this latter body against which the Duma takes its stand, saying that it is wholly self-constituted, self-selected, unrepresentative—save of one small class—and demanding its immediate dissolution. In fiery speeches its acts are condemned, even to the point of treachery, and some members of the Council are even accused of being German spies. "It is a singular fact," says the Duma, "that of a committee of eighteen appointed by the Council to work with (?) the P.G., only four of that number proceed under their own names; it is still more singular," it goes on to say, "that of these others some ten should have names of German origin as their real names." Nor does the P.G.—the ministerial body escape censure. It is accused of not assuming a strong enough hand, of giving in to the socialists, and of putting too blind a faith in Kerensky. This latter individual, after all, they say, has done nothing but speak when action was needed, although it is true he incited the army to advance when not prepared. For all of which it had to pay dearly later. The Duma demands the removal from the ministry of some of the socialist members, or the removal of the present non-socialists in order that stronger anti-socialists may be put in to combat the efforts of socialism. All this, says the Duma, because in this tragic hour Russia's steps must not be guided by one small party. "How can we be calm," say they, "when we find an ignoramus occupying the post of minister of agriculture? The country is near famine now and unless the most energetic and efficient measures are taken famine will grip us; then, the very social-ists themselves will rise, decry the disaster as the work of the bourgeoisie, throw the blame on the Government and incite a hungry, maddened people to counter-revolu-tion; and there we shall have deeds that will make those of Rasputin, Steurmer, and Protopopoff seem mild by comparison."

Meanwhile the P.G. seems to be assuming a firmer grasp on the rudder. It is announced that a Cossack general will be commander of the district, that General Brusiloff will have the task of enforcing iron discipline in the state; each day sees squads of arrests being led to prison, or to the stations for deportation, and the send-ing of old battalions to the front with the arrival of new ones here.

Today we learned of what happened to the "Battalion of Death" during the last advance. This battalion formed of soldiers and officers who sworn purpose is to advance and die rather than retreat, had assigned to it the task of taking two lines of trenches. It took four lines and endeavoring to hold them sent to the rear for rein-forcements. Instead of granting these, the lines in their rear, under the influence of the pro-German agitators opened fire on the Battalion; there, finding themselves between two fires, tried to regain their first position, only doing so under terrible loss. Only eighteen of the whole regiment escaped without injury. Vivre Socialisme! There's brotherly love for you.

Oh these socialistic ostriches drive me to the point of exasperation. Here they are talking, talking, always talking about brotherly love and equality, about the only lasting peace being one made by the social democrats of the world—which all may be true, but do they hear any response from Germany, are the German socialists talking of such things, are they laying down their arms and refusing to fight. You can bet not, the German socialists will protect himself first and argue afterward, and he continues to talk peace from the belching barrel of a rifle. No one tells the socialists that they cannot make the peace they want, but they do tell them that such a peace cannot be concluded with the present German government and this very important fact of the present German government they quite overlook. They desire to come to an agreement with it in spite of the fact that Germany has openly declared that in times of necessity her agreements mean nothing. Don't these socialists understand that they can only conclude peace with representatives of their own people in Germany, and not with them until they are in power there. And at the present stage of the game socialists are conspicuous by their silence in Germany.

21/3 August.

It is rumored today that the remaining three of the original ministry will resign, thus bringing about the complete downfall of the P.G. Of course it all centers around Kerensky. This man, given the permission to go his way and organize a new government of his own has not succeeded in bringing the opposing parties together. Milyukoff and his Cadets [Kadets], whom everyone thought to be down and out, have arisen again, saying that they will not join in the Government until certain of the socialist ministers resign and certain of their laws are repealed. Although the most notoriously incompetent of the socialists, Tchernov,[222] has resigned, the Cadets demand more and are still obdurate. A union seems impossible. What will happen, no one knows.

22/4 August.

From all along the front we hear of the Russian troops retreating under the pressure from the enemy. It seems that now that the wheat is ready for harvest in the southern

---

[222] Wikipedia, "Viktor Chernov," last modified March 16, 2021, 19:37 (UTC), https://en.wikipedia.org/wiki/Viktor_Chernov. Viktor Mikhailovich Chernov (Russian: Ви́ктор Миха́йлович Черно́в) (1873–1952) was a Russian revolutionary and one of the founders of the Russian Socialist-Revolutionary Party. Following the March Revolution, Chernov was agriculture minister in the provisional government. Later, he was chairman of the Russian Constituent Assembly. After the Bolshevik Revolution, he fled to Europe and then the United States.

fields the Germans are starting a drive to obtain it, which will no doubt do. Not bad at all, to have the Russians do all the plowing, planting, and nursing, and then when ready for harvest, have the Germans step in and harvest it. "Our good German brothers," say the Russian ignoramuses. We hear that Kiev is being evacuated, so near are the enemy forces, and that already the Germans have captured hundreds of new locomotives and cars, with which to facilitate the coming advance. We also hear that General Erdeli has been murdered by some soldiers, whom he tried to stop from deserting; shot in the back. General Brusiloff has been arrested and is now at the disposal of the P. G. as well as another commander, Gen. Gurko. The last two ministers, Tereschenko and Kerensky resigned, but their resignations were not accepted (who they resign to, I can't figure out).

It is said that the English Government has placed at the disposal of the P.G. here some half a billion Finnish marks, giving the P.G. financial control over Finland, on the condition that Russia will assume a firm hand over that traitorous province. The firm hand seems to have clenched, for the Finnish Diet has been dissolved by order of the P.G. And so it goes, cowardice here, murder there, treachery on this hand, and bribery on that,—in fact a general breakdown of all the stiffening forces which go to make a country strong, right minded, and progressive. All those forces which tended to keep men in the beaten path have been disrupted and the whole social and governmental structure has fallen like a mere scaffolding under the carpenter's hammer. And before new forces can grow, new practices arise, Russia has a long hard way to go, deep down thru the lowest shambles, and a weary climb to the way again, alone, unaided and pitied.

23/5 August.

It being Sunday, I slept late as usual and when finally I did get up to find it a beautiful day, I regretted that I had not done so earlier in order that I might have gone out to Pavlovsk or Peterhoff. However, I puttered around a bit with a story which is going along somewhat slowly,—this until time for lunch when I made my way to Phillipoff's.[223] Here I purchased a copy of "L'Entente" the French newspaper and settled down to enjoy the lunch and the news in comfort. I've taken to Phillipoff's for meals, not so much on account of the expense of eating at the Hotel Europe as

---

[223] Phillipoff's, or Fillipov's Café was a popular meeting place for St. Petersburg's intelligentsia, located on 45 Nevsky Prospekt.

because of the positively deteriorated quality of the food they serve one in said hostelry. It is actual burglary to sell such stuff. For instance a plate of thin soup costs two roubles fifty, or three roubles, a bit of fish four roubles, one veal cutlet and a few potatoes never less than five roubles, a baked tomato or some green peas (—very, very green—arsenic) three roubles, and a dessert of compote or strawberries three roubles. Before one gets through fifteen or eighteen roubles have vanished, and one's hunger is only teased. So I've tried Phil's and seem to do much better.[224]

By the paper I see that poor Kerensky having conferred and labored practically all day and all night is unable to form the cabinet he wishes. He therefore calls a most important conference to the People's Palace—the former Winter Palace—and stating his present predicament, hands in his resignation. This causes profound surprise and concern among the different parties, who after Kerensky's departure for a rest in Finland, confer far into the night. Although they cannot agree as to party principles they are all agreed—even old Milyukoff and his cadets—who have kicked up a good deal of this last fracas—they are all agreed that the time is one calling for united action, for the thrusting aside of party differences, and for unity as to some means to preserve stable government in Russia. It is therefore agreed not to accept Kerensky's resignation—inasmuch as it was addressed to the P.G. and he was its last standing member—to recall him at once, and invest him with the power to select his own cabinet composed of men who should not be responsible to any political parties, but to their own consciences and to the people.

With this encouraging news in my mind I wandered out and down to the Europe with the intention of looking over some of the French and English papers,—and sometimes the Christian Science Herald or the Brooklyn Daily Eagle—, but the reading room was closed, so that pleasure was denied. I therefore came home and took a much needed nap, before doing some more writing. In the evening, after supper, I read an act of "Hamlet" and went to bed.

---

[224] Pinfold, *Petrograd 1917: Witnesses to the Russian Revolution,* 182. Leighton Rogers was not the only one complaining. On July 29, 1917, British forestry expert Edward Stebbing (who was sent by the British government to northern Russia to assess its potential as a source for timber for the Allied war effort) disdainfully remarked, "At the Hotel Europe, where they did you *en prince* in the old days, in this respect there is a great change. The waiters have imbibed the revolutionary spirit and their service for a first-class hotel, as this used to be, is beneath contempt."

24/6 August.

News comes from home that Lester[225] is in Washington, from whence he will be dispatched abroad at an early moment. This was written in June, so I have no doubt that he is now in France. This brings the war into my home, about as close as it can come. Mother seems worried, and perhaps rightly so, but again it should not be so. It is axiom one in this life that we must die; and the problem is not to put this off as long as possible but to defer it until one can die well. Man's task is to live well, and die well. Besides these, all other considerations fade into nothingness. Rarely have there been such opportunities for doing this. Once in many centuries there come times like the present—when the world is presented with so huge a problem that men can disregard the ways and means of living, the petty cares, toils, worries, and pleasures that characterize the routine, can disregard these as absolutely of no consequence, and plunge his tiny strength into the struggle confident that in so doing he is living to the utmost. And if he die in so doing, confident that he dies in doing the utmost good. Such times are rare; such times are opportunities; such a time is the present.

The war has long ago got by the stage where it is a struggle between rulers for this and that piece of land, or for the assertion of this or that control; it has come to a struggle between two conceptions of living, both of which cannot exist side-by-side. It is a question of whether the few shall rule the many, or the many themselves, whether might makes right, or right makes might, whether the strong are so in order to crush the weak, or in order to serve the weak. With the issue so defined there can be no conciliation, no arbitration, no agreement. There must be a complete, definite, final decision. Let us have it and speedily. Placed in the realm of the ideal, the struggle thus affects each man. It is for him to take his side and join it with all his power. It matters little, how, when, or where he does this as long as the effort is sincere. If he survive it, his is the joy of seeing right sustained; if he die, in that final magnificent moment, his is the realization of having made the supreme sacrifice.

---

[225] Lester Brooks Rogers (1884–1963). Leighton's older brother served as a surgeon doctor in the US Army and achieved the rank of major.

25/7 August.

Today we learn that General Erdeli[226] is quite alive and active, thus refuting the rumor of his being treacherously shot in the back by his own men. Gen. Gurko,[227] who was arrested last Saturday is charged with having written a letter to the Tsar assuring the latter of his allegiance to the old regime. The general, for this inadvertency is now confined in the Fortress of Peter and Paul in convicts uniform. Where Monday there was but one minister, Kerensky, today there are fifteen and three sub-ministers. Kerensky seems to have selected his cabinet from among all the parties in an effort to select as representative a body as possible. His choices are generally endorsed, without enthusiasm, however, by all the newspapers save one,—the widely read "новое время" ["Novoye Vremya" or "New Times"] which alights upon the appointment of чернов [Chernov] as minister of agriculture with hawk-like ruthlessness. Чернов is accused of being an internationalist, one who puts international socialism above patriotism, and therefore not a safe man to have near the helm when Russia's fate is at stake.

This afternoon the regiment in the barracks behind us was assembled out on the Field of Mars and informed that in view of its traitorous actions during the trouble of July 3 and fourth it was to be disbanded. Whereupon all the arms were taken away, the shoulder straps of the men torn off and the regiment marched away in small detachments under guard to be sent to the first line at the front, scattered among different regiments. We are informed that the same thing is being done at the front with the rebellious troops.

26/8 August.

Today the Liberty Loan campaign so rudely interrupted last July by the Maximalist outbreak was reopened. All day long motor trucks, festooned with green, red flags, and brilliant posters have been touring the streets taking subscription to the Loan;

---

[226] Wikipedia, "Erdeli, Ivan Georgevich" (in Russian), last modified April 16, 2021, 10:51 (UTC), https://ru.wikipedia.org/wiki/Эрдели,_Иван_Георгиевич. (Russian: Иван Георгиевич Эрдели) (1870–1939), Russian general of cavalry in World War I and the Russian Civil War. He emigrated to France in 1920.

[227] Wikipedia, "Vasily Gurko," last modified January 25, 2021, 19:35 (UTC), https://en.wikipedia.org/wiki/Vasily_Gurko. Vassily Gurko (Russian: Василий Иосифович Ромейко-Гурко) (1864–1937) served in the Imperial Russian Army beginning in 1892. He was army chief of staff from October 1916 to March 1917 and then commander-in-chief of the Western armies until June. In September 1917, he was exiled to Great Britain for expressing support for the monarchy.

booths have been erected at every convenient corner and hawkers loudly proclaim the necessity for purchasing a Loan of Freedom Bond. Girls in costumes accost one on the sidewalks and press the sale, and even the Boy Scouts, conspicuous in their bright yellow neck piece take your subscription. Crowds seem to have gathered round the machines and booths, whether to buy or only to look on I cannot say, but the lists I saw at some of the booths were generously long. It is not a patriotic crowd, nor an enthusiastic one, things seem to be going in the typical Russian lackadaisical manner with talk substituted for action. What these people need is a Zeppelin raid, an advance on the city, or a few bomb plots. With such they might spur themselves into action. On the other hand perhaps not; at times they seem to me as if exhausted, tired, impervious to it all. That I can understand.

27/9 August

Not much news today, except that yesterday the Maximalists held a grand convention, which few people knew anything about. At their meeting, Lenine [sic] and his pals, now on their way to Switzerland and Germany were elected honorary members! Otherwise from this farcical bit of ostentation the convention was quite mundane. Everyone seems to have forgotten about the Maximalists. So short is the life of an extremist. He burns himself out.

The Freedom Loan sales are still going on, the floats, decorated auto trucks, sidewalk vendors in costume, all as energetic as yesterday. The sales, they report, are very good, and so far the campaign has been a huge success.

28/10 August.

The new government, in spite of the criticism its birth has aroused from all sides— in itself a fair testimonial to its impartiality—seems to be attacking its problems with energy. Undoubtedly one of the most serious problems confronting the army is that of desertion. During the few months immediately following the climax of the Revolution I was informed by a military man that of every company sent from Petrograd to the front, only about twenty percent reached their destination, the others deserting—dropping off here and there to disappear from army service. Only twenty percent. Then, of course, during all this propaganda work carried on among the troops at the front, many, many more were influenced to leave the service. By way of interest it might here be added that in some of the captured German trenches were found printed instructions in hand bill form for distribution to all German soldiers as to how to go about the fraternizing with the Russian soldiers. The topics which they were to drill into the Russian soldiers' mind were printed thereon. They were: 1. That Germany was fighting a defensive war. 2. That England and France began the war and deceived Russia into it. 3. That the Germans wished peace, and were it not for England there would be peace.

There were others but I have forgotten them; these are enough however to show how sincere this fraternizing is.

It is not difficult to understand the delusion which encompasses the minds of these deserters. They have been at this thing for three years, and they are tired; tired of serving a country which for those years has deceived them. The Germans are not such bad fellows after all, and anyway why can't we all be brothers instead of enemies. Why should we kill each other, just because our officers tell us to? It is the simplicity, the childlike trustfulness of these peasants that makes them give way. It is not that they are cowards, but that they are ignorant. Ignorance is not to be damned and punished, it is to be pitied and alleviated.

I said that the government was setting out upon an energetic career. They are treating this vast problem of desertion with an iron hand. Every day sees processions of arrests filing through the streets under heavy guard, and these poor deluded fools are returned to the first line trenches. Today one of the large cafés was surrounded by troops and the passport and papers of every person therein was scrutinized by the officers. All soldiers not having good reason for being away from the front were arrested. A good many young officers were found, some of them even wearers of the St. George's Cross. They stated that their men had held meetings and voted that they should no longer be in command, notifying them at the same time that they must leave the army. Thus any officer, of certain regiments, who happened to have aroused resentment in some of these peasants' hearts, were put out under threat of death, and some popular friend from the ranks who wouldn't demand discipline, elected in his place. Thus it was with these officers in the café, and there are hundreds in the city in the same predicament.

29/11 August (no entry)

30/12 August

Sunday today and I wanted nothing more than to do nothing but follow my own whims and fancies all day long. But early in the week in a rush moment I had promised "Doc" Long to go out to his Y.M.C.A. athletic field and help him with a track meet some of his boys were holding. I slept until eleven and ate a late but large breakfast, and went out to the field. To do this necessitates a ride on a crowded trolley, and at the end of the line a rush for seats a-top a wreck of a horse car which ambles out to the islands. In a discussion with our conductress over the fare a young chap sitting beside us spoke up in careful English and helped us out. Further conversation disclosed the facts that he had only yesterday returned from the Roumanian Front where he has been for the last two years as an aviator. He had lived in Detroit USA for a number of years, as well as being in the American army for two years. He showed us his honorable discharge. Discouraged over the trend of affairs on the Roumanian Front and the general inactivity of the Russians he intends to apply at the American Army Headquarters here for transference to the American forces in France. He claimed to be able to fly any make of machine, with the most experience with the "Spots"—the fastest machine in use. His experience out [ought] to be welcomed in our ranks.

He was a nice chap, quiet, of neat appearance, with soft voice; he spoke of being on his way to the aviation field to see a friend whom he had not seen for two years.

Fred and I went our own way, fooled around at the track meet, which was a disappointment—there being only a handful of contenders there, and then set out for home. It being near meal time we stopped in at a restaurant on the river edge for dinner. Although expensive, the meal was very good, the music excellent, and the fresh air and bright sun on the terrace, comfortable. After lingering there as long as we politely could, we boarded a car and came home. I let the evening slip away in reading without even writing a note to the family at home. Altogether, a lazy comfortable, useless day.

31/13 August.

Yesterday the manager of our Moscow Branch and his assistants arrived and among them was Henry Koelsch. I took him out to dinner this evening, to Contant's,[228] in

---

[228] St. Petersburg Encyclopedia, "Kontan Restaurant," by I. A. Bogdanov, http://www.encspb.ru/object/2804016851?lc=en. Or Kontan. Named after its owner, A.S. Kontan, the restaurant opened in 1885 in the

the garden—where we spent an enjoyable two hours. It was good to get hold of some-one fresh from home who could tell of many of one's friends, how this one is doing this and that one that,—and all about the college and its little world. It seems the old campers were hit hard by this war business—so many of the boys left for camps for training, but an institution is far more than the men that compose it—it is as well what those who have already been have made it—so I guess it will recover. And then too, although this weakening is physical, it is a moral strength to have so many go.

It is difficult and startling to think of these men whom I saw a year ago, shouting at baseball on the campus, sitting astride the Senior Fence whittling canes, strolling to Allen's for a soda, heading for the open fields book in hand, and lying in the sun on the river bank,—strange to consider all this glorious praise of youth living to the utmost, suddenly silenced by the challenge from across the seas; but fine to see the challenge accepted, the happiness turned to enthusiasm and the youth to manhood.

1/14 August

This has been a miserable day. I've puttered around doing one thing and another and really accomplishing nothing all day, blundering and useless, with no fire or energy. After dinner I intended to attend a concert at the Conservatory but upon coming to take a car I found I had no money, not even carfare, so I must needs walk slowly homeward. Of course then I was seized with a fierce desire to stop in a café and eat, but no money; also to go to the movies. But again no money, so there was nothing to do but crawl home here, and humbly get ready for bed. I certainly am an ass.

2/15 August.

Am still in accord with the sentiments expressed above. We hear today that the Tsar and his family are to be moved to Tobolsk in Siberia, "Sic transit gloria mundi."

3/16 August.

Nothing doing today save that there are no more communiqués from the front. All signs point to activity on the Roumanian Front and to date we have heard only

---

Rossia Hotel on Moika River Embankment, 58. Famous for its exquisite cuisine and Romanian orchestra, Kontan frequently hosted banquets celebrating artists and diplomatic events.

discouraging news from that quarter. The situation there is peculiar, according to the information imparted to us by our aviator friend of Sunday. The Allies have a million ready men in Greece, unable to move until the Roumanians are ready, the Roumanians on their part, must await the cooperation of the Russians before advancing, while the Russians are quite unprepared to advance. So there you have it.

I was told today on very reliable authority that at last the obstacles were being cleared from the path of the American Railway Commission and that John F. Stevens, its head, would have complete charge of the organization of the Russian Railroads. There is no doubt that he is well fitted for the job nor is there any doubt that this is a job well worthy of his ability. The great problems are two,—lack of rolling stock and uncertainty of labor. The rolling stock shortage is being alleviated by the importation of many engines and cars from America. The first shipment has already arrived and an enormous shop fitted with American machinery for setting up locomotives has been erected at Vladivostok. But this of machinery is by far the easier of Mr. Stevens' problems. As always man's greatest problem is man, and in the Russian laborer the Commission lines up against a force stubborn, ignorant, and misled. Already the railroad workers of the country are showing signs of uneasiness under the age old economic propaganda of "machinery is taking away your jobs." So it goes, "the Americans are bringing their machinery here to cheat you out of your work," so says the agitator to the soldiers in the trenches and to the laborers behind. "While you are fighting for your country the foreigners are bringing in their machines, and when the war is over and you return, if you do return, you will find yourself out of a job."

Of course these blind ones do not see, cannot see the enormous possibilities open to their country, were each man therein equipped with a machine which would do the work of many men.

There is to be a Congress of Railroad workers in Moscow sometime this month and exciting times are expected there.

Fred and I have had some excitement tonight but of a far different kind. We each snapped up an opportunity to purchase a jar containing about fifteen pounds of jam at three roubles a pound. That makes thirty pounds—fifteen each of raspberry and strawberry—at a cost of one hundred odd roubles, or at the present rate of exchange, twenty three dollars! Thirty lbs. at twenty three dollars makes about seventy-five cents a pound! Whew! It was worth it though, for we had a great time at tea with our bread, butter, sugar, and two kinds of jam. Luxury!

4/17 August

The Tsar and the royal family are to be removed to Siberia. There's irony in that—the very man who for years held Siberia over the heads of agitating subjects is now sent to the very place himself! To Tobolsk, a small village, far removed from railway communication they are to go, to be held there prisoner by the guard of the vast emptiness around them. And the reason for this. It is said that a plot has been uncovered to reinstate the Tsar, and that this movement is a result of the plot. The Tsar is no doubt content at that. Life at Tsarsky Selo could hardly have been happy with the knowledge that in Petrograd one party clambered for one's life, another for deportation, and another liberation. And so, three hundred versts away from freedom the Tsar's also three hundred versts away from his would be murderer.

5/18 August.

Today I was so pep-less after a hard night's battle with the bedbugs that I couldn't even put up a decent game of tennis. It makes me boil when I think of it—this dirt. Here we are living in a supposedly intelligent, respectable family and as a sample of its cleanliness, I relate the following; one evening when I came into my room I killed two cockroaches on the desk, frightened a mouse from the table, and upon going to bed killed a bedbug there! It's a great life! I always thought bugs wouldn't bother me, but they're so damned persistent! But to resume—Bab and I went over for a game of tennis and had to quit because we were so tired—why we did not know. It just goes to show how living here drains one's vitality and leaves one only a shell. I have noticed it—that I have no lasting strength and I can see for myself that I am much thinner than before. And why? I'm saving a little money, to be sure, but hardly enough in proportion to warrant such sacrifice of strength, I have not the time to carry out the plans I had made for writing while here, and third, altho I am getting my experience here in Russia, of what use is the Russian side of it when I know now that I do not intend to return here after my three years are up. And then, far above all these things is the war. It occupies all my attention. I find myself trying to devise plans for the downfall of Germany, scheme of frustration of the submarine menace, and plans of reconstruction when peace is made. I await every new paper with anxiety and long for each letter. The war is everywhere, it encompasses everything, it influences every phase of life today whether it will or no, it is a world problem, and as such it must be met. It behooves every man to consider carefully, take his side, and struggle to the utmost for it. For it must be a decisive victory and whatever side loses must give up all. And my side, of course, is America. And I think Americans little realize what a force for evil they are combating. It is a force which for forty years has been organizing the good around it into an instrument for the service of its evil purpose—so organizing it by the lure of commercial success; for forty years it has drawn, tempered, and polished this instrument until it lay concealed in the show of commercial activity a polished spear with glittering steel head—the German army, and stout well turned shaft—the German people. With little warning, in 1914, it hurled this spear at the heart of the world. It struck deep, but the struggle must not be relinquished until the spear is broken. If it ends with the spear withdrawn unbroken, as General Brusiloff says, life will not be worth the living.

6/19 August.

A day of unparalleled brightness,—like sunshine in a mirror. I tried to stay inside and write but it was far too beautiful outside, and this beauty is far too short lived in Russia. I have heard much about Pavlovsk so I decided at least to see the place once before wintertime.

After clinging to a tram for numerous blocks I arrived at the Tsarsky Selo station in time to stand in a long line for tickets. These purchased I wandered out to the station platform to find that I had just missed a train and would have to wait one hour and a half for another. A large crowd of workers learned the same thing at the same time so we stood there near the iron gate and waited. I might have known that I couldn't compete with these Russians in the waiting game and after reading my two French papers I became aware that I was tired. However, the crowd was so heavy that I had to stay where I was until the gate opened,—when, amidst a great yelling, crowding, and shrieking, I tore down the platform and managed to get a seat in a second-class carriage. The ride out was much like most others on Russian trains, thru typical Russian plains, flat, wet, and only broken now and then by the figure of a lone peasant, motionless in awe at the passing of the train.

We went through царский цело [Tsarsky Selo], adorned with a forest, where stands the summer home of the former emperor now quite invaded by soldiers; and not far beyond came into Pavlovsk. I was much disappointed in this latter, having heard so much about it, but I could not be thrilled over a typical pavilion a la Brighton Beach and a somewhat rundown park. I mingled with the crowd of people wandering thru the park,—just such people as one expects to see in parks—and in my wandering unwittingly trespassed on the grounds of a country estate belonging to one of the grand dukes. The caretaker, sitting in the sun with his wife, was uncommonly agitated at my appearance in his midst, and seemed almost afraid that I might refuse his requests to leave. I only asked him if one was not permitted to walk in the grounds, why were there not signs or warnings at the gates; the question seemed to puzzle him and I left him talking over the solution with his spouse. There were a few listless people gathered around the concert platform at the pavilion where a doll was being auctioned off "Americansky style;" I took a seat at a side table, drank a cup of coffee, and then wandered out to the station again. A tram came along in a few minutes, and it being nearly empty I had no trouble in finding a seat. It was in a second class carriage and I settled down in some comfort. The seat facing me, however, was soon taken by a workman with his wife and baby. He and the lady were in the midst of a discussion when they entered and the baby was prevented from taking part in this by a rubber nipple which it chewed "salivaliciously." It wasn't very satisfactory however, and the child soon set up a howl. Resignedly, I settled down to a ride home midst the din of a howling infant, as I have had to do many times in America. But not so on the Pavlovsk road. Still continuing the argument with her inferior half the lady pulled out her shirt waist, produced a voluminous breast and satisfied "his majesty's" cries at once. The discussion went on, uninterrupted. Being a staid New Englander by adoption I was at first a bit astonished but as the others in the car paid no attention at all, I quit peeping furtively thru my fingers and went on with my reading, or tried to. But the naïve naturalness of it all. It's so in all they do, the Russians, and it is at once their greatest weakness and their greatest virtue.

7/20 August.

Curses! The landlady has returned, and we are informed that our bedroom will be needed for her darling son on Sept. 1. I suppose that means we will either have to remove to the attic or go out on the street in search of other lodgings. Damn these domestic troubles, the struggling young businessman ought not to be bothered with them. It sure is discouraging, just as we get comfortably settled, with our little breakfast in the morning, our nice white bedroom, and our samovar at night, we have to break it all up. If we can get the [Dets?] room though, all will be rosy. High 'opes!

As I came home tonight I heard the news of an Italian and a French victory. About twelve thousand prisoners. Great stuff. If the Allies keep that up, Germany will soon have to admit something. I'm waiting for Lens[229] to fall to the British to hear what the Germans say; they can hardly state that it was of no military importance for the richest iron and coal mines in France are there, so I'm afraid they're going to be up a stump as to what to tell the people. A great problem that, for statesmen now-a-days—what to tell the people.

8/21 August.

It was quite a victory for both the Italians and the French. More prisoners than were first reported and a greater advance. Great praise is due them both, the quiet, struggling French, and the undaunted fierceness of the Italian.

I brought home some books to read tonight, or at least to start. Mrs. Hough,[230] leaving for America, left her library to us at the bank, a gift for which we are supremely thankful. Tonight I brought home three, "Fanny's First Play,"[231] "Tess of the d'Urberville's,"[232] and some O. Henry. Now don't be shocked you literateur, I'm not going to try to mix them anymore than I'd try to mix water, oil, and goose feathers. But a little bit of every side of life hurts no one. But I am not to be judged harshly, for Oh my literary friends into what company have I fallen! One of my fellow workers read with beatific serenity "The Miracle of Right Thought"[233] and "The Nature of Goodness,"[234] while another admits that Joseph Conrad is a good writer but professes to admire Arnold Bennett above all others! So it's environment, you see, that's to blame.

9/22 Aug.

The opera season at the Conservatory has opened and tonight Fred and I took in "Aida." I don't care much for "Aida's" brassy artificiality, but they did it very well this time. Had it not been for the fact that waits of an hour were necessary between the acts it would have been a splendid performance for that organization. As it was, we were unable to stick it out and we left after the fourth act.

---

[229] Lens is located in the Pas-de-Calais department in northern France..
[230] *The Lookout* (published by the Seaman's Church Institute of New York) 27, no. 7 (July 1926), 1. Heloise Leavitt Hough (formerly Heloise Beekman) founded the American Hospital in Petrograd when she "eagerly seized upon an opportunity to establish and conduct a forty-bed lazarette for the wounded of the Russian army." David Leavitt Hough worked as an engineering contractor for the Hough-Kolensky Company in Russia.
[231] By George Bernard Shaw, 1911.
[232] By Thomas Hardy, 1891.
[233] By Orison Swett Marden, 1910.
[234] By George Herbert Palmer, 1903.

10/23 Aug.

There has been a surprising lack of "dope" on the local situation during the last few days. The Prov. Govern. seems to be proceeding stealthily but carrying a heavy club. Agitators are finding themselves suddenly arrested and escorted out of the city, whole factories are being removed further in land, and troops are being moved. There are rumors that in the elections the Maximalists are returning heavy victors and that soon there will be more trouble for the government. Let's hope they'll wield the iron club this time. There are only two ways to treat ignorance, educate it or beat hell out of it. At present there isn't time to do the former so the club must be used. So be it.

A few days ago the Jews market[235] was pinched. It seems that deserters and even soldiers stationed here in the city have been selling their equipment to the Jews, so the P.G. one day sent a detachment of Cossacks down to look the situation over. They surrounded the market, closed all the entrances, and investigated every one of the five thousand shoppers and shop keepers there. An enormous number of guns and packages of ammunition were found, as well as innumerable pairs of shoes. These Cossacks are a great crowd. Yesterday they withdrew their representatives from the Council of Soldiers and Workmen's Deputies or the Soviet, arguing that that body was assuming powers arbitrarily. It is announced that as always, the Cossacks will continue to support the government.

11/24.

I indulged in a little license tonight. Friend Dailey[236] invited Henry Koelsch and myself over to his room to partake of a little drink. Of course we accepted, what Dartmouth man will refuse a drink, and set out for the rendezvous. As we walked up the quay I thought of how with time I had regarded Henry three years ago when we used to stride in the grandeur of seniority about the Dartmouth campus and now here we were in Petrograd walking up the quay on the way for a bit of toddy. As usual the toddy loosened our tongues and we talked all of college, I suppose much to host Dailey's disgust. But two Dartmouth men in one room with a bottle of whiskey is bad company to anyone else who may want to talk. So of course it was inevitable that we should re-tell how Jake Bond prowled around on the lookout for parties, how Jake

---

[235] One name given for the large city bazaar of Petrograd.
[236] Arthur T. Dailey (1886–1953), formerly the private secretary to Ambassador David R. Francis. In late 1916, Dailey joined NCB.

was eluded on such and such a keg party, how so and so got fired, how this game was lost, how that one won, how—but these would be innumerable hours on such a topic. Suffice it to say that we talked the old days over until we almost forgot to eat. And when this subject came to mind we strolled to Donon's[237] and did it up in good style.

12/25

And now we come to the Conference of Moscow. It is to be opened today. Concerning the course of events therein there is much misgivings, hope, and misunderstanding. Back in the early days of the P.G. when the more reserved of the revolutionists were in power—that is Lvoff and Milyukoff there was of course great uncertainty as to the proper course for the baby government to pursue. From all corners of Russia came differing opinions as to the proper conduct of the government. In order to satisfy each of these expressions and to assemble for the country's future good the opinion of the country it was decided to call a conference of representatives from all social-political bodies from all parts of Russia,—this conference to meet at Moscow. In this conference those questions most vitally concerning the destiny of Russia were to be discussed.

Now in spite of the completeness of the overthrow in this Russian Revolution the fact remains that to the present time it is strictly a political revolution; there are those, however, who are striving with all the means and weapons in their power to make it a social revolution as well.

Those who would accomplish this are for the most part extremists—the ignorant workman to whom anything's right that favors him and the over studied impracticalist who mistakes seeing problems for solving them; these men regard ignorance and poverty as the acme of virtue and wisdom and means as the summit of duplicity. They believe in the theory that "what is yours is also mine"—but with one qualification "but what is mine is not yours." They believe in any end to achieve the means, even anarchy—as long as they are the anarchists, but I am sure that should the thinking people resort to anarchy to prove their right, our friends the extremists would be the first to shriek the method down.

[237] St. Petersburg Encyclopedia, "Donon Restaurant," by I. A. Bogdanov, http://www.encspb.ru/object/2804016802?lc=en.
Donon originally opened in 1849 at 24 Moika River Embankment. One of St. Petersburg's most fashionable restaurants, Donon was renowned for its exquisite cuisine, Romanian orchestra, and first-class service (all waiters were Tatars, united in a cartel). Writers, actors, painters, and scientists gathered at the Donon. I. S. Turgenev and N.I. Kostomarov were regulars.

In the exigencies of the times, in fact by taking Russia by the throat when she reeled from the shock of revolution, the extremists have managed to force their will on the country, have succeeded in muffling the voice of the people and having their shrill cry mistaken for it. But comes the Conference of Moscow. In it the blackmailers see the thinkers of the nation gathered together to discuss its future policy; they see moderation and conservatism holding sway, and they see maximalism decried. Naturally the vision does not please them, and it is hence all this talk of strikes in Moscow, riots in Petrograd, anarchy in the army and navy, and chaos let loose; these cries of counter-revolution, of the return of the Tsar, and of treachery to the Revolution.

There is still another danger that threatens the Conference. It is meant to be the unified opinion of the country; there's chance for it to be only a chaos of opinion. If representation came to it with thought of party and theory uppermost in their minds Russia loses much; if they come to it with the love of Russia above all—even above the Revolution, she wins much. If men come to the Conference as to an arena it is a failure; if they come as to an altar its stimulus is inspiring. We shall see.

13/26 August.

Sunday again. Tempus certainly does fudgit![238] I slept late as usual, without my usual guilty conscience however, as it was a rainy morning. Upon arising and partaking of my coffee and rice I sat me down to read. This consisted of a couple of O. Henry stories whose cheerful effect was later offset by a few chapters of "Tess of the d'Urbervilles"—which in spite of its darkness is going to be a commanding story. When it came time to eat again I betook myself to "Phils," and dined palatially for these hard times on "Borscht" and meat and potatoes; whereupon I went to the bank and worked some until nine o'clock on a little story I've been puttering at off and on for the last month or two. I shall now drink my two glasses of tea, read two chapters of "Tess" and retire. A true day of rest!

14/27 Aug.

Of course the first question is, "What of the Moscow Conference?" At this early hour all I could gather was, "All are for the war." Petrograd is quiet, although trouble was

---

[238] Rogers plays with the Latin words "tempus fugit," or "time flies."

or is expected as shown by the guards patrolling the streets. Moscow too is reported undisturbed, save for a tramway strike. That is all.

15/28 Aug.

A holiday today—I slept late and finally dragged myself to the bank to work on a statement which has long been overdue. Incidentally Mr. Stevens called me into his for a little talk, which lasted some time. I think we understand each other quite well now. I explained to him my contempt for office politics,—of which there seems to be a good deal since the new men have arrived from America. I had much rather leave the institution than become involved in them.

Speaking of politics, news comes from the Moscow Conference that all is not in accord there. I had feared it. It seems that while all parties agree that the times call for unqualified unity on the behalf of all, each party refuses to give up its own particular point of view. Thus we have oracular unity, but active dissension. It is regrettable, but I suppose agreement was too much to expect of a people intoxicated with license.

16/29 Aug.

In spite of my hesitant knowledge of French I have managed to read Kerensky's speech opening the conference at Moscow. It is not like the speeches one hears at such functions. It's the speech of a sincere, courageous man, driven to desperation by discord and dissension, expressing his irrefutable convictions. It is almost an ultimatum. "Any attempt at armed violence, or expressions of disapproval through other than the usual channels will be met by blood and iron" says Kerensky, referring to the disturbances of July 3–4–5.

"There are three things necessary for the safety of the country," says Kerensky, "grant of power to the government, establishment of discipline in the army, and economic organization of the country."

The speech was constantly interrupted by spontaneous applause, which, I think was more a tribute to the sincerity of Kerensky's words, than an agreement to follow him. There has been rumor that Kerensky was fading in the popular eye, that he no longer has the full confidence of the people; that Russia is at last tired of words and demands action, and that there is but little action in Kerensky's political record. Rumor had it that General Korniloff would succeed Kerensky; and for a while rumor had some substance in that there was an estrangement between the two as to the method of reorganization. But Kerensky seems to have emerged from the Conference in the increased confidence of those present—convinced by his forceful sincerity—, while Korniloff has again turned his whole attention to the army. The Conference has had the result of giving "carte blanche" to the government and their action is now awaited.

17/30 Aug.

As I have perhaps mentioned before our old friend Milyukoff is by no means out of the game. He seems to have organized his Cadet party to become a power in the direction of affairs, and being conservative, it acts as a counter to the extreme socialists; which is a good thing. And what is more, opinion gradually seems to be shifting to the more conservative side, and while it cannot be said to have shifted to Milyukoff,—as he is keeping out of sight and quiet—he is there just the same and is leading more than people think for. At any other time this lining up of the extremists and the conservatives would be an interesting party struggle, but coming as it does it is much like two groups of fire men fighting to see who should go to the fire, which grows fiercer each second of the time. As Roosevelt says, "Nine-tenths of being wise is being wise in time," so nine-tenths of being wise for the Russians is being unified in time. I often wish for a bolt from the blue or something as arbitrary, to frighten them into unselfishness and cooperation.

18/31 Aug.

Feeling a little lonely I went over to the opera again tonight. It was Tchaikovsky's "Queen of Spades," the second time I have heard it, and I enjoyed it of course more than the first hearing. As ever, one of the most interesting things about the theatre for me continues to be the audience. These opera audiences in Russia are the most varied conglomeration of people one could hope to see. The same gamut of class one sees at the movies at home,—only here they are at the opera. Which shows how much truer their instincts are. Or perhaps how much better their instincts are accommodated. I could not keep my eyes off a group of the girl soldiers, which sat not far away from us. With shaved heads, and regulation uniforms, yet female features they looked like neither men, nor women, nor children, more like some weird new species let loose on the world. And at times ridiculous too, as a husky man would be with long hair and a maternity belt! Oh you fairer sex, truly you are quite capable of fooling men, but you are also bigger fools than men.

19/1 September.

September first! Whew, how tempus fugits.[239] Old Man Time sure has abandoned his sandals for a Twin-Six,[240] and has set out to show the world some real speed. And not only does time seem to move faster but events shift at a redoubled pace, so that the net result is a quadruple increase in the speed of living. Away from home but five years now and the traveler will be as much out of touch as was Rip van Winkle with his 20 years absence.

I forgot to mention that ten new men came from America yesterday. How fresh and healthy they looked, and what strength and enthusiasm. They made me look at myself and consider how far I had fallen in my year here. I feel like a shell of my former self. But I hate to think about it. Now all is whispering and politics around our office, as to who is going to Moscow and who is to remain; as if going to Moscow is a consummation to life's efforts "devotedly to be wished." I'm sure I have no desire to move; in fact I don't seem to care about anything anymore: I seem to be drifting—but to what?

20/2 September.

I have finished reading "Tess of the d'Urbervilles." I find myself surprised at the rapidity with which I went through the book, but there is explanation in the fact that as far as reading goes my mind is dry as dust;—wherefore it soaked up "Tess" like a sponge. There are many things I want to say about the book and its author; but I must be careful.

I have heard "Tess" classed as one of the finest novels in English; and also as almost one of the finest. I should place it in the last named category, for the reason that it is melodramatic. Hardy so concentrated upon the figure of Tess that he quite forgot to make his other characters respond humanly. He is so convinced that a malignant fate sported with Tess that he makes all life ruled by that spirit. And this of course is not so. For life has its happy, farcical, and genial moments if we only will see them; and the generous is just as powerful a guiding spirit as the malignant, and any attempt to depict it otherwise is artificial. You who protest that the characters and events are not melodramatic must answer me why Alec so abruptly becomes convert and so facilely

[239] Another play on the Latin phrase "tempus fugit."
[240] How Stuff Works, "1916–1923 Packard Twin Six," by the Auto Editors of Consumer Guide, https://auto.howstuffworks.com/1916-1923-packard-twin-six.htm; Detroit Public Library Digital Collections, "Driver and passengers in Packard Twin Six automobile, owned by Czar Nicholas II," https://digitalcollections.detroitpubliclibrary.org/islandora/object/islandora:186176. The Packard Twin-Six 12-cylinder touring automobile. More than 35,000 were built between 1916 and 1923. Tsar Nicholas II owned one.

slips from grace just when needed for the story. Why does Tess's father die without warning at so critical a time, why do catastrophes happen, without a preparation or cause other than that of being needed by the author? There are many of them, too numerous to cite.

As I have said, all is subservient, even to the point of melodrama, to the picture of Tess. If Hardy has failed to give us one of the greatest novels he has succeeded in creating one of the most memorable of characters in Tess. I can think of no comparison with her, Juliet, no,—Ophelia, no—Tess stands alone in a peculiar light of her own. Even tho I cannot understand her amazing composition of the slavey[241] and the aristocrat, of the facility—as the author wills it,—of her change from ignorant field girl, to cultured woman speaking and writing the most beautiful English, even tho I cannot understand all this, the pathos of Tess obscures it all. I doubt if there is anything more haunting in literature than the baffled sorrow of Tess when she says,—"I waited and waited for you, but you did not come!" "And I wrote to you, and you did not come"—and—"He is upstairs. I hate him now, because he told me a lie—that you would not come again; and you have come! These clothes are what he's put upon me: I didn't care what he did with me! But—will you go away, Angel, please, and never come anymore?"

It is pathetic, but there is no tragedy in it. Tragedy is catastrophe brought about by some flaw in the character, some wrong choice of the individual, but with Tess there is no wrong choice. She is the victim of a malignant spirit which sports with her with a cynical smile, meets her at every turn with treachery and misfortune, and finally kicks away the platform of the scaffold to end her troubles. Tess is no more to blame than a child, and the evil of the events contrasted with her simple spirit, only deepen the feeling of pity for her.

And now for the author. He is undoubtedly a consummate artist, as he has written merely to arouse emotion and not to demonstrate a theory. The book is quite free from "isms" and contents itself with having a picture of country life taken in all its beauty and reality. But although Hardy sees life accurately, his vision comes through smoked glasses.

---

[241] Slavey. A maidservant, especially a hard-worked one.

21/3 Sept.

The only news is bad news today. The strange silence from Riga way and the sudden collapse of the dwindled rouble on the foreign markets makes us think that after half a year of tottering Riga has at last fallen. In that case of course the Germans could turn their attention to Petrograd; but I cannot see any reason military for their doing so. The capture of Petrograd might make news enough to satisfy the dissenting people in Germany that the Fatherland is still victorious, but otherwise I can't see what good it would accomplish to the German cause. Certainly they could not expect to hold the city after the war, and its capture would be costly. I even think it would be a great thing for Russia if such an attempt were made; it would throttle all this useless verbosity and make concerted action imperative.

Other rumors come from the south that owing to lack of fuel the R.R. cannot run, and therefore no food can be brought to Petrograd. Starvation is predicted in harrowing terms. And to tell the truth, even to the optimist the coming winter bids fair to be a memorable one.

I received a copy of my class booklet from my college today; it is filled with letters from as many of my class as would and could write them. There they are—not letters in cold black and white but voices from a past sweet and all too short. Each one speaks of the present, but it is plain to see that each one thinks of the past. Of carefree, shoulder to shoulder days, rollicking in the crisp snow under the crystal sun, of long walks through scented fields and forests, of droning classes, and of evenings of comradeship and song. They all haunt of it, those letters, each one, in spite of levity; carefree optimism, and youth, breathes a baffled refusal to admit that happier times will never come again. And those that are not there, bespeak it all the clearer. They are far too many, those absent ones, for so young a class. There's John Colby,—a sturdy jolly and trusty soul, whose passing makes us pause: There's Del Albrecht, poor Del, who struggled so to live. I remember when he learned the nature of his affliction; he roomed across the hall from me; he stayed in bed that morning, and called me in to see him; there was much blood, and I knew the hemorrhage had been severe, that the disease had a lengthy start. He soon left college, went to Denver, from whence I used to hear from him off and on. The last time his letter was an invitation to be best man at his wedding,—for he was declared in the best of health; I had to decline and it hurt to do it, and I know it hurt Del too, but I came away before the wedding. That is the last I hear of him until tonight when I read of his death in May; but seven short months after his marriage. Truly there is something wrong in the game played with Del. He would have done much with life, would have given it much, would have appreciated it,—and what more can one do? But a great deal of life was there in his short time, hope, faith, love, and sacrifice; I suppose there's not much more. So there they all are, Bob, Jack, John, and Bill, even myself, my own letter, my sharp phrases come back to haunt me and condemn,—all there, living it over again in the supreme happiness of appreciation.

22/4 September.

It is quite true, Riga has fallen and the Germans have passed through the city. Whether they will attempt to make Petrograd or not remains to be seen. My personal opinion is that they will not. Of course people here are depressed, and pessimistic anyway, are already making plans for departure to Moscow. Gloom is everywhere, even the sky is overhung with heavy clouds, which seem to be hurrying from the south, as if they too were fleeing from the stricken city.

23/5 September.

The Germans subjected the positions of the Russian troops on the Dvina[242] to such a hurricane of fire that the latter were compelled to withdraw, in consequence of which pontoon bridges were thrown across the river, and once across, the German troops had little difficulty in pressing on to the city. And that is not all, they traversed through the city and for a distance of fifty versts beyond scoured the country of Russian troops. The evacuation of Riga was more of a rout according to the report,—a rout of mingled populace and soldiers, ever streaming away from the stricken area, growing as it proceeds, and headed for Petrograd as a haven of refuge. What a refuge! No bread, no sugar, no milk, no eggs, even for those of us here now.

And of course these people here of little faith are frightened. Already they are crying "The Germans will be here in two weeks, a week, three days!" And out of the city they go, taking with them what they can and abandoning the rest. Each day some sixteen thousand leave the city by railway and many others are going back to the villages à la cart.

---

[242] Dvina refers to the Western Dvina River, the major river of Latvia and northern Belarus.

24/6 Sept.

The fear of the Germans coming to Petrograd by foot seems to be fading; but the opinion that they will arrive by sea grows. Having captured Riga they must have also the Gulf of Riga—an excellent base for naval operations. To overcome the opposition of the Russian fleet would be an easy matter—as the Russians would undoubtedly fire on their own ships as they did in the war with Japan—and to sweep the entrance to the Gulf of Finland clear of mines would not be too tremendous a task. Petrograd would then be easy prey.

But things are not done without reason—least of all German things and what reason is there in capturing Petrograd. The government would not be here, the banks would not be here, and it is quite certain that food would not be here. Although it might be strong as an argument for German politicians,—a means of reassuring their weakening subjects that Germany's armies are still victorious, I think Riga's fall is enough for that. Riga will divert them enough, with its "capture after two years of stubborn resistance" to compensate for the loss of Lens on the West Front, and perhaps of Trieste on the Italian Front. So there is no need for Petrograd.

25/7 September.

We read in the papers that Steurmer is dead, after a lingering and painful illness. Steurmer who aimed at a separate peace, Steurmer who played so treacherously with Roumania,—who is in fact to blame for all that doughty[243] little country's misfortunes of war, Steurmer the appointed of the notorious Rasputin. No one mourns him; in fact all seem relieved at being thus freed of the necessity of disposing of him themselves. How accurately the nemesis is working out in Russia's crises. Protopoppoff, the arch villain who sentenced so many to the dungeons of Peter and Paul now fares there on his bread and water and straw; Nicholas Romanoff, whose acquiescence thrust so many into the oblivion of Siberia, now finds himself exiled thither; and Steurmer, whose treachery caused so much pain, now dead of too terrible pain. It is inevitable,—this payment.

---

[243] Doughty. Brave and persistent.

26/8 September.

It is not so certain that the Germans can come to Petrograd by sea. We hear that the Russian fleet still occupies the Gulf of Riga and that twenty English submarines protect the entrance to the Gulf of Finland, so perhaps the waterway is closed. I was told today that soon we should see twenty thousand French soldiers in Petrograd as well as fifty thousand of the Russians that were in France. They are supposed to be returning by way of Archangel.

There are to be two holidays next week and rumor has it that there will be an uprising in the city,—this time against the Bolsheviks!

Sometimes I wish the Germans would capture the city and show its occupants a bit of German thoroughness in forcing them to work twenty four hours a day without pay. It would be the best thing that could happen to them.

27/9 September.

A Sunday, which, as far as my personal actions are concerned, has been productive of nothing. I seem to have lost all impulse to act, all ambition; and seem to be content to rest, to sit and watch and listen. In the afternoon I walked about the Nevsky, crowded as always with its shifting masses of pedestrians. People impelled this way, drawn that, hurrying, draggling, hating, loving, living, in spite of war, in spite of Revolution, pushing on their natural way. I dropped into the Hotel Europe coffee room for a cup of chocolate and a glance at the newspapers. It was only chocolate,—made with water in place of milk, without, sugar, bread or butter; One ordered chocolate and one got just that! While sitting there three large, well fed, men entered and took seats at a table near mine. I had to sit there for the remainder of the time and listen to them converse in quite loud tone in German. No one paid the slightest attention to them. I wanted to have them all arrested, they seemed so responsible for the lack of bread and sugar with my chocolate!—but no doubt I should have been thought the strange one.

Six months ago today—on the 24th of February [March 9 on the Gregorian calendar] began the Russian Revolution. Now a Revolution in itself is wholly a mental process, it is a resolve taken and acted upon. It is too often confused with what follows in its trail, which is, in reality, only the rustling of the leaves after the wind has passed thru them. Now this Revolution was political. It was not so much concerned with a change of systems, as a determination that the system should work better. It purposed to do away with the current leaders, and in the ardency of this desire quite forgot a substitute. So it became wholly negative. Having knocked down their strawman, the people had nothing to put in his place; at least nothing that would work well with the present machinery. This lack is partly explained by the fact that their objective was attained with astonishing ease; and where it had been thought that leaders would arise in the struggle, this was over so soon as to forestall any such developments. Thus the revolutionaries, having disposed of their guide, however poor he may have been, failed to provide a substitute which could keep the whirling factions within bounds. So one feature of the Revolution is its negative purpose.

Another is the all too patent fact that although the Revolution is but political there are those who strive to make it social. Owing to the failure of the leaders of the revolt to provide a sufficiently powerful substitute for the ruler they dethroned there wedged its way into an assertive position in the government a group of the most impractical, selfish, and ignorant minds that ever held a position of power in the affairs of a civilized country. Its first act was to issue an order against discipline in the army, which resulted in turning that body into a mob of ignorant men. Then basing its power on its ability to summon this force in case of need the usurpers in the government set to work. Through some vague idea of consolation they associated all intelligence with duplicity and straightway labeled any attempt of the intelligent to take a hand in the country's guidance as counter-revolution. With this they set to work to achieve true democracy by the abolishment of all restraints;—tax only the rich, divide up all the land, conduct the army by committees of soldiers, work but four hours a day, and achieve as much compensation as for ten hours. Such were the schemes put into operation. In normal times there are things we should all like to see tried out; it would be an interesting experiment. But in the chaos of events, with a powerful enemy hand at work both inside and outside of Russia, the experiments can hardly be viewed with equanimity. But undaunted even by preliminary disasters the work of eliminating the intelligent, the rich, the resourceful, and the substitution of the theorist, the inexperienced, and the uneducated went on. Every effort was strained to make the Revolution social, to place complete control in the hands of those who heretofore had not had it, a complete overthrow of the social strata was the aim.

But the ruling force in any country is the great mass of average people, people of fair education who wish to live and let live, whose need for government is only for protection of honor, territory, and liberty, and a liberty which allows the greatest amount of freedom to all. Any attempt to place the rein of government in other hands than these is bound to meet with failure, simply because majority rules, either by weight of opinion or by superior might. And an attempt of the minority of extremists to rule is as bound to fail as a similar attempt by the minority of court or nobility. One is as futile as the other.

And so after six months of license in which the country has been brought to the brink of the abyss, we find this compelling mass of average opinion exerting itself through its most intelligent representatives. The people are sick of having liberty, freedom, revolution and the like shouted at them as a cure for all the country's ills, and demand immediate steps to prevent the impending disaster. Just what further form this demand will take is hard to foretell but it will make itself heeded. Looking back over the trail the Russian people are hardly proud of the first six months of their Revolution. Their opinion is well voiced by a man of great social, intellectual, and commercial prominence who said "It's a mad, thoughtless joke, this abuse of power by the ignorant, this parading in the limelight of history, while Russia falls into chaos and ruin; the laughing stock of the world, and its despair also. It cannot go on. It must be changed; it shall be changed."

28/10 Sept.

Astounding developments!

General Korniloff, the newly appointed commander-in-chief of the armies has constantly been pleading for absolute control over his armies both at the front and at the rear. He has repeated[ly] asked, almost demanded, of the P.G. that he be allowed to enforce any laws concerning the army that he deemed necessary. His reasons were that by no other means could his army be saved from the dissolution of the others. The necessary powers have not been forthcoming, for first what reason no one knows; it may be that Kerensky is not allowed to give them because of the objection of the Soviet, which hangs like lead around his neck. In them, he has shot his albatross.

But today we hear that Korniloff, tired of waiting and watching his army go to pieces has sent a messenger to Kerensky demanding that all powers of the government be handed over to him, and that he be given complete authority to select a new government for the salvation of the country. Kerensky, of course, refused this astounding request, and at once informed Korniloff by wire that he should consider himself under arrest, should give up his office as commander-in-chief of the army, and proceed at once to Petrograd. Korniloff replied that he would do no such thing; that he would come to Petrograd and unless the powers he requested were given him upon his arrival near the city, he would besiege it and starve it into submission. And what is more, we learn that he has already started on his way to Petrograd with a strong force of picked troops,—infantry, calvary, and artillery. So here we have it,—Civil War.

General Korniloff is in a good way to make good his intentions. He is a Cossack, and therefore has that powerful body behind him; he is a man of wide education, exact and searching mind, and of resolute courage. Moreover his popularity has been growing, and I feel that [if] he could suddenly appear in the city tonight at the head of his troops, the power would be his. The people are so sick of this gibbering of the socialists, their crass inability to deal with facts, and the posing and speech making, that they will welcome any resolute, active, power. And Korniloff is certainly that. His challenge has thrown the city into an uproar. There seems to be a divided split; many are openly for the general and as many against him. As one of his openly avowed purposes in coming to Petrograd at the head of an armed force was to clean out the Soviet, that body is for once taking some active constructive measures—to save its own life! Soldiers have been ordered out to meet Korniloff's forces, but only soldiers would go; the officers would not. The city has been declared under martial law and triple guards posted at all streets; hundreds of arrests have been made,—showing that same strong Korniloff has been at work within the city,—generals, grand dukes, members of the Duma, financiers, in all about eighty important arrests. Excited crowds are gathered at every corner, torn among themselves. While all the time the dictator with his army draws nearer the city. First we hear of him in one place, then in a surprisingly short time, in another, and so he advances, carrying the sentiment of the towns with him as he comes. Meanwhile the city hums with excitement and we go to bed not knowing but that the morning will find the dictator in power, and the experimenters ousted. There are many who would welcome it.

29/11

A holiday today so we slept late, but got up earlier than otherwise to go out and discover whether we were under a dictator or a provisional government. But nothing has happened. There are a few proclamations calling for quiet and order in the city, but nothing more. It has been a lusty day, cool, with a heavy wind chasing the clouds away from a true blue sky. We bought papers but as usual there was much written and little said in them. No further news of Korniloff, save that he is still on his way. The city is surprisingly calm and unruffled.

Today was set for big things too. Counter-revolution, riots, massacres of the Jews, outbursts of the Maximalists,—in fact a regular anarchist holiday, but Korniloff's proposal by far out ramps all the others in daring, so everything has been called off awaiting developments.

We wandered around in the sunshine a while and then proceeded home to read magazines and eat crackers and jam all afternoon. High life. Tonight we took in "Carmen" at the Conservatory and, coming home, went to bed hoping that the Germans wouldn't start a Zeppelin raid at the same time Korniloff begins lobbing shells into the city.

30/12 September.

Another holiday today, and beautiful weather too. However, these two facts are the least of moment; the urgent question is "What of General Korniloff?" From the general and his forces we hear nothing; of him in Petrograd we hear everything. The P.G. brands him as a traitor, who would sell his country to the Germans, would draw troops from the front at so dangerous a time and lead an attack against the government. The Soviet comes out with its stock label for everything, reactionary, contra revolution, an attempt to re-establish the Tsar and all manner of such blatant slander. We hear that his plan has no chance of success, how his officers and men are deserting him for the side of the P.G., how he has been arrested, how—oh but all manner of like things. These are all to be found in the workmen's papers, the socialist and extremists sheets, and that is all for the others have mysteriously been closed down. They are not allowed to put out their editions.

Meanwhile we go our way, wondering what will happen. Food is still growing scarcer, prices still mounting skyward, and many commodities are disappearing altogether. As if it were not bad enough to have to go without milk, sugar, white bread, and butter, our maid today informs us that there is no more coffee or rice to be purchased. We are up against it now, as a good big dish of the latter gave us our start in life every morning. If I can't have my rice at breakfast I cannot last through the day on the slim meals we have at the bank. Oh well, I'll soon be down to one straw a day, like the economical farmer and his cow,—and then what? It's winter now and one can't even turn to eating grass like Nebuchadnezzar.[244]

---

[244] King Nebuchadnezzar, who in the Book of Daniel "was driven from men and did eat grass as oxen."

31/13 September.

Affairs curdle and clot into opposing factions. What I most feared seems to be coming about and of the disorder; it is order coming out of chaos, but a malignant order. We still hear how great a traitor is Korniloff, how he has no chance of succeeding, he will be court-martialed and put to death, but we hear little of his actual actions. It is not denied that he has with him the pick of the troops from the front, ample supplies, and heavy, as well as field artillery. Against this array, the P.G. has the Petrograd Garrison, most of whom could do little effective fighting, and the armed mob of workmen and loafers. It is these last that tinge the situation with red.

The majority of the conservative, thinking people believe Korniloff sincere, and brand as lies all slanders against his sincerity and good intentions towards the country. Prominent merchants, businessmen, generals, and the greater part of the more intelligent people are ardently for him and the success of his bold plan. Against him, as I have said before, are the Maximalists, now fighting part of the army, the Soviet, and the workmen; naturally too they are against all who are for Korniloff. Now in order to strengthen their hand, the powers that be have permitted this mob of miscellaneous persons to arm, and with their avowed intention of "getting" the general and all his "counter revolutionary" sympathizers, they make a dangerous force. Not dangerous to an organized fighting force, but very dangerous to the conservative public. In fact we have the line-up for anarchy, pillage, and massacre. Inflamed with the thought that Korniloff's party wishes to reinstate the monarchy the slightest breath will form them into a raging conflagration.

At first the affair seemed only another of these rumors that would soon be dispelled. But each day's digging only shows its roots to [be] deeper buried. Practically all generals of note are involved on Korniloff's side, many members of the Duma, the majority of the Cadets (Milyukoff's) party, and the leading newspapers. (Else why should they be shut down). It is a difficult problem. Were Kerensky alone I could support him wholeheartedly as he is fearless, sincere, and a straight thinker; but he is under constant pressure from the Soviet, which will not allow him to work his will. Korniloff is a soldier, autocratic, swift, and decisive. I believe him to be sincere in his wishes for Russia's welfare. But it is a question as to whether his usurping the power by force would be a good example or not. Of course much would depend upon whether he was strong enough to hold his place; but his so obtaining it might lead others to attempt the same thing. If one can do it, so can another.

On the other hand Korniloff gains many adherents by his avowal to clean out the Workmen's and Soldiers Deputies if he is successful. And so the argument goes, from one side to the other, from the none too certain established government to the possibility of a stronger one. But whatever the two parties stand for, whatever the outcome of the struggle, it is certain that for the salvation of Russia and perhaps for the Allies is a power at the head that can force her armies at least to hold their present lines, and compel order at home. May the gods give to Russia that power at this vital time in her history!

It is unfortunate that the government finds itself in Petrograd. This is the center of all the various forms of agitation to which it is subject. Stability is next to impossible. It is hardly fair to Russia's good name when a group of hair brained laborers can appear in the streets at the head of a manifestation, perhaps armed, and then overthrow a minister or change the course of the government. In these things so little of this enormous country is represented. The Soviet represents probably three or four million soldiers and half a million workmen; the cultured, the intelligent, and the great mass of peasants are absolutely without voice. If they do succeed in speaking, their words are labeled as "contra revolution" and shouted from the forum. And yet did I not read in an American magazine the other day an advertisement for some peace society saying "Let us unite and express the will of America as clearly and truly as the Council of Soldiers and Workmen's Deputies has expressed that of Russia!" !!?*"!@$! God, what fools some Americans are; and there is not the excuse of ignorance for them either.

But to resume, all this has been intensely interesting and would be more so for me were it not for the fact that I do not appreciate the possibility of being dragged from my perch of an interested spectator down to becoming an excited participant. It really grows serious with civil war impending inside and the Germans stalking around outside, and already [all ready] to come in, what can a poor neutral do? For the French and British residents here the solution is held by their embassies, but as usual the US Embassy is supine. We have heard rumors that it might move, but there has been nary a word from it to us as to what action we were to take in case of trouble. Other embassies have issued their instructions to their citizens, but ours is too busy bent on its own welfare. The people who support it can shift for themselves. I've heard stories of the incompetency of US embassies before and rarely believed them, or believing them have excused their slackness by the fact that they were the representatives in a small country. But here in Russia, in a great power of the world, the American Embassy is so emasculated that one of its secretaries, being arrested for carrying a camera on a trip to an interior town, had to rely on the British Consulate to obtain his release! So I'm going to plan my own salvation. Tomorrow I shall pack my good things, stow em away, get together a traveling outfit, and be ready at a moment's notice to make the wandering Jew look like the oldest settler.

Leighton W. Rogers

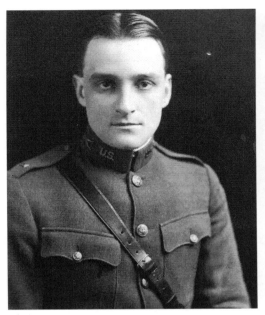

Leighton Rogers in the US Army, 1918

Leighton Rogers at the home of
English publisher Grant Richards
at Marlow-on-the-Thames, 1924

H. Fessenden Meserve

Robie Reed Stevens

The 1916 College Class (National City Bank summer training program)

Frank A. Vanderlip and "his boys." Summer 1916

The SS *Oscar II* in New York

Babcock, Rogers, Swinnerton and Stuart at the Grand Hotel,
Stockholm, October 13, 1916

LEIGHTON ROGERS

National City Bank Petrograd branch staff, 1917

National City Bank Petrograd branch building on Palace Embankment no. 8

Nevsky Prospekt

St. Isaac's Cathedral

International Women's Day march, Petrograd, 1917

American soldiers on parade in Vladivostok, 1918

PART III

The October (November) Revolution. Collapse.

November 1917–April 1918

Seeking to appease the Ispolkom, the executive committee of the Petrograd Soviet whose support he needed, Kerensky failed to pursue serious punitive actions against the Bolsheviks after the July Days. This fatally undermined his credibility. First, the army withdrew its support, despising him for the arrest of Kornilov and his fellow generals, and for giving in to the leftists. For the same reason, he lost the support of the bourgeoisie and the rightists. By September, the vacuum of leadership worsened and social and political polarization grew. US Consul North Winship's earlier warning on May 8 to Secretary of State Lansing resonated: "The power which the Temporary Government now administers is fictitious to a certain extent.... If this power is not handled with the greatest versatility and tact it will pass to the leaders of the Council of Workmen's and Soldiers' Deputies who openly profess and personify the expectations of the majority of the lower classes."[245] That is indeed what happened. In August and September, the Bolsheviks gained influence in the Petrograd and Moscow soviets and made significant gains in the city Duma elections.[246]

The situation in Petrograd grew dire and tense. Ambassador Francis in mid-September wrote to a friend, "The air is full of rumors and general fear is entertained of a Bolshevik outbreak. . . . Many Americans are frightened. . . ."[247] The Allies' confidence in Russia hit a new low. On October 9, the British, French, and Italian ambassadors met with Kerensky and threatened to cut off Allied military aid to Russia unless the country took "immediate, harsh steps to restore order both at the front and in the cities."[248]

Lenin, in disguise, returned to Russia sometime between October 16 and 23.[249] On October 23, with Lenin back in Petrograd, the Bolshevik Central Committee voted to mount an armed uprising (although two leading party members, Lev Kamenev and Grigory Zinoviev, opposed on questions of timing). The same day, John L. H. Fuller recorded in his diary that National City Bank achieved record deposits and that "Pretty soon we shall be the only bank doing business here and we Americans the only ones who are taking a chance on staying." Fuller smartly, or unknowingly, acknowledged NCB's implicit "flight to quality" trade-off. He added

[245] Barnes, *Standing on a Volcano*, 244.
[246] Figes, *A People's Tragedy*, 457.
[247] Francis, *Russia from the American Embassy*, 162.
[248] Barnes, *Standing on a Volcano*, 260–61.
[249] Pipes, *The Russian Revolution*, 482.

the next day that "Trouble is going to come sometime with very little noise—and then it will be real trouble."[250]

Kerensky delivered a speech on October 24 asserting that "Waves of anarchy are sweeping over the land. The pressure of the foreign enemy is increasing, counter-revolutionary elements are raising their heads . . . The Provisional Government presumes that all citizens of Russia will now rally closely to its support for concerted work . . . the defense of the fatherland from the foreign enemy, the restoration of law and order and the leading of the country to the sovereign Constituent Assembly."[251]

The German threat to Petrograd became ominous. After occupying Riga in early September, the German army pressed forward to capture several islands in the Gulf of Riga on November 3 and sent units closer to Tallinn, only 300 kilometers from Petrograd.

Bolshevik intentions became public knowledge. Rogers wrote, "The plans for the outbreak were openly formed; the intentions announced at the Bolshevik meetings." Fuller noted, "It begins to look as though that trouble I have been so anxiously looking for is about to visit us at last; and I am afraid from all I have been hearing these last few days and all the signs, that it is going to be real trouble, trouble of a kind that I shall wish had stayed away."[252]

Kerensky underestimated the Bolshevik threat and was oblivious to his weakness. He wanted it to happen, so he could see it crushed, but made no serious military preparations to do so. On November 5, Ambassador Francis belatedly cabled Washington proposing an emergency loan to the provisional government of $100 million. The next day, Kerensky ordered the closing of several Bolshevik newspapers, which only fueled antigovernment agitation in the streets. Unaware of what was to transpire, Francis paid his daily visit to the Foreign Office and met with Foreign Minister Mikhail Tereshchenko, who told him that he expected a Bolshevik outbreak that very night. Francis replied, "If you can suppress it, I hope it will occur."[253]

The first phase of the Bolshevik coup got under way the morning of November 6 [Julian old calendar date of October 24, thus the "October Revolution"], the very day Rogers and his colleague Fred Sikes decided to move house. Bolsheviks used small, disciplined units of soldiers and workers to seize key government communication and transportation centers, utilities, printing plants, and other strategic locations in

---

[250] *The Journal of John L. H. Fuller*, October 23 and 24, 1917, 22–23.
[251] Barnes, *Standing on a Volcano*, 264.
[252] *The Journal of John L. H. Fuller*, November 6, 1917, 27.
[253] Francis, *Russia from the American Embassy*, 178.

Petrograd by that evening. Only certain districts in the city were affected. Fuller had noticed little when he wrote on November 7: "And yet, as far as I know, nothing has broken loose in spite of the ominous preparations that have been going on all day at the barracks of one of the most rabid of Bolshevik regiments in plain view of my window and just behind the bank."[254] That was because the November Revolution was nearly a bloodless coup d'état and thus differed from the massive armed demonstrations and street skirmishes of the March Revolution. Orlando Figes points out how the popular image of the Bolshevik Revolution owes more to Sergei Eisenstein's "brilliant but largely fictional propaganda" 1927 film, *October*, which portrayed a bloody struggle with tens of thousands, "than to historical fact." In reality, Figes explains, it was "a small-scale event, being in effect no more than a military coup, that it passed unnoticed by the vast majority of the inhabitants of Petrograd," including Fuller.[255]

Lenin released the following declaration at 10 a.m. on November 7:

To The Citizens Of Russia:

The Provisional Government has been deposed. Government authority has passed into the hands of the organ of the Petrograd Soviet of Workers' and Soldiers' Deputies, the Military-Revolutionary Committee, which stands at the head of the Petrograd proletariat and garrison.

The task for which the people have been struggling—the immediate offer of a democratic peace, the abolition of landlord property in land, worker control over production, the creation of a Soviet Government—this task is assured.

Long Live the Revolution of Workers, Soldiers, and Peasants![256]

Late in the evening of November 7, Francis cabled Washington laying out what happened: "Bolsheviki appear to have control of everything here."[257]

The value of the ruble plummeted by 50 percent over the next two weeks.

The November Revolution shattered Russia's political landscape, however weakened it already was. The political parties behind the now-deposed provisional government immediately called for elections to the Russian Constituent Assembly.

---

[254] *The Journal of John L. H. Fuller*, November 7, 1917, 29.
[255] Figes, *A People's Tragedy*, 484.
[256] Pipes, *The Russian Revolution*, 492.
[257] Barnes, *Standing on a Volcano*, 268.

This happened on November 25. The Socialist Revolutionaries won the largest number of seats, while the Bolsheviks won less than one-quarter. This outcome did not augur well with the Bolsheviks, who obtained little support outside their power bases in Petrograd and Moscow. They therefore decided to exclude non-Bolsheviks from membership in the soviets and swiftly implemented the party's platform. On December 14, the Bolsheviks declared nationalization of all private banks, although this decision did not immediately affect Credit Lyonnais or National City Bank. On December 15, they effected a cease-fire and began negotiations for a separate peace with the Central Powers. Woodrow Wilson's Fourteen Points speech of January 8, 1918, in particular the sixth point promising Russia "assistance of every kind that she may need and may herself desire," did not sway Lenin and Trotsky. The Constituent Assembly met again on January 18, 1918, but Lenin wanted no more of it and announced its dissolution the next day. The Bolsheviks then set up their own rubber stamp "All Russian Soviet Congress," condemning all other political bodies' gatherings as "counter-revolutionary." Lenin has been quoted as saying later, "The dispersal of the Constituent Assembly by Soviet authority [was] the complete and open liquidation of formal democracy in the name of the revolutionary dictatorship."[258] This action angered Wilson and Ambassador Francis, and strengthened their determination not to recognize the authority of the Bolsheviks.[259] Then, on February 8, 1918, the Bolshevik government repudiated the debts owed by the tsarist and provisional governments to foreign banks and governments.

Rogers agonized over the weeks that followed the Bolshevik takeover. Red Guards occupied National City Bank's Petrograd branch on December 27 for five days. Rogers lost faith in the Russian people's ability to make responsible choices, and the chaos unleashed by the Bolsheviks convinced him that Russia's cause might be lost. Yet like many other foreigners in Russia and observers abroad, he clung to the belief that Bolshevik power would not last. "Both the people outside and inside Russia will watch for only a short time," he wrote, "and at the first sign of weakness, will pull this socialism down like a tower of blocks."

In January 1918, Rogers acted on his earlier expressed conviction to enlist in the US Army and join the war effort. He chose to leave Petrograd rather than risk being interned by the Germans if they captured the city. A hurried evacuation of Americans and other nationals from Petrograd started in late February. Rogers

---

[258] Pipes, *The Russian Revolution*, 556.
[259] Allison, *American Diplomats in Russia: Case Studies in Orphan Diplomacy, 1916–1919* (Westport, CT: Praeger, 1997), 32.

fortuitously found a space on a dilapidated freight train out of Petrograd on February 23, bound for the Arctic port of Murmansk. He arrived there eight days later only to wait several weeks more to catch a transport ship for a perilous journey across the North Sea to Newcastle upon Tyne, England, where he landed on March 29. Rogers was thankful to get out of Russia when he did, although his mission was far from over. He had his story to tell.

CHAPTER 10

"Affairs slid from bad to worse"

A two-month gap exists in Rogers' journal, from September 16 to November 12. This was a significant departure from his weekly, if not daily practice of writing. Whether he suffered from a malady, lost himself in overtime at the bank, or enjoyed some great protracted distraction, we do not know because he chose not to write about it. His journal entry of November 12 resumed from where he left off in mid-September.

The tone of Rogers' journal entries hardened. He minced no words describing what he saw in Petrograd and abandoned his patience with the Russian experiment in democracy. Instead, he wrote how Kerensky was now a "hated man," and correctly judged that the detritus of the Kornilov Affair presaged failure for Kerensky and opportunity for the Bolsheviks. Leon Trotsky could not have disagreed: "[T]he winding up of the Korniloff adventure . . . had fundamentally altered the correlation of forces in our favour."[260] Rogers saw the Bolsheviks for what they were; there would be no compromise.

Growing anarchy on Petrograd's streets and the approach of the German army heightened Rogers' concern for his personal safety. J. Butler Wright fretted similarly, confiding in his diary on November 12: "I think, frankly, that for really the first time during successive horrors through which we have passed since the March revolution the element of fear for life and property now enters into the thoughts of all of us."[261] Rogers received no solace from the comical efforts, in his opinion, of the US Embassy to ensure the safety of the American colony in Petrograd with an undersized and under-provisioned escape boat. Nonetheless, in keeping with his style, he faced adversity with wit whenever possible. His decision to move home and worldly possessions on the day of the November Revolution, one of the most cataclysmic dates in history, was just another day's adventure.

---

[260] Pinfold, *Petrograd 1917: Witnesses to the Russian Revolution*, 210
[261] J. Butler Wright diary entry, November 12, 1917, cited in Allison, *Witness to Revolution*, 146.

National City Bank continued to attract deposits at a torrential pace. Meserve enthusiastically wrote on September 15 to New York, "I feel that there is a tremendous future in Russia for the National City Bank. . . ," although in the same letter, he assured his superiors that the Petrograd branch was following "in these unsettled times the most conservative policy possible."[262] Meserve set off for Moscow on September 17 to work on the preparations for the opening of NCB's new branch. Two weeks later, National City Bank's assets reached 200 million rubles, double the level in June. The bank had increased its staff to sixty-six employees.[263] Meserve also proposed to open a small department in Vladivostok and to send some staff from the bank's offices either in China or Japan to study the opportunity.[264]

Positive bulletins from Meserve underwrote Vanderlip's attempt to persuade Benjamin Strong, the governor of the Federal Reserve Bank of New York, that the Fed should accept "the securities of the Russian Government among the securities that are eligible as a basis for government deposits with banks . . ." "Nothing but the complete repudiation of its debt by the Russian Government, it would seem, could interfere with the integrity of these bonds," he argued.[265]

Unfortunately, for Vanderlip and National City Bank, that is exactly what the Bolsheviks did.

---

[262] Meserve to Vanderlip, September 15, 1917, Malik, *Bankers & Bolsheviks*, 157, citing documents in the Russian State Historical Archive, St. Petersburg, RGIA/624/1/5/225; Cleveland and Huertas, *Citibank: 1812–1970*, 100–101.

[263] *The Journal of John L. H. Fuller*, November 1, 1917, 26.

[264] Tkachenko, *American Bank Capital in Russia*, 100.

[265] Frank Vanderlip to Benjamin Strong, October 8, 1917, Box B-1-8, Frank A. Vanderlip Papers.

29 [30]/12 November

An interlude of two months since I wrote last. Two months more of chaos with the power of Russia slipping from responsible to irresponsible hands. These two months might well be called "The Downfall" so sure and direct has been the descent of power to the lower orders of society.

(Rogers dated a similar passage in his later manuscript to September 16)

We broke off writing at the very climax of the Korniloff affair. It was a most unhappy thing for all concerned. Korniloff, a Cossack and a life-long soldier deemed strength necessary in the government, and requested Kerensky to come to headquarters. In some way this request became distorted into a command, and a supposition that Korniloff demanded for himself dictatorial powers. There are but two chances for such distortion, into which I shall go later. Kerensky claims to have verified these demands of the Cossack general's over the wire and finding them true, felt justified in denouncing him as a traitor and a counter-revolutionist. Whereupon Korniloff at the head of a faithful division of troops marched against Petrograd; and Russia, among other things found herself confronted with civil war. It looked bad for a while, but with the intervention of General Alexieff,[266] who met Korniloff and persuaded him not to precipitate such a crisis, the doughty leader gave in and delivered himself up to the authorities saying that he did not understand, that he had been greatly misunderstood. He was immediately clapped into prison under a heavy guard, there to await trial by court-martial for treason and plotting to reinstate the old regime. It is certain that nothing was further from this sincere old soldier's mind. Either the whole muddled business arose out of blunder and misunderstanding or else Korniloff was the victim of a hastily decided political exhibition. Lvoff, Korniloff's messenger either

---

[266] Pope and Wheal, "Alexeev, General Mikhail," in *The Dictionary of The First World War*, 21. Mikhail Vasilyevich Alekseyev (Russian: Михаил Васильевич Алексеев) (1857–1918) was an Imperial Russian Army general during World War I and the Russian Civil War. Between 1915 and 1917 he served as Tsar Nicholas II's chief of staff of the Stavka, and after the March Revolution, commander-in-chief until May 1917. He died in October 1918 of heart failure while fighting Bolshevik forces.

did distort his sender's meaning and Kerensky and Korniloff fail[ed] to understand each other by wire, or else Kerensky saw in the determination of the general a danger to his own power and an opportunity, by deflating him and crying out "Traitor," "counter-revolutionist" etc.—to entrench himself in the regard of the extremists of the Soviet who were beginning to apply more pressure on him. This latter seems to be the general consensus. But no matter which was the reality Kerensky suffers. If it were all a mistake he stands condemned for his carelessness and not making his investigation further and for not righting it; if it were a political trick he also stands to lose, for it was easily seen through by all,—by the supporters of Korniloff who immediately withdrew whatever support they had given Kerensky on account of his duplicity, and by the Soviet who also could not trust a man who would go to such extremes for personal prestige. So poor Korniloff was put out of the way with no benefit to those that did it and with great glee by those whom Kerensky hoped least to benefit—the Germans, who no doubt looked upon it as a clever piece of strategy to have got a strong man out of the running at so little expenses, and the Bolsheviks who immediately gave up all respect for Kerensky and rejoiced in the possession of the weapons he had given them to fight with. Ever since these rifles had been taken away from them immediately after the Revolution they had been seeking arms to use against their hated enemy—the bourgeoisie, and now here they were given them by Kerensky to be used in a civilian army should Korniloff get to Petrograd, and if not, free for use in their contemplated class warfare.

If we remember correctly we recall that of the Moscow Conference it was said by the Bolsheviks and the Soviet that the Conference was quite bourgeoisie and therefore quite un-representative of Russia and the Revolution. The Bolsheviks only attended this conference out of curiosity, without any intention of co-operating or participating therein. After it they announced a Democratic Congress to be held in Petrograd which would represent the true sentiments of the Revolution. And in the meantime this body which had started out with no representatives in the Provisional Government then one, then two, and so increasing its power now set out further to increase it in preparation for their demand for all the power. Kerensky's cabinet soon reeled under the blows of calumny and agitation and it was not long before all sides called for a new cabinet, for a bolstering up of a power of some kind which would carry the country along to the Constituent Assembly. Here Kerensky stated his intention of forming a coalition cabinet composed of the strongest members from all classes and parties. Immediately arose a great howl from the Soviet, which at this time came out for a transferal of complete power to its own sweet self. This was done rather haltingly at first and under the guise of a complete rejection of the plan of coalition. And so the argument goes on with much bickering back and forth and with the issue of the Democratic Congress aired before the public view, coalition or no coalition.

(Rogers dated a similar passage in his later manuscript to September 19)

And now here, with the fierce chronology of life we shall leave the arena for the home. Fred and I seized upon an opportunity to leave our bug ridden lodgings of the summer for far more sumptuous ones back on the Vassily Ostroff. So we bid our kind landlady adieu, packed our trunks and upon payment of stupendous ransoms to three *ishvestiks* managed to get ourselves transported back to the dear old island! We really had a very pleasant place though this time. Two huge rooms, beautifully furnished with a bathroom practically to ourselves; they were two of the largest private dwelling rooms and yet two of the most livable rooms I've seen in Russia. We obtained them not without a struggle though. On the day after we had been informed that we could have the rooms I went over to deposit some of my worldly possessions, to be confronted by the horrible news from the maid that a woman had arrived with a letter from the princess—who owned the place—to the effect that she was to occupy one of the two rooms we had engaged,—and of course the prettier one, the pink and white bedroom. This woman claimed to be the sister of the princess, but it seemed more like a gag to me particularly as the maid did not know her, had never seen her before. So I concluded not to be bluffed out of our rooms, but gave the maid ten roubles to bind the bargain and Fred and I am moved in the next day. Much to the lady's surprise, of course; and she raised a great hullabaloo about it, sending telegrams to the princess and sending the manager of the place over to see us. After a long pow-wow it was finally decided that we lost—the woman may always pay, but the man always loses—and we had to take two other rooms next to those we had fixed upon. The old lady turned out to be a good soul and not at all vindictive. She took it upon herself to see that our rooms were adequate and comfortable. And a fine bit of work she did. I never saw two such rooms before in my life. Huge rooms like those in Sir Walter Scott, with heavy draperies yet not oppressive, and with many easy chairs. My bed was the most comfortable one I've ever laid my weary bones to rest in; and taking all in all, we were very comfortably prepared for a long winter.

So comfortable were the chairs, particularly one with a sort of Madame Recamier[267] effect, that straightway [I] began to stay at home o' nights and read. One of the first books that fell into my hands was "David Copperfield," and I read this with evident and often expressed relish. But as always with Dickens, when the reaction set in, even tho I had been pleased at the time of reading, I could not suppress the feeling of impatience that he had not done better. He was content to amuse where he might have amazed; and the ease with which he wrote his lines and drew his characters lured him away from the unpleasant labor of building for inspiration. But in spite of all this I enjoyed the book and its characters, particularly David's aunt. Seldom in any phase of life or representation of it does one meet with a character that speaks and acts under given circumstances just as we would all wish to speak and act if we only dared; Aunt Betsy Trotwood does in this book, and Charley Chaplin does in the moving pictures,—which accounts for much of their fascination.

And now we come to the Democratic Assembly held in Petrograd, which was to decide the fate of the nation. It was held in the Alexandrinsky Theatre. It was supposed to be organized in such a manner as to contain a Bolshevik majority, but when the roll was called the majority turned out to be Cadets! It was opened by a speech from Premier Kerensky; this speech was received with mild applause. Kerensky stated the issue, and clearly. It was to be coalition or no coalition; was the government to be representative, democratic, or was it to be non-representative, autocratic. Was Russia to be led up to the Constituent Assembly by the hand of all the people or by that of an uncompromising labor tyranny? From the very opening of the Assembly it was plain that nothing would be accomplished. The warring factions had come here with no intent to compromise, each intending only to sound out the other's strength. Even with the nation's future at stake the parties were too proud to admit any justice in the opponent's argument. And so it went, haggling and brawling, until the Assembly became but a chaos of vocality. Vote after vote on the coalition issue took place with varying results;—one time the decision stood for and another time against. In one session this august body actually reversed itself twice! In the midst of all this Riga fell to the Germans. It was a sudden stroke and an effective one. Effective in spite of the fact that it had been generally understood that the Germans could take the city whenever they wanted it. A quick concentration of troops, a preponderance of artillery, and the Russians fell back, allowing a bridge to be constructed across the

---

[267] A recamier is a type of couch with two raised ends and no back. It is named after French society hostess Madame Récamier (1777–1849), who posed elegantly on a couch of this kind for a portrait painted in 1800 by Jacques-Louis David.

river, and the rest was easy. It has been said that the Russian soldiers ran, refusing to fight. This is not wholly true. They acted as any mass of humanity acts when all its suffering forces, its collective morale is broken and each unit is thrown upon his resources as an individual;—some of them ran away as cowards and others held their ground to die as heroes. But Riga fell and the Kaiser came thither and reviewed his troops midst a great show and it was reported over all Germany that the German steel will to victory and iron strength was still triumphant. And so it was against a demoralized opponent. But meanwhile things began to happen on the Western Front,—more of which later.

One would think that such a military disaster would sweep away all this party bickering like so much street-dust, but no, even with the stake changed to whether Russia should be Russian or German these political dwarfs played it as they always had,—shall the government be Cadet or Bolshevik. I've forgotten now what the final decision of the Democratic Assembly was on the question of coalition, but whatever it was Kerensky went ahead and formed his Coalition Cabinet, and to us uninitiated seemed to have done it well. In addition an Assembly of the Republic was formed, made up of representatives of all parties and of all parts of the country; to this Assembly the Provisional Government was to be responsible; was to submit its proposals for approval, and was to come for advice. During the first meeting of this Assembly the Bolshevik representatives left the hall, thus signifying that they agreed to no compromise, and intended to carry on the class war to the end.

Meanwhile, with Riga in the hands of the Germans, and here it must be related that they are said to have hung all the Bolsheviks there, who had made it so easy for them to rout the Russian soldiers, this showing their appreciation of their worthlessness—with Riga German, the danger of aerial attacks became imminent. The city prepared as best it could. Ambulance and first aid stations were established; the few aeroplane defense guns were polished up, the searchlights cut the sky nightly, and everyone lived in expectant dread. The Germans were not slow to follow up their Riga victory, by an attack on the group of islands which commands the entrance both to the Gulf of Riga and the Gulf of Finland. These islands, though heavily fortified, fell after a good fight, thus giving Germany a commanding finger on the jugular vein of Petrograd. In this battle the Russian fleet participated but of course was outweighed by the German dreadnoughts and battle-cruisers. One Russian battleship was sunk, the "Slava," and others badly damaged. A day or so after the fight I happened to meet a group of sailors just returning from Reval whence they had been brought in after the "Slava" sank. They were a discouraged looking lot in their dirty battle jumpers, some with wounds. I wondered what they thought of their German "brothers," just then, but I hadn't the nerve to ask them. The fall of the islands further demoralized the city and preparations for evacuation were laid.

Day by day bulky river barges lined up first in single, then in double rows along the quays and a continuous string of vehicles brought great packing cases of valuables to be stowed away and so saved by being towed up the river into the sea of ice forty versts away, down its shores and eventually down the Volga to safety. Museums, libraries, household paraphernalia, government offices, banks, and even the State Bank moved a large part of their valuables away from the danger zone in this fashion.

Even people themselves planned to escape in the same way. Nearly every foreign embassy has maintained a boat for the last two months. These are river craft with a fair amount of cabin room, in some cases stocked with food, with steam always up, and moored ready and waiting at different places in the river. Such plans must be guarded so it befell the foreign residents by turns to watch over their particular boat. The plan was that if serious trouble broke out here in Petrograd or if the Germans managed to persuade their way through Finland, the foreign inhabitants would betake themselves to their respective boats and steam up the river to the Great Lake and there down the Volga, or stop at a small lake town on the Murmansk Railroad, there get a train for Archangel and from Archangel take a boat to England.

(Rogers dated a similar passage in his later manuscript to October 20)

It came the turn of Fred and myself to guard the American boat.[268] We prepared for the worst and got into old clothes, loaded our pockets with food, even taking my alcohol stove and a can of beans and a thermos bottle of coffee. At the appointed time we were at the appointed place. We crept aboard a tugboat moored to a landing just above the Litania Bridge and in silence, even the steersman said nothing more than the necessity of his orders in the speaking tube, and we set out up the river. It was not long before we approached a mass of hulks hovering in the blackness; our whistle called shrilly, its echo drowned out in the answer from up ahead and we veered in towards the shore. As we slid quietly up alongside a river boat two figures appeared around its stern, one

---

[268] *The Journal of John L. H. Fuller*, October 19, 1917, 20. Fuller also performed guard duty. He called the boat *Getaway* and wrote that it "is a tub but I suppose a hundred and fifty or two hundred could be crowded on her in case of necessity. She is almost our only chance of getting away safely if things come to that pass and she is at least well provisioned. The duty of the guards seems to be to keep anyone but Americans from coming aboard and to see that the provisions are not stolen by the crew. There won't be much use in guarding it for very long for it won't be many weeks before the Neva will be frozen solid."

carrying a dim lantern. They helped us clamber aboard, and as silently as it had come the tug slid away. Groping in the dark we were led across this boat onto another and down into a small cabin lighted by a struggling oil lamp. The Captain greeted us smilingly with a side long glance at a huge Colt 45 that lay on a small table, as if wondering if we were quite safe with such a piece of artillery. We talked with him a moment, and after assuring us that all would be quiet he went below to the engine room. We stowed our belongings away as conveniently as possible, prepared our books and writing materials, set the gun to one side and the watch began. I was disappointed in the boat. It would hardly have accommodated half the Americans in Petrograd, and there was not an atom of food on board. We were fortunate though, just to have a boat so I tried not to grumble about it. But just up ahead of us lay one of the largest and most luxurious river steamers, with an adequate amount of cabin space for hundreds in an emergency, and this boat had been rumored to me as belonging to the French. I was smitten with another attack of that disturbed wonder which strikes the man in a strange land where he sees other strangers faring better than himself. But surely Americans should be safeguarded as well as others; what are embassies for?

During one of my watches, after mid-night, I went up on the upper deck. I stuffed the pistol in my pocket as best as I could in abeyance to the sheet of written instructions which counseled the guard always to carry the weapon concealed,—one must needs have the pockets of a giant to hide it from view,—and which by the way ordered the guard to shoot to kill in case of trouble; as I could make out this "to kill" clause was quite superfluous, as if one but pulled the trigger the killing part would take care of itself; where such a weapon exploded someone in the vicinity was bound to drop. But I stuffed it in my pocket and went up on deck. There was a chill in the air but I found a seat near the funnel which purred comfortably and was warm.

The air had the stillness of death. The sky was an arch of spangled blue-steel. And the night had the silence of wonder. Some lamps on the further shore thrust rigid blades of light deep down into the glossy water, which now and then warped like the crinkled daggers the Persians had, as some unfelt breath floated by. Once a black shape glided past behind a red and a green light, with a fiery geyser spurting from out a slender funnel, and at its passage the water rolled up from the darkness and patted the side of the boat. I considered the relevancy of all this destruction and discord. Was it not all due to the fact that there is a confusion of two questions,—a question of life, and a question of living. Shall the motive of life be artistic or political. Shall we expend our lives to live perfectly for perfection's own sake and to let live so, or shall our life be an effort to demonstrate something, the pride of power, or the efficacy of might? Shall the world be a lovable place to live in or shall it be a field for the struggle of wits and arms? These are translations of the first question. And the second? Shall not environment be so equalized that but very little of the individual's happiness or success shall depend upon the accident of birth? Shall not man's life be the result of his own direction and determination. Shall not the life of the individual be self-determined as well as that of the state? These are the two questions in amplified form. The great pity of this enunciation is that it is simultaneous. No one denies the validity of the second, nor denies that its answer is imperative; but thinking people do deny that they can both be effectively solved at the same time. The first is the greater, the more fundamental; the second the more visible, the more seductive. One appeals to the educated, the other appeals to the ignorant. Thus it is that we have the class industrial war, an outgrowth of the war of ideals, superimposed upon it; and just as surely as every victory in the industrial war strengthens the cause of "government by the governed," first as surely does it shackle their strength for the greater struggle between artistry and policy. Expounded in these words the cause of the Allies in the Great War does not seem so much to fight for, does not impel the unseeing to fight for it. But understood or not it is a cause which must be defended, must rebuff and gradually absorb the boisterous German politic philosophy. If not in this war, then in the next. And unless the question is settled once and for all now, there will be another war, and another, until it is solved. I never wanted to explain this point and drive it home more eagerly than two days ago when my attention was attracted to one of these revolutionary soldiers walking down the Nevsky. He carried a little boy on his shoulder, his own; who loved him so demonstratively that passersby turned to watch and smile as they went on their way. I wanted to stop this soldier and tell him as best I could that unless he and his fellows saw this thing through, unless they gave up temporarily all this hare and hounds game of forcing a social revolution onto Russia's already overoccupied attention, the thing would come up again for settlement in a more terrible struggle which would no doubt snatch away the life of his son. I wanted him to understand that; but of course in these times I could not myself explain it to him. So I had to content myself with stopping with the others and watching them, the little lad held tight in his father's arms, his little tip tilted nose pressed flat over his father's ear, his Slav blue eyes bright with the things he whispered, riding to his death on his father's blunders.

But I did not speculate further. An envious cloud looms up from the gulf; a slight breeze is driving a chilling mist down upon the city, my blades of light in the water are always crinkly Persian blades, and with a shiver I hurry below to sleep. I was awakened by the sound of bells as they are rung in the Russian churches. A monotonous boom of the big bell which fills all the air, and is inter-woven with the oriental jangle of the myriads of small ones, shaken without thought of harmony and only eastern rhythm.

Thru the oblong of the cabin window I saw the hazy dawn as blue as old china and the city's shapes immersed in it as dim. Gradually it faded, and left things stark and bright. The relief soon came and I hurried home.

(*Rogers dated a similar passage in his later manuscript to October 29*)

The Bolshevik agitation became more insistent and more shrill. Meetings took place in all parts of the city day after day; and at these the Bolsheviks, led by one Trotzky alias Bronstein expounded their doctrine. It runs something like this: The Russian Revolution is the greatest event in the world's history. We made the Russian Revolution. But even though we did it we are oppressed by the "bourgeoisie,"—all laborers are oppressed. The Russian Revolution still finds the power in the hands of the bourgeoisie; and the Revolution is therefore failing; it is being killed; it is endangered. The bourgeoisie only wish to keep on making money out of it, and will eventually re-instate the Tsar and betray the Revolution. Therefore the Revolution must be saved. But we cannot fight the war and "save the Revolution" at the same time for to save it we must make war on the bourgeoisie. Then we must make peace as soon as possible. Alright, peace then. To hell with treaties, agreements, and such that were not made by the labor democracy. To hell with France, Belgium, Serbia, Roumania, Italy, America and England; let the Germans destroy them if they can,—they are all bourgeoisie and capitalists anyway! So give us the power and immediately we shall have peace; immediately shall the secret treaties be published, immediately shall we give you more bread, and all shall be well. Or if you will not give us the power we shall take it, we shall kill the bourgeoisie and take the power.

Such words were ominous and coupled with the whisperings of Dame Rumour it was no wonder that the populace became nervous. All the Bolsheviks were fully armed; a "Red Guard" was being formed by the workmen; the army would all support the Bolsheviks.

Affairs slid from bad to worse. Railroad strikes hovered over the head of the Provisional Government, food almost ceased coming into the city; the rations were cut down to three quarters of a pound of bread per day per person, with the privilege of having one egg a month if you were fortunate enough to get it. Meat became out and out horse meat.[269] Wood was scarce, making it necessary to save electric power, in conse-

---

[269] Pinfold, *Petrograd 1917: Witnesses to the Russian Revolution*, 233–34. Florence Farmborough, an English nurse, wrote in her diary in January 1918: "If one is hungry—as one always is—one does not enquire too closely into the kind, or quality, of the meat. Horse flesh provides the main meat supply; it can be cooked and served in a variety of

quence of which all lights were turned off until six o'clock, a veritable hardship in these dark days. Clotted anarchy raised its head in a prophetic warning at scattered places over the country. An officer murdered here, there a merchant stabbed and robbed; in one place an entire estate despoiled; and in another place, particularly Petrograd, thieves plied their trade in open daylight. Loafers and soldiers stopped pedestrians, demanding their money and jewelry; women were trapped and their clothes stolen, and even school-children were robbed of their apparel. Petrograd overflowed with the scum of the land. The government would do nothing but hold its meetings. Kerensky, was powerless; what could one man do against this all, and a hated man at that. The Bolsheviks hated him because he was against their program of civil war, and the bourgeoisie hated him because he seemed so powerless against the Bolsheviks. The members of his Coalition Cabinet were all disregarded save Tereshchenko, the Minister of Foreign Affairs, and he was hated by the Bolsheviks,—for was he not a rich man, a capitalist, and moreover wasn't he pro-English?—a heinous crime in the eyes of the powers that were trying to be. The Council of the Republic held its sittings but they were mangey affairs. The speeches echoed in the bare hall and as an advisory or legislative body it was as impotent as a phonograph. The plans for the outbreak were openly formed; the intentions announced at the Bolshevik meetings. Dates were even set, and the 20th, 21st, 22nd, or 23rd were given. [Gregorian calendar: November 2nd, 3rd, 4th, or 5th] From the side of the government came only silence, which meant that they had the situation in hand or that they had nothing. On one afternoon troops of cadets paraded the streets, and the battalion of woman soldiers, fully armed, also made its appearance on the side of the government. This last was one of the neatest looking bodies of troops I have ever seen; dressed in the regulation Russian uniform, with long belted coat, hat tilted at the proper angle and bright, determined, feminine faces kept straight ahead, guns on shoulder, they moved up the street in perfect step, with the full arm swing. No one knew where they had come from or what their purpose. One morning people in the streets noted that wherever there was stationed a government guard, a Bolshevik "Red Guard,"—a shaggy workman in rusty clothes, with a white and red armband, and evilly armed; had taken his place too. At this an air of suppressed excitement spread over the city; and with the atmosphere thus, the stage was clear for the beginning of the tragi-comedy.

---

ways in order to disguise both origin and taste. . . . At the first mouthful, I knew what I was eating; but, as hunger is the best sauce, I had no qualms in demolishing every scrap."

CHAPTER 11

"When I walked down to work in the morning I did not realize that I was living under a new government"

Who moved home and worldly possessions the morning of a revolution? Leighton Rogers did. Petrograd was on acute alert. Throughout October, the Bolsheviks, capitalizing on their gains following the Kornilov Affair, threatened outbreaks of demonstrations and violence. Rogers welcomed new colleagues Boies Chittenden Hart and Henry A. Koelsch, who arrived in Petrograd in the beginning of September. Newcomer Hart wrote in his memoir: "We hear there will be an uprising of the Bolsheviks and that there will be mobs rioting in the streets, killings, etc. None of these stunts have been pulled off yet, so I won't believe anything is going to happen until I see it."[270] In early October, after meeting John Reed,[271] John L. H. Fuller noted: "The Reeds prophesied trouble in a couple of weeks when the combined soviets hold their meeting here, but I have heard them prophesy many things that haven't come true so perhaps this is another of their false alarms."[272] Rogers shared his colleagues' doubts.

In the first days of November, the Bolsheviks publicized their intent for a call to arms, but each day passed with no sign of the avowed uprising. No one was certain whether this threat was real. Rogers cautiously postponed his home relocation three days in a row. He decided that the Bolshevik warning for a fourth day would be another false alarm and thus began his move in the morning of November 6. Bad decision—the Bolsheviks had just launched their coup d'état, forcing Rogers to circumnavigate a full-fledged street and bridge calamity. By evening, ensconced in his new digs and satisfied with his courageous feat, he detailed his daredevil

[270] Hart, *Petrograd, Rio, Peking and Points Between*, entry dated September 25, 1917, Chapter 3, 37.
[271] John Silas Reed (1887–1920) was an American political activist and journalist, best known for his account of the Russian Revolution, *Ten Days that Shook the World*, published in March 1919.
[272] *The Journal of John L. H. Fuller*, October 4, 1917, 15.

adventure with a good dose of bravado. But, outside his window blew the chilling winds of a new revolution.

Uncertainty and bedlam reigned in Petrograd in November and December. Papers were closed, streets became lawless, rumors abounded, and facts were scarce. No one knew whether the Bolsheviks could maintain their control and who, with what forces outside Petrograd, approached to dispatch them. Rogers and his colleagues witnessed another killing, this time of an unarmed young soldier outside the windows of the bank's office on the Palace Embankment. Rogers fearfully wrote, "One can rarely walk about in the evening or night without hearing the crackle of rifle firing somewhere in the city. Twice I've heard the bullets whine too close to my head for comfort." Philip Jordan, Ambassador Francis' valet, bewailed: "The Bolsheviks got the city in their hands and I want to tell you it is Something awful. Streets are full of all the cut throats and robbers that are in Russia."[273]

H. Fessenden Meserve, along with his wife and stepdaughter, was in Moscow finalizing preparations to open NCB's branch when the Bolshevik Revolution erupted. Fierce street fighting and gun and cannon fire raged across the city, forcing the Meserves to hole up for days in the basement of the Hotel National, right off Red Square. US Vice Consul DeWitt Clinton Poole in Moscow helped extricate the Meserves and other Americans on November 16 when the fighting had subsided. "They had had a pretty bad time of it—little food and little sleep, and also a little panic," Poole recalled. "They were particularly concerned by the existence . . . of large wine cellars and the fear that the soldiers would get in, with unforeseeable results."[274] Rogers poked fun at his colleagues who traveled to Moscow: "I would have given much to have seen the group hiding in the potatoes cellar."

Circumstantial evidence points to the possibility that Meserve fled Russia. He wrote to Ambassador Francis from Moscow on November 8 uncharacteristically requesting help to travel out of Russia to accommodate an "urgent business trip to America."[275] The nerve-wracking episode in the National Hotel cellar likely stiffened his resolve. The Meserves returned by train to Petrograd on the evening of November 19, arriving there the next morning.[276] That week, the US Embassy, J. Butler Wright wrote in his journal, was trying to induce as many Americans as possible to leave

[273] Barnes, *Standing on a Volcano*, 272.
[274] Lorraine M. Lees and William S. Rodner, eds., *An American Diplomat in Bolshevik Russia: DeWitt Clinton Poole* (Madison: University of Wisconsin Press, 2014), 29.
[275] Tkachenko, *American Bank Capital in Russia*, 97.
[276] De Basily, *Memoirs of a Lost World*, 102; Tkachenko, *American Bank Capital in Russia*, 99.

Russia "due (1) to the fact that there is as yet no government with which to deal with here; and (2) that food difficulties will undoubtedly lead to shortage and then rioting and pillage."[277] The embassy had reserved a special car on the Trans-Siberian Railway Express train for eighteen Americans to leave on November 20 without "Smolny approval."[278] Meserve would have known of this plan. Back in Petrograd, Meserve likely met his client, William Boyce Thompson of the American Red Cross, who also lived in the Hotel Europe. The American Red Cross had recently opened a $1 million account at the bank.[279] Thompson so feared for his life then that he abandoned his luxurious suite in the hotel and slept on a cot in the apartment of the US Military Mission. His American Red Cross colleague Raymond Robins later recalled that Thompson said to him, "It means if we fail you get shot." And Robins replied, "Colonel, if I get shot you will get hung."[280]

What was behind Meserve's "urgent business trip" to America? Meserve cultivated private clients such as Grand Duke Boris Vladimirovich, General Count Alexander Grabbe, and other noteworthy members of the tsarist aristocracy.[281] He may have feared those relationships and his prominent cooperation with the tsarist and provisional governments made him persona non grata, or worse, with the Bolsheviks. And yet, on the day after he returned to Petrograd, he advised New York that NCB should continue its activities in Moscow and Petrograd as usual.[282] Meserve left no correspondence that explained the circumstances or reasons for his departure. No one who worked for or with him mentioned it (e.g., in the letters and diaries of Rogers, Fuller, Hart, Vanderlip, and others), nor did any announcement of his departure or reassignment appear in the NCB monthly employee magazine *Number Eight*, which frequently reported on the activities of personnel in Russia. The 1922 National City Bank internal report on the history of its Russian business was silent. Meserve just packed up and left. He informed Ambassador Francis he planned to

---

[277] J. Butler Wright diary entry, November 16, 1917, cited in Allison, *Witness to Revolution*, 149.

[278] US State Department, Office of the Historian, Papers Relating to the Foreign Relations of the United States, 1918, Russia, Volume 1, "The Ambassador in Russia (Francis) to the Secretary of State [Telegram]," File No. 861.00/718, https://history.state.gov/historicaldocuments/frus1918Russiav01/d247. J. Butler Wright, in his diary on November 18, 1917, wrote "About 35 men, women, and children will leave on Tuesday [November 20] together with the majority of the Red Cross mission . . ."

[279] Norman E. Saul, *War and Revolution: The United States & Russia, 1914–1921* (Lawrence: University Press of Kansas, 2001), 162.

[280] Strakhovsky, *American Opinion About Russia*, 31.

[281] Tkachenko, *American Bank Capital in Russia*, 88.

[282] Ibid., 100. The author could not find this correspondence from Meserve in the Frank A. Vanderlip Papers at Columbia University. Tkachenko cites this particular document which is in the Russia State Archives in St. Petersburg.

take a Trans-Siberian train to Harbin, China, leaving Petrograd on November 27, and then board a steamer leaving Kobe, Japan, on December 26 to America.[283] Meserve's stepdaughter, Lascelle Meserve de Basily, confirmed in her memoir that her family boarded a Trans-Siberian train at the end of November.[284] US Immigration passenger manifest records show they sailed on the RMS *Empress of Russia,* which left Yokohama on December 28, 1917, and arrived in Vancouver on January 8, 1918. Meserve never returned to Russia but remained closely involved in NCB's Russian business. He continued to misjudge the political risk situation in Russia, excepting, perhaps, this one time, his own.

"All foreigners seem to be leaving as fast as they can as evidenced by the crowds which come up here whenever we are open," Fuller remarked in his diary. "Many of them are transferring their accounts from Russian banks to us because our deposits are guaranteed by the home office. The whole atmosphere feels of trouble."[285] "Flight to quality" reigned supreme.

The Bolshevik Revolution and Meserve's sudden departure notwithstanding, National City Bank opened its Moscow branch for business on November 26.[286] The Moscow branch had a turbulent, short-lived history. Controversy surrounded its opening. NCB's 1922 internal report contained questions surrounding the decision to open at the very time revolutionary bedlam engulfed Russia. Fuller and Hart, who helped open the branch, described how business strategy abruptly changed. Fuller wrote on December 4: "The home office sent instructions not to pay interest on any more new accounts, which amounts to saying that we are not to take on any more accounts. In other words, the home office is responsible for all of our accounts and they are getting leery about conditions over here themselves. The Moscow branch opened its doors for one day when it received orders from New York to shut down until affairs became more settled. Perhaps they will give us orders to move on one of these days—when there will be no moving."[287] On December 10 and 17, the branch received cablegrams from New York to limit liabilities.[288] The Bolsheviks decided to move the capital to Moscow and commandeered premises in the city that included the National Hotel. This forced the

---

[283] Ibid., 97.
[284] De Basily, *Memoirs of a Lost World*, 102–3.
[285] *The Journal of John L. H. Fuller*, November 29, 1917, 40.
[286] The Moscow branch was located in the National Hotel at 8 Brusowski Pereulok.
[287] *The Journal of John L. H. Fuller*, December 4, 1917, 42.
[288] *History of the operations of the Petrograd and Moscow Branches*, Memorandum for Charles Schwedtman from George Link and William Welsh, July 7, 1922.

Moscow branch to move to the lower floor of International Harvester Company's office on Mesnitskaya Street on January 26, 1918.[289] Boies Hart then noted, "The Soviet finally took possession of our Bank, but they were quite decent about it."[290] On February 8, after the Bolshevik repudiation of tsarist and provisional government loans, NCB stopped paying interest on all current accounts.[291] Thereafter, the Moscow branch principally focused on winding down its business, maintaining its records, and safekeeping its remaining securities and bills received for collection. "We devote all our time to finding depositors and trying to get them to take back their money," Hart wrote, "It is a harder job than one would think. Many of them have disappeared. Those we do find prefer to have us owe them the money rather than take it back and run the risk of being robbed or having the government seize their funds."[292] The Moscow branch officially closed on August 26, 1918.[293]

Rogers surveyed the carnage. He admitted he had underestimated Russia's desire for peace, and that its willingness and ability to fight was over. Rogers self-debated this problem in his journal. The Bolshevik political platform demanded peace, Russia was going to stop fighting, and for the Allies, this matter threatened their prosecution of the war. Rogers wanted to see the Bolsheviks gone from the stage. He detested the brutality of the Red Guards and their incessant ugly street violence, and decried the Bolshevik dissolution of the Constituent Assembly. He lost hope in the Russian people's ability to assert themselves against the Bolshevik usurpation of power, lamenting, "I am forced to believe that the Russian people are more apathetic than any other race with which I have come in contact."

Weighing his duty to National City Bank versus his desire to contribute to America's war effort, Rogers admitted: "I do not see how I can stay; it's not because I fear the coming of the Huns but because I could not stay here unresisting and witness what I feel to be evil triumphing over what is right."

Surrounded by mayhem, Rogers still managed to see Russia's finest perform in the ballet and opera. He enjoyed a traditional American Thanksgiving Day holiday dinner at R.R. Stevens' apartment, which Fuller so blissfully described: "But to cap the climax came Mr. Stevens' Thanksgiving dinner Thursday night when all the twenty four or so Americans in the bank turned out in all their glad rags for a feast which

---

[289] Ibid., Letter of Henry Koelsch, May 12, 1922, 19.
[290] Hart, *Petrograd, Rio, Peking and Points Between*, entry dated January 28, 1918, Chapter 4, 67.
[291] *History of the operations of the Petrograd and Moscow Branches*, Letter of Henry Koelsch, May 12, 1922, 18, commenting on the *History of the operations of the Petrograd and Moscow Branches*, 13.
[292] Hart, *Petrograd, Rio, Peking and Points Between*, entry dated January 28, 1918, Chapter 4, 68.
[293] *History of the operations of the Petrograd and Moscow Branches*, 22.

beat anything any of them had ever seen before. Petrograd had been searched over for food and as one of the fellows said before we saw it, there was five pounds of everything for everybody, and there was enough wine to drown a toper."[294]

National City Bank organized a big Christmas party for the American colony in Petrograd at its branch office. Rogers joined the party and described a harrowing adventure that happened to one of his colleagues that evening.

[294] *The Journal of John L. H. Fuller*, December 1, 1917, 41.

(Date attributed to October 24/November 6)

And here Fred and I stepped into the scene for our little act. Although we were by far more comfortable in our new quarters than at any previous time in Russia we never closed our eyes to opportunities for still better lodgings. When the good Mr. and Mrs. Hutchins[295] went away we found that they were leaving their apartment open; they were kind enough to put in a good word for us and we obtained it rent free for a period of at least six months. I probably shall never live in a nicer place. It is an apartment on the French Quay,—the Riverside drive of Russia; a comparatively new place, comfortably and beautifully furnished, and equipped with a cook and a maid. Our only expenses were to be the current ones, the greatest item of which are of course wood and food; these would have been far too heavy for our salaries so we engaged Stuart and Swinnerton on the subject and soon had them signed up with us. Fred and I gave notice at our place and set Tuesday the 2 th as our moving day. I rather regretted leaving the old place; there had been so much comfort there; I wouldn't be able to lounge in my easy chair reading, and eating candy, perhaps listening to the girl upstairs play her scales or practice the Grieg compositions she was so fond of; nor could we further "cuss out" the folks upstairs when they stamped too hard during their Saturday night dances or when they played the American ragtime piece "Get Out and Get Under"[296] for more than an hour at a session. At first I was a bit wary at moving during a time when street riots and civil war were threatened; but as two days on which trouble had been scheduled passed by without disturbance, it seemed all right to chance the third day, which was Tuesday the 2 , our day.[297] Consequently we left the bank early and went to our

[295] H. Grosvenor Hutchins, vice president of the New York Bank of Commerce, left Russia in September 1917 on a mission to convince the American government to send funds to support favorable propaganda for Kerensky's government.

[296] Wikipedia, "He'd Have to Get Under—Get Out and Get Under (to Fix Up His Automobile)," last modified January 21, 2021, 10:45 (UTC), https://en.wikipedia.org/wiki/He%27d_Have_to_Get_Under_%E2%80%93_Get_Out_and_Get_Under_(to_Fix_Up_His_Automobile). https://ia802705.us.archive.org/8/items/BillyMurray_part2/BillyMurray-HedHavetoGetUnderGetOutandGetUndertoFixUpHisAutomobile1914a.mp3. *He'd Have to Get Under–Get Out and Get Under (To Fix Up His Automobile)* is one of the lengthier titles in the history of popular songs. The song was published in 1913, with music by Maurice Abrahams and lyrics by Grant Clarke and Edgar Leslie. It poked fun at the trials and tribulations of the average young car owner of the 1910s, especially when he wanted to get down to some serious "sparking" with his female passenger. It was a hit for Al Jolson in 1913.

[297] Rogers refers to Tuesday, October 24, on the Julian old calendar, which was November 6 on the Gregorian calendar. We don't know why he didn't add a "4" after "2."

home on the Vassily Ostroff to gather our belongings together. Even on the way over one could feel a nervous tensity in the air and already there were soldiers guarding the Dvortzovaya Bridge. The streets, especially the quay, on the V.O. were crowded with hurrying people. After some difficulty we managed to garner in three "ishvestiks"—it was very difficult as people seemed in such a hurry to get somewhere, and the trams had ceased running. However we finally brought three as shaggy looking pirates as you ever saw, around to our abode and after much haggling agreed on ten roubles a piece, and loaded in our baggage. One of them was in an especial hurry as he expostulated with me for being so slow, and in general for trying to move on such a day. He explained that there was to be great fighting in the streets. We at last got ready to set sail, oiled all the outstretched palms behind us and set out. By this time, pedestrians were actually running towards the Dvortzovaya Bridge, even overflowing the sidewalks to the street; some with bundles, boxes, and luggage of all kinds. It just swept over me at this point that it did look like trouble after all, and knowing of their cute little trick here at such times of raising the bridges, I advised our little caravan to speed up. Unfortunately one of our drivers was a bit "piannie" [Russian "пьяный" for "drunk"], or exhaled the charming odor of alcohol, and this worthy one had fallen behind in the race with two of our trunks in his rig. We had to take turns watching him over the back of our carriage to see that he did not accidentally or otherwise drift down a side street with all our worldly belongings. We all three came together again at the bridge. We arrived there amidst a whirlpool of humanity. A guard had just been thrown across the entrance and crossing was prohibited. People were running this way and that in black streams, shouting and arguing, but it was of no avail. Crowds gathered onto corners, on the steps of neighboring buildings, and in a black mass on the platform around the Bourse, watching with that fearful strained anticipation with which one watches great pressure being applied to a rubber band, wondering to when it will snap, and how much will be its sting. Our "three musketeers" tried to sneak by the guard, but were hastily turned back by the hairy shaggily hatted Siberian guards, and then a great howl fell upon the air; they rose in their seats, yanked at the reins, screaming with fear; and each scream only added fuel to what fired it and automatically, like a thermometer, the price of our ride mounted and mounted. It got to such a ridiculous figure that I could not agree, could laugh at them and consider the heroic figure they presented. The next bridge, the Troitzky, seemed to be open for traffic so we ordered our charioteers to take us over by this route. One of our friends, the obstreperous one at the very beginning of our wanderings—threatened to throw our trunks out onto the street and run to safety; saying that he was a Bolshevik and would do as he pleased. As best as I could I informed him that I was a Bolshevik too, and if he tried any funny business I'd beat him over the head and drive the outfit over there myself; the threat of force was added to that of words by a few preliminary waves of the fist in his face. To tell the truth we were in a great fix; stranded in the worst district of the city with a social revolution and all its street fighting impending, with all our worldly possessions in danger of being thrown overboard at any minute,—it was not a situation conducive to comfort. However, one driver was reasonable, the other scared, and the third drunk, so we managed to get them started for the Troitzky Bridge. Traffic was still passing here and we got across in safety. On the way over, however, I happened to think that there was not enough money in our party to satisfy the demands of the "three musketeers;" so after discussing the matter, and when we arrived on this side of the river Fred slipped out and ran down to the bank to mobilize our resources,—the plan being that upon arrival at our new residence I should stall and parley with the brigands until Fred could come up with reinforcements. This I did. But it was hard work; they were scared, or pretended they were, and howled and raged for their money, threatened to run away with our luggage etc. But I stood my ground until reinforcements came up with the money and then gratified them with twenty-five roubles a piece. I tried to make it a lesson as well as a payment, by telling them that they had done well by me in the fracas at the bridge and that now I should do well by them. But although they were grateful and even waived their moth-eaten hats in the air, I think their minds were too occupied with the vision of the cartons of cigarettes and bales of tea they could buy with twenty-five roubles. They drove away and we moved into our new quarters.

Hardly had we got our things unpacked, and were we seated in the living room reading than the sound of machine gun fire drummed into our ears like the beating of a hellish drum. How I hate that sound! In its place, on the battlefield, it wouldn't be odious, but to hear it in a peaceful city populated with defenseless folks and to see in one's mind's eye the results of its bloody work on a mass of people, to experience this fills me with an implacable hate. They were really at it, then. We had to wait, of course, until the next day to learn the result.

In the night the Bolshevik army, "The Red Guard" attacked the Winter Palace, the headquarters of the Provisional Government. Kerensky, as it was said, had left for the front; at any rate he was not in Petrograd. The palace was defended by a regiment of "Junkers" or future officers, and by the battalion of women we had seen the day before. The Red Guard, attacked from all points of vantage around the palace, and the defenders retorted from the windows of the palace and from a barricade of wood in front of the building. It was a furious fight, if not a bloody one; the machine guns beat out their message, and the rifle fire crackled like a great conflagration. The defenders could have beat off the Red Guard, but for one thing,—the arrival in their midst of solid shot from the guns of the Fortress of Peter and Paul across the river and the guns of a cruiser anchored below the Nicholas Bridge. There shells tore their way through the thick walls of the palace like paper and the defenders soon realized that their cause was hopeless. Detachments of the Red Guard also attacked the barracks of the Junker regiment, principally the Vladimirsky barracks. The young chaps put up a stubborn fight and like the defenders of the palace were only brought to surrender by the action of heavy guns brought against them,—this time field guns.

They were all disarmed; some were arrested and marched away to prisons, while the others were left in the barracks incapable of putting up any further struggle.

Perhaps the most intense fighting occurred at the Post Office and Cable Office; here the defenders held out all during the first day, fighting from barricades in the streets and from the roofs of buildings. The State Bank, too held off the enemy for a long time and for two days it was unsafe to approach in this place. It was an uneven struggle though. The Provisional Government had no one on its side willing to fight save the women's battalion and the Junkers,—the rest looked on in terror or apathy. And those who did fight had but meager arms, which were futile against the soldiers' ammunition supplies, the machine guns, field guns, and cruisers of the Bolsheviks.

(Date attributed to October 25/November 7)

When I walked down to work in the morning I did not realize that I was living under a new government.[298] A government of anarchy,—if that anomaly can be. But it was true, the Bolsheviks had won, and at the same time; it seemed to me had lost. By force they had gained for themselves, as they said, the right to direct the country and the people. But in their failure to realize that this is a duty and not a right, lies their downfall. They pried their way into government, into the fierce carbon-light of public demand, where their faults will show mercilessly black in the public eye. They have abandoned their strongest position, that of being the attacker against the existing order, that of always being the protester, a position which of great influence and absolutely no responsibility. Now they had given all this up,—they have become the government, and in the public mind are held for its obligations. They must fulfill

---

[298] At 10 a.m. on October 25/November 7, Lenin announced that the provisional government had been deposed.

or fall. From now on, they are on the defensive, it is they who must defend themselves against the scathing criticisms of the government of which they had been but a part.

Although I wish them to succeed I know they will fail. That's one of the tragedies of the war,—that its imperative demands will make [im]possible the patience necessary to follow through this great experiment. For it is a great experiment. That which the socialists the world over have been laboring for for years has at last come to pass; for the first time in history a first state of the world has come under the direct control of the most socialistic of socialists. In ordinary times I am sure the world would watch with interest the outcome of the experiment and perhaps in it would be engendered the spark that would rehabilitate civilization; but the war precludes that patient, interested, audience. Both the people outside and inside Russia will watch for only a short time, and at the first sign of weakness, will pull this socialism down like a tower of blocks. It will be judged speedily and harshly. So, it is not what the Bolsheviks have done that will win censure, but the time they have chosen for doing it. It is much like commencing to re-paper one's house when the roof is on fire. If these Bolsheviks win out and do succeed in bringing Russia up out of the ashes a free and straightforward nation, why then, all honor to them. But if they fail, let us hope they take their failure like men. There must be no crawling out of this, no sidestepping, no shifting of the blame. The task is a difficult one but they took its doing upon themselves by pure physical strength. There are many obstacles in their way: they will have to combat the opposition of the so-called "bourgeoisie" which will be just as determined and relentless as was their own opposition to the "bourgeoisie" government. They have taken the burden of proof upon themselves and they must prove or retire. In case of failure I half suspect that the good socialists will disclaim the Bolsheviks entirely; but their implication in the affair is inescapable. They have never disclaimed them before; they have urged them on, have pampered them in their present self-approving state of mind, and are as responsible for their action as were the monarchists for the criminal inefficiency of the bureaucrats of the old regime. But we shall see.

Their initial efforts were hardly encouraging. In the first place they formed their new cabinet, or Commissary, as they labeled it, and elected our old friend Lenin president. Lenin, who was granted free passage through Germany on his way to Russia, who, in July, was found guilty of receiving enormous sums of money from German agents. He explains this rather naïvely, however. "Of course I receive money; but I am an internationalist, money has no nationality for me, so I care little where the money comes from." After him, Trotzky, otherwise Bronstein, received the post of Minister of Foreign Affairs. With these two in office,—the long dream of the Bolsheviks was realized, and backed by the others of their party there seemed to be no reason why they could not carry their program to a conclusion. Let us go over once more the articles in their program. Briefly the Bolsheviks promised these things if the power came into their hands; (1). An immediate general democratic peace based upon the text "no indemnities and no annexations;" (2). immediate distribution of the land among the peasants; (3). an immediate organization of production, distribution, and direction, so that all these three should be under the absolute control of the proletariat, the "working classes;" and (4). (a sort of attractive sop but I think destined to be one that dribbles all over the offerer) the immediate supply of the people with food. With these declared purposes in mind we can continue to what happened.

During the day a band of "Red Guards" again attacked the Junkers in the Vladimirsky School, and in spite of the fact that all arms had been taken away from them in the early morning when they surrendered, the guard murdered some thirty odd of them in cold blood; and afterwards were seen stripping the bodies of their clothing and valuables.

Prince – – – was murdered at the entrance to his own house and his body tossed into the Moika Canal. The Junkers from another school were attacked without provocation and although they surrendered after only the momentary instinctive struggle of surprise, they were led away to prison and left there to terrible hardships. The women's battalion, after having surrendered was also imprisoned, its members suffering unprintable degradation.[299] One thing I saw with my own eyes. A group of us were standing in the bay windows of Mr. Stevens' office watching the crowds go by; one of the little groups which composed it consisted of a band of ten workmen and sailors escorting three disarmed Junkers whom they had captured. Just as they got in front of our window we heard the crack of a rifle shot, the last Junker's hat shot straight up into the air and he pitched face forward to the roadway. Someone remarked, "There goes a shot, where was it?" Someone else, "why that chap's fallen

---

[299] John Reed, *Ten Days that Shook the World* (London: Penguin Books, 1977), appendix to chapter 4, note 29, 306. According to John Reed, "All sorts of sensational stories were published in the anti-Bolshevik press, and told in the City Duma, about the fate of the Women's Battalion defending the Palace. It was said that some of the girl-soldiers had been thrown from the windows into the street, most of the rest had been violated, and many had committed suicide as a result of the horrors they had gone through. The City Duma appointed a commission to investigate the matter. On 16 November the commission returned from Levashovo, headquarters of the Women's Battalion. Madame Tyrkova reported that the girls had been at first taken to the barracks of the Pavlovsky Regiment, and that there some of them had been badly treated. . . . [Another commission member] testified dryly that *none* of the women had been thrown out of the windows of the Winter Palace, that *none* were wounded, that three had been violated, and that one had committed suicide, leaving a note which said that she had been 'disappointed in her ideals.' On 21 November the Military Revolutionary Committee officially dissolved the Women's Battalion, at the request of the girls themselves, who returned to civilian clothes."

down." And we all stood in silent wonder for a few seconds, at the strange picture of the astonished guard and the boy outstretched in their midst. Then the realization dawned; in the street people started to shout and run: we in the room, sickened, turned our heads away, and swore softly. One of us remembered having seen a sailor in the group on the corner level his gun at the Junker the second before the shot, and having seen him jump into an automobile the second after and hasten away. Why had he done this? We should never have our question answered. They picked up the body with the bubbling gash in the head, and carried it away. The street cleared so that traffic could pass, leaving only a knot of curious ones gathered about the corner and the cerise blot on the paving blocks. We left the window and returned ostensibly to our work but really to consider on the strange swiftness with which the Junker had passed from a striding, hating, loving boy to – – –?

Many many incidents of this kind happened all over the city and all over Russia; part of them intentionally and part accidentally. One of the strangest was of course an accident. A maid working in the apartment of one of my friends here was giving a betrothal party that evening. All the guests arrived on time save one and the festivities were delayed into the night on her account. When finally her knock did come they opened the door on a pale and bewildered guest. She told her story. A friend of them all, also invited to the party, had come to her home to spend the night. Her bedroom was on the ground floor and the two girls occupied the one bed. In the night and early morning, when the fight broke out, it festered about the corner where she lived. Lead flew thick and fast, and one stray bullet ground through the window and into the heart of her friend beside her. She knew something terrible had happened, she could not get up and strike a light for fear of other bullets and for three long hours, till the struggle lurched itself away she had to lie there beside her dead friend.

Private property was at public mercy. A band of brigands broke into the Winter Palace and despoiled it of many of its marvelous art treasures,—tapestries, rugs, hangings, jewelry, pictures and vases. In the streets was no law but that of force. Every man went armed, and thus thrown back into the medieval times when each man was his own police force, when the sole public protection was the individual's suppleness of wrist and the worth of his steel, thrown abruptly back to this, it was no wonder that ghastly things happened.

It was a blasting day for peace of mind. The Bolsheviks had won in the city but for how long. Dame Rumour had it for but a short time. It was said that Kerensky had joined Korniloff at the front, that they had influenced many soldiers there, that they were marching on Petrograd thousands strong with the unchangeable interest of exterminating the Bolsheviks. This was pleasant news for us in view of the fact that the approaching army was known to have heavy artillery and the missiles of such are not reputed to select their landing places. The Bolsheviks did not lose their nerve but immediately got together a crude army from among the garrison of Petrograd and the workmen. It was mostly made up of the latter, however, and I imagine they had their difficulties even in getting that comparatively small army together; When it became known that good Bolsheviks must needs fight for Bolshevism, Bolsheviks became scarcer than when only verbal opposition to the powers that were was the backbone of resistance. This crude army, however did get together, and we watched it march in a semblance of order across the Troitzky Bridge and down the Millionaya. A tattered, black coated, rusty looking crew, and evil looking too, they were, with long bayoneted rifles, heavy cartridge belts, and swords. Along with them were women carrying bundles of "first aid" things, evidently prepared for the worst. It was sad to think what a well drilled battalion would do to such a motley gang, and I, for one, fervently hoped they would not meet. Moreover, the Bolsheviks brought up a cruiser and two torpedo-boat destroyers from the Baltic Fleet, which they anchored just below the Nicholas Bridge; and let it be known that should the attacking forces of Kerensky and Korniloff succeed in capturing the city, they would find nothing but tattered ruins! Yes it was a pleasant situation for us innocent bystanders. Then the rumor came that the attacking forces would not attempt to take the city by violence, but would camp outside and by cutting off the food supply and allowing it to fester away within itself, would compel it to give in; but our friends the extremists countered with the statement that if this were done they would plunder every "bourgeoisie" house and apartment in the city. Which was of course, also very pleasant for us who had just taken a very "bourgeoisie" apartment! The next rumor we heard was to the effect that the troops really were on the way; that to delay them the tracks were being torn up; and that people living in buildings near the Baltic Station had been given warning to move away from that district as serious fighting was expected there. And so it went all through the day. In the evening it was not pleasant walking home. On the street corners, hovering around wood fires, were bands of these gaunt, rusty individuals known as the "Red Guard," shouldering their rifles, wearing their insignia on the arm, and shouting and laughing in boisterous, evil glee at the success of their coup d'état. Nor at night was it pleasant, sitting there in suspense, not knowing what might happen next, robbery, murder, bombardment, and unable to keep our minds off the subject because of the sudden crack of a rifle shot, or the tattoo of a machine gun, spitting, in some far corner of the city.

But when the morning came and we had not been murdered or blown up through the roof, we began to see and hear some of the lighter, amusing facets of the affair. We heard how Trotzky had gone to the foreign office to take up his duties as Minister of Foreign Affairs and had been met at the door and refused admittance; "Who are you?" the clerk asked. "I am Trotzky, the new Minister of Foreign Affairs;—show me my office." "No, you are Bronstein, the Bolshevik, we shall have nothing to do with you." Whereupon the whole clerical force went on a strike. Trotzky, once seated in his office chair, demanded the "much heralded" secret treaties at once. The clerks met him with, "We know of no secret treaties; in the files are ten thousand dossiers, if you wish to look through them, you are quite at liberty to do so," and they all left. This was a new idea to Trotzky and his Bolshevism—this idea that the "bourgeoisie" also could strike. In all his urging the workmen to strike to extort gratuities from the capitalists it had never occurred to him that their method would work both ways. And now, on his very own self, the new Minister of Foreign Affairs; it was being done, and he could do nothing but stamp about the room in impotent rage. We also hear how Trotzky went to the British Embassy to call on Sir George Buchanan and how Sir George was not at home—to him. Then again how Lenin and his closest companions sit up in his office, write out these decrees, and laugh uproariously at the damned fools that carry them out. Of course even the Bolsheviks needed money, and upon presenting their check at the State Bank for ten million, the director refused to honor it. Force was tried, but that was in vain also as there are three keys to the massive vaults of the State Bank, and the Bolsheviks could only find one. Moreover the employees of the bank struck at once, and with them the government printing force, which prints the new money; so there could be no more from that source either. Somewhere along in this time a new form of money made its appearance. We had all been astonished and a bit skeptical when the new forty and twenty rouble bills made their appearance about a month ago,—nothing but crudely printed designs on cheap green and tan paper; but even this gave out, so the Bolsheviks appropriated a batch of Liberty Loan bonds from the State Bank, which had not been sold, or any way delivered, cut the coupons from these and issued a decree to the effect that they were to be accepted as money. Printed on these coupons is a caption that it will be redeemed to the bearer on or after a certain date; one can imagine what chance there would be of receiving anything but another coupon in exchange! The Bolsheviks soon found that these would not suffice; they must have money. So they presented their check for ten million and their own sweet selves accompanied by an imposing show of arms to the State Bank once more. Again they were refused. But this time they finished by arresting the director of the bank and carting him to let him "rot in prison" until the check was honored, as they remarked.[300] This holding for ransom was effective temporarily for a group of the commercial banks got together a pool of five millions which they sent to the Bolsheviks as the price for the release of the director, Mr. Shipoff.[301]

All this time came rumor after rumor that a new government had been formed by Kerensky, Rodzianko, and perhaps Korniloff, that its army was marching on Petrograd with the intention of cleaning up the Bolsheviks and reestablishing a sane government. These rumors kept our new rulers on the qui vive[302] as much as our innocent and eager selves. Detachments of the Red Guard army were sent this way and that; and the bridges across the Neva opened to allow, cruisers, torpedo boats and destroyers to pass up the river to anchor opposite Smolney Institute, the Bolshevik headquarters. These could not remain there for long, as it was getting colder and colder each day, and the river gave promise of freezing up in record time.

I forgot to mention the fact that even the telephone girls refused to work under Bolshevik direction. Upon learning that a strike impended the Bolsheviks sent a woman representative over to conciliate the girls, but her efforts were not crowned with success. I guess the girls did not like the way she did her hair; anyway they prepared to leave. Whereupon the lady informed them that she would have them all lined up against the wall and shot. This sample of socialistic equal rights for all did not alarm the girls, however, who marched out not to return for many a day. One must admire the girls for adhering to their beliefs, but it sure is hard on the rest of the people. For when one wishes to phone and rings up Central and hears a guttural "что" [English "what"]? followed by a "нельзя" [English "impossible"] and the click of the plug being withdrawn, and that is as far as one gets. Of course the mail service is blocked too, and we hear that all cables are being held—even the diplomatic messages. This, it seems, to me is a sure way to start trouble, and one of the most effective methods I know of for ensuring recognition!

---

[300] Pipes, *The Russian Revolution*, 528; Figes, *A People's Tragedy*, 501. Rogers' recapitulation of the Bolshevik heist differs substantially from Richard Pipes' and Orlando Figes' summaries, which cited various Russian sources. They write that on November 20, the new Bolshevik commissar of finance, V.R. Menzhinsky, appeared at the State Bank with armed sailors and demanded ten million rubles, only to be rebuffed. On November 30, he returned, fully armed, and forced the workers to open the vaults. He put five million rubles into a velvet bag and placed it on Lenin's desk at the Smolny Institute. Pipes and Figes both write that "The whole operation resembled a bank holdup."

[301] Wikipedia, "Ivan Shipov," last modified April 13, 2021, 19:06 (UTC), https://en.wikipedia.org/wiki/Ivan_Shipov. Ivan Pavlovich Shipov (Russian: Иван Павлович Шипов) (1865–1919), governor of the State Bank of Russia from 1914 to 1917. The circumstances of Shipov's death are uncertain but seem to coincide with many political arrests and executions by the Bolsheviks in 1919.

[302] French: On the alert or lookout.

And of course recognition by the foreign governments is what the Bolsheviks are playing for now. They can really do little to affect the war and peace until they are accorded this recognition. But the Allied powers are very wary of granting it. They do not wish to recognize a government of Russia which is not backed by the majority of the Russian people; nor do they wish to recognize one that they know intends to conclude a separate peace with their enemies. The only thing they can do is to await the decision of the Constituent Assembly which is scheduled to meet on November 25th, old style. I have no doubt but that the Bolsheviks will do all in their power to prevent the meeting of the Assembly; or if it does succeed in getting itself together that they will prevent its decisions. They mean to attain their greatest aim,—peace—at all costs, and if the Constituent Assembly meets, and even represents a majority of the people of Russia as against a separate peace,—the Bolsheviks will overthrow it. Of course it is tyranny. The whole Bolshevik program, if carried out, will not lessen the weight of evil in the scale one whit, it will only transfer it from one side of the balance to the other. But I am indulging in speculation which is not good. It might bear repetition that the Bolsheviks are playing for recognition, and it seems to me, playing badly. That they are eager for it is shown by the shouts of "Recognition," "Triumph," which break out whenever anyone connected with a foreign power applies to Smolney[303] for an automobile permit, or a permit to leave the city.

Of course there are many taking this opportunity to leave the country. On the Siberian Express last Tuesday was a special car for Americans leaving for home. Some of the newspapers had it that all Americans were leaving and predicted that this meant trouble between Russia and America; but the car was occupied by a few women and one or two men, engineers and Red Cross people. This only goes to show, however, how alert the enemy agents are to seize upon every point available. Of course we at the bank have not even considered going; I sometimes think we'll stay so long that it will finally be impossible for us to get out. We can no longer depend upon our boat, as the river is freezing making it necessary to discontinue that avenue of escape. But that is the least of our worries.

The vital question at present is food. We hear that the peasants refuse to send it to Petrograd, as they do not agree with the Bolsheviks' aim; we also hear that what food there is will be distributed to the workmen, and that the "bourgeoisie" will be

---

[303] Wikipedia, "Smolny Institute," last modified May 7, 2021, 04:29 (UTC), https://en.wikipedia.org/wiki/Smolny_Institute. The building, constructed from 1806 to 1808, originally housed the Smolny Institute for Noble Maidens, borrowing its name from the nearby Smolny Convent. Lenin chose it as Bolshevik headquarters immediately before and during the November Revolution. Today, it is the official residence of the governor of St. Petersburg and houses a museum dedicated to Lenin.

left to take care of themselves. It was announced in the papers yesterday that in the absence of wheat, which would be shortly, potatoes would be distributed on the cards in place of bread.

Meanwhile we hear exciting tales from Moscow. The fighting has been far more prolonged and intense there than in here in Petrograd. The Junkers there were fore-warned and forearmed and when the outbreak commenced, they retired to defendable positions in the Kremlin and in important buildings about the city. The Bolsheviks, who outnumbered them by far, laid siege with every kind of weapon in their power and for six days and nights Moscow endured the hottest battle of her career. Meetings of Junkers and Red Guards in the streets left them dotted with dead, and doorways and stairways became depositories for the bodies. Our party in the Hotel National underwent a siege, spending most of the time in the cellar.[304] The Bolsheviks used the front part of the apartment as a sniping position and the place was riddled. Formerly, when in possession of the Junkers, it had been bombarded with field guns, which roar caused the defenders to flee. I would have given much to have seen the group hiding in the potatoes cellar. When in Petrograd and about to leave for Moscow, they had bewailed the fact that they probably would miss the fight which was then impending. I'll bet that during those six days they retracted all those lamentations.

The common opinion has it that the Bolsheviks will not remain in power long; that their downfall will be the result of a split in their own ranks between the more and less radical branches. And in fact it already does begin to appear so. For Trotzky, throwing all restraining influences to the winds, reiterates his demands for merciless warfare on the bourgeoisie; he would exterminate them by murder from the streets of Russia; but fortunately there are more conservative heads around him, and he does not have his way. It is either the split in their own ranks or external force of arms which will depose Bolshevism from its self-appointed throne,—according to popular conversation. Some think that General Dukhonin,[305] the recently deposed

[304] De Basily, *Memoirs of a Lost World*, 99. Lascelle Meserve de Basily described the ordeal on November 14: "It became necessary to seek safety underground. Many people had already spent several days in the cellars, but now word was given and a general rush ensued. We ran to the cellar, past windows where bullets were raining. . . . Our nerves were high keyed but I felt no fear. . . . Herded into a subterranean passage, we spent the night—men, women and children—sitting upright on a pile of boards, our heads against the rough stone wall. Sleep was impossible."
[305] Holger H. Herwig and Neil M. Heyman, "Dukhonin, Nikolai Nikolaevich," in *Biographical Dictionary of World War I* (Westport, CT: Greenwood Press, 1982), 135-6. Nikolai Nikolaevich Dukhonin (Russian: Николай Николаевич Духонин) (1876–1917) was the last commander-in-chief of the Imperial Russian Army. In September 1917, Dukhonin became chief of staff in Mogilev. When Kerensky fled Petrograd and then Russia following the Bolshevik seizure of power, Dukhonin became de facto supreme commander. Lenin ordered Dukhonin to discuss an armistice proposal on November 21, but Dukhonin stalled, and Lenin ordered his dismissal the next day. A Bolshevik mob of soldiers and sailors murdered him near the Mogilev railway station on December 3.

Commander-in-Chief will succeed in foisting a sufficient force to him to come to Petrograd and clear out the nest of Bolsheviks. Of this I have my doubts. I even think that the Bolsheviks have a fair chance of continuing in power and of obtaining what they desire. The surest way to make a conservative is to give a radical responsibility. The extremists have assumed responsibility from which there can be no honorable retreat and we can now settle back and watch the mass of this responsibility turn the edge of their keen radicalism. It may be that in the chaos of the time, in the space of that dangerous moment when the machinery of the commonwealth is running on its momentum alone,—is more or less independent of the driving power of popular needs,—it may be that in this moment the Bolsheviks may be able to substitute for the old a new economic order, without stopping the wheels. They must realize fully that their stay in power depends upon their ability to satisfy the popular demands; and it is just these popular demands which will engross their time and attention and withdraw them from the problem of executing their national radical conception. But in being brought down from the altitudes of theoretical radicalism by the demands of the people as a whole the Bolsheviks will undoubtedly raise the people's demands to more radical level, and thus will a new basis of conservatism be established. This will be a good thing. The question is at what cost will it be gained?

Of course axiom one of the Bolsheviks is peace. It has been their cry from the first, and in face of all kinds of opposition and accusation they have adhered to it. Peace, general peace, separate peace, any kind of peace. Peace thus must be in order that they may begin their experiments on the new economic structure of Russia. But the Germans also desire peace, not because he wishes to construct a new social structure, but because he happens to have his arms full of spoils and sees an opportune time to quit. A general peace if he can get it; if the Russians can make their Allies agree to such a thing on German terms; and if not a separate peace which shall leave Germany free to turn her full strength on the Allies, possibly backed by Russian resources. But some kind of peace too, the Germans want. Here it is that the wager of German intrigue mingles with and curdles the purity of the Bolshevik purpose. It is just this coincidence with the German desire that casts a ghastly mist of doubt over the whole glowing extremist structure; and it is the mist of distrust that, like the very German poison gas itself, will rot the lungs of those who should carry this edifice on their shoulders, causing them to drop it and let it shiver on the ground. For if there is one virtue the Russian people have above all others it is sincerity. And if once they see that Bolshevism is stabbing their friends in the back and so be-germanizing Russia's fair name; I believe they will drop Bolshevism. Of course there are sincere Bolsheviks, but they are led on, by Germany, their way made easy by Teuton money and their action guided by Hun suggestion. Thus is this new green growth but another cursed German blind. It is the product of one more poison seed, planted this time in fertile soil. By its very nature it cannot stand alone. And in itself twining about the German trunk it begets its own downfall, as it is a trunk dying and rotting, fit for the woodman's axe.

But I am wandering, and not even concisely. Once in power the Bolsheviks turned their efforts to obtaining peace. Not being recognized by the Allies they could not expect much from that direction, so they turned to the enemy. Receiving intimation somehow or other that the Germans would enter negotiations with them they have sent a party to the front to make plans for these negotiations. These have not been announced as yet and we can only await them. Nothing else can be done.

Although most of the performance has not been hopeful, there has been one thing to admire. That is the conduct of the Petrograd City Duma. This body but recently elected by the ballot of the city's inhabitants has from the first deplored and actively opposed the "might makes right" policy of the Bolsheviks. During the first day of the outbreak the members of this body issued proclamations calling on the citizens to ignore the usurpers as much as possible; and authorizing them to form committees for public safety and private protection. The inhabitants of each building were requested to form a House Committee which should stand guard, and defend the house. These committees were to provide arms, and the Duma urged their full use in defense of private property. They have been ordered to be silent, and forbidden to meet time and time again, but they persist in carrying out their duties, and in this insistence on duty they present one of the most cheering spectacles I have seen in Russia. All support to them and to their like.

It is a fearful thing to contemplate how faintly the spark of inspiration burns in breasts of the masses. It fails to burst out in a blaze even when fanned by the tremendous winds caused by the present rush of events. While the fate of a nation is being fought for by a few, the great majority look on in wonder, without realization, without understanding, turn their shoulders and proceed on the daily path. I am forced to believe that the Russian people are more apathetic than any other race with which I have come in contact. I cannot imagine similar events taking place in America and any person of my own age remaining a spectator! I know as surely as I know my own existence that every one of them would be actually involved in it on one side or the other; there would be few spectators. And yet here in all this I have hardly become aware of any organized resistance by anyone save the few Junker cadets. To be sure they are the young men of the country; but such a very small part of them. Meanwhile, in spite of the struggle the public goes its way, and I believe that even more curiosity would be evinced from them if the whole affair were a moving picture in the taking. Bands of armed men march the streets, or race to and fro in machines; there is fighting about some public building, scurrying of the pedestrians, momentarily for shelter, and when they emerge again a government has fallen, a new one stands with swinging arms over its body, and another tremor goes through the world. But things as they are still are; Ivan Ivanovitch still drives his "droshky,"[306] Sasha Ivanova still patters to the market, standing perhaps in a slightly longer line, and Olga Spiradonova still walks to school. And if the new order fits it is put on and worn, if it does not fit it is discarded. For the minds of the people are not concerned with experiments in government, but with problems in comfort and happiness.

9/22 November. 1917

The most important news of the day is the announcement that each "rich" apartment must furnish at least one blanket, and food for the soldiers. A committee will be formed in each apartment house which will collect these things and deliver these with a report to the Bolshevik government at Smolney. The words "rich apartment" are further defined as apartments whose rent is 2400 roubles per year or over. In case of refusal to give up these things the dweller will be fined heavily and perhaps imprisoned, and his apartment subject to complete confiscation. Thus are the "rich" to be made to pay. How will we fare under this I cannot say; the rent of our apartment is just that sum, when there is any, but we are getting it free of rent. And we are not Russians, whether that will make any difference or not we should see. Taxation? Socialism, Communism, or—robbery. I suppose it all depends upon the point of view. The next important bit of information was that the Bolsheviks are in favor of the meeting of "The Constituent Assembly."

10/23'd. November.

And today we are informed that the Bolsheviks have all the secret treaties in their hands and that very soon they are to be printed. According to Trotzky not only treaties with the Allies but also those with Germany will be published, and the revelations disclosed

---

[306] A *droshky* (Russian: дрожки, plural) is a term used for several types of carriage, including a low, four-wheeled open carriage. It consists of a long bench on which the passengers ride sideways or astride, as on a saddle.

therein will stop the war. Millions of copies will be printed and when distributed among the soldiers at the fronts, will disclose to them what they are fighting for; and according to Trotzky the disclosures will be such that soldiers will refuse to fight longer. (Perhaps Russian soldiers; it is no new thing for them). I sincerely wish it would be so easy to stop the war as this. If the publication of any document would accomplish that end; I am heartily for its publication. So out with your secret treaties Trotzky.

11/24 Nov.

Today, under the heading of "secret treaties" they published a few telegrams interchanged between Sazonoff and the Russian ambassadors in France and England; they were harmless affairs, mostly concerned with expressions of confidence, and with agreements that Russia should have Constantinople. Altogether their tone was such as to place England and France in a very good light, a generous one. It is said that this is only the beginning, that there are many more to follow, and that the disclosures will be startling. Sounds like the conjurer at a children's party keeping his audience in suspense until the ice cream is brought in.

But while Rome burns we shall eat drink and be merry; this to wed two good old proverbs. Tonight we're giving a party,—a sort of combination affair in honor of our new quarters—a housewarming, and to the honor of Mr. Stevens, whose birthday it is tomorrow. There's much food got together at terrific expense, and an extensive wine list. Here's a part of the expense column:—

12/25 Nov.

This has been an immoral day for me. I have done nothing save sleep, eat, drink, and be comfortable. After last night's party, which was a great success, I slept until two o'clock this afternoon! Upon getting up lunch was served, and after stalling off some guests who came in the afternoon and outstayed their welcome, we had dinner at nine. We should have invited our guests to dinner had we not known that they came with that express and avowed purpose; so we fooled them instead. Aren't we the big, generous, manly creatures though? I've read a little of Samuel Butler's "The Way of All Flesh" and find it a keen satire; but its keenness is that of a blade devoid of the exhilaration of the keen wind. However, we must reserve opinion until we are finished and qualified to give it.

We heard today of a great French and English advance,—a gash cut six miles deep into the German line, and some eight thousand prisoners taken. If so, it is good. Good logic, the only kind the German mind can understand.

13/26 Nov.

Yesterday the voting for the Constituent Assembly began. Fighting had been prophesied for it was rumored that the Bolsheviks had planned to break it up, knowing that a large vote is sure to be polled against them. And if I remember correctly that was part of their plan, to hamper the formation of the Assembly. But, at present, they seem to be encouraging it, with the best of their efforts. This change of heart is explained by some who say that the German answer to the offer of armistice and separate peace, which everyone knows that Trotzky made, was an emphatic refusal to deal with any Russians until after the meeting of the Constituent Assembly. Hence the Bolsheviks have had to swallow their wrath and howl for the Assembly. In the City Duma a telegraphic answer from the German troops to Trotzky's armistice proposal was read. It said that if the Russians really wanted an armistice let them withdraw one hundred versts from their present lines. This insulting proposal was received with cries of "Shame" at Russia's degradation.

But this election is an interesting affair. There are nineteen parties and nineteen groups of men up for election. The groups or "speecok" [Russian: список, or "list"] as it is called, which receives the greatest number of votes gets a proportionate number of representatives into the Constituent Assembly. There are all kinds of "speecoks" Bolsheviks, No.4, Menshevik, church, Party of People's Freedom which is No.2 and so forth. The campaign seems to be a battle of posters. All buildings and available spaces are plastered with them, ten deep, as it is considered a great feat for a party to sneak out in the night with a sheaf of posters and a can of paste and conceal every enemy poster under one of its own. Speecok No. 2 has an office downstairs in our building and two or three times have I seen their representatives set out on such an adventure. So there is some truth in the statement that the side with the most paste and posters will win! (Do they call that sticking to it?) Shoot him, quick!

We also learned today that Trotzky had sent a note to all the neutral representatives here requesting their cooperation in his efforts to secure a democratic peace.

14/27 Nov.

The best news of the day is that an increased amount of supplies is coming into the city and that the bread ration is to be raised to one half pound per person per day. From Grey,[307] who has been up at Smolney Institute talking with some of these Bolsheviks—and he says they're not half as bad as they are made out to be—I learn that they recognize the seriousness of the food problem; and are taking all steps within their power to meet it. Thousands of soldiers and sailors have been sent into the country to bring food to Petrograd.

The voting for the Constituent Assembly still goes on quietly. It is not known who leads but the race is said to be between the Bolsheviks and the Party of People's Freedom, Milyukoff's party.

An answer from the Spanish Embassy to Trotzky's neutral note was published today. It stated that the embassy took pleasure in forwarding the note to Spain. This is considered a big victory by the Bolsheviks!

15/28 Nov.

Results of the Petrograd election were published today, and they show victory for the Bolsheviks; but not a great victory. Of the thirteen delegates elected to the Constituent Assembly from this district six are to be Bolsheviks, four Cadets, two Social Revolutionary, and one some other party whose name I have forgot. As this district is said to be the most rabid Bolshevik of them all, I cannot see where the latter can expect to come out over the whole country. Not that it makes much difference whether they do or not, for I firmly believe the Bolsheviks will pay little or no attention to the Constituent Assembly. I think at one time they had made up their minds to abolish it, and were only got to change their attitude by intimations from Berlin that some sort of semblance of abeyance to popular opinion should be made, even if it were to a perverted one. So I think that if the Assembly does meet, it will be nothing but a chaos of sound as ineffectual as a moving force as was the Moscow Conference or the recent Council of the Republic. It seems rather an ignominious ending for a gathering which was to have determined the future of this mighty country, and it makes one's blood boil to consider how little the usurpers listen to the voice of the people. And these men were the very ones under the old regime that bewailed

---

[307] Frederick Gray, the English secretary to H. Fessenden Meserve.

their impotence in the loudest cries; they are now treating the popular will with far more contempt than theirs was ever subject to.

Today we hear the details of the opening of the peace negotiations with the German army. In truth, not the negotiations but the preparation for them. The Russian Committee upon arriving at the front, proceeded to the neutral zone prescribed in the German conditions. Here they were met by the German party, blindfolded and taken in automobiles to the Teuton headquarters. It was arranged that on 19th. of November, old style, the negotiations should begin. The Russian representatives should come to the meeting on the appointed date, accompanied by representatives from the army; there they would find the German Committee, and the negotiations would commence at once. Each party was to be allowed to have telegraphic connections with army and its government. I could not but remark the naiveté with which these men expressed their delight with this business. Especially were they pleased with the blindfold. It was mysterious and strange to them,—like the atmosphere pervading a fraternity election in some college at home.

Trotzky announces to the Allies that negotiations begin on the 19th. and unless they have representatives there, the blood will be on their own heads. Sir George Buchanan, in a typical diplomatic reply, points out the fact that it is physically impossible for the Allied ambassadors to send the news to their respective governments and receive an answer before that date, which casts a bit more suspicion on Trotzky's sincerity. As the matter stands, then, the Allies have not recognized the Bolshevik government,—they will not take part in the negotiations, and as a result these negotiations will be separate in character.

16/29 Nov.

I write this early in the day because I know that later in the evening I shall not feel much like writing. Today is Thanksgiving and by way of celebration Mr. Stevens is giving a dinner to all Americans employed in the bank. This is to take place in his apartment, and I know the place, and knowing Mr. Stevens is enough to make me prepare to out-Neb-Nebuchadnezzar. (?). I have heard rumors of a real New England Thanksgiving Dinner with turkey, stuffed with chestnuts, corn, beans, apple pie, plum pudding; and the like, but I can hardly believe it.

Personally I have much to be thankful for. Good health, a restless mind, the fortune of being allowed to witness these current events at such close quarters; my Mother, Father, sister, and brother, and their happiness and health; good books, pictures, music, the out-of-doors and this passionate play of life. It is more than enough.

I get so damned mad at the attempts at clever work of these ambassadors—at this thing called diplomacy, that cannot contain myself. They've gone and put their fingers in the broth again. Why, oh, why can't they be gifted with brains enough to mind their own business? The embassies, not being accredited to this present government of course have no relations with it. But the military mission of each of the Allied country's at the front has presented a letter to General Dukhonin, the recently deposed Commander-in-Chief—informing him of their disapproval of the intentions of the Bolshevik government to talk peace with the Germans, and informing him that the consequences of a separate peace will be severe for Russia; they also inform him that the letters are sent with the knowledge and approval of their respective ambassadors. Of all the asinine tricks this seems to me the greatest. What can be the use of sending notes to a deposed general condemning the policy of a government with which he has lost all connections and in which he has not one whit of influence. And if there is not any use in it why did the ambassadors allow these notes to be sent. I'm afraid the name of these representatives of foreign countries, ought to be spelled without the "amb."—To my mind this internal problem is wholly Russia's; it is one she must solve alone as that is the only way any permanent solution of any problem is attained—by the efforts of those most vitally concerned. Any unsolicited outside interference is bound to pervert the solution and incur the enmity of the people. It is certain that although this is a Russian problem the interests of the Allies are vital in it; but their efforts to affect the issue should lie confined to arranging the external conditions; conditions within their own countries, decisions of their own people, to which Russia must adjust herself. That they should arrange these conditions is only reasonable and just, but any attempt at interference in the affairs of another country is rank intrusion. If the foreigners in a country do not like the conduct of affairs there it seems obvious that they should be decent enough to confine their disapproval to moving out. Instead of that they must play their old-fashioned games of mental hide and seek, verbal tennis, and physical masquerade in a house that's not their own. The whole system is rotten; to the junk heap with it.

17/30 November

It was a Thanksgiving dinner to be proud—or ashamed of—it depends upon whether one can contemplate it from before or after enjoying it. We had all those things to eat that I mentioned and more besides. As far as food went, a combination of New

England and Russia; really a tremendous combination. And as for things to drink Bacchus himself must have turned his face away in shame. Of course S – – – got tighter than a drum and regaled the party all the evening with song and dance; we played cards, listened to our piano-playing brethren; sang, and enjoyed ourselves according to our various whims. I was almost ashamed to eat so much, when I thought of the privation and hunger in the city; but the stomach makes cowards of us all—I go back to Karl Marx for that statement—so I did my share with the others. At the end I had eaten so much that I could hardly stand and sing "The Star Spangled Banner." This makes me think of a dream I had last night.

I did not awaken but the beginning and ending of my dream were as clearly defined as if I had awakened. I found myself in a room whose walls were concealed with American flags fastened to their staffs and leaning at various angles. I was examining them, taking the cloth in my hands, rubbing it between my fingers, and holding it outstretched so that the colors might show. Many of the flags had too much red in them; the white stripes were imperfect, or soiled, or, as in some cases obliterated. And I remember I passed each one by, saying to myself, "no—that won't do; I must have a flag with the white stripes clear and pure. Don't you see, the white stripes must be pure." Then I found one, a magnificent banner with clear stripes and shining stars, larger than all the rest, and I took it out with me.

It has finally dawned on me that there may be some method in the Allied notes to Dukhonin after all. I see now what they are trying to do. The scheme is, of course, to encourage him to start a revolt against the Bolsheviks, and to assure him that in case he sees his way clear to do so, the Allies are giving him their support. The notes come from the military missions as they are the only foreign representatives who can speak without committing their governments to too much. It is a steep political game and unlikely of success. The Bolsheviks are too well established in power and any such movement would have to have the army behind it to ensure success; and I think the army is most all Bolshevik. The Allies make their great mistake in not recognizing that the majority of the Russian people, including the army and navy, do not wish to fight. Any attempts to drag them further into the fight are bound to end in failure and to engender only hate for the intriguer. I think the Allies have known this, but they have refused to believe it. Had they believed it, and acted upon it; had they supported Russia in her desire for peace and aided her in an effort to spread the Russian democratic doctrine throughout Germany, the situation would now be different. Russia would be still fighting an effective battle for the Allies,—true only a diplomatic battle—but an effective one just the same. As it is now they have alienated

Russia from themselves; and while she has not exactly thrown herself into the hands of Germany, she is acting independently. There seems to be no way to rescue Russia from the step she is contemplating. We hear that if she makes a separate peace England will set Japan upon her; and not only do we hear this but the Russians greatly fear it. I have my doubts though if America would stand by and see this done. That the Russians have these same doubts also was ably expressed in one of their papers the other day. If such a thing were done, however, it would only drive Russia into the open arms of Germany, which is just what the Germans want, and the Allies do not want. It is no time to cry over spilt milk or to bemoan neglected opportunities; the question is, "what's to be done?" Are we going to sit calmly by while Russia evades her obligations because she cannot fight more, makes peace with our enemies thereby making it possible for them to throw their whole weight on us? It is a cruel question.

18/1 December.

There is little news today save that Krylenko, the Bolshevik Commander-in-Chief, has set out for headquarters with his army to dispose of General Dukhonin, who refuses to leave that post.

It is difficult to hear anything but rumor now, as all the newspapers are closed down save one or two rabid Bolshevik sheets. Talk about tyranny and oppression, the Tsar and his secret police were babes in arms compared to this new freedom. There's no freedom of action, print, or speech,—and even freedom of thought is frightened out of the heads of these poor people by the constantly flourished rifle of the Red Guard. They shoot at any time, upon the slightest provocation. One can rarely walk about in the evening or night without hearing the crackle of rifle firing somewhere in the city. Twice I've heard the bullets whine too close to my head for comfort. It's a great life if you don't weaken!

19/2 December.

Whenever I consider the business of a separate peace I am divided within myself. There are in me two forces constantly at odds with each other, for convenience's sake I shall call them "Will" and "Kan." As we shall see one is masculine the other feminine; one takes no account of facts, the other all account of them. The controversy goes something like this:—

Will:—Above all things I despise a coward; and these Russian soldiers are cowards.

Kan:—I'm not so sure. How do you make it out?

Will:—I call soldiers that refuse to obey their officers and run away from the attack cowards.

Kan:—But you must consider that for three years these men were heroes; they fought without adequate training, without arms, in many cases going into the attack armed only with clubs, tearing the barbed wire with their hands. For three years they did this only to find that their officers were traitors, throwing them against the enemy's strongest positions knowing and intending that they should be slaughtered; that ammunitions meant for them somehow got into enemy hands, that ammunitions ordered abroad were made to fit German guns and not their own, that supply trains were invariably captured by enemy men, leaving them to starve. And above all this, that their ruler himself was only a tool in enemy hands. Can you call men cowards because, realizing this, they distrust their officers and refuse to fight further?

Will:—But the Russians began the war.

Kan:—No. Their Tsar was dragged into it. In those days the Russian soldier fought because his Tsar told him to, for no other reason.

Will:—But they relied on the help of England and France; and at this stage of the game they have no right to desert their Allies.

Kan:—But what can they do? It is a physical impossibility to continue the fight as the organization of the country is disrupted; there is nothing to fight with. You must recognize that.

Will:—They can at least hang on.

Kan:—And by doing so lose everything. Germany can swallow them in a military way anytime she pleases.

Will:—But that consideration of fear does not give Russia the moral right to desert her Allies in time of need.

Kan:—It is not a question of morals; it is a question of facts. The great fact is that it is a physical impossibility for Russia to continue the fight, and no amount of moralizing can alter this fact. Why not recognize that, and make the most of it?

Will:—But for Russia to withdraw now is weakening the cause of the Allies. It permits Germany to concentrate all her forces on the French Front and this comes just at a time when the Allied forces stood in a fair way to begin to punish Germany with her own weapons. You can talk all the humanity you please, but there is none of it in Germany and until there is the world will have no peace. Only by stern harsh punishment can they be made to see the error of their ways; only punishment with just such weapons as they sought to conquer other peoples with. They will not understand until they have been done by as they sought to do,—until German towns are blown to dust as French towns have been, until German orchards razed as they have razed the French, until their cities have been bombed as they have bombed the English. These things they could begin to understand; nothing less. To take from the Allies at this time the power to inflict this understanding, to teach this lesson is to rob justice of her sword; and I agree with Wilde that there is no more pitiful spectacle than that.

Kan:—But I do not think her withdrawing will have that effect. It seems to me that the Germans have had their best troops away from this front ever since the Revolution, leaving only a few landstrum[308] here. Surely anyone could see at the time of the Revolution that it marked the end of Russian participation in the war. That was the most outstanding fact.

Will:—It is easy enough to see that now. But at the time of the Revolution anyone who made a prophecy about it was either a diviner or a fool.

Kan:—But if the Allies did not see this and act accordingly surely it was their own error; you cannot blame Russia for the Allies' mistakes.

Will:—Nor does Russia's weakness justify her traitorous action.

Kan:—She is not attempting to justify it.

Will:—I know it, and that's what makes me so impatient. The utter moral irresponsibility of these people. And how they would yelp and scream if their Allies deserted them. Look here, we agree that Russia is up against a fact and not a theory in the sense that it is physically impossible for her to fight. Well, you will agree that if possible the Allies would be within their rights to alter these facts.

Kan:—Yes.

Will:—Then if Russia makes a peace it is certain that the Germans will be in control here and doing all in their power with Russia's vast resources to further Germany's cause. This being the case why shouldn't the Allies step in and take the resource for themselves. Why not let Japan come in and take things over rather than allow Germany to do so. Why not have Japan declare war on Russia if she makes a separate peace if only in order so the Russians so absorbed with their new problem that they could give no assistance to the enemy of the old.

---

[308] German term historically used to refer to militia or military reserve forces.

Kan:—That would indeed place Russia in a dilemma. Either step would mean ruin.

Will:—Such problems have to be faced sometimes. What does a man do when he finds himself washed overboard into the ocean. He either swims for his life or loses it. There's no excuse possible. If he can swim he has a chance if not he drowns. It's a cold engulfing fact, not a theory.

Kan:—Of course; but sometimes people rescue him. And that's what the Allies should do in this case. They should aid Russia instead of making it difficult for her.

Will:—Yes. You know that these people would not tolerate the kind of aid the Allies would give them; it would be military and their whole purpose is to avoid fighting. You know that all along their sympathies have been with the Huns, they have always shut their eyes to the faults of the Germans and concentrated on the failings of their Allies. The only kind of aid they would accept would be submission to the German will; which even the most reasonable man cannot expect them to grant. That is the very thing Germany has played for all this time—to get Russia to inveigle her Allies into a peace conference with no guarantees made beforehand. It's for the purpose that she has flooded Russia with spies and agitators and money.

Kan:—You believe that the leaders of the present movement are spies and traitors purchased by German money?

Will:—I believe that some of them are sincere, but blind and had by spies and money.

Kan:—Then you cannot blame the whole Russian nation for the work of a few traitors who happened to be in power.

Will:—I do not; but I indict them for apathy, for their sitting by as witnesses while a group of hired Jews in the name of Russia gives civilization the Judas kiss.[309]

Kan:—But the great majority of the people is deceived; it is ignorant, it cannot even read or write. And you cannot indict ignorance, you can only pity it.

Will:—By pleading thus, you surrender the whole reason for education. Isn't its purpose to overcome ignorance, to lead it? And if those here who do know and understand are too apathetic to overcome or lead the ignorant, then they are to be indicted. Only God can help them.

---

[309] Leonard Schapiro, "The Role of the Jews in the Russian Revolutionary Movement," *The Slavonic and East European Review* 40, no. 94 (December 1961): 148-167. Schapiro comprehensively studied the role and prominence of Jews in the Russian Revolution and concludes: "It could not be said that before 1917 Jews exercised any really decisive influence inside the Bolshevik faction and certainly nothing like the influence which they had among the Mensheviks. Bolshevism as it developed before the revolution was essentially a Russian creation, and Lenin's creation at that."

Kan:—I guess that's the way we shall have to leave it. God help them.

20/3 December. 1917.

There never are any newspapers on Monday, but we hear today that all of them have been shut down absolutely because of a proclamation by the former Provisional Government, which appeared in all the Petrograd dailies. This message, signed by as many of the old government as could be got together, called on the people to remember that they were still the power in control, although momentarily deposed; it urged them to oppose the Bolsheviks with all strength and to put faith in the Provisional Government. Kerensky did not sign it and this omission brings up the question of his whereabouts. No one knows where he is. Not a word has been heard of him since the first day of the outbreak.

21/4 December 1917.

Today we read in the "Russian Daily News" the only paper printed in English in the city and the only one that seems to be allowed to print as it thinks,—we read that the troops of Krylenko have taken the General Headquarters, dispersed the troops of General Dukhonin, and lynched him. If true it is a true Bolshevik answer to the Allied notes of encouragement. There's no getting around the fact that the Bolsheviks have it on the diplomats when it comes to getting results.

We also read that in different parts of the city Austrian and German prisoners have been seen in full uniform and armed! We read that their "manner was haughty and over bearing, but the people seemed to take their presence as a matter of course."

It is also stated that the Russian representatives to the Peace Council have arrived at the neutral zone and are ready to begin negotiations.

22/5 December.

No news today. The newspapers were all closed down,—save one which came out very late, not affording me an opportunity to look it over. This paper, originally called "The Day" was suppressed by the Bolsheviks, so it turns itself into an evening paper and calls itself "The Night." Score one for the Editor!

I haven't heard any but bad rumors all day. The powers that be seem to fill the air with them. Of revolution in Ireland, India, and Egypt. Of disaster in Italy, of a

German advance on the West Front, of—but so they go, all anti-Ally,—so to be taken with much salt. There is another thing which I suppose I must doubt too, and that is the current rumor that there are three German officers at Smolney Institute taking active part in the Councils of the Bolsheviks.

We went to the ballet tonight. The Russian ballet is the stage put to its finest use—the depiction of pure romance. Here, abetted by beautiful people, lyric scenery, and the poetry of motion, we see things as they ought to be, as we would all have them be if dreams would but come true. Art takes us by the hand as a mother takes a smudged child, and leads away from the dirt and strife into the land of fairies, hob-goblins, and perpetual youth. The practical considerations of the day fade into nothing, their place taken by the fascination of kaleidoscopic color, the lull of the rilling music, and the curving grace of youth. It is romance. I know of no greater blow for the poor struggling realists in art than the ballet. The very acme of the artificial in execution, it is the essence of beauty in effect. To the tired heart it is as dew to a dusty flower. The dusk, the soothing music, the tender green of the woodland setting, the silver glow of the moon, and Karsavina[310] floating like a rose-petal in a fairy breath.

Oh, if these people would only learn from their art. If they would consider how in it obedience and cooperation make beauty supreme and apply this to their daily lives, what suffering would be saved. If they could learn that in all things as well as in art happiness comes from joy in work well done, and beauty from perfection for its own sake alone—if they could consider the stage and appreciate these things, truly they would be the children of earth.

23/6 December.

Rumor upon rumor today. That Siberia has broken away, declared her independence, chosen Kerensky as Minister of Justice, sworn to stop all shipments of food to Petrograd and Moscow, and to oppose Bolshevism to its utmost. That the Cossacks of the Don have done like, and have sworn likewise. That General Korniloff has escaped from prison and has joined the Cossacks and Kaledin,[311]—that the peace

---

[310] Wikipedia, "Tamara Karsavina," last modified July 5, 2021, 09:41 (UTC), https://en.wikipedia.org/wiki/Tamara_Karsavina. Tamara Platonovna Karsavina (Russian: Тама́ра Плато́новна Карса́вина) (1885–1978) was a Russian prima ballerina renowned for her beauty. She was a principal artist of the Imperial Russian Ballet and later of the Ballets Russes of Sergei Diaghilev.

[311] Wikipedia, "Alexey Kaledin," last modified May 3, 2021, 01:32 (UTC), https://en.wikipedia.org/wiki/Alexey_Kaledin. Aleksei Maximovich Kaledin (Russian: Алексе́й Макси́мович Кале́дин) (1861–1918) was a cavalry general who led the Don Cossack White movement in the opening stages of the Russian Civil War. At the beginning of

negotiations are delayed, for perhaps a week owing to the fact that the Germans refuse to discuss other than the technical details of the military situation and refuse to stop transferring troops from the Eastern to the Western Front. That the Japanese have landed troops in Vladivostok "to protect our interests." That President Wilson has again declared that durable peace can only come thru the defeat of Germany, that the American ambassador, Francis, is to be relieved and replaced by Raymond Robbins.[312] There you have a day's gleanings; take your pick.

I can quite believe the one about the hitch in the peace parleys. And I don't know whether to believe or not the implication that the Germans will take a week to transfer all the soldiers they want to the West Front and thus allow the Bolshevik tools to say "we lived up to our promise, not a troop moved to the Western Front during our truce." That about the new ambassador I should like to believe. Our present representative's claim to fame is the fact that he is one of the most successful grocery merchants in St. Louis and that he managed the St. Louis World's Fair! Current opinion has it that his ambassadorial qualifications are nil.[313] On the other hand Raymond Robbins is an American Bolshevik. While heart and soul in the present strivings of labor the world over he is at the same time blessed with reason and much common sense, so that his sympathies would not be so powerful as to lead him to indiscretion. His appointment would demonstrate to the Russian proletariat that America is in sympathy with its cause but not with its extremes and impracticalities. A self-made man with vision, and a fighter, Raymond Robbins is a man I would gladly trust with the fair name of the United States of America in Russia.

the November Revolution, Kaledin stated that until the authority of the provisional government in Russia was fully restored, the Don Cossack Army would assume control of the Don region. This statement marked the beginning of the Kaledinschina, a rebellion in the Don region. Negative developments soon led Kaledin to believe that the situation had become hopeless. He shot himself on February 11, 1918.

[312] Wikipedia, "Raymond Robins," last modified February 8, 2021, 17:43 (UTC), https://en.wikipedia.org/wiki/Raymond_Robins; American National Biography, online ed., "Robins, Raymond," by Thomas Winter, https://doi.org/10.1093/anb/9780198606697.article.1500575. Raymond Robins (1873–1954), an American economist and writer, advocated for organized labor and diplomatic relations between the United States and Russia under the Bolsheviks. In July 1917, he headed the American Red Cross Mission to Russia. After the Bolsheviks took power, his activities and influence extended far beyond his office, tantamount to acting as the unofficial US ambassador in Petrograd given the State Department's refusal to allow Ambassador David Francis to directly communicate with the Bolsheviks. Although not philosophically sympathetic with the outcome of the November Revolution, Robins felt it was popular and that counter-revolutionary efforts were counterproductive.

[313] Dosch-Fleurot, *Through War to Revolution*, 151. The ambassador's valet, Philip Jordan, once told Dosch-Fleurot that Francis knew only two words in Russian: "Amerikanski Posol" (American ambassador).

24/7 December 1917.

This morning on my way to the bank I was greeted by the sight of the personification of free Russia disporting itself in the street—a soldier gloriously drunk. With one end of his shirt held fast by a sober friend who seemed to have him completely under control, the drunken one gyrated from side to side, his arms whirling wind mill fashion and his dribbling lips opened wide in curses and song. He saw our little group making its way down the street, and dived for it head long, shouting, "Bourgeoisie, kill them." The firm grip on the shirttail hauled him back, and he turned to strike, lost his intention in the muddle of his mind and threw his arms about his friend's neck kissing him effusively. And so he went up the street, alternatively springing murderously at the "bourgeoisie" and making violent love to his captor. This latter finally shoved him into a passing wood sleigh, sat on his chest, and went out of sight with him around the corner.

There were more in similar condition on the streets during the day and we finally learned that the soldiers had broken into the wine cellar in the Winter Palace. The cellar is half full of water, and the men sent to inspect it with a view to bailing it out I suppose, only got drunk and had to be bailed out themselves. But an enormous party has been going on there for a day and a night now; the square is littered with splintered glass, the corners piled with drunken soldiers and the vicinity crackles with the shots from the rifles of the drunk, shooting at nothing or anything. They roved up the streets in bands, fully armed, working their will on whomever they meet; new groups hurry down the quay, eager to share in the festivity, some even with baskets for carrying the stuff away. I walked home behind a group whose combined breaths would have run a steamboat; their arms and pockets were full of bottles, they sang and laughed and swore. They were planning to sell what they had taken and I learned later that this was being done, at the rate of ten roubles a bottle. The whole city shows sign of the carousal. Broken bottles along the sidewalks and strewn on the ice in the canals all signify to it. In all it is said that three regiments are helpless. The Winter Palace itself is a wreck and we hear that many in the cellar slipped into the water and being too drunk to save their lives by swimming, lost them there. Free Russia!

25/8 December.

Concerning this levy of a warm article of clothing exacted from each "rich" apartment, which I mentioned not long ago, when the list came around we wrote down one very good blanket. We received notice from the door tender, who heads the

Committee in our home, that this was not enough, that we must give more. The colossal nerve of it. Here we are strangers, we have to give nothing at all, but when we do offer a very good article, more is demanded. It fairly makes one's blood boil to think that American citizens are subject to such things as this. We are forced to do it under threat of violence.

Should we refuse and take the matter to the embassy we would be met by the question "what are you over here for?; you have no business here!" It isn't that I mind giving, it's the threat of violence that accompanies the demand that I object to. Do you think the English and French embassies allow their countrymen to be robbed? Not a bit of it. These things are said to be for the army and if it were any other army in the world I would gladly give much that I actually need myself, but I know these soldiers will sell what they receive for money to buy cigarettes and vodka with, their very lack of warm things now is due to their selling the equipment given them by the government. Can one be blamed for not feeling generous towards such sodden bits of humanity as leered about the streets last night after the raid on the Winter Palace wine cellar?

26/9 December.

I haven't done a thing all day save get up late, eat two very good meals, sit around before the fire, and dream. Mr. Jacobson came in to dinner bringing with him a bottle of cognac and some of his very excellent champagne. We had great fun with him, talking about his various business exploits; and he had just as much fun with us too. He particularly enjoyed the fireplace and the Caruso records on the gramophone.

I think I'll spend the rest of the evening in trying to do something—I'd hardly say of use—but something I like to do; I shall start a little story that's been running around in my mind for a long time.

27/10

There is nothing save apprehension as to what will happen tomorrow. This is the day set for the Constituent Assembly—the day towards which all Russia has been looking since the overthrow of the monarchist government. It was to be one of the most momentous days in Russian history. And now what has become of it. The Bolsheviks, with their avowed policy of force, say that the Assembly will be allowed to meet but that if it shows signs of a bourgeoisie majority, they will dissolve it and hold another election! Naïve! We hear that the Assembly will not convene tomorrow, that it is to be postponed; also that if such is the case the streets will run with blood etc. etc. There will be nothing of the kind. The Assembly will not meet because the Bolsheviks fear it and will not permit it, and there will be no disturbances in the streets. The fire of the popular rage will consume to ashes the very spirit which kindled it and the populace will settle back with a gasp into the old apathy once more.

Played bridge at Mr. Stevens' tonight and particularly enjoyed some raspberry tarts he had. A great journal this—from Constituent Assemblies to raspberry tarts! I don't know which I consider more important.

28/11 December.

Big holiday today;—the sun shining and low, as if by request, flags flying from all houses, banners flung across the streets,—at night the streets brightly lighted and special performances in the theatres. For it was the day upon which the Constituent Assembly was to meet. No, gentle reader, it did not meet,—the Bolsheviks postponed it until they announced "four hundred of its delegates should arrive in Petrograd." So all this celebration was for nothing and the people did nothing save walk around and look at it. Nothing.

A little excitement did come from a group from the Convention of Peasants which is meeting in town today. Chernov, the leader of the more conservative wing made speeches in the streets condemning Russia's present policy, and affirming that what Russia should be striving for were the American aims as set forth in President Wilson's speech in declaring war upon Austria. Chernov was loudly cheered and carried about the streets on the shoulders of his admirers. What else came of it I do not know.

Even though the Germans have got the Russians off their backs and have exacted an armistice from them, I imagine they are in a bit of a hole. President Wilson announces that America is in the fight to a finish and that there can be no peace until Prussian spirit is broken, saying that even if by some chance Germany should win a military victory over the Allies, the latter still hold the all-powerful weapon of economic boycott over her head, the German people are a bit disturbed at the prospect of another winter of the war after being promised absolutely that the submarine would finish it, and are beginning to question their government's refusal of the Russian peace offer. The government has been telling the people "We wish peace, but the Allies turn a deaf ear to our offers." And now the people murmur "The Russians have offered you peace and you turn it away. Why?" A venturing voice suggests that it is because the Russians offered peace "with annexations," and this being refused intimates that the imperial government is fighting for aggrandizement after all. No I would not want to be in the German Government's position. It's beginning there, the foment,—we can see it in the changes of ministers, in the hurried goings and comings of the Kaiser, Hindenburg and Ludendorff, and the gigantic hysterical efforts on the Italian and French Fronts. Hold fast Allies! Put more lead in the club America!

29/12 December.

Of local importance there is nothing much today. All business is nearing the point of actual immobility; at present it is but running on its momentum. The strike in the State Bank and the ministries continues; the banks can get no cash, and consequently can do no business. It has been thus since the end of last week, with a spasmodic opening of the doors for an hour on one or two days. And at these times no more than one thousand roubles can be paid out to one customer. When a check is presented, the client receives one thousand roubles in cash and the remainder of his check in checks drawn on various banks. All other transactions are impossible, merchandise, securities,—all are not. The clearing house has not been open and in consequence the banks are clogged with checks on other banks for which they have been unable to obtain credit. I understand that if our bank is open tomorrow it will be only for the payment of one thousand roubles to each client against checks drawn on us only; no other checks will be received! So we drag along each day; on each one hoping that the following will disclose an improvement in the situation. But we have been hoping this for eight months now and it has grown steadily worse. It is not a cheerful future.

The city sinks deeper into the slime of anarchy each night. Every morning brings an augmented report of looting, holdups, rapes, and murders; and so bold has lawlessness become that now she does her work in broad daylight. My Russian teacher boarded a tram which took up the Nevsky to the square where are the Hotel Europe and the City Duma. A crowd had gathered here about a group of men in an argument, consisting of some members of the Red Guard and a most respectable looking man in civilian clothes and carrying a leather portfolio. As her car approached she saw this man leaning over as if looking for something; farther and farther down he went until he was doubled up jackknife fashion. She ejaculated to the man beside her in the tram, "Look at that man, what is he doubled up about; what is he looking for?" The answer came, "Didn't you hear the report; he has just been shot." And sure enough, the victim suddenly relaxed like wire untempered, dived to a heap on the snow, and lay still. Roger Smith, at the bank, was on his way home from the theatre in an "ishvestik" last night when they turned a corner to find themselves almost in the midst of a group of workmen, all armed, two of whom were screaming in argument. One of these broke away and ran towards Roger's sleigh, another darted from the crowd shouting, "я иду товарищ" ["I'm going, comrade"], leveled his gun and shot the runner in his tracks about ten feet from the rearing horse.

This evening Fred started out for the Y.M.C.A. and had no more than closed the door behind him when a fusillade of shots broke out behind him, several drunken members of the Red Guard ran past, and more shooting followed. He felt a sudden distaste for exercise and returned home. Even as I sit here writing this I can now and then hear shots, and not long ago one cracked out not more than one hundred feet from my window. We are in strange times, times far back in the ages, times of the cave-man and the mastodon, when the latter is master of the earth because of his enormous tusks and thick skin—weapons and armor.

By the way the Bolsheviks are arresting important personages, it must be that they scent trouble in the making for their cause. They have announced that if the Constituent Assembly, when it meets,—proves itself more Cadet than Bolshevik, they, the Bolsheviks will arrest the bourgeoisie members, expel them, fill their places with appropriate appointees of their own and thus starts the "Representative Congress" on its way! I venture to say that if these things were done in any other democratic country on the globe's surface—if a meeting of the people's representatives was prohibited from meeting by sheer force,—I venture to say that the city would be knee-deep in blood before it would submit; even the women and children would be fighting such audacity. But here in Russia it seems to have aroused only disconsolate discussion in the tram cars. These are the forums of Russia, sort of perambulating affairs which can hardly be accused of not being progressive. In them all kinds of people meet shoulder to shoulder and with frankness speak their opinions. The only people not afraid to speak their minds are the Junkers and the women. It is a sad truth that the very best of Russian youth flung itself, as young officers in command of cowardly men, into the leaden trail of the German hound, recklessly, heroically in a futile endeavor to arouse a faint glimmer of stability in the wavering hearts. If this had not been so and Russia still had her youth the story might be different. What few of these there are left, however, are of the same stuff. I heard one tell two members of the Red Guard what he thought of the Bolsheviks, "We did not put up with Rasputin," he said vehemently, "why should we let Lenin live?" Another, when a workman in a tram, involved in argument, mentioned the word "Imperialism," snapped out, "Imperialism, what do you know about it. What does it mean to you?" The workman had to admit that it meant nothing, that he had only heard it used. Another tram debate. A soldier bemoaned the fact that some sixty odd soldiers died in the carousel in the wine cellar of the Winter Palace; shot by their fellows in quarrels or too drunk to swim in the flood of water which engulfed the place; a woman across from him, upon hearing the number, heaved a sigh, saying "Thank God!"

30/13 Dec.

I have just got hold of a copy of President Wilson's speech to Congress declaring war upon Austria-Hungary. It is not a speech; it has the solidity of a fact, the ringing clarity of a bar of steel—flawless along its length. It is essentially an American speech, setting forth both for the inspection of the American people and for the American people, their own opinion in this vast matter. But it is also an international speech. It is for America in that it speaks her will, and keeps ever clear in the forefront of her mind the conviction that for them it is primarily an American war. It is for England in that it contains a suggestion that the war's purpose is not to crush the German nation. It is for France in that it re-affirms that gross wrongs done her shall be expiated. It is for Italy in that it implies against the complete commercial blockade of Austria. It is for Belgium, Serbia, Roumania, in that it sets up once more before their burning eyes, the figure of Justice with keen sword in hand waiting, preparing, patiently her time. It is for Austria in that it condemns her vassalage to Germany and if there is a spark of individual pride left in her it is appealed to. And finally it is for the German people in that once more it affirms the refusal of the American people to covenant with the present rulers of Germany and drives still further home the wedge between those people and the government.

I see that in this long application I have not mentioned the name of Russia. Although there is much in this speech for Russia, Russia as a whole will not even know of the speech, let alone read it. The spirit of these people has snapped, they have heart for nothing—country, friends, pride—all these things mean nothing to them when opposed by the dread of carrying on the struggle further. They do not wish to fight more; they want rest, quiet, and they will sacrifice anything to attain it.

Honor, pride, duty,—all those sinews which bound the unrelated parts of the nation's body together into a willing, active force—have all been severed by the subtle blade of German propaganda and in the place of Russia stands a vacant, idiot mass of humanity, into whose unknowing hand the German has thrust the knife which shall stab civilization in the back; behind the leering agent stands shaking with pleasure at having found so malleable a subject.

It is difficult to confront the separate peace situation without expressing rancor; but I should say the present was by far the darker outlook. There will come a time, when the Allies refuse to join the negotiations, when the Russians get a glimpse of the mailed fist at the elbow of the extended hand, when Germany makes an offer of peace to the Allies and it is refused, and when Americans and French and English are battering the Hun troops back in France,—there will come a time I say, when Russia will realize her wrong and will hasten back to the faith. Let it be imminent.

1/14 December 1917.

On our way to work this morning we passed the corner where all the firing seemed to come from last night. The building there is a fine residence, and as we approached the odor of wine was distinct. Before the doorway, were two hay wagons empty of hay but being filled with the stiff-drunk bodies of members of the glorious Red Guard, who in the fulfillment of their duty had only smashed their way into the house shooting as they went, and drunk themselves to quietness in the wine cellar.

We read in the paper today that the peace delegation has again left for Brest-Litovsk to open negotiations. One of its members, a general sent to represent the army, immediately upon his arrival, went to the room reserved for him and committed suicide. People are unable to explain it but my Russian teacher shed some light on the event by recalling this general in former times was in command of the fortress at Brest-Litovsk, and in fact built the place; she thinks that upon arriving back there at the spot that had been his little kingdom, that he had grown to love as such, he was sunk in remorse at the deed he was abetting and shot himself. It may be so.

Coming home this evening, far behind me, as if coming from the Nicholaevsky Bridge, I could hear an intermittent rattle of shots. It is like that everywhere, in all parts of the city.

2/15 Dec.

My friend Ramage[314] at the bank had a bit of an experience the other night. After the opera he took an "ishvestik" homeward, and while driving down one street to cross a side street shots were heard. As these noises are common here, he kept right on until

---

[314] Spelled "Ramadge" by John L. H. Fuller, who called him the "little Scotsman." *The Journal of John L. H. Fuller*, October 29, 1917, 24.

too late, in the cross street they found themselves in the midst of a battle between a band of Red Guards firing from one direction on a group of soldiers firing from the other. Ramage says that rarely in his two years of trench experience has he heard bullets whistle so, and he wondered whether he was to survive a gas attack and the explosion of an eleven inch shell which landed him in the hospital for three months and out of the army,—if he was to survive these only to be struck down by a Bolshevik bullet. One of these just then struck the horse, which keeled over in the road, spilling the sleigh. Ramage crawled to the gutter and hid there until the skirmish was over, when he caught another "ishvestik" which was streaking down the street for dear life. He said the "ishvosch" [Rogers uses a diminuated word, again improperly transliterated (*izvoz*), for *izvozchik*, driver] drove a mile before he realized he had a passenger.

3/16 Dec.

On my uptown this evening there was a crowd of soldiers and loafers—really a very fine distinction—gathered about the house on the corner of the alley just below the bank and the Millionaya. As I passed there was much talking and frequently I could hear the word "wine" used, so I guessed they were getting a large enough gang together and summoning up a high enough courage to raid the wine cellar. I did not stop to investigate, but went on thinking of the direct proportion between courage and size in such mobs as this.

4/17 December 1917.

My surmise about raiding the wine cellar seems to have been correct. Last night just as I got in bed an outburst of shots came from that direction; and this morning the street and especially our corner was littered with broken bottles; and smelled rank of wine. The windows of the house were broken, and the iron guards over the gaping cellar windows had all been pried off.

But I am wasting time writing about trifles, when there are tremendous things afoot. One of them is that if I wish I am free to go home. Home! How that word sounds in my ears.

The day's gleanings of news result in the impression that the Bolsheviks have already concluded a separate peace with Germany, and are concealing its terms until a time when it will be too late for the Russian people effectively to resist. The terms are said to include a 15 year free-trade clause, which if true, will of course give commercial

Germany plenty of opportunity to get its fist well clenched about Russia's throat; and a clause to the effect that in order that they may "protect their interests in Petrograd," the Germans are to be allowed to send two army corps here! Rumor has it also that in this case, the Germans will of course take possession of the city, control both it and the resources of the country, set the young Tsarevitch on the throne with a German regent and settle down to pour raw materials into Germany with which to make it hot for the Allies. A most cheerful outlook! Mr. Stevens, however, said that as far as he could ascertain this was the truth. He was quite convinced that the city would be in German control and that we would of course have to close up; he added that no matter what happens he would stay on the job thru the whole business, and it would of course make it immeasurably easier for him if we would too. But he did not wish to bind us in any way. If we wanted to leave, now was the time to do it before it was too late, for once in control, the Germans would make it difficult to get out of the country,—especially for Americans. Such might even be interned or deported. Such news as this is likely to make a sky rocket of the human mind,—to make it shoot up into the air and spit out sparks. If all this is true I do not see how I can stay; it's not because I fear the coming of the Huns but because I could not stay here unresisting and witness what I feel to be evil triumphing over what is right. A spectacle of that sort puts it up to me to take some other than mental action in behalf of the side which is mine. On the other hand I hate to desert Mr. Stevens just at the time when my feeble services would be of the most use to him. For the bank, I should not stay a minute; but for Mr. Stevens,—yes.[315] It is a difficult question and whichever way I decide it will be much the same as Socrates' comment on marriage,—"if you do you'll regret it, and if you do not you'll regret it." So there you are. Anyway, it's not a question to be the decided at this late hour; far better wait until tomorrow morning after a bath and a good breakfast.

5/18 December.

There is no getting around the fact that I've been stalling and kidding myself along for some time. Had I been in America I should have been in this war long ago,—from the very first of our entry into the war. But being over here in absorbing work, comfortable quarters, and able to save money and send occasional sums back to my family, I

---

[315] *The Journal of John L. H. Fuller,* July 18, 1918, 78. Fuller similarly praised Stevens: "He's a fine boss and good fellow but in spite of his good fellowship no one takes any liberties with him. He'll make bankers out of us yet."

have been pleased, and careless in my perceptions of issues. I have felt all along, far back of my thoughts, that I should eventually be with my friends in the ranks; but just when—? When I did not know. I have passed the decision by time and again, held here more or less by what I thought my duty. Unless the need was urgent I could not run away and leave those I worked with just at the time they needed me. But now that need seems lessened. On the other hand by being here I have had no opportunity to select my service voluntarily, as my friends at home had; all these commissions, all these places I might have felt myself best fitted to fill are now closed. And no man, I care not how patriotic he is, likes to feel himself dragged into the struggle by the draft without any voluntary part, any choice in the matter at all. So before taking up the question of staying here and going home, I have cabled to my brother in London to find out whether or not there is any work there I can do in connection with the war office there. If I can get to London the step from that to the aviation corps or the artillery school in France will be easy. So I see that even before making my choice I am leaning in one direction, but even though it would be cruel to desert the staff here at a critical time I cannot suppress the feeling that woe will be to the man, that when this war is over, cannot feel his moral stand to have been a sound one. He will never be able to show his face on Memorial Day!

6/19 December.

There's nothing to do now but await the answer to my cablegram; to wait and hope that Lester comes through with something. I haven't stopped to figure, though, that all this going away business is subject to the physical possibility of doing it or not; which is no mean condition. Many of the railroads have ceased operations owing to strikes and the others all threaten strikes. Then there are the diplomatic impediments to be overcome, the obtaining of permits which the consulate is loath to assist in getting owing to the fact that it necessitates going to the Bolsheviks for it, and the US government has not recognized the Bolsheviks yet.

A sign on our consulate door says that unless those desiring to leave the country apply there at least two weeks before the day they wish to leave, they can give them no aid. If the answer to my cable takes a week and two more are necessary to make arrangements, it looks as if my chances are slim. I am foolish to get my hopes up. Then too, God knows where one can find a ticket these days.

7/20 December.

One of the boys met a young chap with an interesting story. Born of German parents on the high seas en route to America he lived there eighteen years. Early in the summer of 1914 he and his parents were visiting then old Germany again when the war festered out. The young fellow, in spite of all protest, was haled[316] into the German army and made to serve on all fronts. During September last he found himself on the Roumanian Front in a propaganda squad,—a squad whose duty it was to fraternize with the opposing forces. At this time he first heard of America's entry into. This was too much for him, or enough, as he put it, and he deserted, coming to Petrograd. What his plans now are he did not say, but very likely he will attempt to get back to America to join her forces. He should be an experienced man with a well-founded knowledge of what he is fighting. Think of the Germans, though, keeping their men "buffaloed" even up to September.

8/21 December.

The American colony is to blow itself to a party on Christmas night. It is to take place in the bank,—which is far more adapted to parties than to banking. Mrs. Farwell[317] seems to be the generic spirit of the affair and if so, the party is sure to be a success. She seems to be having the time of her life over here,—in fact enjoys it so evidently that among the colony she is known as "Alice in Wonderland." As far as I can gather the idea is to make the gathering as informal as possible and with this end in view she has asked me to print some "fresh" signs containing some of my "sparkling bits of humor!" These to be tacked up around with the other decorations just to scare away the formal guardedness which chills a good time. Then of course there will be the punch,—and from all I can gather that too will be a gloom chaser. It looks to me like a good time "was going to be had by all."

---

[316] To hale. Archaic. To drag or draw forcibly.

[317] House Histree; "Mallow 31 Yellow Cote Road, Oyster Bay Cove, Nassau County, New York," https://house-histree.com/houses/mallow. Mildred (Williams) Farwell (1878–1941) was called "America's Most Beautiful" war correspondent. In 1902, she married a multimillionaire fifteen years her senior, Walter Farwell (1863–1943), of Chicago. In 1917, she became the special correspondent to the *Chicago Tribune* and was caught up "in the thick of the riots in Petrograd," finding herself in "a hailstorm of bullets." France awarded her the Croix-de-Guerre military decoration.

9/22 December.

Tuesday is Christmas and I have been fortunate enough to have a friend invite me to attend a gala performance at the Narodny Dom for the benefit of Shaliapin. It ought to be wonderful with such an assembly of stars as Shaliapin, Smirnoff, Karsavina, Kuznetsova,[318] and Smirnova![319] Enough to satisfy even the most rabid beauty-seeker. In spite of the fact that it comes on the same night as our Xmas party at the bank, I shall go to the theatre and take in what's left of the party afterwards.

10/23 Dec.

Sunday, and another wasted day for me. I only got up just in time to greet our guest, Joe Sommerville.[320] He seemed to enjoy our dinner greatly and was quite content when seated about the fire with us. In fact everyone says we have one of the most homelike places they've seen. It is nice. But I can't take upon myself any of the house holders pride, for all swellings of this nature are burst by my abject thankfulness that we are here. That man's indeed near destruction who builds pride upon his good fortune.

I finished Kipling's "The Light That Failed" this evening. I had my mind all made up not to approve of the book in deference to the many opinions I have heard of it; but contrary to them all I admire Kipling's strict adherence to consequences as he saw them. I admire the fine friendship of hero and friend and the splendid despairing courage that drew the hero to his end. It is an exquisite relief to find a writer who makes more of the bond between man and man than that between man and woman; to discover a tale in which the hero does not throw over everything, even his friend for the feminine mirage. True it may be that this is because the feminine mirage will not realize for him, but never mind the why, the fact's the thing.

---

[318] "Kuznetsova, Maria Nikolayevna," in *Grove's Dictionary of Music and Musicians*, Vol. 4, ed. Eric Blom (New York: St. Martin's Press, 1954), 879. Maria Nikolaevna Kuznetsova (Russian: Мария Николаевна Кузнецова) (1880–1966) was one of the most celebrated opera singers in Imperial Russia and was renowned for uniquely combining her talents in operative singing and ballet dancing.

[319] Wikipedia, "Elena Smirnova," last modified June 23, 2021, 18:36 (UTC), https://en.wikipedia.org/wiki/Elena_Smirnova. Elena Smirnova (Russian: Елена Александровна Смирнова) (1888–1934) was the last prima ballerina of the Marinsky Theater in Imperial Russia and starred in many leading roles. After the November Revolution, Smirnova fled with her husband to Berlin, where they founded the Russian Romantic Theater. They performed throughout Europe until 1926.

[320] Joseph Sommerville and his wife were sent to Petrograd with the YMCA, according to the February 1917 edition of *The Key*, the official organ of the Kappa Kappa Gamma (KKΓ) sorority, in which Mrs. Sommerville was a sister.

11/24 December.

Christmas Eve,—my second one away from home; and each time the voices in the air grow louder. Christmas is a time for the heart and not for the head; and upon its ability finally to recognize this depends the welfare of mankind. For it is on Christmas that the divine spirit taps gently at our hearts once more to see if we be ready to take him in after these long years of waiting.

Christmas is for children and for old folks only through the children. How well I remember when I was a small child and lying breathlessly in bed heard the bells of Santa Claus jingling around the house; and what little change in the happiness of that memory makes the present knowledge that they but jingled at the bidding of my father, who ran through the drifts with them around the house. The spirit is the thing, and the spirit of Santa Claus was ringing those bells even tho that spirit was in the heart of my father. God bless him. How we children used to hop from bed at unearthly hours, light tiny candles and haul our stockings down from the mantelpiece; great bulky sausage-like things now, stuffed with nuts, candies, popcorn and always with a large orange at the very tip toe; how we crept noiselessly downstairs, shielding the candles with our hands, mostly because the huge shadows on the walls frightened us, and repressed our screams of delight at the gorgeous exhibition of the Christmas tree,—brighter than heaven it seemed; with the heaps of toys and books under it,—how we hastened thru the picture books, tried all the toys, took the best beloved with us and lest our candle should go out and we be left in the cold darkness, hastened back to bed and glistening dreams. Happy days! Happier memories! And I remember well the Christmas I received a soldier suit,—a brilliant red affair all fastened to a card,—hat with cockade, golden epaulets, crimson breast piece cross laced with gold braid, and a shining sword. Hastily I was dressed in it by my scheming older brother and sent out to meet my neighbor cross the street who appeared almost simultaneously in one of blue. We met and fought, for there could only be one general in that small village; my sword was stouter, his bent and broke, and there was nothing for him but ignominious and tearful retreat. I was not at all magnanimous and returned home flushed with victory with a keen desire to use my sword on the turkey in lieu of knife and fork!

And how faithfully we attended Sunday School for a month before Christmas! And how certain was our faith to be rewarded by the book, the bag of candy, and the orange. Sometimes we spoke a piece,—my sister did once, refusing to take off a red Turkish fez cap she had received—much to the consternation of the audience that could not fathom the masquerade—and other times we just joined in the carols. I'm afraid the boys soon forgot their religious zeal, perhaps as soon as the effect of the candy wore away, but what matter? Their very action shows that being children they little need it.

12/25 December 1917.

What is this life of ours? It is a world of providence and beauty; and we, its children, strutting in the image of Him who made us, selfish, intolerant, and unseeing in our willfulness, scatter its providence to the winds and trample beauty down with bloody feet. We are gone far from the way of good, and the divine spark within us barely flickers in reproach. Oh may we call halt and pray you our pitying God to take us in your arms as fathers do their children, and give us to understand, give us to understand.

13/26 December 1917.

Yesterday was a full day. To begin with we had quiet but very tasty little dinner here at home, which for all its simplicity did not lack decorations at that. For with it we had two kinds of wine, port and white, the former from the wine cellar of his imperial majesty the Tsar in the Winter Palace, and the latter from the cellar of Mr. Tereschenko, the former minister of Finance and later of Foreign Affairs. Not so bad. I think that with a supply of liquids of this calibre I should be a confirmed "booze fighter." As Bert Williams[321] says, "If Hell is paved with Wine, Ladies, and Song, Oh death, where is thy sting?"

In the evening we attended the opera and it was a rare performance. Kuznetsova, the soprano sang two Spanish songs and executed four Spanish dances with amazing color and finish,—one is tempted to say that as a singer she is a capital dancer; Shaliapin gave an adequate performance in the short opera of "Motzart and Salerini" [Rogers means *Mozart and Salieri*] no doubt did far more with it than anyone else could have done; and in the third act from "Boris Gudonoff" quite brought the house to hysterics with his work in the part of the wandering monk. I have never seen anything to approach linking of song and action. As for Karsavina, she was the same Karsavina, incomparable,—who can depict her? She had to repeat the little two-step she danced, and would no doubt still be repeating it if such were a physical possibility.

---

[321] Wikipedia, "Bert Williams," last modified July 15, 2021, 00:18 (UTC), https://en.wikipedia.org/wiki/Bert_Williams. Egbert "Bert" Austin Williams (1874–1922) was a Bahamian-born American entertainer and a pre-eminent entertainer of the Vaudeville era.

We quitted the opera in a haste and after great argument with an *ishvosh* finally cajoled him into taking us to the bank for a price somewhere within range of our monthly salary. Here the party seemed to have gone right well if one can judge by the debris, composed mostly of chicken bones and broken punch glasses. We managed to get a little of the feed and Mr. Stevens mixed up an extra bowl of punch[322]for us, so we fared well in spite of our lateness. The dance was still going on in the salon and it really presented a fine sight with its cream and gold walls, gold furniture, tapestries, the glinting chandeliers, and the still more glinting women whirling about. Music was offered up by a balalaika orchestra, and when that got tired, piano and gramophone. Of course the good old Stars & Stripes was everywhere in evidence and in addition an opera singer,—a real one, who came as one of the guests, sang the Star-Spangled Banner.

I waltzed around a couple of times with "Alice in Wonderland"—Mrs. Farwell, at every step bumping ambassadors and causing great jingles of brass work among the generals present, and finally gave up in despair to retire to the home hearth. Four of us came home thus, early, and by so doing missed much of the excitement that followed. It came about in this fashion.

One of the boys from the bank, Jesse Hawley,[323] but recently arrived from America had invited a very nice young lady to attend the party with him. On his way to her house to fetch her and escort her to the festivities, Jesse got lost in the dark streets. At last he saw an apartment house which he felt sure must be hers. Entering to look around he found that the place was in the process of being ransacked by the Bolshevik Red Guard, ostensibly in search of a counter-revolutionary plot. Poor Jesse, snooping around, looked suspicious, and as the guard had not found anything as yet they pounced upon him as a great find and subjected him to questioning and search. As he could not understand their Russian the questions yielded little, but the search yielded two "account opened" slips which he had taken from the bank at some time or other for scratch paper. Alas, this was suspicious, a stranger who cannot speak, in evening clothes, wandering about a strange apartment with two "account opened" slips in his pocket! To headquarters with him! So our miserable hero was lugged off to Smolney where he was kept some five hours, stark-naked, his captors having stripped him in search of counter-revolutionary plots! Finally someone came in who knew a little

---

[322] "Local Man Sees Hope for Russia if People Rise," *Grand Rapids Press*, Grand Rapids, MI, February 23, 1918, 12. Charles "Chuck" Stuart also attended the Christmas party. In his letter dated December 29, 1917, Stuart described the punch as "composed principally of vodka, rum, champagne, cognac, sherry, whisky and a little—a very little seltzer."

[323] Jesse Hawley (Reginald Galusha Hawley) (1896–1980), was in the same summer 1917 NCB training class as John L.H. Fuller and traveled with him from New York to Petrograd in August 1917.

English and Jesse explained himself. Still suspicious his guard doubly armed itself, packed him into a machine and brought him down to the bank. In the very midst of a dance these burly thugs burst into the party with their prisoner. Great was the consternation. The music stopped, people edged for the door, and bejeweled dames thrust handfuls of earrings and necklaces down their bosoms. Finally Mr. Stevens took the gang into his office and explained who Hawley was, and the wherefore of the suspicious documents. The hairy cops were much overcome at their error and in addition to begging pardon all around wanted to kiss Hawley. But Jesse figured he'd suffered enough and wouldn't allow this, thus spoiling a touching tableau.[324] The thugs departed and the party went on. Meanwhile it was one-thirty and poor Hawley's girl was still waiting for him to come and take her to the ball! He says he is ruined.

Ramage was up in the night, came home with us when we left the party. He is an interesting little chap. It would seem that when one has been in the war for over two years, has been barely brought to life after a gas attack, and has survived being blown sky high by an eleven inch shell and being in the hospital one hundred days,—and had been sent abroad to recover one's health,—it would seem that after all this, one was entitled to well-earned rest. But no, the British government wants Ramage again for the army, and back he's going for it. He takes it well, without protest or bravado which makes one hate the more to see him go. He is a man and has done more in his brave spunky way to raise my opinion of the English than any other one of them I have met. Here's to him.

The answer to my cablegram to Lester has come and he tells me to report to the Liaison Officer, US Army, London. I have quite decided to go in spite of all these things that tend to hold me back. The great problem of the war has been ever in my mind and no matter what sentiment of loyalty to individual or institution kept me here, I should never be able to justify myself before myself if I did not do my active part in it, no matter how small that part is. Knowing this, there is no use trying to deceive my own self to anyone else, I must go. By far the most difficult part of the whole business is telling Mr. Stevens; I dread it the more because he will say nothing. My going at this time will add to his already too crushing burden, but I know that if I go to him and tell him my feelings, he will in his heart agree, and let me go. Such a man he is.

---

[324] Tableau. Picture.

CHAPTER 12

The Red Guards

"The country is in complete and utter chaos," wrote J. Butler Wright on December 20.[325] Seven days later, Red Guards burst into National City Bank's Petrograd branch and for five days, preposterously posed about the office and forced work to an utter halt. Rogers alternatively restrained his anger or unleashed intellectual sarcasm against his unwanted occupiers while John L. H. Fuller bemoaned, "I don't see how we can continue to do business under these conditions."[326] This was the end of business as usual, if business in 1917 could have been anything resembling "usual."

Petrograd had become terrifyingly depressing. "A walk up the Nevsky this afternoon convinced me beyond doubt of this country's social and economic disintegration," Rogers wrote. Wright, ensconced in the American Embassy less than two kilometers away, grumbled about "A heavy fog, practically no lights, the streets almost impassable owing to the snow, no trains, stinking *isvozchiks* charging outrageous prices, etc. . . . the most depressing, forlorn, hole in the world."[327] Boies Hart, in Moscow, bewailed, "it is hardly safe to be out after dark. We have no police control. Hold-ups and murders occur every night. Many of my acquaintances have been robbed of their money and their overcoats as well."[328]

Virtually every state and municipal institution viewed the Bolshevik takeover as illegitimate. Civil servants went on strike and work in key ministries came to a standstill. Bolshevik pressure tactics on the Russian State Bank that Rogers described in November proved a harbinger of what would befall National City Bank in December.

Rogers informed R.R. Stevens of his plan to leave National City Bank to join the US Army. To his credit and Rogers' great relief and appreciation, Stevens responded

---

[325] J. Butler Wright diary entry, December 20, 1917, cited in Allison, *Witness to Revolution*, 161.
[326] *The Journal of John L. H. Fuller*, December 29, 1917, 49.
[327] J. Butler Wright diary entry, January 15, 1918, cited in Allison, *Witness to Revolution*, 170.
[328] Hart, *Petrograd, Rio, Peking and Points Between*, entry dated December 23, 1917, Chapter IV, 66.

sympathetically, even though Rogers' departure would mean an untimely loss of critical personnel to the bank.

No one at this time imagined the fate of National City Bank in Russia. Rogers and his colleagues believed Russia was going through another change, and more uncertainty. The promise of Russia's potential still glimmered; the United States was not yet giving up on Russia, and so they carried on. Messages the staff in Russia sent to the bank's *Number Eight* magazine did not convey the actual situation in Russia and some were even flippant. "The boys at Petrograd have many worries—besides watching the mobs and longing for chocolate," Boies Hart wrote in the December 1917 issue. Two of Rogers' other colleagues, W. Welsh and A.R. Smith, wrote in the same issue, "anticipating a pleasant and comfortable winter," going as far to state that "the present conditions of affairs in Russia promises to take some of the mob out of Petrograd, and thus make it an even more attractive place to spend the winter." The January 1918 issue contained a remarkable understatement: "It seems that these are exciting days for the Petrograd and Moscow Branches."[329]

More accurately, they were disastrous days, given the situation National City Bank faced that winter. Red Guards occupied the Petrograd branch and briefly arrested branch manager R.R. Stevens; the bank's representative for Russia, H. Fessenden Meserve, abruptly left Russia never to return; the Moscow branch opened on November 26, only to close days later and soon thereafter be commandeered; Stevens admitted the accounting books would be in a terrible shape;[330] the Soviet government declared nationalization of private banks on December 14 and seven weeks later repudiated all debts owed by the tsarist and provisional governments. In December 1917, National City Bank had $33 million of risk exposure in Russia, which amounted to over 40 percent of the bank's entire capital. A crisis of the greatest proportion loomed.

Rogers later candidly summarized the situation in *Wine of Fury*: "Those who had never worked day after day, night after night, without the nourishment of good and sufficient food, who had never known the nervous tension of walking bullet-swept streets—they could never comprehend the sheer nervous power required to push the routine under such circumstances."[331]

---

[329] *Number Eight*, The National City Bank of New York, December 1917, 40–41, and January 1918, 67. *Number Eight* featured serious essays on important banking issues and world affairs, organizational updates, as well as lighter, often entertaining personal dispatches. These quotes fell in the last category.

[330] *The Journal of John L. H. Fuller*, January 10, 1918, 51. Fuller wrote of R. R. Stevens' fears that the bank's books "would be in a terrible shape to turn over to the home office or to be inspected by auditors."

[331] Rogers, *Wine of Fury*, 251.

Rogers' colleagues wrote of the carnage and ruthlessness they witnessed to their friends and family in America, as did Rogers in his journal. Were the messages in *Number Eight* crafted to understate or play down the bank's troubles in Russia? Unlikely. Rogers and his teammates were diligent and committed people, ready to challenge jeopardy and depredation with bravado and wit. And so read their messages.

Bravado and wit, however, were no match for the gauntlet Bolshevism would throw their way.

14/27 Dec.

Today brings its excitement too. We had no more than got started to work this morning than in walked a little red-headed Jew[332]soldier at the head of a gang of roughnecks; he strutted up to the counter, pounded upon with his revolver, and announced that the bank was closed by order of the People's Commissaries. Under threat of being shot, we had to put away all our books and papers, watch him place a guard over the Current Account book, and arrest Mr. Stevens, and march him off to the State Bank. I could have committed murder at that. Mr. Stevens, one of America's best, marched through the streets of Petrograd at the bayonet's point, by a gang of low down Jews. Oh, for a handful of marines! But the arrest was for short duration. Mr. Stevens already had papers from the Bolshevik manager of the State Bank providing against just such an incident and he was soon free to return. He came back to his bank to find us members of the staff playing cards, and dancing to the tune of the Victrola left with us from the party, much to the disgust of the little red-headed Jew who couldn't figure out why we were so happy when he had tried to make it so unpleasant for us. Mr. Stevens' sense of humor saved him. He said that when it was announced that he was arrested and the order was given to go to the State Bank the little Jew said, "We'll go in your automobile." Said Mr. Stevens, "But I have no automobile." "What?" says the red topped son of Israel, "a director of a bank without an automobile. It can't be." Mr. Stevens replied that Americans were plain democratic people and didn't need such luxuries. But his captor was lost in consideration of this strange anomaly. Then while walking up the middle of the Nevsky under his heavily armed guard who should he meet but his friend Countess Nostitz in her machine. The countess almost fainted out of her machine, but Mr. Stevens merely grinned and plodded on as if getting arrested was one of the daily incidents of his life. The news spread like quicksilver and it was not long before many subtle influences

---

[332] *The Journal of John L. H. Fuller*, December 29, 1917, 48; *Hearings on Bolshevik Propaganda Before a Subcommittee of the US Senate Committee of the Judiciary*, 65th Cong. (February 11–March 10, 1919) 255 (testimony of Rogers Smith, National City Bank officer), digitized by Cornell University Library, https://babel.hathitrust.org/cgi/pt?id=cool.ark:/13960/t3fx7vk2j&view=1up&seq=9&skin=2021&q1=smith. Rogers' calling the Red Guard in question a "red-headed Jew" was the same language used by Fuller and Smith referring to this event. Rogers deleted all the references to Jews that he made in his journal when he prepared his later manuscript, "Tsar, Revolution, Bolsheviks."

were camping on the Bolshevik's trail; but Mr. Stevens was out without any of their aid, thanks to his own forethought. The bank was closed up and we went home.[333]

I did not go, however, until I had showed him my cablegram telling me to come to London and told him of my desire to go. He said he knew we all wanted to fight; that he had been expecting the sword to fall but was not certain first where. But he told me to take plenty of time to think it over, to consider only myself in so doing, and to decide it with my conscience. With the decision made he would do all he could to help me no matter which way it came out, and if I left I could always return to Petrograd should I desire to continue banking. In college we used to have saying of admiration "I vote for him for the greatest man in the world," half humorous but sincere admiration for all that. Well, Mr. Stevens gets as many votes for the "greatest man in the world" as I can stuff into the ballot box.

15/28 Dec.

We are still closed. The little Jew struts around in great pride now. He calls it his bank and gets real peeved because we smile at him. This is the greatest thing he has ever done in his life and he sure is making the most of it. He is not born to command and cannot understand why people sit and grin when he gives out his orders in stentorian tones. Even his own men don't pay much attention to him, as is the way with the Russian soldier now-a-days. I heard him talking over the phone to his headquarters today, it was something like this. "Say, send me over nine more soldiers. These I've got here now say they're tired and want to go home. They've slept on better beds than they ever saw before, eating better and more food than ever before, eaten like horses, and now they say they're tired and want to go home. Send me some more. Fine soldiers! Oi oi oi."

Soon even these Bolsheviks will learn that it's not because of their principles or theories that the soldiers have supported them; it's simply because the Bolsheviks promised the soldiers they wouldn't have to fight. As soon as the Bolsheviks tell them they'll have to work or fight,—good night Bolsheviks, they will be army less.

We engaged our hero in argument over the Bolshevik peace effort for a little while today. He seems quite excited and sincere about it but his valiant soldiers

---

[333] Louis de Robien, *The Diary of a Diplomat in Russia, 1917–1918* (New York: Praeger Publishers, 1970), 178. National City Bank was not the only bank occupied that day. Louis de Robien, a French diplomat, reported that on December 27 "all the banks were occupied by detachments sent by the government, and they were all put under direct state control."

harbor no illusions. When I asked him how he could believe that the Germans would be true friends with them after all their deceit he was quite offended and said, "Of course they will be true friends; there's no doubt about it. Why do you think they fraternize with us at the front if they don't want to be friends?" Here one of his soldiers broke in with "I can tell you that. We've got soap and they haven't and they want it!" That broke up the argument.

16/29.

Still closed, and the would-be Napoleon gets more tyrannical. If something is not done soon I fear war between the bank force and the Bolsheviks! There was nothing to do today save hang around for lunch and then come home to read. For this boon the Israelite has my thanks even though for others he has my ire.

I can quite well understand the Bolsheviks' actions toward us however. His greatest enemy is capitalism and of course to a patriot this enmity would naturally increase for its being in addition foreign capitalism. We come under both of these classifications,—and we are therefore the Bolsheviks' worst enemy. Were I a Bolshevik and were I free to act I should abolish foreign banks. Thinking thus and judging our present treatment by this thought, I must confess that they have been lenient with us. Satis est. [Latin for "near enough is good enough"]

17/30 Dec.

Sunday today and I intend to do a lot of work on a maudlin short story I have started. However, I failed to arise at my usual early hour (!) and Mr. and Mrs. Long came to lunch so there went the whole morning and afternoon. "Thus are enterprises of great pith and moment—etc." "But," thought I, "there's the whole evening left and I can accomplish much in it." About eight, however, not long after supper, Capt. Crosley, the US Naval Attaché,[334] dropped in on us and before his capital humor and wide experience all my plans of labor fled.

We fell to comparing stories of weird experiences in revolution-ridden Petrograd. By far the most numerous of these are the hold-up stories. The one about the man who

---

[334] Wikipedia, "Walter S. Crosley," last modified May 25, 2021, 12:37 (UTC), https://en.wikipedia.org/wiki/Walter_S._Crosley. Walter S. Crosley (1871–1939). Recipient of the Navy Cross, the second highest decoration for valor, for his diplomatic service in Russia. Crosley advanced to the rank of rear admiral in 1927. The destroyer-escort USS *Crosley* was named in his honor and launched on January 1, 1944.

in the street suddenly discovered that his watch was missing, and remembering the man who had just bumped into him and had passed into the court-yard of a house, followed him and cried, "give me that watch." The culprit meekly delivered the watch without a word, and the owner stuffed it into his pocket contented that he had thwarted the thief. Upon arriving home, however, he found his watch lying on his bureau where he had left it in the morning! Putting an advertisement in the papers to the effect that the man who gave up a watch at such and such a place at such and such a time could have it back by calling for it, he received an answer in person. "My dear Sir," said he, "why did you give me the watch when you knew it to be your own." "Because," replied his victim, "I had four hundred thousand roubles in my pocket, and felt lucky to be let off with only the loss of my watch!" Then about the man who was forced into exchanging coats with a soldier and found in the pockets of his ragged new possession a huge roll of bills and a couple of watches,—swag which the soldier had forgot to remove!

And how another enterprising American found a revolver pressed against his side, the butt gripped in a thug's fist; the holdup ended in the purchase of the revolver for a fairly reasonable price!

We heard also of one happening not so humorous, from Captain Crosley's own experience. On the island of Oesel, recently captured by the Germans lived a Captain Knupfel, a Russian military engineer the builder of the fortifications there and the commander of them and their garrison. He was possessed of a beautiful wife and two famed, beautiful children, a daughter of twelve and a son of ten. When the German fleet appeared off the island and subjected it to bombardment Captain Knupfel remained in the fortifications until the very last. He then hastened to his home to get his wife and children aboard a destroyer which he had held ready for just such an emergency. What he saw upon arriving home made him commit suicide. His beautiful wife and two children dead,—his own men having ravaged her and the little daughter, and beaten the little boy to a pulp when he tried to defend his mother and sister with a candlestick.

18/31 Dec. 1917.

Our Bolshevik friend and his indolent band of soldiers are still with us. They do nothing and compel us to do the same. If he waxes much more impudent however I greatly fear a pogrom. Today, upon finding that work was forbidden, four of the boys started a game of bridge. Our friend came up, snatched the cards away, and tore them to pieces saying that he could not allow it! He will never know how near he was to being beaten out of shape. That's the way with these people though, throughout the whole business, they go out of their way to make trouble for any of their Allied friends. This is particularly so in the case of the English, and there is a known reason for it.

When Trotzky, the present Minister of Foreign Affairs, came to Russia from America he was detained by the English at Halifax. His conduct and reasons for departure were not satisfactory to the authorities there and he was taken from the ship and held in a detention camp for a month. Not without resistance, however, for it is said that Trotzky refused to leave the ship, cried and screamed, lay down on the deck and held fast to a stanchion, bit and scratched,—in fact acted as one would expect a Prime Minister to act! He was finally allowed to come, but his experience embittered him against the English. Since his accession to power, he has done every-thing in his means to create trouble with England, so far being only ignored. It seems criminal though that the foreign policy of a nation should be formed on the personal animosities of its tyrant. Such policies and their holders cannot be permanent.

19/1 January 1918.

New Year's Day! I have started the new year by resolving not to make any resolution. As I have said earlier, every day is New Year's Day, and there is no particular reason for selecting any one of them in preference to all its fellows for making good resolutions. Use them all in that way.

This afternoon we attended the Ambassador's reception at the embassy and had a quiet little time there. We embarrassed his Nibs[335] a bit by dancing on his Persian rugs but he soon got over it and the party went merrily on. There were not many there as most Americans had left while the leaving is good.

20/2 January 1918.

Attended a box party at the ballet tonight; it was by far the best performance I have ever seen. The audience was in fine form and the dancers responded magnificently. Karsavina was—well she is not human, that's all. The piece was "Giselle" and her pantomime work in depicting the delicate innocence of the country maiden was

---

[335] His Nibs. English slang from 19th century. A person in authority, especially one who is demanding and tyrannical. Sarcastic reference to someone seen as aloof or stuck-up.

amazing and her dancing out-spirits the spirits themselves. In truth, the world is more beautiful for her having danced in it.

21/3 Jan.

In spite of the fact that it was such a night out doors as to elicit, "God pity the poor sailors on a night like this," from comfortable hearts, I took an opportunity and went to the Marinsky to hear "Rigoletto." It was only a fair performance, the great quartet being weak and the Rigoletto failing to make the most of his opportunities.

I do not care much for Verdi's vocal gymnastics anyway. They are clever pieces of workmanship but are hollow of feeling. And the voice above all things is an instrument of feeling.

22/4

I finished reading Maxim Gorky's "The Man Who Was Afraid" and I have no patience with it. Like the majority of these Russian novels it is not one at all. It's but a flat piece of life of two dimensions only length and width, cut out and set before the reader. There is neither beginning nor end; nor is there any depth. I do not deny that a novel should be a piece of life, but I do claim that the piece should have all dimensions,— and above all depth. And it is depth these Russian novels lack; they are like friezes on a nursery wall. The character of the hero—Foma Gordeyeff—is typical. A will-less misanthrope,—refusing to obey all the rules of life,—moral, physical, mental, and dissatisfied with life because it is not pleasant. Like a pig which violates all the laws of cleanliness in his pen and then grunts because it is dirty. But of course I have no intention of committing the grave error of judging Russian novels by Maxim Gorky—that would be absurd for his is the exaggeration of their faults.

23/5 January 1918.

A walk up the Nevsky this afternoon convinced me beyond doubt of this country's social and economic disintegration. The street itself piled high with dirty snow and ice, the worn out trams jammed with people, the buildings sadly in need of paint and repair—studded with bullet holes—and the frantic throng on the sidewalks; ragged, gaunt, worried, with a look of a fugitive imprinted on their faces they hurried along as if driven before a storm of unknown forces. People with rude bundles, some with hard won loaves of bread under their arms, and others with neither bundles nor bread,—only the hunger for it. Thin, aged children forced to labor before their time; crippled soldiers turned out of hospitals by their native country with no other payment for their sacrifices than the privilege to beg on its streets, and professional beggars everywhere, blind, you say? Absolutely eyeless. The whole thing was more like a conception of Doré[336] than reality,—a panorama of les miserables.

24/6 Jan.

Only work today. Man's life is a conflagration: his body the wood, his spirit the flame.

25/7 Jan. 1918.

Today being the Russian Christmas we were invited over to have dinner and to celebrate with Mr. Jacobson.[337] We accepted gladly and were told to be on hand at seven o'clock. After giving one of our party the wrong address and having to hang around waiting for him for half an hour we finally arrived at our destination intact. "Jake" has a very nicely furnished home, which includes an office in which six employees are kept busy on his personal affairs alone. In the living room stood a beautifully decorated Christmas tree, which he explained to us was the result of his four hours labor the night before. All kinds of fine gifts for the children were scattered about the room, and the kids themselves were in the midst of a gay time when we arrived. Shortly after tea was brought in, and the side table loaded with sweets, upon which we pounced being right hungry. Guests and relatives dropped in in a steady line until we wondered whether this was to be a quiet dinner or a picnic. The candles on the tree were lighted and we were to wait until they burned out. In the midst of it all Santa Claus came in much to the kids' amazement and delight,—and they exhibited all their presents to him and sang two or three little songs very sweetly. Still the guests kept coming; "Jake" rapped on the wall with a hairbrush and the relatives next door came in, then he stamped on the floor and someone from downstairs came up,—the place was a regular rabbit-warren of relatives. We played with the

---

[336] Paul Gustave Doré (1832–1883). French romanticist artist.
[337] Affidavit of George B. Link dated November 19, 1925, 32 and 47, Supreme Court, Appellate Division-First Department, New York County, Matthew A. Moosbrugger vs. Moskovsky Koupetschesky Bank. Heinrich Ivanovitch Jacobson engaged in the cotton business for the Great Yaroslav Manufacturing Company, one of the biggest companies in Russia. Jacobson borrowed more than $150,000 from NCB's Petrograd branch, which he secured with 1,400 bales of cotton. The loan was never repaid.

children, listened to the gramophone, and chatted as best we could with the guests. Our host showed us various Christmas presents received by members of the family; they included a very rare and very ancient Japanese tea set of china with a lacquered tray, an enamel cigarette case set with precious stones—an amazing piece of work, and a diamond bracelet valued at one hundred seventy-five thousand roubles,—formerly the property of the Tsar's sister—which Jake gave to his wife. About eleven o'clock the last candle on the tree sputtered out, the lights came on and we went into the dining room. A sight to make old Epicurus[338] turn over in his grave. The huge table set for twenty-seven places—fairly bended with good things, meats, fruits, cakes, candies, entreé of caviar, ham, fish,—in brief a variety and amount beyond imagination. Wine flowed free and our four glasses at each of our places were never empty. By the time the "pièce de résistance" came,—two huge pheasants in their glorious plumage—the dining had become fast and furious. We sang and laughed and ate, listened to the chatter and added our own. Much to our relief our host had us all seated at the head of the table around him, and there he sat as pleased as if he had been the father of us all, beaming smiles and hospitality. No one understood our English so we could say what we pleased, and they had no cause to be shocked at the harsh words of some of the college songs we sang. Our singing pleased them and one would have thought we were giving a show so avidly did they call for more. We did the best we could and I'm certain they did the same for us. In spite of the fact that my Russian is poor, that I was in a strange family in a strange land, that our hosts forgot their Russian and spoke German as the party progressed, in spite of all this I had a memorable time. So said they all. About three-thirty we arose from the table and retired to the living room. Here we danced a while, talked a little, and then took our leave. It was a party I shall not forget.

26/8 Jan.

We hear today that both Lenin and Trotzky have left the city for parts unknown. It is mysterious; no one seems to know what is up. Some have it that they know the jig is up, that they never can get the peace they counted on from Germany, and that in view of the threats made against them from all sides, they have fled. If so, then Russia, or at least Petrograd is without a government, and anarchism reigns. To all outward

---

[338] Wikipedia, "Epicurus," last modified July 18, 2021, 03:07 (UTC), https://en.wikipedia.org/wiki/Epicurus. Epicurus, an ancient Greek philosopher and sage, founded Epicureanism, a highly influential school of philosophy. Epicurus and his followers were known for eating simple meals and discussing a wide range of philosophical subjects.

appearances the city should delight the heart of even the most deep dyed anarchist. There are no police, no guards, no order except the natural self-restraint of the people. Of course the Christmas holidays explain it, but the industrial life of the city seems to have run down. No trams are running, the trucks are obliterated under the layers of snow, the street cleaners have not been busy and the level of the streets are far above their natural level,—bulging and rolling as would the ocean were it suddenly frozen. At night the streets are black save here and there for a stray streetlamp, which has somehow got lit, stores are closed, no banks are allowed to do business, and there is a scarcity of bread. Uneasiness reigns in the city. One can expect anything to happen.

27/9 January.

Rumor has it today that Lenin and Trotzky have not fled the country, but on the contrary have gone to Brest-Litovsk; the seat of the peace negotiations to engage in a last parley with the Germans. Rumor also has it that these are not going any too well,—the Germans are demanding so much—and that the Bolsheviks are preparing to declare war again on the enemy, re–mobilize the army, and fight it out.

Perhaps that may be the intention of the leaders but if so, they reckon without their fellows. They forget that to tell their followers, most of whom are soldiers that they will have to fight more will knock the "plat" out of their platform; the Bolsheviks obtained the support of the army by claiming that if they were in power peace would be made at once and all fighting over. The Russian soldiers joined them not because they wanted a separate peace, but because they did not want to fight. And the fact that it is the Bolsheviks who are calling upon them to do so instead of Kerensky or the Tsar will not change their disposition one whit. The Bolsheviks will first drop out of sight and the next party that steps up and informs the soldiers that to elect them means an instant cessation of fighting, will accede to the power. That may be the anarchists. To have anarchists at the head of the government would be the sublime paradox, for does not anarchism mean the abolition of all government of whatever nature?

CHAPTER 13

"A depressing glimpse of revolutionary Russia"

Hardship and disappointment outweighed hope that winter. One year in Russia and Leighton Rogers had experienced two revolutions and several coup attempts, narrowly escaped death by bullet and saber, and witnessed killings in front of his home and office. National City Bank reached the pinnacle of success only to have it yanked away. In what must surely have been an apt description of himself at this time, Rogers later wrote of the protagonist of *Wine of Fury*: "Alone in this immense emptiness, the strangeness of his position enveloped him. A stranger in a strange land, immersed in strange ideas, involved in strange events. Strange convolutions of circumstance which had brought him thousands of miles from home to involve him and his work with these people."[339] J. Butler Wright was more blunt: "*Personally, there is nothing in the world that I want more than to leave this filthy place . . .*"[340]

Rogers grappled with the reality of the Bolshevik takeover. He thought their power couldn't continue, but the lack of enmity of the Russian masses to the Bolsheviks disappointed him. "These people are *not* going to remain in power long—but they *are* in power now. It's like Mexico," prognosticated J. Butler Wright.[341] He was wrong. The Bolsheviks moved to destroy old state hierarchies and push power to soviets and in doing so, slowly centralized their control. The defeat of Russian democracy convinced the Allies that they now had two enemies: the Central Powers *and* the Bolsheviks.

John Reed makes an appearance in Rogers' journal and the National City Bank saga. Rogers wrote disparagingly of him. Reed was a controversial character in the American colony in Petrograd, where his activities and reputation were common knowledge. Biographer Eric Homberger writes that the community widely regarded Reed "as a fool who failed to understand that he was being used by others for devious

---

[339] Rogers, *Wine of Fury,* 265.
[340] J. Butler Wright diary entry, January 30, 1918, cited in Allison, *Witness to Revolution*, 176.
[341] J. Butler Wright diary entry, December 4, 1917, cited in Allison, *Witness to Revolution*, 156.

ends."[342] Ambassador Francis declared he "naturally regarded Mr. Reed as a suspicious character and had him watched and his record and acts investigated."[343] When Reed left Petrograd on February 7, 1918, to follow his wife, Louise Bryant,[344] Rogers wished him no goodwill. Neither did the US military attaché in London, Lt. Colonel S. L. H. Slocum, who sent an intelligence report to Washington referring to Reed as "an anarchist and Bolshevik sympathizer" and warning of his travel plan.[345]

John L. H. Fuller and Boies Hart got to know Reed and his wife. When the Reeds left New York for Petrograd on August 17, 1917, they sailed on the same ship with Fuller and six other NCB men.[346] Fuller became acquainted with Reed on the train journey from Christiania to Petrograd, where they arrived on September 14. At an intermediate stop at Beloostrov, someone stole most of Reed's belongings and his letter of credit. Fuller had lent Reed some money to help him buy certain things and noted in his diary on October 4 that Reed came to see him at the bank that day to repay the amount of 71 rubles, equivalent then to about $14.50.[347]

In the last week of September, the Reeds, Hart, and another NCB colleague, Milton B. "Colonel" Rogers, were temporarily staying at the Hotel Angleterre. Hart's memoir entry of October 3 related that Reed:

> knocked at our door the other evening, introduced himself and said he had noticed on the board downstairs that we were with the Bank. He asked us to inquire about some money he has been expecting as he said he has been so busy attending meetings of the Bolshevik convention that he hasn't been able to get to the Bank during business hours. His name is John Reed and he is a correspondent. I have learned from the embassy that he is over here representing some socialist paper in New York and that he has been indicted for some 'anti-draft' activities. Anyhow, he is a likeable cuss. His wife, who calls herself Louise Bryant, is a peach. They have been dropping in our room every evening. I think it is our pipe tobacco that draws him, as I gather they are hard up. He seems to know more about what is going on among the Bolsheviks

---

[342] Eric Homberger, *John Reed*, (Manchester, UK: Manchester University Press, 1990), 164.
[343] Ibid., 137.
[344] *Hearings on Bolshevik Propaganda, 565* (testimony of John Reed, journalist).
[345] Homberger, *John Reed*, 164.
[346] "A Letter From John Reed," published in *The Masses*, November–December 1917, 14. John Reed wrote, "My shipmates are a strange blend of various sorts of Scandinavians, Russians, a knot of young college boys from the States going to Russia as clerks in the Petrograd branch of an American bank...."
[347] *The Journal of John L. H. Fuller*, October 4, 1917, 15.

than anyone else I know, and if what he predicts comes true there is going to be 'hell-a-popping' around here and no mistake. He says the Bolsheviks will get Kerensky before long.

Although Reed and his wife are very radical in their views and sympathies, they don't try to influence us—probably figure it would be wasted effort, but they do go out of their way to tell us what they hear. We are glad to stake them to tobacco and cigarettes in return. Thanks to Reed I had a thrilling experience last night that still makes me tingle.

He came drifting in last night and asked me if I wanted to go with him to the Crystal Palace, where a big anti-Kerensky meeting was being held. The Crystal Palace was a barn of a place that must have held five thousand people. Every seat was taken, so we crowded against the wall about half way to the stage. It was a rip-roaring meeting. Mostly soldiers, with a sprinkling of laborers. There were plenty in that meeting with the power of speech, and what power![348]

Hart composed his memoir some twenty-five years after he left Russia. The passage of time either fogged his memory or encouraged historical creativity. No anti-Kerensky event occurred at the Crystal Palace. The Crystal Palace, in fact, was a popular moving pictures theater on Nevsky Prospect with a seating capacity of about 500 people. It still exists today. Did Hart refer to the Democratic Congress that opened on September 27 at the Alexandrinsky Theatre and where Kerensky and Trotsky made speeches? John Reed, Harold Williams and other journalists reported on that event.[349] But the Alexandrinsky seated upwards of one thousand people, not five thousand, and delegates from Russia's many political parties, not soldiers and laborers, filled the theater. Hart implied the event was on October 2, i.e., "last night," and wrote that Kerensky surprisingly appeared and "played upon that audience skillfully." The *New York Times* reported that "several thousand members of the Bolsheviki" attended a mass meeting in "a big circus tent" on September 30.[350] That was the Cirque Moderne, a popular locale for mass rallies, which was located across the street from the Kschessinskaya Mansion. Kerensky, however, did not speak at that event. John Reed described the Cirque Moderne as a "bare, gloomy amphitheater with its five tiny lights hanging from a thin wire. In it was packed from the ring up the steep

[348] Hart, *Petrograd, Rio, Peking and Points Between*, entry dated October 3, 1917, Chapter 3, 39–40.
[349] Harold Williams, "Kerensky Dominates Petrograd Congress," *New York Times*, October 3, 1917, 2.
[350] "Kerensky Cabinet Defies its Enemies," *New York Times*, October 2, 1917, 5.

sweep of grimy benches to the very roof."[351] Reed spoke there that evening, along with the Bolshevik Bill Shatov, "before an audience of 6,000 Russian workers."[352] David Francis called Cirque Moderne a "place of assemblage of all the radical elements in Petrograd."[353] Francis had sent a telegram to Secretary of State Robert Lansing on September 29, which referred to the event: "Following is being placarded about the city: 'Free' America wants to execute a Russian emigrant, revolutionist Alexander Berkman.[354] All the soldiers and workers of Petrograd must attend a mass meeting which will be held in Cirque Moderne on Sunday, September 17 [/30] at 7 p.m. to find out how this 'free' country deals with its revolutionists. Admittance free."[355]

Hart neglected to mention the noteworthy detail that Reed spoke at the Cirque Moderne event to which Reed supposedly invited him. His account confuses two different events. Perhaps he attended neither.

The Supreme Council of the Soviet government repudiated all national loans concluded by the tsarist and provisional governments on February 8. American banks by then had lent $233 million to the tsarist government, and the US government advanced nearly $200 million in loans and credits to the provisional government in 1917 alone. The United States was not the only big creditor to Russia. France, Great Britain, Italy, and other Western countries also had significant investments at stake, and not only in commerce and finance, but in the military and political spheres as well. Secretary of the Treasury William McAdoo suggested to Lansing and Wilson that the United States should withhold recognition of any new government in Russia unless it respected existing obligations to the United States.[356] This position hindered the establishment of diplomatic relations between the Soviet Union and the United States for more than a decade to come.

---

[351] John Reed, *Red Russia: The Triumph of the Bolsheviki* (London: Workers' Socialist Press/Warwick Digital Collections, 1919), 15.

[352] Homberger, *John Reed*, 137; Francis, *Russia from the American Embassy*, 166.

[353] Francis, *Russia from the American Embassy*, 136.

[354] Wikipedia, "Alexander Berkman," last modified July 13, 2021, 17:37 (UTC), https://en.wikipedia.org/wiki/Alexander_Berkman. Alexander Berkman (1870–1936) was a leading member of the anarchist movement in the early 20th century, famous for his political activism and his writing. He served 14 years in prison for attempting to assassinate businessman Henry Clay Frick and was sentenced to another two years in 1917 for conspiracy against the newly established US war draft. He killed himself in Nice, France.

[355] US State Department, Office of the Historian, Papers Relating to the Foreign Relations of the United States, 1918, Russia, Volume 1, "The Ambassador in Russia (Francis) to the Secretary of State [Telegram]," File No. 861.00/564, https://history.state.gov/historicaldocuments/frus1918Russiav01/d165.

[356] Foglesong, *America's Secret War Against Bolshevism*, 178.

On March 3, the Bolsheviks concluded their peace talks with Germany at Brest-Litovsk, which included terms J. Butler Wright considered "monstrous" for Russia.[357] The separate peace between Russia and Germany, of which Rogers anxiously wrote, seriously undermined the Allied war position. It enabled Germany to redeploy up to forty army divisions to the Western Front and gave Germany access to Russia's precious natural resources in Ukraine and in other ceded territories. Lenin's peace, however, was not true peace. Russia descended into five and a half years of civil war resulting in casualties, including civilians and noncombatants, of seven to twelve million and more than one million refugees outside of Russia.

During those trying winter months, companionship, old and new, buoyed the spirits of Rogers and his colleagues. Frequent social visits and rummaging for meals together lightened their burdened lives. Everything changed by the end of February, when the German army threatened Petrograd. The foreign community fled the city for Moscow or Vologda,[358] or exited Russia via northern routes through Finland or to Murmansk, or across Siberia to Vladivostok, or points beyond. Rogers left Petrograd for Murmansk on Saturday, February 23, and the next evening, ten of his colleagues left for Siberia and exited Russia from Vladivostok by ship to Yokohama, Japan.[359]

National City Bank evacuated its Petrograd branch operations to Vologda on March 9 "rather than have our branch fall into the hands of the Germans."[360] The remaining NCB staff left Petrograd on the same day except Stevens, Welsh, and Gray, who left on March 19. National City Bank's 1922 internal review of its Russian business stated that "while all property of the Petrograd Branch was in Vologda and consequently Vologda was the base of operations, the Petrograd Branch, in charge of a neutral,[361] remained constantly open. This was desirable because of the provisions of our Russian charter as well as for the sake of prestige and the convenience of our clients. To have closed our Petrograd Branch would have subjected us to severe criticism, whereas, our keeping it open resulted in many expressions of appreciation."[362]

---

[357] J. Butler Wright diary entry, February 23, 1918, cited in Allison, *Witness to Revolution*, 185; Figes, *A People's Tragedy*, 548. Figes writes that Russia gave Germany "34 per cent of her population (fifty-five million people), 32 per cent of her agricultural land, 54 per cent of her industrial enterprises, and 89 per cent of her coalmines." The peace treaty also prioritized German economic interests within Russia.

[358] Vologda is a major transport hub in Russia's northwest, located approximately six hundred and fifty kilometers from St. Petersburg. In February 1918, Allied embassies in Petrograd moved there to avoid the approaching German army. Vologda thus became the "diplomatic capital of Russia" for several months.

[359] *Number Eight*, The National City Bank of New York, September 1918, 37–43; *The Journal of John L. H. Fuller*, February 25, 1918, 56–58.

[360] *History of the operations of the Petrograd and Moscow Branches*, 15.

[361] A Dutch national, Guillaume Heuts.

[362] *History of the operations of the Petrograd and Moscow Branches*, 16.

NCB's woes in Russia found their way to NCB in the United States. In mid-February, Chairman James Stillman called Frank Vanderlip to New York, where they had, as Cleveland and Huertas surmise, a very difficult discussion involving the question of responsibility for the "Russian fiasco."[363]

---

[363] Cleveland and Huertas, *Citibank: 1812–1970*, 101.

28/10 Jan.

Nothing doing today, save that they set the clock back an hour which gave me an extra hour's sleep. It threw me all off my base when I got up this morning and discovered how early I was.

I forgot to mention that yesterday I had a talk with Mr. Stevens relative to my leaving the bank and going to England or France. He had just received a cable from New York in which the authorities at the home office of course wanted to discourage my breaking my contract in this manner, but leaving it wholly up to him. He stated that in that case should I decide to go he would rather I not leave the bank entirely, but ask for leave of absence for the duration of the war, and return to finish out here afterwards. That suits me exactly, and if I decide to leave it will be on that basis.

29/11 Jan.

We hear today that President Wilson has made a speech outlining the terms upon which America will make peace. In this speech he makes the statement that the voice of the Russian people have been heard in a sincere effort to make peace. It is also said that he speaks not for America alone, but for the Allies. If these statements are in accordance with the facts why do not the Allies recognize the Bolsheviks. If they approve of their policies why not recognize their government? It is very strange. In his speech before the Labor Congress at Buffalo the President denounced the Bolsheviks as dreamers and fools; scarcely two months later he praises them. What has happened? No one can tell; and it is better to put off further discussion until I can read the speech in English. I have made arrangements to receive a copy.

30/11 Jan. 1918. *(Rogers writes the date incorrectly. It should be 30/12 Jan. 1918)*

I did not get my copy of Wilson's speech so must reserve comment. Received a letter from home and one from Lester in London today.

31/12 [13] January 1918.

Mr. Stevens gave me a copy of the President's speech today and I read it through many times with great care. It is the voice of a mighty and generous people. It clears the diplomatic atmosphere of all the fears, doubts, and suspicions which have clustered in it of late, and by so clearing it, blows away the last vestige of the German peace setting, revealing these arch-plotters to the full view of the peoples of the world. As do all the President's speeches it rings true from every viewpoint. I doubt if with all the differences of race and creed, and purpose that exist among the Allies there will be a single dissenting voice. To Germany it is the challenge direct to state her war aims. Silence can only be construed as refusal and refusal of any kind on any basis must only develop the proof of Germany's guilt the more clearly. Through all the speech, forming an integral part of every one of the fourteen conditions which the United States incorporates into its peace terms and war aims, runs the principle of self-determination of peoples,—the privilege of government "of the people, by the people, and for the people;" to deny any one of the conditions is to deny this principle in part, while to deny this principle is to deny the all that the world is fighting for. There is no getting around it. If the principle is accepted it must be lived up to in the peace negotiation which entails Germany returning everything she has conquered, to deny it prolongs the war until Germany sees fit to change her mind and accept. Of course what the Germans would like to accept [is]the principle and deny the execution of it, to squirm around it in the peace negotiation. But I fear that the principle is in the hearts of too many and too powerful people; under the leadership of such men as Wilson and George, there need be no fear that it will suffer. Moreover, now, there is no misunderstanding possible over war aims, the German octopus can no more envelope the minds of its enemies in the inky cloud which it spews over the subject of war aims, the people of the Allied nations understand clearly and have determined to stand by their principles.

As applied to the Russian situation the speech again rings true. In its realization and acceptance of existing facts, and its effecting all that is immediately possible by way of remedy it is magic. No other nation in the struggle, save perhaps Germany, has understood the actual helplessness of Russia. America does. No nation, if they have realized it, has dared admit it. America does. Nor has any other nation placed herself unequivocally behind the Russian people. America does. This speech places the strong arm of Uncle Sam in back of the Russian people and insures them support. If the leaders of the present movement are sincere they receive powerful support; if they are traitors, this speech gives them an opportunity to reform and make good, and if they will not, their immediate actions will show them up in their true light.

Considering all phases of it, I should say that the President's speech is a great success. We can await the German answer with a calm spirit.

1/14 Jan.

A holiday today for the Russians and consequently for all of us. I utilized it by writing letters and copying on the typewriter a part of a story I have written. There is very little news. No papers. We hear that Lenin and Trotzky are greatly pleased with Wilson's speech, and have departed for Brest-Litovsk with copies of it for distribution amongst the German soldiers. I doubt if they will have much success. The only thing that will impress the German soldier is a crushing blow on the "dome."

2/15 Jan.

No bread today and people are getting restless. Already the voice of the anarchists is heard protesting that the Bolsheviks have turned "bourgeoisie," so away with them. There have been threats of an anarchistic uprising and once more the streets are filled with armed soldiers and ruffians on the lookout for trouble—in order that they may join it! The fifth is the date set for the Constituent Assembly, but I have my doubts as to its meeting. I do not see how the Bolsheviks can permit it to meet unless they have stuffed the ballot so as to give their party an overwhelming majority of delegates. Left to the natural course of events, the vote of the Assembly would be against the present powers that be.

3/16 Jan. 1918.

Indeed it was a depressing glimpse of revolutionary Russia caught during the short space of my walk home tonight. A blinding snow, the streets piled high, tracks hidden so that no trams were possible, only a stray light here and there, a dead horse half buried in the snow forming a hillock in the center of the quay, and hurrying, silent throngs of people, here and there a voice protesting against the lack of bread.

4/17 Jan.

Someone took four shots at Lenin the other day and missed; the Bolsheviks are up in arms and it looks as if it would go hard with anyone connected with the affair. They place the blame on the Social Revolutionary party and charge that a great "counter-revolutionary" plot is afoot. And rumor confirms it. Tomorrow is the day set for the meeting of the Constituent Assembly and as the Social Revolutionary party has a large majority of delegates it looks as if the Bolsheviks would endeavor to prevent the meeting. A fight is advertised, and the papers advised those not taking sides to keep off the streets! It will have to be a well laid and well executed plan to succeed, because the present powers that be have taken all precaution and strong, armed forces are in evidence. It must be said for them too, that they wasted no time in haggling over details, they cut right to the heart of the matter even though it be a human heart. Knowing this the plotters must make their plan a bold and energetic one; if they win,—all's well, and a vast majority will be on their side; if they fail—! We shall see.

5/18 Jan.

The day of the Constituent Assembly. Quite early this morning the parades began streaming across the Troitzky Bridge as of yore—the black mass of people, and the scarlet flags and banners with the golden mottoes. Most of these last were against the Bolsheviks and for the Assembly. This peaceful demonstration was met by the Bolshevik Red Guard, concealed behind barricades on the Litania and the Spalernaya [Shpalernaya. Russian: Шпалерная] with volleys which killed some fifteen of the innocent paraders. This is all I could find out about the Assembly today.

6/19. *(No entry)*

7/20.

These two days have been the first holidays we have spent as such since our arrival in Russia. Having signified our desire to spend a day or two in the country we got permission from one of the artelschiks[364] at the bank to use a house of his out in Pargolova,—a village about 40 versts away from Petrograd. Rather, he invited us

---

[364] Russian: Артельщик. John L. H. Fuller described this position as a cashier who handled all the cash.

out there, saying that he could guarantee us a warm cottage and plenty of food. This sounded enticing so we accepted the kind invitation and for a safe measure sent out a lot of food to be prepared for us. There were six of us going and we prayed for good weather. When we got up early Saturday morning it looked as if our prayers had been held up by the censors as the wind blew like the devil, and snow and sleet fairly cut into the flesh. However, we had made up our minds to go, and go we did, all decked out in our oldest clothes, each carrying a blanket and a toothbrush in a suitcase. Although I thought the wind would blow our dinky little train off the track but we managed to hold it down until we got started. The journey was not long and upon arrival at Pargolova we were met by our friend who conducted us to his house not far from the station. It was a rugged, well-built affair, of solid eight inch beams throughout, caulked like a ship with creosoted[365] felt. Not a bit of draft or cold air could force its way inside. It sat within an ample yard with a garden at the back, and in the front a modestly proud brass sign proclaimed that this was the house of Mr. Y.E. Ekeemov. He told that as yet the place was unfinished owing to the high cost of materials since the beginning of the war. He took us inside and introduced us to his wife, a dark, flashing little woman who fitted into the scheme of things about the neat little home like a charm; and his daughter, Nina, a bright eyed girl of thirteen with a mass of beautiful hair. Hot coffee awaited us, and was more than welcome. We drank it as a sort of defiance to the whistling wind outside. Then we stripped to few but heavy clothes, as near snow-proof as possible and set out for a romp through the snow. This was like the good old college days for me, and I thoroughly enjoyed it. We were unable to obtain skis that morning, so we plowed our way across country on foot. The sky was clear by now, the sun out, and the wind not keen; the fine crystal snow flew in clouds around us, plunging, swirling, and wrestling in it, the clear air acted like a tonic and we cut loose in a disgraceful manner. In our rambles across country we lost even the semblance of a road in an endeavor to make a shortcut and had to plough through the snow, waist deep, until exhaustion halted us. I for one felt I couldn't walk another step; I wanted nothing better than to sit there in the snow and rest. But that would not do at all; we must get to the road; some crawled along on all fours until we could take advantage of a line of trees where the snow was not so deep, and which we could follow to the roadway. It was a worn-out and hungry gang that descended upon Mrs. Ekeemova's dinner table and we completely demolished the most excellent

---

[365] Creosote. A complex mixture of coal tar derivatives. Commonly used as a wood preservative protecting against wood-destroying insects and wood-rotting fungi.

repast of soup, roast turkey, potatoes, cabbage, bread and butter, and cocoa. In spite of all the big dinners I've been to since arriving in Russia, I think this one tasted the best of all. There was some vodka at the beginning, at least a species of vodka, but it was so brutal that I couldn't down much of it. Whew! It burned like an acetylene torch! Yakob Efeemovich told me it was made from black bread and had sweet grass crushed in it to conceal the scorch. Or to make it "хорошо пахнуть" ["smell good"] as Nikolai Vassilievitch constantly says.

After dinner our sole desire was to sleep, or if too early in the day for that to sit around and talk, play cards, read, or listen to the gramophone. We did all of these things until supper time, and more too, for instance, got acquainted with the dogs. There were two,—a strange little cuss part dachshund, terrier, and spitz, which had a habit of sitting quietly up on his hind legs until someone gave him something to eat; or again, if someone lay down on the sofa, "Jack," for that was his name, would lay down too, and woe be to the bold one who tried to disturb the sleeper; Jack would fly at him in tremendous rage; then there was another dog "Shaliapin" we nicknamed him because of his deep voice,—a huge bull,—so ugly as to be handsome, which they kept chained up in the kitchen. When they brought him in for exhibition Jack flew at him jealously and hung on his lip until shaken off, but the big dog with fine chivalry would not harm the smaller. Finally supper was announced, how it came to be ready I can't figure out as Mrs. Ekeemova had been sitting around with us, laughing, talking, playing cards,—only now and then stepping out to the kitchen humming her little tunes,—but it was ready and a fine one it was. We did justice to it and then returned to our diversions for the remainder of the evening.

In the time of the old regime we would have been social outcasts for visiting with an artelschik and his family. But society or no society we were having a thoroughly happy and comfortable time; and moreover with worthy people, sober and industrious. I've never seen a woman that made her home so happy and accomplished her household tasks with such ease and joy as this one did. Snatches of a song, the clink of silver, a laugh and lo! the table was set. Away you perfumed, bejeweled, cigarette puffing town creatures!

At nighttime, mattresses were dragged out and placed on sofas and divans, and on the floor; upon these we laid our weary bones to rest. Outside it was gorgeous,—silver moonlight, bright stars, and only a gentle wind. In spite of the fact that from time to time the rattling of the bulldog's chains in the kitchen jangled in our ears inspiring dreams of the "Hound of the Baskervilles" and such like, we slept well, and arose early the next morning ready for another day.

This one we spent in riding to a place called Uké and hired "ishvestiks," perhaps an hour's drive through somewhat broken country, and in trying out three pairs of skis we engaged there. None of us are experts at this game and the aerial hierographics described would have done good to the seeker of the mysterious. Although the snow was soft and we clung to gentle hills we were a bit bruised, and it was not long before we crept back to the sleigh and headed for home and the most excellent meal we knew would be awaiting us. After dinner we were too tired to stir out again so we confined our efforts to indoor sports. Here I must mention a book I found on the living room table of this worthy family. It was an album of postcards, such as most everyone has at home,—with the exception of the postcards. Some of these were vile, obscene, dirty; I could not understand how people so obviously respectable would have such things around. But then I reflected that this is the way of the Russian. Whatever is natural he accepts, and even a distorted and exaggerated form of the natural touches his sense of propriety not at all. It is all in the point of view; what shocks us Westerners of finer sensibilities, the Russian accepts as a matter of course.

When it fell dark again and after another meal, which completely did us up, we left our hospitable Russian friends and, catching an evening train, returned to Petrograd after having experienced two exceedingly enjoyable days far from the maddening crowd.

It had indeed been quiet there; we had not heard a bit of politics or business. We were engrossed only in the great outdoors and the problem of enjoying it. But our return to Petrograd plunged us headlong into the stew of events once more. We discovered how the longed-for Constituent Assembly had at last met, how an anti-Bolshevik majority had elected an anti-Bolshevik president, how three questions were brought up for discussion, that of peace, of land, and of governmental form; how the voting had been always against the Bolsheviks; how the Assembly had refused to recognize the Bolsheviks; how the meeting conducted itself in disgraceful fashion,—mostly due to the efforts of the B's—who "boohed" and "caterwauled" the opposition speakers; how the Bolsheviks brought up machine guns and ambulances to encourage the speakers, how there was no respect for order at any time; and finally how the Assembly was adjourned by the Bolsheviks never to meet again, accused of being "counterrevolutionary." How sick of hearing that word! Applied to everyone and everything that works not for the Bolsheviks, we have it dinned in our ears day after day. Even the weather at times is counter–revolutionary. It is supposed to be an indictment damning beyond all redemption, while I half believe most of those to whom it is applied are rather proud of it. Indeed the trend seems to be away from the powers that be; the pendulum is swinging back—to what, I cannot say. Perhaps to the anarchists, they are the lowest rung on the ladder. But, as I have remarked before an anarchistic government would be a paradox. But the Maximalist government is doomed to failure as are all governments that are not practical. The essence of all government is not so much the expression of a fine idea as it is a means; a means which will furnish the order, liberty, and organization for the satisfying of material needs, out of which the ideals arise. Never have I known of a more glaring example of impracticability than the present government; it is as inefficient as the old one, and just as surely doomed. Gaining its following through glowing words it is now discovering that mere words will not hold the following. The Bolsheviks leaders promised negotiations for an immediate general peace, they promised an increase in the food allowance, they promised an immediate division of the land amongst the peasants, these things and many more they promised in return for the support which gives power. Not a one of these promises has materialized; the leaders themselves recognize how utterly impossible their realization is, but they dare not admit it. For as soon as the truth of their impotency becomes known the popular support shifts naïvely to those who make more glowing promises. It is only after trying them all, after dragging through the lowest depths of anarchy that Russia, through sheer gorge of license, will demand a strong hand to take her over and guide her to the path of order. As my father aptly expressed it in a letter not long ago, "The Russians cannot set up a heaven upon earth until they fight hell more efficiently than they have." They have failed to recognize the essence of a republican form of government, the self-restraint that substitutes for tyrannous force and keeps men in line. In all the things imperative for the success of a republic, self-restraint, honor, duty, vision,—in all these products of education, the Russians as a mass are singularly lacking. And yet, as if the efforts of mankind for centuries had all been for naught, they proclaim them wrong and themselves right. Ignorance is not bliss, it is potential tragedy.

But I am astray. Another bit of news we heard soon after our arrival was of the murder of two of the former members of the Kerensky ministry,—Shingareff and Koshkoshkin.[366] A baser deed I have rarely heard of. These two men were imprisoned in the fortress by the Bolsheviks for no particular reason save that they had been

[366] Wikipedia, "Andrei Ivanovich Shingarev," last modified May 9, 2021, 01:33 (UTC), https://en.wikipedia.org/wiki/Andrei_Ivanovich_Shingarev; Wikipedia, "Fyodor Kokoshkin (politician)," last modified May 9, 2021, 03:19 (UTC), https://en.wikipedia.org/wiki/Fyodor_Kokoshkin_(politician). Andrei Ivanovich Shingarev (Russian: Андре́й Ива́нович Шингарёв) (1869–January 20, 1918) was a Duma deputy and one of the leaders of the Constitutional Democratic Party (Kadets). Fyodor Fyodorovich Kokoshkin (Russian: Фё́дор Фё́дорович Коко́шкин) (1871–January 20, 1918) was a Russian lawyer and politician, a deputy in the first Russian State Duma,

members of the Kerensky government; not long ago they both became very ill and upon advice of the medical authorities were transferred to the Marinsky Hospital. Thither came a band of the Red Guards, forced its way into the hospital and shot the two sick men in cold blood in their beds, shot them as they lay flat on their backs, barely able to move. Brave deed! Mighty Red Guards! I've often thought that the only hell we humans would experience was right here on earth, but there must be some other lower place for such animals as this!

Then we heard of the editorial in the official paper of the anarchist party to the effect that if Berkman, the anarchist, was not released from jail in America at once, the life of the American ambassador was in danger. They demanded an arrest for arrest, imprisonment for imprisonment and execution for execution. Truly the drug of power doth make men mad.

8/21 Jan. 1918.

Today was a holiday for the simple reason that a parade was scheduled as a protest against the murder of the two ministers, another by the Bolsheviks on general principles, and when two parades are on tap, the city must needs take a day off to see what will happen.

Nothing happened, however. The parades were out with their red banners but evidently the route masters planned better than they knew, for the two groups never met.

9/22.

I was told today about the valiant sailors at Kronstadt expelling 20 officers naked into the snow and chasing them through the streets, beating them with whips. Just another glimpse at the chivalry of their large natures.

10/23 Jan.

Four letters from home today, first like that. Four all at once; from Mother and from Father with snapshots enclosed too. This is too much.

---

a founding member of the Russian Constitutional Democratic Party, and the controller general of the provisional government.

11/24 Jan. 1918.

No dope today.

12/25 Jan.

I heard a little inside information about the threat on the American ambassador's life. It seems that the day after the threatening messages were received a woman called up the embassy on the phone and told one of the secretaries there that she had some important news for the embassy which she could not tell over the phone, requesting that someone meet her at a certain corner at a certain time. Two secretaries kept the appointment and the woman in question—a Russian who had married an American,—informed them of a plot to destroy the embassy. A sailor had come to her home trying to sell her some wine, and in the course of the transaction, being drunk, I suppose, had revealed this plan to her. The sailor incidentally boasted that he had been one of the gang that broke into the hospital and murdered the two Kerensky ministers in their beds. The secretaries carried their news back to the embassy. All of the availables were called upon and fully armed, they sat up that night, prepared to give the raiders a suitable reception. Until three in the morning they waited but nothing happened, so the staff dispersed and went to their various homes to sleep.

13/26

I seem to be learning many embassy tales. It just goes to show the reversal of the times,—ordinarily an embassy is considered one of the safest of places in a foreign country, but here in these times, they are singled out for all kinds of enterprises. This one concerns the Italian Embassy. About ten o'clock one evening ten fully armed Russian soldiers appeared at the Italian Embassy carrying sacks. They forced their way by the doorman and demanded some wine, requesting that the sacks be filled with bottles. Their demand was refused so they made a search themselves and carried off fifty-one bottles from the ambassadorial wine cellar. Evidently the comrades of their regiment were not pleased for not long after some fifty odd members of the regiment came to the embassy demanding wine. They backed up their demands with force. The ambassador naturally refused to be held up in such a manner so the valiant soldiers scattered round the house to search for the stuff. Meanwhile one of the Italians procured two revolvers, went out on the street, concealed himself from view, and began firing them off into the air as fast as he could load. The fifty soldiers inside became panic stricken, cries of "murder!"—"a plot to kill us," "Help!" and such like resounded through the house, and dropping their guns they fled. Two of them hid in the attic and were apprehended by the house guard, turned over to the authorities—such as they are—at Smolney, and jailed! Such is the life of an ambassador accredited to revolutionary Russia.

27/10 [9] Feb. 1918.

More than two weeks have sneaked by since I last wrote here. I have been very busy on other things and both this and the fact that little of note has happened during the period accounts for my neglect.

The event of prime importance was the ejection of the Roumanian minister and his staff. It came to the knowledge of the Bolsheviks that Roumania had undertaken to make away with a part of Bessarabia to compensate herself for the territory lost to Germany when she made her unfortunate entry into the war. Poor little Roumania,— led into the awful business by Russia with the promise of support, betrayed to her ruin by Steurmer, the German Prime Minister of Russia who saw to it that Russian relief never came, and now, having reorganized herself—by a superhuman effort, to have the opportunity for getting back what she lost snatched away by the total breakdown of the flanking Russian armies. Is it any wonder she at last turns upon the cause of all her troubles, especially when all the efforts of the Bolsheviks have lately been directed to the end of initiating revolution within her shrunken borders? But as I said, the Bolsheviks discovered this scheme to annex Bessarabia and gave the Roumanian staff twenty-four hours to get across the border. They of course protested but the protest only elicited the information that if they were found in Russia at the expiration of the twenty-four hour period things would go hard with them. They got out. In spite of the fact that civil war reigns in Finland, that tracks and bridges are blown up, entailing it upon passengers to drag their baggage a mile or two, and ride in sleighs to the next train, in spite of this, and the insult to the ambassadorial dignity, they got out.

The wine-cellar escapades have broken out once more and at night the streets reel with drunkards. It is not safe to go out alone. A good deal of the stuff, after being stolen is sold on the streets by the soldiers, at from two to twenty roubles a bottle.[367]

---

[367] Dosch-Fleurot, *Through War to Revolution*, 195; Meriel Buchanan, *The City of Trouble* (New York: Charles Scribner's Sons, 1918), 212–13. Petrograd denizens took advantage of a "fire sale" of fine spirits perhaps never before seen. Arno Dosch-Fleurot wrote, "Many soldiers made off with their arms filled with bottles, some of them passing the apartment I occupied in the neighborhood. One offered to sell me part of his loot, and finding it to be

The Red Guards have been on the rampage again. They broke into a church last week, killed one of the priests who tried to defend the place, looted it of much of its gold, silver, and precious stone ornaments, and among other things threw the body of the dead priest and his golden robes into a canal. This feat of bravery has excited much hatred, and has led to the Bolsheviks, as a party, being excommunicated from the church. Many and large religious processions were held last week, I think, with a view to arousing religious fervor against the Bolsheviks. But these Russians are a spineless lot; their religion meant no more to them than so much idol worship of the ikon and image; they will talk much about it and do nothing as usual. I have great faith in the power of talk over this people, but none in their power of action. They'll talk themselves into and out of anything. Rumor has had it lately that the separate peace with Germany and Austria has been signed and that Trotzky is returning from Brest to Petrograd to report upon it. Of course this arouses great indignation amongst the good Russians and if true, great will be the excitement of protest. But it will all be verbal; they will talk about it until they have utilized all their vocal powers expressing to the world how such a deed does not represent the true will of the people, how they wished to remain faithful to their word, how they were forced into it,—and when this is done accept it calmly. The facts of the case are that these people will do anything to quit fighting; although the majority of them will not admit it, they admire Germany and want to be on her side. The sooner the Allies recognize this and take strong action accordingly the better off they'll be. Germany has played the game well here, and unless positive steps are taken to prevent, ten years will find Germany in the saddle here with Russia and all her vast raw materials at her back. I am perfectly willing to admit that Russia is worn out economically, that her physical strength is gone; but these people are far too willing to admit that this implies lack of moral strength. Perhaps Russia cannot fight more; neither can Belgium, but she has not wavered in the moral conflict for a moment. The issue comes to this, then, Russia cannot fight; if she refuses to accept the German offer of a separate peace, the Huns will punish her with their armies. What to do? I should say cling to the moral conviction, defy the Huns when you know he is wrong, let his armies come, fight him if you can—run away from him if you can't, but don't submit to him. Hang on. If Germany does attack Russia

---

Château-Yquem, Didesheimer, and old brandy I bought. And once we had wine in the house again after the long drought of the war-prohibition in Russia, we wanted more." Meriel Buchanan witnessed the street bacchanalia as well: "Women, their arms full of bottles, could be seen trying to sell them to passers-by in the streets. Even the children had their share of the plunder, and could be met carrying a bottle of champagne or, perhaps, some valuable old liqueur."

further it will be much like fighting a sofa pillow, what land she takes she cannot hold at the peace conference and what troops she uses here will weaken her by so much on the Western Front. I would say to Russia, then, die clean with honor rather than accept the German bribe and give to civilization the kiss of Judas!

Meanwhile the internal convulsions here continue to be of interest to those social-istically and anarchistically inclined. Six hundred roubles a month is supposed to be enough for any citizen to live on and this amount at the rate of one hundred fifty per week is all that he can draw from the banks. The private banks have been abolished, created into branches of the State Bank, so that now in Russia there are but three banks, the State Bank, the Crédit Lyonnais, and the National City Bank of New York. What they will do with us I don't know. Of course there is much agitation against us,—arising from Germanic sources, and many would have us closed out altogether; but the more conservative heads are not of that opinion; they realize that it is inevitable for America and Russia to carry on commercial relations and that therefore it is advantageous to have the most powerful banking institution in America represented here. But we shall see. All industrial enterprises, factories, mines etc. have been taken over by the state and are under control of committees of workmen; all stocks and shares have been abolished and from now on are considered worthless, while the interest on a number of the State Loans, the War Loan of 1916 and the Liberty Loan, for example, has been repudiated. All the while the throb of the commercial heart of the country grows weaker. Food supplies are gradually exhausted, famine reigns in many districts and threatens others, while epidemics of cholera and typhus run their horrid course.

Fairly to judge the Bolsheviks we must understand the composition of their party. It is made up of three parts. First there are the sincere and competent same interna-tional socialists who started the movement and are making a faithful effort to control it. It is they that are attempting the social reorganization of the country,—workmen's control of industry, nationalization of the banks; and federal ownership of property, and such radical projects as the changing of the calendar. Second, come the paid German agitators, whose work is to strain every effort to lead the few sincere ones into a separate peace, to thwart their attempts at bringing order out of chaos, and in general to keep the country in such a state of turmoil that it cannot aid the Allies and must offer every opportunity for German occupation either by peaceful means, or otherwise. Theirs are the separate peace cries, the insults to Allied ambassadors, the strikes, civil war, in general playing of one class, one force against another, which results in such internal disruption. Third, we have the anarchistic riff-raff, thieves, thugs, murderers, drunkards, all the red flag-waving, scatterbrained scum which is the product of the tyranny of such systems of the government practiced by the old regime. This group is responsible for the violence, the murders, and the general lawlessness. There we have the composition of the party known as Bolsheviks. In order to obtain the power before the session of the Constituent Assembly and so prevent the country from falling under control of the conservative, bourgeoisie party, the sincere Bolsheviks had to appeal for and enlist the sympathy and aid of the insincere,—the second and third named groups above.

Once in power, the first group has found it impossible to control the other two, and such is the growing strength of the anarchists, that many see in them the overthrow of Bolshevism. Whether the anarchists or the German agents will win out, it is difficult to say,—but certain it is that the real Bolsheviks are finding it more difficult to govern each day.

Only day before yesterday the official paper of the anarchists "Pravda" (Truth) came out with a flaming editorial reminding all good members of their brotherhood of the duty to choke the bourgeoisie wherever they were met, and in general advocating wholesale murder and slaughter. This was incited by the fact that, in spite of official Bolshevik reports to the contrary, the civil warfare against the Cossacks around Kieff [Kiev or Kyiv] is not going well, and some fifteen hundred Red Guards have been killed in the fighting.

Welcome to the case of John Reed. This gentleman, though an American, has been appointed Russian counsel to the Port of New York. The sole object of this action is to involve the United States in a bicker-fest with the Bolsheviks over the release of certain anarchist criminals now held in America, namely Berkman and Goldman. There is an indictment out for Reed and as soon as he sets foot in New York, if ever he is allowed to do that, his arrest is almost certain to follow. The Bolsheviks would arrest the American consul in retaliation here and perhaps other Americans, and then demand the release of Reed and whatever other anarchists they happen to favor. An incidental purpose in the appointment may be to obtain for Reed, who is as low an anarchist as they make 'em, an opportunity for Bolshevik propaganda in America. For the Bolshevik purpose is to spread their doctrine, or lack of it, through every country on the globe, and turn it all into a red flag waving haven of lawlessness. Their activities are not directed against any one country or any group of countries; world-conquest is their aim.

Rumor has it that Reed is a dangerous man, also that the world is a dangerous place for him. It is said that he went to Germany in the early part of the war as a correspondent, that in a visit to the first line trenches he seized a rifle and fired at French soldiers in the French trenches across the way, exclaiming as he did so, "whoopee, there goes another Frenchy!" that for this boasted feat the French government is holding a warm reception for him should he ever fall into French hands; that while doing correspondent work in Roumania he followed the refugees behind the Russian lines, and here, without a passport or permit of any kind was discovered taking pictures of Russian positions; that for this, with his characteristic swiftness, the Grand Duke Nicholas ordered Reed executed; that the American Embassy in Petrograd hearing of the affair got the sentence revoked by promising the Foreign Office here that they would be responsible for Reed; that Reed gave his parole that he would not attempt to leave the city and on the strength of his word was allowed to live unmolested at the Astoria Hotel here; that one morning the police called up the embassy asking where Reed was, and at the reply of the embassy that he was at the Hotel Astoria, they were informed that he had left there for parts unknown a day or so before; that hid on a train for the border Reed was accosted by a couple of secret police agents who told him he was headed the wrong way for Petrograd and took him in custody; that he was soon sent back to America; that upon arrival there, he wrote an article for the paper he represented or mis-represented, the "Metropolitan Magazine," deliberately distorting the facts so as to place himself in a jovial light and the American Embassy, whose standing with the Foreign Office he had appreciably lowered, in a ridiculous light; And that soon after the Revolution he appeared once more in Petrograd as a representative of American socialism, while he has ever been cursing America and things American at every opportunity. Ought he be allowed to set foot in the United States?

I must not forget to relate of the time I saw the ballet from the imperial box! Last Sunday, having been indoors all day I set out in the evening for a walk and a little after seven o'clock finding myself near the Marinsky Theatre went in and endeavored to get a seat. But it was too late, there wasn't a place in the house for sale. Just as I was going home one of the ushers signaled to me and informed me that he could find a seat for me. I gave him ten roubles, which almost knocked him down, and he conducted me to a seat in the first box on the belle-etage tier—a very fine place. He soon discovered another "sucker" and I had the company of a young Russian chap with whom I soon became friendly. We saw the first ballet from this place and went out to take our promenade. During this I met a number of my friends. I returned to "my box" early and was serenely contemplating the people below with a superior air when there came a knock at the door and my usher friend whispered in my ear that the real owner of the box had come and that I'd have to scoot. I whizzed by the rightful possessors as fast as I could and was informed by my guide that as soon as the lights went off he would find another seat for me. Meanwhile the second ballet began. Soon my Russian friend came around the corner laughing to himself. He told me that he had returned to the box later, that he had rapped and rapped on the door, that the owner had stuck his head out the door asking him "what in Hell he wanted?" that he was so surprised he nearly fell over. Soon our pussy-foot friend, the usher took us by the corner and led us into the huge royal box where we sat in state! I didn't dare go out in the row of front seats where my friends could see me, so I stuck to the shadowy rear. After about half an hour another usher, evidently not in the same fraternity as our friend, steered a big party into the royal box, and asked for our tickets. As they all had tickets and we did not, we had to exit as gracefully as possible. Meeting our helpful friend once more we told him that his "tovarisch" [Russian: товарищ, comrade] didn't know the signals at all; he grew quite peeved at the insult to our persons and conducted us to one of the ornate grand ducal boxes at the sides where we viewed the remainder of the ballet from the softest of plush and gold chairs!

29/11 Feb. 1918.

Trotzky has returned from Brest with the announcement that although the Bolsheviks refuse to accept the German peace program of annexation they cannot fight longer and will therefore disband the army! Strange state of affairs, unparalleled in history,—refusing to sign a treaty of peace and yet refusing also to defend oneself from the arrogant enemy. As usual the Bolsheviks have taken the middle course, that between the signed separate peace which it may be certain would read so as to hand Russia commercially over to Germany—and the active prosecution of the war. It is perhaps the best course to pursue. Certainly they do not bind themselves in any way to Germany,—if the latter wants Russia she must come take it,—it will not be handed over to her on a velvet pillow. This is as much as the Allies can expect of Russia under the present circumstances and they must be congratulated on having refused to sign the German terms. The Bolsheviks have left their hands free for future action also. Of course there will be much clamor and cursing from all sides, but this will come mostly from people who do not appreciate the situation. When considering the state of affairs in the east one must remember that the war is virtually won if Germany manages to gain commercial foothold in Russia to the exclusion or in preference to the Allied nations, and every move which makes the possibility more remote is as good as a military victory for the Allies' side. This one seems to obviate the danger from the point of view of Russian treachery or concession. There still remains the possibility that the Germans may step in and take what parts of the country they desire, but it is up to the Allies on the West Front to keep them busy enough to prevent this.

30/12.

Today we hear that the army will not be demobilized, but only parts of it. This is another step in our direction. The naïveté of these people. The government today published a decree requesting all criminals to leave Petrograd! Does the government fear competition?

31/13 Feb.

We read in the paper today that the Allied and neutral ambassadors met at the American Embassy last night to confer on the question of protection of the respective citizens and their private property. The results of the meeting which the newspapers say was a "lively one" was a note signed by all and sent to the State Department of the Russian government stating that the foreigners did not recognize the Bolshevik decrees abolishing private property, real estate, government loans etc., and that all losses incurred by foreign holders would have to be made good by the Russian government, which must indemnify the foreigners against losses.

The reply to this note will be interesting. I should not wonder if it turned out to be the beginning of very serious negotiation.

1/14 Feb

"What is Caesar's, render unto Caesar" and this time it is praise we must accord to the Bolsheviks in power for inaugurating a reform in Russian custom that will be second only to the abolition of vodka in its beneficial effects on the future of the country. Without any of the quibble and interminable debate that would have delayed such a step under the old regime the system of dates has been changed and the Georgian [Rogers meant the Julian] old calendar abolished, and that used by all the civilized nations of the world adopted. Thus today, under the old style, the 1st of February is the 14th of February as it is everywhere else. Not only is this a significant stroke against the masses of tradition and custom which have held Russia in ignorance and darkness but it will also have effect of far-reaching benefit on the commercial life of the country. It may be superfluous to add that it never could have occurred under the old powers because of the opposition from religious quarters. The Tsar was at once the head of the state and the head of the church, and this latter exercised a strong influence over the state. The church has always fought stubbornly any movement that would tend to the education and liberation of the masses, as such events would weaken its position. It took the Revolution which overthrew both the rule of the church as well as the domination of the Tsar to make this reform possible.

This afternoon while walking up the Litania I came to a group of men and women hard at work clearing away the snow from the streets. There were men in fur coats and fine shoes, women in furs and feathers, all armed with picks and shovels, presided over by burly soldier guards, who stood by while their charges worked. I was witnessing the "bourgeoisie" being forced to labor by the "proletariat;" it was the translation into action of the words of the recent governmental decree to the effect that all must work for their living, that there should be no one idle. A worthy principle, but how distorted in application!

I suppose from the point of view of the long suppressed laborer and the moujik there is a keen sense of ultimate justice and of enjoyment at the sight of these people doing manual labor, based as it is on the supposition that they have never worked before. But there is where the injustice comes in, for many of these people who are now suffering most from the antics of the Bolsheviks have worked hard all their lives, if not with their hands, with their brains, and now that they had just saved enough as a result of this labor to make them comfortable, it is hardly just to deprive them of it. What adds more to the resentment and the injustice is the spirit in which the oppression is exercised. Were there a crying necessity for the efforts of these people, such as absence of labor, or questions of public safety and health involved nothing could be more just than that they should be called upon to neglect their private tasks for the more fundamental public ones, but there is no such necessity. The streets are crowded with loafers, with idle soldiers who do nothing, and have done nothing for the past year save eat, drink, sleep and steal; ten of them from the hilarious group of spectators that attended the band of impressed workers I mentioned above, could do the task in half the time and better. The spirit then is not of necessity, it is of travesty. And it is just this insincerity which shows itself in the vindictiveness, travesty, imitation, which underlies so many acts of people that most threaten their new freedom. For above all things a revolution must have something great to give the world, some sincere purpose for being, if it has not this the many crimes committed in its name, the innumerable cases in which the good suffer with the bad, the right with the wrong, are all unpardoned, inexcusable, and they only brand the movement as a mob uprising, a riot, instead of a revolution. Therefore unless the leaders in this revolution cease doing this thing because there is an element of keen satire about it, and that thing because the French did it,—making it good revolutionary form as it were—they are likely to find themselves, when the novelty wears off and people are tired of idleness, they are likely to find themselves only rioters after all.

I like to think that this will not be so, because to me there was behind the Revolution the pent up desire of a suppressed people for expression; expression not only political but, commercial, artistic, and Christian. It was another link in that great chain of popular rule that is connecting together, harmonizing, the civilized world, another chapter in the great history which is making the world a humanity and not a collection of nations and individuals. Because I saw all this in the Revolution I keep my confidence in it and prefer to think that these petty acts are due to minor minds and not those in direction.

The motive behind the actions against the wealthy, mercantile, and land owning classes is plain. The intention is by confiscating their wealth, assuming control of their industry, and taking over their land, to break their power forever, to grind them out of Russian life. For it is true that upon them or their ancestors lies the guilt of the age long neglect and oppression of so huge a majority of the Russian people. The "intelligentsia" as they are called, had centuries of time and uncountable wealth to devote to the education and uplift of the masses. Did they make the most of their unparalleled opportunities. No! On the contrary, they used these things to tread down every attempt of the masses to crawl up out of the slime and darkness. Viewed in the broad sense of human progress these people, then, have failed, and we cannot complain at the justice that sweeps them aside to make way for those who will undertake to do what they failed to do. If the methods used against them are ruthless and rough we must console ourselves with the thought that it is not as ruthless as they deserve.

2/15 Feb.

I have been assured that I shall receive permission to leave the country and I am now at liberty to set about my other preparations. With any kind of fortune at all I should pull out within two weeks. Perhaps the hardest of all the preparations is telling the boys about it. We've been together now through thick and thin for fourteen months and I hate to break away from the circle. But such things must be done and tomorrow I shall let it out.

3/16 Feb.

Went over to the control office this morning and learned that my application to leave has been granted with an "A" recommendation, which means that I should not have much trouble on the way. From there I went to the Foreign Office and presented my application for the Bolshevik permit to leave. In the office I entered a young, red-headed little chap presided over his office force of one mangey soldier. On the desk in front of me lay a list of people to whom it was forbidden to leave Russia, and this had to be run over carefully twice to make sure my name was not on it. Not being there, my name was taken as well as my passport and I received a little slip which, I was informed, on Saturday next will enable me to receive the necessary permit. While standing there I had to notice the many maps, war or otherwise, pinned on the wall; all good old German maps made in Germany and printed in German. One of them, showing in pink all the territory over which Germany has control, was very careful to emphasize the Bagdad Railway, running in a heavy blue line from Berlin to the east.

It was announced in the papers today that the Metropolitan of the Petrograd district had been murdered by the Red Guard yesterday. The Metropolitan is the lead of the church of his district, and Petrograd being the governmental district, its metropolitan is by far the most distinguished in all Russia. Nevertheless, this man was dragged from his home and murdered. The reason given was that he had blessed the Ukrainians in their struggle against the Bolsheviks.[368]

Besides being another stain on the Bolshevik banner this act in a way signifies one thing they stand for,—the separation of the Church from the State. A decree to this effect has already been issued. While I am always glad to see this decision made, it is always attended with serious strife of some kind, and if I am not mistaken we can expect to see the Bolsheviks, in their warfare against the church, meet with acrid resistance.

17 Feb. 1918.

During the last week we have been hearing of famine and sickness among the poor, and I have no doubt that the rumors are true. Some four or five hundred cases of

---

[368] Orthodox Church in America; "Saint Vladimir, Metropolitan of Kiev and Gallich," https://www.oca. org/saints/lives/2014/01/25/100311-saint-vladimir-metropolitan-of-kiev-and-gallich. Metropolitan Vladimir (Russian: Владимир) (1848–February 7, 1918) was metropolitan of Moscow and Kolomna from 1898 to 1912, metropolitan of St. Petersburg and Ladoga from 1912 to 1915, and Galitch from 1915 to 1918. Rogers cited February 15 as the date of his murder, but it happened on February 7.

typhus have been reported and already there are many deaths from it. The food situation continues to get worse I don't see how the poor live at all. Today, "Count"—who too is the steward of our flat, said that for the six of us for the last two days three quarters of a pound of bread had been issued to us!

CHAPTER 14

"Well, we fooled the Bolsheviks, we fooled the German subs and I arrived . . ."

Exhausted, hungry, and desirous of a hot bath, Leighton Rogers reached Murmansk after a grueling eight-day journey across broken rail track between Petrograd and Murmansk. Today, the same 1,350 kilometer train passage takes one day.

In 1918, Murmansk resembled, as historian George Kennan put it, an early American logging camp consisting of log cabins, wooden barracks, and storage sheds.[369] Murmansk was Russia's closest northern port for Allied ships to transport much-needed military, Red Cross, and other supplies. It significantly grew in population and activity by the winter of 1917–18 not only because of increased military traffic but also because of the growing stream of refugees seeking ships sailing for the West. One train of refugees arrived per week. Rogers waited for three weeks in Murmansk before a run-down British transport ship arrived to take him and other refugees to England.

Major Allen Wardwell served as the Red Cross officer in Murmansk. He vividly described the scene:

> We have nearly every nationality here now—it is a queer conglomerate crowd. There are French, Italian, English, a few Americans, Russians, Roumanians, Czechs, and with the Chinese working on the railway and the Greeks and Finns with us, we are well represented. There are Germans and Austrian prisoners not far down the line and every day or two some Lapps come in to town to trade . . . There are French officers and men, some Italian singers who bellow all day in their car and once in a while sing in front of it

---

[369] George F. Kennan, *Soviet-American Relations, 1917–1920, Volume 2, The Decision to Intervene* (Princeton, NJ: Princeton University Press, 1958), 23.

in true operatic style with all the approved gestures. There is a famous singer of gypsy songs, a number of Russian aviators trying to sneak out of Russia to America, a Russian professor of mathematics, with all kinds of letters permitting him to go to America, who, with his assistants bribed someone in Petrograd to the tune of 1500 rubles, for the privilege of riding in an ordinary box car five or six days to Murmansk, and living in it while here. [370]

Rogers and his fellow refugees' arrival on March 2 complicated things for the Allies. The British Embassy sent a memorandum to the US Department of State on March 4 detailing its concerns over the situation:

> The British Rear Admiral at Murmansk has reported to His Majesty's Government that a serious situation exists there owing to the anti-Ally attitude adopted by the Bolsheviki garrison, and to the reported intention of the Finns who, acting at the instigation of the Germans, propose to advance on the Petrograd-Murmansk Railway. The arrival at Murmansk from Petrograd of refugees who are seeking passages for England and of repatriated Russian sailors and soldiers, the attitude of whom will probably be hostile, is complicating the situation. . . . A British cruiser has been sent and the British Embassy are instructed to ask the United States Government to dispatch a man-of-war to join the squadron now on the spot as soon as possible, as the situation may develop rapidly and the matter is therefore extremely urgent.[371]

American authorities also worried. Frank Polk of the State Department wrote to Ambassador Francis on March 9, requesting information "covering political situation, accumulation of supplies if any and condition of railroad transportation" in Murmansk.[372]

Rogers noted the presence of British and French cruisers in his journal. The British warship H.M.S. *Cochrane* arrived on March 7 and the French cruiser *Admiral*

---

[370] Steven D. Corrsin, "The American Red Cross in Revolutionary Russia," *Columbia Library Columns* 30, no. 1 (November 1980): 22–23.

[371] US State Department, Office of the Historian, Papers Relating to the Foreign Relations of the United States, 1918, Russia, Volume 2, "The British Embassy to the Department of State," No. 232 Memorandum, File No. 861.00/1233, https://history.state.gov/historicaldocuments/frus1918Russiav02/d572.

[372] US State Department, Office of the Historian, Papers Relating to the Foreign Relations of the United States, 1918, Russia, Volume 2, "The Acting Secretary of State to the Ambassador in Russia (Francis) [Telegram]," File No. 861.00/1401a, https://history.state.gov/historicaldocuments/frus1918Russiav02/d573.

Aube on March 19. These deployments represented the Allies' first step to secure the Murmansk-Petrograd rail hub from the threat of German forces. George Kennan doubted any "serious danger of attack on Murmansk by Finns under German command" in March and April, but concluded "by the time the British and French had spent some weeks acting as though there *were* such a danger, they had succeeded in conjuring it into a real existence."[373] In April, Woodrow Wilson reluctantly sent the cruiser USS *Olympia*.[374] Later in June, British General Frederick Poole arrived in Murmansk and occupied the railway as far south as Kem, declaring it "Russian territory under Allied protection." In August, he acted similarly in Archangel, Russia's other key northern port, located thirty hours' nautical travel farther east.

Leighton Rogers sailed across the North Sea providentially without incident and arrived in Newcastle upon Tyne on March 29. In England, he joined the US Army, where his firsthand experience in Russia brought him to the attention of senior Army intelligence officers.

---

[373] Kennan, *Soviet-American Relations 1917–1920, Volume 2, The Decision to Intervene*, 43.
[374] "Murmansk | Spring 1918, from 'Russian Sideshow: America's Undeclared War' by Robert L. Willett, 2003, Potomac Books," *Notes on the Jesse Halsey History Project (blog)* February 26, 2013, http://halseyhelgesontree.blog-spot.com/2013/02/murmansk-spring-1918.html.

(Rogers left Petrograd by train on Saturday evening, February 23, 1918)
17/2 March

So this is Murmansk! Let's see, the last time I wrote in this book was on the 17th of February and I doubted then whether I should be able to leave Petrograd before three weeks were up. Here it is a bit over one week and I'm out. You never know what you can do until you try. A very old saying, but a very true one. So much has been crowded into these short eight days that I shall probably omit much but the way I feel now I don't care about ever having it recalled to me in the future, let alone read about it in my own handwriting. But here goes; it was like this:—

It was a dark and stormy night when—but seriously it was just that kind of an afternoon when I received in a neat little envelope a summons from the Bolsheviki to appear before their committee at Headquarters the following morning at nine o'clock. No further invitation or warning was needed; I don't know exactly what it was about, nor did I care to wait and find out. I had my permit from the British to leave for Great Britain but my passport was in the hands of the Bolsheviks at the Foreign Office. There was a chance that I might get it. I hustled down to doleful red building in the Palace Square, fought my way up to the office and presenting my little numbered slip, requested the little sorrel topped soldier to return my passport. He fumbled around amongst the papers, found a list, looked it over and replied that I was too early, according to my number the visa would not be ready for three days yet. "But I want my passport" I said, after much argument, with him telling me that it would be impossible to leave without the visa and with me saying it did not matter, that I needed the passport at once, he sent a messenger out in search of it. I waited breathlessly to see whether he would look for my name on the black-list of people who were not to be allowed to leave the country, but he did not. It may not have been there anyway.

In half an hour his emissary returned with the passport bearing the Bolshevik visa to leave the country, but lacking as he explained another stamp, without which I could not leave the city. But I took it and went out.

The American Consulate was the next stop; here I was received a bit sharply as were most Americans, and informed that nothing could be done towards assisting me to leave the country. The consul, however; in spite of himself, did assist me, because he gave me a letter of introduction to the British consul, which I requested.

Armed with this I proceeded to the British Consulate, made my way through a mob of Britishers who had besieged the place, growling and protesting at having to leave the country. (They had been notified by their country to get out). Most of them wanted a few days to pack, to arrange this, and to see this and that person and the irate consul had about lost his patience. "My dear friends," he finally observed, in the voice of a college professor, "You are not taking a pleasure trip out of the country. You are refugees, you are running away, and will have to make the best of it. There's a train, a freight, pulling out for Murmansk at midnight tonight, now who wants to go on it?"

"I do," I chimed in, stepped up and presented my letter. He read it and looked me over. Just then a British major came in and after hearing the consul's few words about the contrariness of the crowd, provided to "bawl them out" in great style. He had a marvelous flow of language, that major and even invented extemporaneously several new oaths. The consul spoke to him about me. He, in his turn looked me over. "You want to get out?" he demanded.

"Yes," said I meekly.

"Can you be ready to go tonight?" he asked.

"Certainly," I said. "I can go now for that matter."

"No you can't," he contradicted, "but go to your home, pack up food enough for fourteen days in something you can carry on your back, roll up a few warm clothes, go to the Nicholas Station at twelve tonight, and on the first track in the freight section at the left you'll find a train ready to pull out. Get in one of the cars and you'll go. I don't guarantee it; but the chances are fifty-fifty you'll make it, and those odds are good enough for anyone these days."

"Thanks" I replied, heading for the door, "I'll be there."

This was something encouraging at last and I got home as quickly as possible to prepare. Food for fourteen days that I could carry on my back! That was a problem. En route to the house I stopped in two provision stores to try to get some canned meat of some kind. One shop had two rusty six pound cans of corned beef, but they demanded seventy-five roubles a piece for them—nearly nine dollars for six pounds of old corned beef,—and this was impossible; the second shop had a small ham, weighing at the most ten pounds, an heirloom from the look of it, for which the keepers asked three hundred roubles—or more than thirty–five dollars,—impossible also. I tried to buy a cake of chocolate, but there were none. The shop was practically bare of food! Finally I gave up and hurried home. Here I told the boys of my plan and all was excitement to help me.

For months we had treasured a little horde of extra good things we had been fortunate enough to purchase here and there or have given to us by departing friends. A can of chicken, some of cold tongue, deviled ham, canned fruits, and such, they were that composed the little stock; luxuries we had not tasted for many months. All of these the boys generously offered, as well as some bread made from some real American white flour we had saved up. I accepted the bread but couldn't deprive them of the rest; and therefore proposed a grand feed at which we should share these things. This would give me a chance to eat to a finish, get a flying start, and enable me to live "off the humps" like a camel for at least a day and thus save what I would carry until absolutely necessary to open it. The suggestion was immediately translated into action and we sat down to a fine feast, while the cook dried the bread in the oven for me, packed it away in a wicker basket, stuffed in cheese, yard lengths of sausage, some tea, a small teapot, a can of condensed milk, a bottle of alcohol, a few small tins of solidified alcohol "Sterno" they call it, and, as a luxury—a bottle of Heinze's Pickles!

After the feast, I packed away in my trunk all my clothes save one suit I planned to carry with me in a suitcase, and a sweater; packed away and bid a fond farewell to all my worldly goods, clothes I had bought for the next three years, suits I had never worn, overcoats, evening clothes,—everything, including a box full of very valuable ivories, tapestries, linens, embroideries, and laces, I had purchased to take home with me at the end of those three long years. In my suitcase I put the suit, the sweater, some warm underwear, a blanket, and this journal. The hamper of food was duly strapped up, and with my available funds in my pocket, I hoisted the basket over my back, took leave of the boys, and left with "Chuck" who insisted upon going to the station with me and carry the suitcase. Without him I should have been ruined, because in the great coat I wore I could hardly have sneaked the basket and suitcase past the first circle of guards we found around the station. A howling mob besieged the station, but was kept out by the Cossack guard which forced those who would go to form in a long line which led thru a narrow fenced in passage to the still narrower gate of entrance. At the gate a grimy workman stood examining the papers of those who came thru. I thought I saw my finish right there, but I picked up the suitcase, Chuck tossed the hamper to me over the fence, I caught it in the face of the astonished inspector, and was by, bag and baggage before he knew what had happened. He had no time to give for pursuit because the yelling mob outside threatened to trample him down at any minute. And moreover, I suppose, he left me to be captured by the second circle of Red Guards inside the station. The one of these I struck, however, was happily drunk, and a handful of roubles sufficed for him.

Inside I happily met a friend, who introduced me to a young English engineer who planned to get out the same way. We waited until nearly twelve, and then walked out to the freight platform where the train stood. There seemed to be numerous others going also, and here in the search for a place, I lost friend C – – –. After clambering in numerous four wheeled freight cars,—goods wagons—they call them, and thinking them unsatisfactory I found what had once been a sleeping car attached to the train and got aboard. C – – – was here, and in it there was but one place left, half the upper platform in a compartment meant for two. I made the fourth occupant. Although it had once been a sleeper it was now sadly out of commission—no heat, no water of course, no light, here and there no glass in the windows, with dirt and ice inches deep on the floor, and icicles hanging from the ceiling. One of the freight cars would have been better, because there would at least have been room in that and here I was cramped up on half the shelf like a monkey. I was about to make the change, when the whistle screeched, and we started.

It was the good quantity of food I'd eaten that got me through that first night; without, I would have been as stiff as a board by morning. It was the worst weather I'd seen in Russia, blasts of wind and stinging snow which fairly shook the train on the track and held it down to a speed of ten miles an hour. Moreover, the outlook did not seem bright, because we were going north all the time.

But morning finally came and things looked better. There were four of us in the coop, making it possible for only two to stand up at the same time. There was friend C – – – and two Englishmen—no one Englishman and one Scotsman (horrible error) from the great British mills in Narva. It was not long before we were acquainted, and had what few things we carried packed away so as to leave us as much space as possible.

For eight days we rumbled northward. Eight days of intense cold, of cramped sleep on the half shelf, of going without wash or shave—there was no water save what we could get when the train passed at some tiny northern village, and this went for hot tea with our meals, eight days of eating the dried bread, cheese and sausage, of four hours of light and the remaining twenty of darkness, and eight days of wondering when we should be stopped and hauled back.

At one stop it did look as though the game was up for me. Soldiers boarded the train, came down through, making those in the cars show their papers; there were men on the train, they said, without the Bolshevik permit to leave and they were instructed from Petrograd to take them off. I was quite prepared to be hauled off when, just as the search party had got to the car ahead two Russian sailors walked down the track, having come from the forward car of the train. "What are you delaying us for?" they demanded of the searching Red Guards. "There are men on this train [without] permits and we're going to take them off" was the reply. "Who told you?" demanded the sailors. "We got orders from Trotzky in Petrograd," replied a soldier. "Well, never mind 'em" retorted the mariners, "We're going to a wedding in the next village and we're late now. Get out and start the train. This is a Republic now, and we're just as good as you, or Lenin or Trotzky or anyone else, and moreover, we've got no permits and you're not taking us, so start the train, comrades!"

The "comrade" and the "just as good" stuff did the trick; the soldiers withdrew, the sailors returned up ahead, gave the word to the engineer, and we were off, they to their wedding, and I to Murmansk.

As we went north it grew colder and colder, and of course darkness came earlier each day. The road bed got in poorer condition also, due to its being built across the swamps and there were places which at times it seemed impossible to cross.

All of this lowered our daily mileage. Of scenery there was none but the endless, melancholy, impassive waste of ice and snow, now and then broken by a scrabble of bushes and blasted spruce trees; once in a great while we crawled past a tiny village of crude log shacks and mud huts where German and Austrian prisoners of war lived under horrible conditions—more like animals than men, imprisoned by the vast emptiness around them.

At the first town of any size we stopped at,—a place called Petrozavodsk—we managed to buy some candles and a little vodka, these were godsends, the light cheering us up and the vodka helping in the battle to keep warm. From Petrozavodsk to the next sizable town of Kem must be well over three hundred miles of the same desolate white spaces as we lumbered across them in the face of a stinging snowstorm. The food question had begun to trouble a bit and I was by this time good and tired of dry bread, cheese or sausage and weak cold tea. My bottle of wonderful pickles and cinnamon had frozen, and broken and soaked my edibles with the vinegar. But it was welcome as a variation;—a pure case of variety being the spice of life.

The railroad station at Kem is a mile or so from the town, but I had no desire to visit the latter. Across the white swamps we could just see the low roofs of the town and beyond them the vast waste of the White Sea. The station contained a restaurant at which we stocked up for the last lap of our journey. At Kem also, encamped in a train on a siding was a regiment of French artillery, or part of a regiment—which had been with the Russians on the Galician Front, and was now on its long way home. I talked with some of the young officers a while and even considered their offer to come in with them in their freight car, but remained where I was upon learning that they were to follow directly behind our train. They helped us out considerably here too. A train load of Russian soldiers en route to Petrograd crawled in with a damaged locomotive. They tried to take ours and our little resistance would have been puny without the French and their superior show of rifles and machine guns. We won the argument and after eighteen hours in Kem set out once more, not however, before giving our hands and faces their first wash and shave in four days and nights.

From Kem to the next place with any right to call itself a town, Kandalashka [Rogers meant Kandalaksha], must be another 300 miles of precarious riding across frozen swamps and ice. But this passed much more quickly and pleasantly due to the fact that by this time the four of our compartment were the best of friends. Being the only American on the expedition, altogether there were some sixty odd on the train—I was somewhat of a curiosity; but after the surprise at my appearing without tomahawk and feathers wore away, we got along famously. Without "Scotty"—the Scotsman member of our quartet, to swap stories with and teach college songs to and learn Scottish ballads from the trip would certainly be drab. But with his keen wit, inimitable sense of humor, and vast experience of some forty-five years to draw upon, his companionship is priceless. No claim to a school education has Scotty but his unerring knowledge of literature, of music, of art in general, and of social, political, and historical subjects label him as a man of the best education—the natural, self-obtained brand. Before it, ye narrow, university-learned savants, bow to the ground. (Scotty would put ground glass in my tea if he saw this). Then too in the pocket of my overcoat I found a book, Joseph Conrad's "Nostromo," and this I welcomed as a long absent friend, reading it as avidly the third time as I did the first.

At this time I gave up writing until we arrived in Murmansk to wash and shave and when the train stopped to allow us to get water for tea, performed these feats in snow. It was difficult at first, but not so bad as it sounds after one or two times. I threatened to disrobe and take a bath in it too, but Scotty demurred, saying he couldn't waste good vodka bringing me back to consciousness if I tried it. It could be done though.

Kandalashka really has some claim to beauty, set as it is among a series of hills, for the most part naked of foliage, but covered with snow which the low-lying sun, escaping from the clouds for a few delirious moments, turned to burnished gold. Not for long, however, and simultaneous with the fading of the color we took up the iron trail again for Murmansk.

Thus, after eight days, we arrived; and here we are.

Just a word about Murmansk. It is a town under British and French control which serves as a port of entry for supplies which are to be sent into Russia over the Petrograd-Murmansk railroad. This single track line, completed in late 1915, is the only route over which Britain and France can help Russia,—hence, while Russia was an active factor in the war, it was very important. It is a small place of not more than two thousand people, mostly Russians, Laplanders, and Mongolians; its buildings, of the low hewn log type, ramble up the hill side from the water edge. Along this, skirts the track with spurs branching out to the docks constructed by the Allied forces. Beyond, in the harbor, a natural land locked haven which does not freeze, in spite of the fact that it is some three hundred miles beyond the Arctic Circle and nearly five hundred north of Archangel which is frozen nine months of the year. (This because the Gulfstream takes a final curve around the peninsula into the harbor; hence the water is comparatively warm—only comparatively though.) Encircling the harbor and the tower are rugged hills which afford no little protection from the tundra winds. Out in the harbor lies a dirty, ancient Russian battleship whose obsolete guns and red flag with difficulty look squarely at Britain's symbol of power the battleship "Glory" and her four twelve's and Union Jack which flutters in accord with that waving over the consulate on the hill.

Here we must live in the cars which are back up on a siding, one week, two weeks—we don't know how long, until a transport comes in. But it will be in comparative luxury because the battleship is sending us food tomorrow, we are to have a little stove put in, and the Russian bath in the village—to be cleaned and opened for us alone each morning.

18/3 March.

Have that "grand and glorious feeling" today, having just come from a short walk about the village and the Russian bath. This latter was cleaned especially for us and we took possession this morning. For the first time in ten days I got my clothes off and had a grand time throwing the hot water about, rubbing away pounds of soap in suds, slipping on the wet wood floor and in general disporting myself in a wasteful, wonderful manner.

The town certainly is a disreputable place,—no order in its make up. It just rambles where it pleases and everyone in it seems to do as he pleases, in consequence it is filthy with refuse. The docks and land there about are cluttered with machinery, once new, now rusting from disuse, and the greater part of this is American,—the huge cranes, the locomotives, donkey engines, and the like. On the shore lie the remains of two very small submarines transported here in pieces to be shipped overland by rail to Petrograd and the Gulf of Finland for assembling and possible use against the German fleet. These too are fast rotting away. At one of the docks are tied up four Russian torpedo boats now manned by skeleton crews as is the battleship in the open harbor; the majority of the sailors have gone home. But a few weeks ago there was a Russian admiral here with whom the British dealt officially, but there arose some trouble or other between him and some delinquent members of the ship's crew which resulted in his being shot in the back one evening as he came from his house. The sailors, however, maintain that none of their number did it, saying that they respected the admiral and that the Bolsheviks sent Reds up from Petrograd to commit the crime. It may be.

We are getting settled now, a stove was put in the car this morning and we are now warm once in a while. When we get the food from the battleship this afternoon, "Scotty" intends to cook on it. He has already fashioned a sign for our car, it hangs over the door and reads "The Better 'Ole."[375]

19/4 March.

The food has come. We carried it bodily up from the dock and now have it apportioned out. Fine. Canned meats—rabbit, corned beef, white bread—just like cake—oleomargarine, jam, coffee, crackers, and some miscellaneous canned vegetables and fruit. We elected Scotty cook and he brewed a concoction this evening that knocked us stiff. All I can do is sleep, after finishing this. There are now only three in the coop meant for two, C – – – having left us for quarters at the consulate. At one time I should have counted him lucky; but this isn't so bad now. I wouldn't miss Scotty for anything, he's a show in himself.

Another car of refugees came in today—all British. We're getting to be quite a colony. Must quit now; Scotty wants to sing over some of our "close harmony" stuff, and after doing this and keeping the others awake, we shall sleep.

---

[375] Wikipedia, "The Better Ole," last modified January 23, 2021, 05:11 (UTC), https://en.wikipedia.org/wiki/The_Better_%27Ole. *The Better 'Ole*, also called *The Romance of Old Bill*, was an Edwardian musical comedy based on the cartoon character Old Bill, an infantryman, drawn by Bruce Bairnsfather. The original London production in 1917 was a hit, running for more than 800 performances, and had success on tour and on Broadway the following year. It spawned two film adaptations and a sequel.

21/6 March. 1918.

The populace here rides about in reindeer sledges. They are not bad at that—the sledge is very light,—constructed of two skis kept parallel by cross pieces upon which is constructed a light framework and seat for the riders. The reindeer are usually hitched in threes, one experienced leader at the head, a less experienced one first behind and at the side, and a young deer still further back and to the side. They pull the sledge by means of long hide thongs and the driver guides the leader and the trio by poking them with a long light pole at the end of which is fastened a knob of padding. The deer have wide flat soles or pads on their feet and pull the sledges over the snow at a snappy pace. In addition they are tireless and easy to keep, eating almost anything,—like the Harlem bloodhounds, the goats.

25/10 March 1918.

There's a hill over to the south-east that has attracted me ever since our arrival. Its rounded top, of course deep in snow, bears the three massive towers of the British wireless station, and this, coupled with the rugged beauty of it as the sun in rare moments burnishes it with gold, has at last drawn me out on a walk to climb it.

It was not a bad day today considering the season and the place, and with a thick woolen shirt and a sweater I was right for a walk. With a thick stick for use against the somewhat wild dogs that infest the region I set out for the golden mountain, like the boy in the fairytale. There seemed to be something magic about it too, because although I walked vigorously I could not see that I got nearer, and at last I modified my resolution and thought it would be well should I arrive at its base, let alone climb it. A Lapland village intervened and my passage thru created quite a commotion among the skin and fur clad residents.

At last, seeing that the trail I was on led around the mountain I gave it up and returned. While on the way the sun suddenly dropped from sight and it was dark. I arrived at the "Better 'Ole" first as the Northern Lights began their nightly fantasia of sinuous movement and eyree light.

28/13 March.

Tempus sure does fudgit. Nearly two weeks have flown by and still no boat. There's not much to do and hence not much to write about. Went for a long walk along the shore this afternoon and around the bend where the watchtower is, but found the same bleak, forbidding emptiness there as here. On the way back we stopped at the tower where the two Russian sailors living there gave us tea and bread and entertained us with their playing on the accordion and balalaika. These people are by nature so simple and generous that it is a crime against humanity that they are misled.

Thus the waiting goes,—once in a while a walk, but the greater part of the time is spent in sleep. At meal times, Scotty awakens us with the clatter of the instruments he uses and his northland oaths, but I cannot watch him, —I would rather eat. So we close our eyes again while he prepares the mixtures; we eat these concoctions meekly and lie down to sleep again. No one knows what he puts in them; but I lost a pair of heavy rubbers one day, and I am beginning to have my suspicions! At night we light our little candles and read out of the mangey periodicals sent us from the battleship. Scotty and I then sing our mournful melodies and sink back into the twenty-hour darkness.

1/14

I see where I'm due to have my troubles. So far on the trip everyone has treated me with the utmost consideration and courtesy, so much so that I have felt as much at home as if among my own countrymen. But there is a pretty little British second lieutenant in charge of the passport control here who has remarked that he has no use for Americans; and moreover he has demonstrated it to me. So, as he is in command, I suppose I'm in for it. I'll meet him again somewhere however, for it is a small world, and then we'll see what's what. Meanwhile I suppose I might try the Hun hate business and indulge in my morning hate before breakfast, or I might hope his white mice die, or something terrible like that!

9/22 March 1918

The time has flown by so swiftly that it has left me far behind. Why I have not written here, I don't know. But my sins come back to harry me, because much has happened and I must make up what I lost and get it set down here before my pencil gives out!

In the first place a whole flock of ships has come in. Four, in fact, a British cruiser, a French cruiser, and two transports. The British cruiser and the first transport arrived some time ago. The transport is a wheezy old skiff and will be held up here until engine repairs can be made. The one we are going on has just arrived, a former German ship taken by the British and put into the service. She is preparing to take us aboard now.

Outside lie the two cruisers, the British trim and neat, and the French more like a floating tenement house with red underwear and geraniums in the portholes. Rumor hath it that an American cruiser is coming also, and I'm getting ready to cheer.

Previous to this marines were landed from the "Glory" and quartered in buildings on the hill taken over for barracks. They brought their colors, field pieces and machine guns with them ready for business and tho, in reality, took over the port from the Russians, although nothing official was said about it. These were the first British troops to land on Russian soil as enemies since the Crimean war. We ate at their mess with some of the boys who became acquainted with us and it was good to be with a crowd of young men again. They were hardly more than boys, though, and seemed to regard it as a great lark to be off ship. This move of landing was taken to forestall a Bolshevik attack on the place which had been threatened. It was reported one day a force of one thousand Bolsheviks had passed Kandalashka en route to take Murmansk. Twelve British marines with a machine gun in a flat car went down to meet them! But the meeting did not occur.

The French troops we had passed at Kem came in and encamped in their cars, and added to the life of the place. Up on the plain beyond the tower I joined some of the younger officers one day in racing reindeer sledges. It was great sport, and on the spot we formed the Racing Club of Murmansk.

Following them came many more refugees, French, men and women, more British, and finally a troop train of Czechs. These are men from certain provinces in Austria who rebelled against fighting for the Central Powers, deserted and are now on their way to France to form a Czech unit to fight with the French. It is said that capture is certain death for them. Perhaps this knowledge has helped give them the wonderful esprit de corps they have. Certainly they are a fine looking body of fighters and they should give a good account of themselves.

Some members of the American Red Cross from Petrograd also put in an appearance, riding luxuriously in the rolling palaces from the Tsar's royal train. I stopped in to see them one afternoon, but even though they had two extra beds and a good supply of food, and even tho I was the only American besides their own party in the place, I got no offer of help from them. I must have looked like a roughneck. Or else, maybe they are not supposed to help stray and distressed Americans. I may be all wrong in thinking it queer.

With them came a member of the Y.M.C.A. who promptly got a cabin and opened a hut; which has been greatly appreciated by everyone. Moreover, as we are having to get out of these cars tomorrow whether we sail or not, he has thrown the place open to us for use.

Arrangements are now underway for our boarding the ship. Cabins have been doled out to some lucky members of the British section, but I shall be with the majority in a hammock in the hold. Tickets have to be purchased,—they are being sold at a very fair rate for the passage—and here is where our friend the little British "looly" is taking his digs at me. He refuses to see me and refuses to sell me a ticket. But, there is another American in the place besides myself and the Red Cross people. An army lieutenant[376] in charge of our passport control and he is helping me conspire for the Englishman's downfall. Tomorrow, I get the ticket by going over our British friend's head directly to the naval commander of the port, and then with that in hand we have a scheme whereby I get aboard in spite of the young son of John Bull. It's not that you've got to get up early to beat the Americans; you've got to stay up all night.

Thus tomorrow we shall be packed away on board the transport and after hanging over in port tomorrow night, will no doubt set out for England the following morning. As I want to take no chances of losing this journal I must now tuck it away in my suitcase. Hence if we dodge the submarines, I shall have to finish the account of the trip somewhere in England, London, I hope; and if we don't dodge them,—why, I'll be saved all that work!

London
April 3'd. 1918.

Well, we fooled the Bolsheviks, we fooled the German subs and I arrived in this city of many people on April Fools' Day.[377] Who's the joke on?

It was a great trip; but I'm glad it's over. But to begin back where I left off.

The American lieutenant's scheme worked to perfection. I saw the naval commander, he sold me my ticket with the best of courtesy and laden now with but the suitcase we made for the boat. At the gangplank stood my nemesis the British "looly"

---

[376] US Army Lieutenant Hugh S. Martin (1891–1931), assistant military attaché of the American Military Mission who also acted as passport control officer. Martin was the senior US representative in Murmansk and worked with Major Allen Wardwell (1873–1953) of the American Red Cross and Reverend Jesse Halsey (1882–1954) of the YMCA. Halsey then also acted as American consul in Murmansk.

[377] A copy of a page from Rogers' wartime passport is found in the Leighton W. Rogers Papers, Scrapbook Folder, at the Library of Congress. It shows a British immigration stamp from Newcastle dated March 29, 1918, and a British alien registration stamp dated March 30, 1918. Therefore, he could have arrived in London on March 30, not April Fool's Day. Unfortunately, we can't ask Rogers now to reconcile these dated stamps with his journal entry.

who scrutinized carefully everyone getting on board. My ally, however, indulging in Ruse No. I of the Machiavellian code called him to one side for a moment's official conversation during which I clambered aboard the ship, and the deed was done with no trouble whatsoever. Simple.

Nearly the entire night was needed to get everyone on board and stowed away,— the refugees, both British and French, the French artillerymen, for whom the boat had really been sent by the British, a detachment of the British armored car unit which had been fighting with the Russians, and the Czechs.

I drew a hammock far down in the hold where, as I lay in it, I could hear the water rushing by, far overhead, where a life preserver would have been quite useless in case of accident, hence I was spared that encumbrance while below decks. And let me add here, that for a rough ocean voyage give me the hammock every time; it swings with the boat and you avoid the bumps you get when in a state room berth.

We cast off about two in the afternoon and were escorted by tugs down the long narrow, bleak harbor and around the cape to the open sea. The Arctic Ocean. And believe me it was the coldest looking water I've ever seen, not excepting the salt slush you pour from the ice cream freezer. I remained on deck to get my last glimpse of Russia for some time and had it just as darkness came,—a low-lying, brittle streak of ice on the horizon fading from sight in the sullen clouds and eternal snow.

A British officer of the ship came and talked to me and we got to be good friends. He gave me the use of his cabin for washing, shaving, and dressing, which was most considerate and greatly appreciated. While sitting there during the evening talk over things in general he remarked, "I don't want to make you nervous, old chap, but you might like to know that our wireless in Murmansk picked up two interesting messages last night. One the Bolsheviks sent from Petrograd to Berlin to the effect that this transport was sailing today with eighteen hundred men of military age on board and intimating that if Germany wanted to make a good impression on the Bolsheviks and really was any good at all with her bully subs, she would sink this boat."

"H–m–m–m!" I commented, "Yes, very interesting."

"And the other," he continued, "came from Berlin to Petrograd; we managed to decode it and it assured our Red friends that this transport would never reach Newcastle, because two subs had been withdrawn from operations around the north coast of Scotland and sent over to get us." "But, of course, they won't, you know," he added.

"No," I agreed. "Of course not." Gee, what a cheerful guy! Why tell me this cheering news?

As in all good British transports there was a bar on this one. In the following morning often looking long and hard at the green, cold water of the Arctic, I visited said bar, came away with a bottle of liquid dynamite in my pocket, resolved to swallow it when the torpedo hit and go down in a blaze of glory at least. This because the life-saving facilities as far as we men were concerned were nil. The lifeboat capacity was barely enough to take care of what women there were on board and the cabin passengers. Of course there were rafts and preservers, but in this cold water one could cling to a raft about thirty seconds. And at that, including rafts and boats, there were accommodation for about nine hundred and we were eighteen hundred. Hence my "blaze of glory" stuff was a good bet.

Orders had it that preservers must be worn at all times on deck and we were a queer looking crew as we paraded around bundled up in them. But we saw nothing of submarines, although they did get a ship just ahead of us as attested by the rafts and empty lifeboats we passed one evening.

The second day out I managed to make an arrangement with a steward whereby I could eat in the main mess instead of down in the hold,—which was a great relief after as many weeks of shift-for-yourself-eating. The bar, too, became such a popular resort that within four days it was dry of everything save gin, vermouth, and angostura bitters which we drank as a mixture. I shall never forget it; with the taste like hair tonic. The bar was Scotty's undoing; he feared being seasick and forestalled it by consuming plenty of gin, which left him in more than his usual jovial mood. Out of compassion for those who were ill he tried to render them all sympathy possible, but as his idea of being sympathetic was to place his hand on the sick one's shoulder and say "Don't be shy, darlin', cough it up in mother's hand," he did not get very far with his patients!

It was on shipboard that we first heard of this great German offensive which is now in progress. It came over the wireless to be tacked up on the bulletin board. "Thirty five Mile German Advance. Hun shatters British Line and advance to within six miles of Amiens, where our troops have halted him. Now bombarding Paris."

This news set the ship in an uproar. There was amazement everywhere save in the ranks of the armored car troop; one of whom greeted the news with, "Bli' me, so, we've lost the war, again, have we?"

The smoking room was hectic with excitement, the British trying to suppress theirs and the French, particularly the officers, fairly jumping up and down before their maps as they tried to trace the course of the attack from the meagre details of the wireless report. The bombardment of Paris was inexplicable to them because the bulletin had not mentioned a break through the French. "Impossible, C'est pas vrai,

C'est un erreur," were the remarks. And it was not until the next day that details of the marvelous long-range gun came thru and settled it all, leaving them open mouthed at this latest exhibition of German audacity and constructive genius. The British were staggered as the extent of the blow to their forces became known and the atmosphere on board became heavy with gloom. It looked as though the Russian defection had told at last and the Huns were on the road to the Channel ports once more.

One day and a half from land two destroyers picked us up and acted as our escort from then on. Their presence acted as an immense relief to all on board, and this coupled with the more encouraging news from the front lightened the atmosphere considerably.

When a day from land while walking about the rear deck for the first time I met quite by chance a young French officer escorting a lady. The latter was muffled up in furs and a low hat so that only part of her face was visible. I could not recognize her for some time, but gradually it dawned upon my feeble mind that she was none other than the beautiful landlady mentioned at various times in the course of this journal. This then was her last and so far successful chance to escape, to come with one of the officers, and she had taken it. She avoided me carefully and it was not until ready to disembark, when she found I had recognized her, that we spoke. I congratulated her on the success of her expedition.

After a week of steering off course, zigzagging and indulging in all known ruses to outwit submarines, the last day spent with the destroyers cutting circles about us, we came into Newcastle. The misty shore looked good to me and for the first time in many months I felt at ease. We were towed up the Tyne to our dock and the landing stage. It was a motley looking gang that came down the plank from the landing ferry. Dirty, unshaved, with old, worn clothes, laden with blanket rolls, miscellaneous luggage of all description, some carrying skins and reindeer antlers purchased from the Laplanders at Murmansk, we were atypical refugees.

The Y.M.C.A. had a canteen on the dock and its free hot chocolate and sandwiches were a godsend. After passing through the British military control, where rigid examinations were given, we were free to do as we pleased. A special train had been provided for London, pulling out at five o'clock. I spent the afternoon getting my bag checked on the train, eating a good meal, and wandering about the town. Returning to the station about 4:45 I found a crowd around the forward coach. Asking what the trouble was, the reply came from two or three different sources. "There's a couple of Scotland Yard detectives in there with a famous spy." I pushed thru the ranks, peered in the window and there sat our friend the landlady of beauty and youth, between two gentlemen as patently detectives as if they had worn labels to that effect. So she was caught at last. I wonder what has happened to her.

The train rolled out at five o'clock, and deposited us in London about two in the morning. After wandering about, staggering under the weight of my suitcase and heavy sweater and lack of food, I found the hotel at which the Y had made arrangements for us. Learning of the excellent Turkish Bath attached thereto I spent the greater part of the night in that being pummeled like the Caesars of old by a couple of burly Numidians. Retiring to my room for the few remaining hours of night I found the bed far too soft and luxurious and could not sleep. When a respectable arising hour had come around, I descended, surrounded a fine English breakfast and went forth into the sunshine for a walk. On Victoria Embankment I met Lester, a major in the A. E. F., [American Expeditionary Forces] much to our mutual surprise. And here I am stopping with him until he crosses to France or until I join the army and am sent elsewhere.

In spite of the fact that I have been nearly crushed in an automobile accident, and that this is the great German air raid season, it is a relief to be here at last. Just to see the sun, feel its warmth, see the bright faces, the smiles, the green grass and trees is—is—well, it's life.

A week or so of this and then the army as soon as possible, and my chance to do my little bit. It's been a long time coming, but it has arrived.

(Leighton Rogers typed the last pages in his journal)

Paris
April 20th, 1919

Since my last entry of more than a year ago I have been commissioned First Lieutenant of Infantry in the American Expeditionary Forces and assigned to Military Intelligence, G-2. Only recently attached to an Intelligence unit serving with the American delegation to the Peace Conference, I was ordered a few days ago to appear before a group of ranking officers and diplomatic representatives for the purpose of answering questions about "the Russian problem." Thinking that a record of the meeting might make a fitting, albeit belated Finis to the Russian phase of my Journal, I shall set it down to the best of my ability for insertion therein.

Colonel Van Deman[378]of the General Staff, known as "the father of American Military Intelligence," told me beforehand that I could make a statement prior to the interrogation if I wished. I decided to do so, and took a few notes to the meeting. It was not a large group but contained plenty of rank,—major and brigadier generals, staff officers, colonels, an embassy secretary, and two representatives from the American Delegation to the Peace Conference.

To begin I'll reverse the order of the program and comment first on the question-and-answer period. It lasted almost an hour and at times lapsed into heated arguments among those present. I stayed out of them as much as possible, and the few times I found myself involved the sight of some of those "ram-rod swallowers" ready to jump down my throat didn't make the going easy for me. But Colonel Van Deman proved a stalwart and stood up for my right to answer queries as I saw fit.

They were many and varied: Should the Allies organize or support an army for invasion of Russia and overthrow of the Bolsheviks? What did I think of the American troops landing in Murmansk and Vladivostok? Should the Allies recognize the so-called Soviet government? Etc., etc.

The questions touched upon matters of such high policy that I didn't think many of those present expected to be much influenced by my answers; they were asked, it seemed to me, with the aim of providing grounds for discussion and argument.

To those of a military nature I had to plead ignorance, since I am no more than a lieutenant and amateur soldier. I pointed out, however, that the German army had not been able to conquer Russia, even after killing two million of her military, but had brought her down with propaganda; and that many of the conditions which effected Napoleon's defeat were still prevalent. I was able to describe fairly well some of the geographic, climatic and economic difficulties hampering military operations in Russia,—the vast distances, the meagre and woefully inefficient railroads, the almost total absence of paved highways rendering motor transport hopeless, the mud, snow and ice. We think the United States is a big country but the former Russian Empire occupied one-sixth of the total landmass of the globe.

A question about the Russian population welcoming an Allied or Allied-supported invasion brought my reply that since the rank and file of those Russians who would

---

[378] Wikipedia, "Ralph Van Deman," last modified April 16, 2021, 15:38 (UTC), https://en.wikipedia.org/wiki/Ralph_Van_Deman. General Ralph Henry Van Deman (1865–1952) is honored in the American Military Intelligence Hall of Fame. The Military Intelligence Section, War College Division, War Department General Staff, was created on May 3, 1917, with Van Deman, then a colonel, as its head.

fight hadn't chosen to support the Provisional Government against the Bolsheviks, it seemed to me that they would refuse to join forces with a foreign invader.

As for the American troop landings in Vladivostok and Murmansk: I know nothing of Vladivostok, which is nearly 6000 miles from where I spent most of my time in Russia. But although while in Murmansk I had hoped for American troop landings, later reflection had brought about a change of mind. In those white wastes the troops were prisoners of their environment, and the American supplies and machinery which they were supposed to be guarding had deteriorated to the extent of being worthless or obsolete. I did not, however, presume to indulge in after-the-event criticism of the decision which had to be made in war time.

My answer to a request to say something about possible diplomatic recognition of the Soviet government was as strong as I could make it: No, I would not recognize any government in Russia unless and until elected representatives or the people had been allowed to express their consensus about the form of government Russia should have. And I recalled that the Constituent Assembly, organized for this purpose after the first Revolution, had been dispersed by Bolshevik force of arms.

With the aid of notes, my general statement, which was largely a repetition of writings in this journal, went about as follows:

Of all the influences arising from the World War I venture to say that the future will show the most portentous to be that of the Russian Revolution, and the most important problem confronting the world to be the Russian problem. Old Russia's influence upon the Western world is appreciated, especially in the fields of literature and music; and now in sociology and economics it is the Russian action expressed in dangerous experiments which is giving us pause.

The unique character of these influences is a product of the Slav philosophy, which has a lot of the Oriental in it and is difficult for us to understand. The Russian, his freedom fettered by his imperial government, has always lived in protest against the system. This, controlling his industry, education and religion, had all the opportunities of time and wealth to adapt itself to the demands of its people and meet their desire for a more free, fuller life; but it failed to liberalize its controls and tried to entrench itself in reaction. Hence the people thrust it aside.

If the decision were left to them the Russians would, I am sure, choose to be a republic like the United States or a constitutional monarchy of the British type. In fact a delegate to the Assembly told me, shortly before its dispersal, that there would be a better than two-thirds majority vote for one of these two forms. But as things stand at present no choice will be allowed. The Bolsheviks have stolen the Russian

Revolution and they intend to organize the country and operate it to suit themselves. They don't give a damn for the Russian people or their welfare. What they want is a Russian base from which they can promote their scheme of world domination through the addition to the Soviet Union, as they call it, of one foreign country after another in the form of additional Soviet states brought into the Union by means of revolution, propaganda, conquest, or any other convenient method. In early 1918, for example, they were confident of instigating a revolution in Germany and of bringing that country into the fold; but they failed and were vociferously disappointed. They still have hopes, however; not only for Germany but for every country in the world.

This sounds fantastic, but they are fanatics. It is their dream, their conviction, their religion; and as long as the Bolsheviks last it will be the pattern of their efforts in international affairs. They have deluded a large segment of the Russian people into following them, and those they cannot continue to seduce by one means or another they will destroy. Already their Terror is beginning. To date I have learned that five of my former good Russian friends have been executed, with more to follow. The Russia we knew will be a nightmarish shambles for years to come.

Since my arrival in Great Britain a little over a year ago I have been asked about the possibility of two things happening in Russia: Following the stipulations of an old saying, that a good way to make a conservative is to give a radical responsibility, won't the Bolsheviks in time become conservative in order to ensure to themselves the support of the property-owning and working people? My answer has been, Not necessarily. Their plan is to have no property-owner other than the State, the government—themselves; with labor working for them only. This, of course, with the exception of agriculture, in which field they have urged the peasants to break up the huge estates and operate the land for themselves. Once this transfer of ownership is accomplished—the Bolsheviks had to further it in order to obtain the support of the predominantly agricultural population—I doubt that they will ever dare an attempt to take the land away from the peasants.

The other possibility that I've been asked about has been: Don't you see any likelihood of the Russian people overthrowing the Bolsheviks? Well, judging by the way things appear to be going at present—No. But it is a possibility, none the less, because of the unpredictability of the Russian character. With those people, anything can happen. For example: No one, not even representatives in the Duma who were in close touch with Russian politics, expected or ventured to hope that the imperial government would be done away with—modified perhaps but destroyed, never. Yet, in one city of that vast empire a popular uprising with no more organization than a college campus rush brought that imposing façade down in a crash of lathes and plaster. Yes, it could happen again. If and when, no man can say.

Over and beyond all this, keeping in mind Russia's influence in the past and the baleful repercussion of events there on the World War, we come to consideration of what it may be in the future. Is it not logical to think of it as being even more powerful when Russia emerges once more a united nation, and isn't that possibility a staggering one? With natural resources comparable to those of the United States, though scattered and undeveloped, with one hundred eighty millions of people impelled at some time to unite by a Slavic bond or by machine-guns, Russia's potential power for good or evil is almost beyond conception.

Meanwhile it seems to me that our policy should hold us ever ready to help the majority of the Russian people as soon as their will in the matter of their form of government is made known—freely, honestly, and unmistakably.

Such was the gist of my talk. With two or three exceptions, I don't think the members of my audience took it very seriously. On my way out I overheard two of them discussing it, with one commenting, " . . . very young." Yes, it's true—I am young. But maybe a little time will take care of that criticism, as I fervently hope it will of "the Russian problem."

Epilogue

L eighton Rogers wrote his own conclusion to this book. This made the author's job a little easier.

Rogers confessed years later that "ever since 1916 he maintained interest in Russia and its enigmatic people"[379] and indeed, Russia featured in subsequent chapters in his life. Having persevered through five weeks of deprivation during his escape travail, Rogers gratefully embraced the psychological and physical relief that greeted him in England. Although his Russian experience ended not as he originally envisioned, it nevertheless afforded him an extraordinary opportunity to engage Russia as few other Westerners could. Admittedly, he often viewed Russia through an American set of lenses, unintentionally foisting ill-fitting ideals and cultural assumptions onto a Russian psyche. "I cannot imagine similar events taking place in America and any person of my own age remaining a spectator!" wrote Rogers, exasperated; but in fairness to him, it was the rare American in that era who thought otherwise.

Rogers left a message in the past for the future of our relationship with Russia. The biggest problem confronting the world, Rogers wrote, was the "Russian problem." Writing in 1919, he meant Bolshevism. When asked whether he thought the Russians would overthrow the Bolsheviks, he could not answer with certainty, citing the unpredictability of the Russian character guided by its unique "Slav philosophy." Yet Rogers draws our attention to a question we face in our contemporary relations with Russia: Does the current leadership in Russia care about its people, and can we in turn understand the Russian people and how they will react to those leaders?

He did not lose hope in the Russian people. Rogers instinctively believed the Russians would ultimately reject communism, and time proved him correct. "We should always be ready to help the majority of the Russian people as soon as their form of government is made known—freely, honestly, and unmistakably," Rogers advised. He makes an important point: Provide help to the Russian people once they have made their own decision and call out their leadership if it denies its people the right to do so.

His following piece of advice is eternal: He warned against any intervention in Russia, militarily or otherwise, and believed Russians would never accept a foreign presence in their land regardless of its stated aim.

---

[379] Leighton W. Rogers Papers, Box 1, Folder 2, 4, Library of Congress.

Rogers referred to the ill-fated Allied intervention in Russia, which unfolded at the time he left Russia. The Allies experienced an unmitigated setback when Germany transferred hundreds of thousands of battle-hardened troops to the Western Front. On March 21, 1918, German commander Erich Ludendorff launched his Kaiserschlacht, or "Kaiser's battle," against the Allies in France. On the Eastern Front, German troops stood only 135 kilometers from Petrograd. Great Britain and France, and the United States as a reluctant third partner,[380] decided to reestablish a second front in Russia, otherwise known as the Allied intervention. Apart from the obvious goal of preventing Germany from exploiting its advantageous peace agreement to access and exploit Russian natural resources, the Allied intervention aimed to create a nucleus for non-Bolshevik control in Russia and bring Russia back into the war against Germany. The Allies believed Bolshevism threatened the stability of the international system, the viability of foreign investment in Russia, access to Russian markets and natural resources, and the basis for economic revitalization after the war.[381] "(I)f these damned bolsheviks are permitted to remain in control of the country," Ambassador Francis fumed, "it will not only be lost to its devoted people but bolshevik rule will undermine all governments and be a menace to society itself."[382] The Allies also kept a close eye on Japanese intentions and wanted to prevent the Japanese exploitation of the Russian Far East, Siberia, and the Tran-Siberian Railroad. The intervention plan called for military landings in the north at Murmansk and Archangel, in the south through the Crimean Peninsula and Transcaucasia, and in the east, with closely monitored Japanese cooperation, at Vladivostok.

The United States imposed economic sanctions on the Bolshevik regime. Foglesong writes how in 1918, the "U.S. War Trade Board, Federal Reserve Board, and Shipping Board had imposed strict controls on the licensing, financing and shipping

---

[380] The US Department of State aide-mémoire to Allied ambassadors issued on July 17, 1918, impractically outlined the American position to avoid hostilities: "It is the clear and fixed judgment of the Government of the United States . . . that military intervention there would add to the present sad confusion in Russia rather than cure it, injure her rather than help her, and that it would be of no advantage in the prosecution of . . . the war against Germany. It cannot, therefore, take part in such intervention or sanction it in principle. . . . Whether from Vladivostok or from Murmansk and Archangel, the only legitimate object for which American or Allied troops can be employed, it submits, is to guard military stores which may subsequently be needed by Russian forces and to render such aid as may be acceptable to the Russians in the organization of their own self-defense."

[381] Anne Wintermute Lane and Louise Herrick Wall, eds., *The Letters of Franklin K. Lane, Personal and Political* (Boston and New York: Houghton Mifflin and Riverside Press Cambridge, 1922), 195; Foglesong, *America's Secret War Against Bolshevism*, 177. For example, US Interior Secretary Franklin K. Lane on March 1, 1918, wrote about a Cabinet meeting he attended with President Wilson the day prior where Lane said, "Russia, when she 'came back,' should not hate us, for there was our new land for development—Siberia—and we should have front place at that table. . . ."

[382] David C. Francis, August 4, 1918, cited in Foglesong, *America's Secret War Against Bolshevism*, 211.

of goods to Russia, which allowed them to block almost all exports to Soviet Russia while permitting trade with White regions."[383] Support for these measures was not unanimous in the United States though, amid concern that by ignoring the Russian people's hardships they strengthened, rather than weakened, the Bolsheviks' hand.

Within months, The United States sent 5,500 troops to Murmansk and Archangel, to be under British command, and 9,000 to Vladivostok starting in August 1918 until early 1920 in a joint action with 75,000 Japanese troops to secure the Trans-Siberian railway. Wilson agreed to take part on the condition that the United States would use its forces only for defensive purposes, but that was impractical, if not wishful, given the hostilities the Allies faced from Bolshevik forces. Wilson wanted to make Russia "safe for democracy" without going to war, declared or undeclared, but doubted whether the Russian masses could be counted on to create, no less support, an effective democratic government.[384]

The Allied intervention failed. It was neither large enough nor adequately supported by the political leadership in London, Paris, and Washington. American troops withdrew from Archangel and Murmansk by June 1919, and Wilson authorized the withdrawal of American troops from Siberia on December 27, 1919. The United States lost 235 dead in the north and 189 in Vladivostok.[385] Rogers correctly predicted that the Allied troops in Murmansk and Archangel would preside over a disaster and that "troops in Vladivostok would be prisoners of their environment." Although the Allies had thwarted Japanese intentions in Siberia, they engendered distrust and suspicion from the Russian people, who regarded the intervention as an invasion of their land. The Soviets would not forget this.

Rogers warned that Russians would refuse to join forces with a foreign power since they chose not to fight for their own provisional government against the Bolsheviks. The US consul in Archangel, Felix Cole, concurred. In July 1918, he cabled to Washington stating, "Intervention cannot reckon on active support from Russians."[386]

"Russia's potential power for good or evil is almost beyond conception," Rogers wrote. That remains true. Will Russia play a constructive role in international affairs or act as a spoiler? And can Russia's great promise, with its rich, undeveloped frontiers, once glowingly praised by Frank Vanderlip and his contemporaries, lead to a

---

[383] Foglesong, *America's Secret War Against Bolshevism*, 248.
[384] Ibid., 9.
[385] Ibid., 189, 186 and 180.
[386] Ibid., 204.

new chapter in international relations or remain unfulfilled by a series of missteps and disappointments? We may not be in great suspense about the answers to these questions at this time, but what may the future hold?

The *New York Times*, reviewing Rogers' *Wine of Fury* upon its publication in 1924, commented that Rogers "gives an illuminating, clear cut, plausible interpretation of Russia during the great upheaval."[387] In closing, we may say the same. Rogers experienced perhaps the best and worst Russia could offer. He navigated a full range of emotions and experiences: excitement and boredom, hope and fear, confidence and uncertainty, beauty and repulsiveness, kindness and cruelty, feast and famine, and life and death. He urged us to remain interested in and engaged with Russia. And never to lose hope.

---

[387] "Latest Fiction: Whom the Gods Destroy," *The New York Times Book Review*, May 25, 1924, 22.

NATIONAL CITY BANK

At the end of 1917, the balance sheet of National City Bank included over $5 million of Russian government bonds, $2 million advanced by New York to its two branches in Russia, and $26 million in liabilities to depositors at its Russian branches at the official rate of exchange. This $33 million exposure represented over 40 percent of the bank's total capital, which, in retrospect, was nothing short of mind-boggling.[388]

"Kerensky fell and so did Vanderlip," quipped Clarence W. Barron, called by many the founder of modern financial journalism, and a prominent figure in the history of Dow Jones and Company.[389] Vanderlip and his senior managers envisioned a great postwar future for American business and banking in Russia. They thought they understood how Russia worked, and that Russia's path to democracy would usher in unparalleled opportunities for capital investment. National City Bank's fast-growing, immediately profitable Petrograd branch only bolstered their conviction. But, exhilarated by success, Vanderlip and team failed to grasp the reasons behind the "flight to quality" the bank questionably enjoyed. They underestimated the huge geopolitical risk Russia embodied in 1917, even though Leighton Rogers and his colleagues daily experienced its ramifications and continually wrote and spoke of them. Less than twelve months after the bank published its positive analyses of Russia, the situation there had significantly deteriorated in every sphere: military, political, economic, and societal. The consequent Bolshevik Revolution ended National City Bank's dream in Russia and ultimately Frank Vanderlip's banking career. Why didn't Vanderlip ever question Meserve's judgement about Russia?[390] He should have spoken to one of Meserve's fellow bankers in Petrograd, the head of Great Britain's London City & Midland Bank, John Frederick Bunker, who was sensible enough to admit that "the centre of the burning house is naturally not the best place from which to observe the progress of the fire."[391] Or queried American diplomat Fred Dearing, who closely watched National City Bank, and warned that "somebody is going to lose some money."[392] Blind before the oncoming Bolshevik wrecking train, the bank learned the costly lessons of country risk, nationalization, and sovereign default. Many other

---

[388] Cleveland and Huertas, *Citibank: 1812–1970,* 101.
[389] Ibid., 102.
[390] De Basily, *Memoirs of a Lost World,* 51. Meserve's stepdaughter mentioned that her father "admired [Vanderlip's] fine qualities and was devoted to him."
[391] Malik, *Bankers & Bolsheviks,* 141.
[392] Fred Morris Dearing, Unpublished papers, May 25, 1916, 291, Folder 509.

investors shared the same fate, or worse. Singer Sewing Machine Company, for example, calculated that its losses in Russia exceeded $84 million.[393]

Foreigners and Russians alike initially believed that the Bolsheviks could not hold on to power. R.R. Stevens "gave the Bolsheviks a length of life of about nine months."[394] National City Bank management shared this view and therefore decided to "wait it out" until the Bolsheviks met their expected demise. The immediate situation, nevertheless, required a bifurcation of strategy. Tactically, the bank focused on maintaining the integrity of its operations, ensuring the safety of its staff, and quickly reducing its balance sheet. Strategically, it aligned itself with the Allies' interventionist policy toward Russia, namely to "restore Russia back to its democratic path," which essentially meant the removal of the Bolsheviks from the stage and Russia rejoining the war. Following the Bolshevik coup d'état, National City Bank would support the Allies' cause in several ways.

H. Fessenden Meserve resurfaced in Washington, DC, in January 1918. Upon his return, he requested a meeting with President Wilson. The reason for his request apparently did not specifically relate to National City Bank. While he transited through Japan back to the United States, Meserve met with the Japanese foreign minister, who asked him to relay to the president Japan's request that the United States not send troops to Vladivostok or Harbin, China, to keep order "as any such movement . . . would create a very unfavorable impression in Japan." Meserve failed to get a meeting with the president and instead delivered the message to Frank Polk, who relayed it to Wilson.[395]

National City Bank worked with the Russian Embassy in Washington, which continued to represent the deposed provisional government. Foglesong provides many details: The Wilson administration rejected the "temporary nature" of the Bolsheviks and supported the anti-Bolshevik ambassador, Boris Bakhmeteff. One week after the Bolsheviks seized power, the US government deposited earlier approved, not-yet-spent funds to the provisional government's account with National City Bank in New York. Foglesong cites Frank Polk assuring NCB that despite "the 'rebellion in Petrograd,' the bank was 'justified in going ahead'

[393] Robert Bruce Davies, *Peacefully Working to Conquer the World, Singer Sewing Machines in Foreign Markets, 1854–1920* (New York: Arno Press, 1976), 329–330; "Singer War Loss Was $106,024,543; Soviet Confiscated Sewing Machine Co.'s Russian Business Valued at $84,302,231," *New York Times*, July 1, 1923, 18.
[394] *The Journal of John L. H. Fuller*, May 8, 1918, 70.
[395] US State Department, Office of the Historian, Papers Relating to the Foreign Relations of the United States, The Lansing Papers, 1914–1920, Volume 2, "The Acting Secretary of State to President Wilson," File No. 861.00/1047a, https://history.state.gov/historicaldocuments/frus1914-20v02/d181.

in making payments from those funds 'on order of Embassy.' "[396] By December 5, National City Bank lawyers and Serge Ughet, the Russian Embassy's financial attaché and chargé d'affaires, worked out the details for disbursements according to a procedure Bakhmeteff and Polk devised.[397] Vanderlip knew Ughet well, as Ughet had earlier provided him with documents concerning the proposed budget of the Russian Empire for 1917.[398] On December 20, the Russian Embassy made payments through National City Bank of $325,000 to the Remington Company for rifles and $2,075,000 to Westinghouse for arms.[399] Also, in December, the Russian Embassy directed NCB to transfer $500,000 from its accounts for silver to pay Russian soldiers in Persia and the Caucasus. This transaction drew the criticism of Basil Miles, a top Russia expert at the Department of State, who argued that the transfer (the Russian Embassy sent the bullion through the British to the anti-Bolshevik Cossack cavalry general Alexey Kaledin) constituted a "grave responsibility" "for purposes which may well be regarded as inimical by the Russian people."[400]

Vanderlip maintained a high profile regarding Russia. He attended a conference in April 1918 organized by two leading business executives, Thomas Lamont of Morgan and William Boyce Thompson (Meserve's valued client from the American Red Cross mission), with the aim to set up the "American League to Aid and Cooperate with Russia."[401] Many other prominent businessmen supported this initiative, including George P. Whaley of the Vacuum Oil Company; Charles Coffin, the co-founder and first president of General Electric; Daniel Willard, president of the Baltimore and Ohio Railroad and Henry Ford.[402] Designed to publicly support Wilson's policy to "stand by Russia" by providing economic and relief efforts, notably and specifically in areas not controlled by the Bolsheviks, e.g., Siberia, this "League" ultimately achieved little. The thinking behind it, however, survived. Wilson, during the Paris Peace Conference Council of Four meetings on March 28, 1919, remarked, "The only way to kill Bolshevism is to establish the frontiers and to open all the doors to commerce."[403] "Nonrecognition and nonintercourse" with the Bolshevik regime

---

[396] Foglesong, *America's Secret War Against Bolshevism*, 59.

[397] Ibid., 61.

[398] Vanderlip to Ughet, April 30, 1917, Box B-2-4, Frank A. Vanderlip Papers.

[399] Foglesong, *America's Secret War Against Bolshevism*, 64.

[400] Foglesong, *America's Secret War Against Bolshevism*, 86; Tkachenko, *American Bank Capital in Russia*, 101.

[401] Roberts, *Frank A. Vanderlip and the National City Bank During the First World War*, 157.

[402] "Mission Planned to Free Russia From German Control," *New York Tribune*, May 15, 1918, 5; "America Not to Renounce Russ Nation," *Sioux City Journal*, Iowa, May 4, 1918, 1–2.

[403] Wilson's declaration to the Council of Four in Paris, cited in David W. McFadden, *Alternative Paths: Soviets and Americans 1917–1920* (New York: Oxford University Press, 1993), 166.

would be State Department policy until the United States recognized the Soviet Union in November 1933.

In July, Vanderlip agreed to join an economic mission, approved by the president, to (non-Bolshevik-controlled) Russia to be led by Daniel Willard. The *New York Times* reported that "the mission was an outgrowth of conferences of businessmen in New York and other large commercial centers where it was recognized that a vast field of trade lies waiting in Russia and Siberia," and further stated, "If it all works well, the project will probably take the form of a corporation for Russian relief with a capitalization of $50–100 million."[404] This mission, however, never materialized.

Meanwhile, Meserve worked to open an office of National City Bank in Vladivostok, where Allied intervention forces needed certain financial services. On July 21, Admiral Austin Wright, commander of the warship USS *Brooklyn,* harbored in Vladivostok, warned that any military mission to support the Czechoslovak Legion in Siberia would create a monetary crisis there and recommended that National City Bank or International Banking Corporation establish a branch bank in Vladivostok.[405] On August 23, NCB cabled William Anderson of the International Banking Corporation that it would open a branch in Vladivostok pending the authorization of the Russian finance minister. This authorization, however, never occurred because no Russian government existed that the United States recognized.[406] Meserve informed Vanderlip on August 28 that he had met with Commerce Secretary William C. Redfield, who advised him to see US Secretary of War Newton Diehl Baker Jr. "immediately about this matter as he considered it very important." Meserve met Baker and separately with V. J. Novitzky of the Russian Embassy the next day. Meserve again wrote to Vanderlip on August 30 to relay "intelligence" he garnered from his meeting with Novitzky and about the sending of small denominations of Russian currency to US forces stationed in Vladivostok.[407] Meserve also maintained close contact with his previous contacts in Petrograd. He coordinated the visits in Washington of two leaders of the Society for the Economic Revival of Russia, Aleksei Putilov, the former president of the Russo-Asiatic Bank, and Alexander Vyshnegradsky, the former president of the St. Petersburg International Commercial Bank. These émigrés supported the anti-Bolshevik White Russian generals Dmitry Khorvat and Pyotr Wrangel.

---

[404] "Willard to Head Mission," *New York Times,* July 17, 1918, 7.
[405] Leo J. Bacino, *Reconstructing Russia: US Policy in Revolutionary Russia, 1917–1922* (Kent, OH: Kent State University Press, 1999), 106.
[406] Ibid., 111.
[407] Meserve to Vanderlip, August 28, 29 and 30, 1918, Box A-67, Frank A. Vanderlip Papers.

National City Bank opened a short-lived agency in Vladivostok on February 3, 1919. Leighton Rogers' Dartmouth friend and colleague Henry A. Koelsch became agent.[408] Meserve moved to Europe in January 1919 to become vice president for European business. There, he stayed involved in the Russian business. He sent a cable from London to New York advising, "If Petrograd depositors wish to draw roubles in Vladivostok make it plain to Koelsch to give them the right and true answer namely that they are an agency and not a branch and therefore cannot take in or pay out deposits. It ought to be clearly understood that the powers of an agency are strictly limited to gathering commercial information and cash letters credit as courtesy."[409] National City Bank closed its agency on March 13, 1920, two-and-a-half months after Wilson ordered the evacuation of American troops from Vladivostok.

In Russia, R.R. Stevens leveraged his network of business and diplomatic contacts. On December 24, 1917, he became director of the Tovaro-Obmien (in English, Goods-Exchange) Purchasing Company, formed to purchase strategic commodities in Russia including copper, manganese ore, platinum, hides, oil and fats, and military supplies and war materials stockpiled in Vladivostok, Archangel, Petrograd, and other locations.[410] The mission of the Tovaro-Obmien was to "purchase goods for the purpose of keeping them out of German hands," according to US Vice Consul Poole. The American commercial attaché in Petrograd, William Chapin Huntington, managed US government interests in Tovaro-Obmien's dealings and consulted with Stevens on matters of foreign exchange.[411]

Stevens knew Raymond Robins, who was then acting as an unofficial intermediary between the US government and the Bolsheviks since the United States refused to recognize the Bolsheviks. Robins met Stevens in Petrograd on March 5, 1918, to ask what Stevens thought of his plan to propose Anglo-American government aid to the Bolsheviks if they canceled the Brest-Litovsk peace agreement signed with Germany on March 3.[412] Robins, however, failed to bring his plan to fruition and the Extraordinary Fourth All-Russia Congress of Soviets duly ratified the peace

---

[408] *History of the operations of the Petrograd and Moscow Branches*, 29. Koelsch worked in NCB's Petrograd and Moscow branches until March 1918.
[409] Cablegram from H. Fessenden Meserve, undated, Box A-67, Frank A. Vanderlip Papers.
[410] Bacino, *Reconstructing Russia*, 48.
[411] Lees and Rodner, *An American Diplomat in Bolshevik Russia: DeWitt Clinton Poole*, 104 and 106.
[412] *Hearings on Bolshevik Propaganda*, 804–5 (testimony of Raymond Robins, former commander of the American Red Cross mission in Russia). Albert Rhys Williams stated in his book *Journey into Revolution, Petrograd 1917–1918* (Chicago: Quadrangle Books, 1969), 253, that Harold Williams, an anti-Bolshevik correspondent for the English papers and *New York Times*, R.R. Stevens, and Charles Smith of the Associated Press, "all appealed to Britain and the United States to seize the opportunity."

agreement on March 14. Later that month, Stevens, having then moved to Vologda, asked Robins for help in the bank's dealings with the Bolshevik government. Robins persuaded Lenin to relax banking regulations to enable NCB to continue, temporarily at least, its operations in Russia.[413] Several weeks later, the State Department, which opposed Robins' actions, forced his recall to the United States.

National City Bank played a role in helping the Allies prevent Russian strategic metals and other supplies from falling into German hands. Norman Saul writes that a "hastily organized" Anglo-French-American "Inter-Allied Trade Board," otherwise known as the Michelsen commission, "backed mainly by American money," funneled at least $1 million through National City Bank in New York in March and April to facilitate the purchase of "a large quantity of nickel, copper, platinum, furs, sunflower seed oil, food stocks and so on" to transfer to safer places in Russia or abroad. Stevens, along with Major Henry Crosby Emery,[414] then working for Guaranty Trust Company and acting as a special military agent, facilitated the initial operation.[415]

On March 30, the American consul general in Moscow, Maddin Summers, received a report from Ernest Harris (former NCB officer in Petrograd in 1917, who became the consul general in Irkutsk in March 1918) informing of plans to immediately ship one-half of the cotton crop of Turkestan, or roughly 200,000 tons, to Moscow, ultimately destined for Germany. Summers urged Secretary of State Lansing and Vanderlip to immediately authorize the consulate and Stevens to buy the cotton to prevent it falling into Germany's hands and keep the cotton in Tashkent until Russian mills could buy it later.[416] Harris followed up with Lansing on June 15, but the State Department never authorized the transaction.

The Inter-Allied Trade Board executed another $5 million in purchases in June. Interestingly, the Bolsheviks permitted the export of one carload of platinum to the United States, given their need for sizeable sums of money, not to mention personal graft, according to commercial attaché Huntington.[417]

---

[413] McFadden, *Alternative Paths*, 119.

[414] Major Henry Crosby Emery was sent to Petrograd with Guaranty Trust Company in September 1916. In March 1918, while transiting through Finland, the Germans seized Emery and held him prisoner in Germany until October 1918.

[415] Saul, *War and Revolution*, 298.

[416] US State Department, Office of the Historian, Papers Relating to the Foreign Relations of the United States, 1918, Russia, Volume 3, "The Consul General at Moscow (Summers) to the Secretary of State [Telegram]," File No. 861.61321/7, https://history.state.gov/historicaldocuments/frus1918Russiav03/d151.

[417] US State Department documents and Petrograd diplomatic posts (National Archives and Records Service), cited in Saul, *War and Revolution*, 299.

In the summer of 1918, everything changed for the worse when the Soviet government expelled nondiplomatic foreigners from Russia. On August 5, Stevens and the entire NCB staff (there were then fifteen employees in Vologda) were required to leave Vologda for Moscow. Upon arrival, Stevens transferred the bank's books and records to the Swedish Consulate General for safekeeping. National City Bank's Petrograd and Moscow branches were officially closed on August 26. NCB staff traveled to Petrograd on August 27, remained holed up in Finlandia Station for four days, and during the night of August 31–September 1, along with more than one hundred other Americans and Europeans, finally left Petrograd for Finland and onward destinations. They almost didn't make it out. The day before, Moisei Uritsky (1873–August 30, 1918), the chief of the cheka (Russian abbreviation of "All-Russian Extraordinary Commission," the secret police) of the Petrograd soviet, was assassinated. Pandemonium erupted in Petrograd. US consulate officers "deemed it necessary to bribe the Russian official at the frontier" with 10,000 rubles (then equivalent to $1,000) to facilitate the NCB staff and other foreigners' safe departure.[418] The next day, the Bolsheviks launched a wave of mass political persecutions and executions later referred to as the "Red Terror."

The Bolsheviks seized NCB's records from the Swedes on June 9, 1919.[419] In a flabbergasting footnote to history, the Russians never returned the documents to the successor of National City Bank, Citibank. As of this book's publishing, the "great mass of [NCB's] records and books"[420] are kept in the Russian State Archives in St. Petersburg. Perhaps, one day Russia will return them to their rightful owner.

Robie Reed Stevens suffered a nervous breakdown in the summer of 1919, shortly after he returned to the United States. He never recovered.

The armistice on November 11, 1918, ended World War I but the expected quick demise of Bolshevism did not occur. Vanderlip started to publicly and stridently argue for the continuation and intensification of the Allied intervention. On December 6, 1918, the *New York Times* quoted Vanderlip: "We must get the workers to see that Bolshevism would bring about the disorganization of society." The newspaper

---

[418] Lees and Rodner, *An American Diplomat in Bolshevik Russia: DeWitt Clinton Poole*, 160; Francis, *Russia from the American Embassy*, 289–90; US State Department, Office of the Historian, Papers Relating to the Foreign Relations of the United States, 1918, Russia, Volume 1, "The Second Secretary of Embassy in Russia (Armour), temporarily at Stockholm, to the Secretary of State [Telegram]," File No. 861.00/2687, https://history.state.gov/historicaldocuments/frus1918Russiav01/d613. Ambassador David Francis had earlier instructed American Embassy Second Secretary Norman Armour to oversee the safe passage of the NCB staff from Vologda.

[419] *History of the operations of the Petrograd and Moscow Branches*, 30.

[420] Ibid., George B. Link and William W. Welsh statement, August 14, 1922, Exhibit "C."

wrote that in discussing the matter of surplus army clothing and supplies after the war, Vanderlip suggested giving it to Russia in return for its products and its credit, stating, "It would relieve the prevailing situation in Russia, and we would make firm friends for the future ... I think that she would part with a great many products we could make use of, and in that way we would help to compose the commercial and political chaos now going on there."[421]

Vanderlip joined Meserve on his steamship journey to Europe in January 1919.[422] In Europe, Vanderlip met with the finance ministers of Great Britain, Spain, France, Italy, Switzerland, Belgium, and the Netherlands. He returned to New York on May 19 and on May 26 previewed the key points of his hastily written book titled *What Happened to Europe?* in a dinner speech to the Economic Club at the Hotel Astor. There, as the *New York Times* summarized, he accused the Bolsheviks of flooding Europe with counterfeit currencies and concluded that "America alone could save Europe."[423] Vanderlip's book focused on the role America could play in the revitalization of Europe. He admitted, though, that in Europe he "gained a view that was contrary to the beliefs of most persons."[424]

Vanderlip's call to provide massive American financing for Europe, akin to a post-World War I Marshall Plan, did not appeal to National City Bank's board of directors, who likely considered it impractical and outside the bank's profit-seeking remit.[425] They wanted to disassociate the institution from Vanderlip's outspoken public pronouncements. Vanderlip may have guessed as much, for in his speech to the Economic Club he rhetorically challenged his audience: "Now a lot of you may say that Vanderlip is excited; he has got too imaginative a brain in looking at this thing..."[426] By this time, the state of affairs in the bank had aligned against him. The board of directors was digesting the bank's impending loss in Russia. Moreover, Vanderlip had a strained relationship with the recently elected chairman, James A. Stillman, the son of former chairman James J. Stillman. Thus, at a board meeting on June 4, 1919, Vanderlip "resigned, packed up and walked out of the National City

[421] "Vanderlip Would Give Russia Clothes," *New York Times*, December 6, 1918, 11.

[422] Vicki A. Mack, *Frank A. Vanderlip: The Banker Who Changed America* (Palo Verdes Estate, CA: Pinale Press, 2013), 211.

[423] Vanderlip, *From Farm Boy to Financier*, 302; "Europe Paralyzed; Our Task to Save, Says Vanderlip," *New York Times*, May 27, 1919, 1 and 13.

[424] Vanderlip, *From Farm Boy to Financier*, 301.

[425] Roberts, *Frank A. Vanderlip and the National City Bank During the First World War*, 159.

[426] "Europe Paralyzed; Our Task to Save, Says Vanderlip," *New York Times*, May 27, 1919, 13.

Bank for good."[427] The board probably eased him out. In his memoir, Vanderlip never mentioned the bank's misfortune in Russia, as if it never happened.

At about the time of his resignation, Vanderlip had written an essay intended for publication titled "The Actual Situation in Russia," which conveyed his vehement anti-Bolshevik position. Vanderlip bemoaned "the apparently meek submission of a whole nation to the sanguinary sway of a small group of fanatic visionaries, with their following of murderous bandits, whose openly avowed aim has been the destruction of the social fabric and consequently the ruin of the country." He had "no hesitation in affirming that this so-called government, far from representing after all the will of the Russian people as one sometimes hears it said, is bitterly hated by the overwhelming majority of the people... " Concluding, Vanderlip urged recognition of, and material support for, Admiral Alexander Kolchak's Omsk government. He saw Kolchak as a temporary military dictator who could address the "task of evolving law and order out of the prevailing complete chaos... "[428] Vanderlip's call, however, was too late. Kolchak's forces were already in retreat and by November 14, the Red Army took Omsk, Kolchak's capital.

Even after Vanderlip's resignation, Meserve continued to support his vision. In August, on a trip back to the United States, Meserve declared he was working on a national loan to support American purchases of raw materials from Europe and that "The National City Bank intended to open branches all over Europe, even if it cost a million dollars."[429]

LESSONS LEARNED

National City Bank ultimately reduced the scale of its loss in Russia to close to $10 million. This still amounted to over 10 percent of the bank's capital, a serious financial blow. The damage could have been much greater if the bank were required to repay its depositors in Petrograd and Moscow the US dollar equivalent of their original ruble

---

[427] Vanderlip, *From Farm Boy to Financier*, 303.
[428] "The actual situation in Russia" manuscript, 1, 8 and 9, Box F-8, Frank A. Vanderlip Papers. A note written on the manuscript states "Accepted by the *Saturday Evening Post*. Will appear on July 5th." The essay, however, was not published, as confirmed by a microfilm reel search of the *Saturday Evening Post* June and July 1919 issues by a Library of Congress librarian in May 2021.
[429] "New York Banker Brings New Loan Plan from Hague," *Great Falls Daily Tribune*, Great Falls, MT, August 8, 1919, 15. The article intimated that Vanderlip resigned from NCB because his project for a general loan, which should be shared by enemy and Allied countries alike, met disapproval.

deposits. Although the bank paid some depositors' claims in US dollars in New York in individually negotiated settlements, American courts determined that the bank's liability to depositors was payable in rubles in Russia.[430]

National City Bank documented its history in Russia in an internal report titled, *The History of the operations of the Petrograd and Moscow Branches of The National City Bank of New York, compiled during January and February 1922, from material available in New York.* The report incorporated written statements from employees who had worked in Russia. Besides creating a chronological narrative of the bank's actions and the events surrounding them, the report focused on reconciling the details of the accounts of the branches, an arduous task given the Bolsheviks' seizure of most of the bank's documentation.[431] Missing from the history were questions asking why country risk was never sufficiently analyzed and acted upon, and where and with whom the responsibility should have lain.

Could National City Bank have avoided its loss in Russia? The answer is no, but in theory, the bank might have further reduced its losses if Vanderlip and Meserve saw fit to act earlier, which, as history showed, they did not. "As long as the music is playing, you've got to get up and dance," Chuck Prince, a future chief executive of Citibank, National City Bank's successor, eerily remarked eighty years later.[432] NCB averted a potentially larger loss because it did not extend a significant amount of commercial credits, paid interest rates on deposits lower than what competing Russian banks offered, and once the Bolsheviks took over, took steps to reduce its balance sheet.[433]

The inflection point was January 1917, when National City Bank opened its Petrograd branch and started taking customer deposits, which grew exponentially in months and correspondingly increased the bank's liabilities. Prior to the branch opening, NCB had no brick-and-mortar investment in Russia, no customer deposits, and risk exposure limited to several positions in Russian government securities it earlier syndicated. NCB could have implemented a measured "wait and see" posture after the March Revolution, slowed the rate of client and deposits acquisition and accordingly moderated the growth of its securities investments. Communications between Petrograd and New York, however, only praised the bank's rapidly growing business and the allure of future opportunities. Meserve still felt there was "a

---

[430] Cleveland and Huertas, *Citibank: 1812–1970*, 101.

[431] The report also recounted the bank's drawn-out, ultimately unsuccessful efforts to regain the seized documents.

[432] David Wighton, "What we have learned 10 years after Chuck Prince told Wall St to keep dancing," *Financial News*, July 14, 2017, https://www.fnlondon.com/articles/chuck-princes-dancing-quote-what-we-have-learned-10-years-on-20170714.

[433] *History of the operations of the Petrograd and Moscow Branches*, 3.

tremendous future in Russia for the National City Bank."[434] The bank's asset level actually reached its all-time high of 226.8 million rubles on December 22, six weeks *after* the Bolshevik Revolution.[435]

Although National City Bank's troubles in revolutionary Russia paled compared to more recent financial calamities, such as the Asian currency crisis in 1997 and the financial crisis of 2007–08, management shortcomings noteworthy in National City Bank's case represent key business risks today. What lessons can we learn? First, the timely collection, analysis, and communication of on-the-ground intelligence about markets, geopolitical developments, and other risk factors remain paramount. Today's technology makes this task infinitely easier, faster, cheaper, and more efficacious than the limited tools available a century earlier to Frank Vanderlip and H. Fessenden Meserve. Second, management diversity matters. National City Bank's Russia team and management in New York did not include women, staff from more diverse backgrounds, with differing skills and experiences, or even Russians (not one Russian served in any management function in any of NCB's branches, thus forfeiting the value of local insight). A business ecosystem built on talent diversity might have engendered varied perspectives on the bank's prospects in Russia and offset the strain of paternalism prevalent among the bank's senior management. That was a different era, but this does not excuse ignoring the importance of diversity today. Third, the ineffectual American missions to aid the provisional government and the Allied intervention underscore the lesson not to overestimate one country's ability to influence another. And last, never assume that Russia should act or behave like your home country. Never.

History sometimes repeats itself. Citibank returned to Russia in 1993. On August 17, 1998, the Russian government defaulted on its domestic debt, declared a moratorium on repayment of foreign debt, and simultaneously devalued the ruble.[436] Citibank incurred significant losses attributed to Russia that year, many times those it suffered eighty years earlier. [437] "We simply missed it," John Reed, the chairman of Citibank, later told financial journalists Carol J. Loomis and Jeremy Kahn. He recounted that Citicorp board member John Deutch, a former director of the CIA,

---

[434] Meserve to Vanderlip, September 15, 1917, cited in Malik, *Bankers & Bolsheviks*, 157.
[435] Tkachenko, *American Bank Capital in Russia*, 84.
[436] Abbigail J. Chiodo and Michael T. Owyang provide an excellent study of Russia's default in 1998 in "A Case Study of a Currency Crisis: The Russian Default of 1998," Federal Reserve Bank of St. Louis *Review*, November/December 2002, 7–18, https://doi.org/10.20955/r.84.7–18.
[437] "5 Big Lenders Report Losses From Russia, At Citicorp, Profit Drain of $200 Million is Seen," *New York Times*, September 2, 1998, C1 and C7.

had drawled out, "Stoo-pid!" But Reed, not known for holding his tongue, noted that Deutch had not warned him in advance.[438]

Citibank in Russia has grown profitably and responsibly ever since.

But Russia is still a place where the unthinkable can become thinkable. Leighton Rogers' journal, then—in which smart people don't know how to read the signs of impending calamity—is a word to the wise, a cautionary tale for every new generation of bankers and investors with ruble signs in their eyes.

---

[438] Carol J. Loomis and Jeremy Kahn, "Citigroup: Scenes From A Merger The marriage has smooth spots, but it's been rocky. There are too many chiefs—and none is Jamie Dimon," *Fortune,* January 11, 1999, https://money.cnn.com/magazines/fortune/fortune_archive/1999/01/11/253777/index.htm.

DESTINIES AND FATES

"It was interesting to watch the change come over Americans—see them arrive full of steam and the notion of getting a lot done in a hurry, and gradually lose their energy and optimism until they either went home defeated or got a sort of second wind, and understood that the game in Russia was a new one and called for an amount of patience, leisure, politeness, and apparently aimless palavering which they never dreamed of at home."[439]

LEIGHTON ROGERS

Leighton Rogers left an autobiographical sketch that provides much detail and color about his later life.[440]

Commissioned a second lieutenant in the American Expeditionary Forces soon after he arrived in London, Rogers served in the G-2 Military Intelligence section of the US Army's Seventh Division. In 1918, the army promoted him to first lieutenant and sent him to France. He worked with the American delegation to the Peace Conference in Paris and Versailles in January 1919 and in September, returned to the United States, where he was demobilized at Camp Devens, in Massachusetts.[441]

In 1920, Rogers spent a few weeks speaking about Russia, or as he described in his autobiographical notes, "Of the menace of Bolshevism," before the chambers of commerce and Rotary clubs in various New England cities. He then returned to National City Bank, where he worked on the staff of a vice president handling foreign business.

On August 15, 1921, he resigned from National City Bank. He sailed to Europe on the RMS *Aquitania* to become a US trade commissioner for the US Bureau of Foreign and Domestic Commerce. After brief stays in London and Paris, he moved to Berlin, where he also served as a Russian specialist for the US Department of Commerce in charge of investigating "any rumored business being done in Europe by Soviet Russia." His reports went up the line to Herbert Hoover, then US secretary of commerce. After Berlin, Rogers became a commercial attaché at the US

---

[439] Ruhl, *White Nights*, 50.

[440] Leighton W. Rogers Papers, Box 1, Folder 1, 2–4, Library of Congress. *Autobiographical Sketch* prepared by Leighton Rogers at his home at Chateau Lafayette Apartments, Greenwich, CT, between 1957 and 1959.

[441] US Army, "Devens Reserve Forces Training Area," https://home.army.mil/devens/index.php/Misson%20and%20Vision/history. Camp Devens was established in September 1917 as a temporary cantonment for training soldiers during World War I. After the war, the camp became a demobilization center.

Embassy in Warsaw. While in Warsaw, he completed his novel *Wine of Fury,* which was published in England and the United States in 1924. Rogers wrote that the novel received widespread notice, chiefly for its picture of the Russian Revolution.

Family concerns forced his return to the United States in 1926. Later that year, he organized and administered the Aeronautics Trade Division of the Bureau for Foreign and Domestic Commerce in the Department of Commerce. His mission: expand foreign trade in American aircraft and assist in the establishment of US airlines in South America and the Far East.

In October–November 1927, on loan from the Department of Commerce, Rogers served as a secretary on the staff of the American delegation to the International Radiotelegraph Conference.

From August 1928 through January 1929, again on loan from the Department of Commerce, Rogers served as organizer and executive officer of the first International Aeronautics Conference held in December 1928 in Washington DC. President Calvin Coolidge called on the conference to begin work on treaties governing international air transportation and to celebrate the 25th anniversary of the Wright brothers' first flight.

In February 1929, France made him a Chevalier of the Legion of Honor. Later that year, Rogers obtained a leave of absence, went to flying school in St. Louis, and learned to fly, getting a commercial pilot's license.

Rogers went to the Senate Appropriations Committee in 1930 and argued for funds in the Department of Commerce budget to pay to send trade commissioner specialists in aeronautics to the Far East and South America. The Senate approved funding and an American flight training school was established in China. Although the training school supported civil aviation, no clear-cut distinction existed between civil and military aviation training. The disparity became more pronounced when, in 1937, Major Claire Chennault retired from the US military and went to China to become Chiang Kai-shek's chief air adviser. Chennault championed American support for China's air force in the fight against Japan and in 1941, organized the famous Flying Tigers American Volunteer Group of pilots and mechanics to serve in China in World War II.

In June 1933, Rogers resigned from the Department of Commerce to become executive vice president, and later president, of the Aeronautical Chamber of Commerce of America, the national trade association for the aircraft industry. In this capacity, Rogers worked with the US government on matters of national defense, negotiations for the industry of wages and hours agreements, and testimony before Congressional committees.

From March to September 1935, Rogers took part in an American economic mission to Japan and China to promote good business relations, led by former US ambassador to Japan, William Cameron Forbes. Rogers represented the US aviation industry. During this trip, he met with Chiang Kai-shek in Chongqing. Near Shanghai, Rogers flew in an amphibian airliner owned by the China National Aviation Corporation, which stalled and fell into the Huangpu River. He suffered a sprained leg in the accident and wore a cast for six weeks.[442]

Rogers resigned from the Aeronautical Chamber of Commerce in 1939. The aeronautics industry was expanding rapidly, and he established a consulting business. Rogers frequently commented on the American aircraft industry's ability to produce vastly greater numbers of warplanes.[443]

In February 1943, Rogers joined the Bell Aircraft Corporation of New York as an assistant to the president. He subsequently headed a four-man mission to Russia during October 1943–February 1944 to oversee how Russia used the P-39 Airacobra planes sent under the Lend-Lease program. It was the first American manufacturing group that received such permission. Rogers wrote, "Although this was a return visit to Russia 25 years after my first experience of it before and during the Revolution, and therefore, especially interesting, it was a relief, when the time came to go home, to leave these fear ridden people who have allowed themselves to be enslaved by a small group of homicidal maniacs." Upon returning home, *March of Time* radio invited Rogers to present a program. Rogers also wrote an article titled "Russians Like Our Planes. An American Aircraft Man Visits the Soviets," for the September 1944 edition of *Harper's* Magazine. In 1945, at the end of World War II, he finished his work with Bell Aircraft and resumed his consulting work on aeronautical matters. Rogers became a consultant to the President's Committee on International

---

[442] "Narrow Escape," *Nottingham Evening Post*, UK, May 18, 1935, stated: "Five occupants of an amphibian airliner had a narrow escape near Shanghai today when the machine plunged into the Whang-Po [Huangpu] River as it was taking off for Hankow. The occupants, which included two members of the United States Economic Mission, were in it." It is interesting that a British newspaper reported such an incident. At that time, there was Anglo-American rivalry for military and civilian aviation orders in southern China. Perhaps one intent of the article was to highlight the mishaps of the Americans.

[443] For example, "US Aircraft Industry Can Double Output," *Santa Cruz Sentinel,* Santa Cruz, California, January 13, 1939, 4.

Information Activities from January to June 1953 and a dedicated participant of the American Friends of Russian Freedom Inc.[444]

In his last years, Rogers pursued the possibility of publishing his journal, which was "written in ink and pencil on paper of poor quality which has deteriorated."[445] In 1957, he prepared an edited version he titled "Tsar, Revolution, Bolsheviks." This excluded "purely personal comments as well as references by name to the National City Bank of New York, . . . on the staff of whose Petrograd Branch I worked in Russia."[446] As footnoted earlier in this book, Rogers removed the references to Jews he made in his original journal.

Rogers never married. His last home was in Greenwich, Connecticut, where he lived with his sister, Edith. Leighton Rogers died in West Haven, Connecticut, on January 27, 1962. He never published his journal.

LEIGHTON ROGERS' FIVE COLLEAGUES WHO SAILED WITH HIM ON THE SS OSCAR II

Rogers was one of the six young men who graduated from the National City Bank training program and sailed together for assignment in Petrograd on September 28, 1916. Their paths diverged in 1918. Rogers joined the US Army in London, Edward Babcock exited Russia via Vladivostok, and Rogers' four other "batch mates" left Petrograd in March 1918 to work in Vologda until August, and then returned to the United States via Scandinavia in September 1918.

Rogers impishly shared his first impressions of his colleagues in a letter to some friends back home.[447]

Chester "Count" T. Swinnerton (1894–1960) graduated from Harvard before joining National City Bank. He continued to work for NCB in South America for three decades. In 1921, he moved to Havana, Cuba, and several years later moved to Mexico City, Mexico. Later, he worked in Medellin, Colombia, and in Caracas, Venezuela, where he was branch manager. The bank promoted him to resident vice

---

[444] "Russian Friends Change Name," *New York Times*, November 17, 1952, 16. The purpose of the organization was to "Assert the friendship of the American People for the Russian People, as distinct from the Russian Government."
[445] Foreword to "Tsar, Revolution, Bolsheviks," Leighton W. Rogers Papers, Box 3, Folder 7, Library of Congress.
[446] Letter of Leighton Rogers to the John Simon Guggenheim Foundation, written sometime after August 25, 1959. Charlotte Roe, the grandniece of Leighton Rogers, provided the original copy of this letter to the author.
[447] "Letter from Leigh Rogers," November 23, 1916, *Class of 1916 of Dartmouth College: First Annual Report, 1917*, 82–83. A copy of this letter is also found in Leighton W. Rogers Papers, Box 1, Folder 2, Library of Congress. Rogers added, "They are all good boys, though, and I suppose, at that, I'm the queerest one of the bunch."

president in 1949, and he retired shortly thereafter. In an account Swinnerton wrote during the 1917 March Revolution, he declared, "The whole affair was no sudden unreasoning uprising. The people had simply reached their limit."[448] Rogers puckishly described Swinnerton sporting a "mustache, goatee, and 'so help me God' expression."

Frederick "Fred" Gilbert Sikes Jr. (1893–1957) continued to work for NCB in Antwerp, Belgium, from 1919 to 1929, and afterward for many years in New York. He retired as an assistant vice president in 1955. Rogers called Sikes "a very likeable kid, in spite of the fact that he has been sheltered all his life from the cruel world, especially in his four years of college at the Country Club at Princeton, and the fact that he would rather have a Japanese valet than a wife."

Edward "Bab" Howard Babcock Jr. (1894–1976) graduated from Columbia University. He was also a Psi Upsilon fraternity brother of Rogers. He left Petrograd by a Trans-Siberian train (which he, Boies C. Hart, and eight other NCB colleagues who traveled with him nicknamed the "Express Get-Away")[449] on February 25, 1918, and arrived in Yokohama, Japan, on March 25. Babcock worked for the International Banking Corporation in Kobe, Japan, until October 1919 and returned to San Francisco in November. If we are to take Rogers at his roguish words, Babcock was "an intellectual Victorian china doll, unable to give birth to an original thought even with the aid of all the Twilight Sleep powders this side of the meridian of Greenwich."

Charles "Chuck" Moore Stuart (1896–1923) died young of appendicitis. In a captivating letter from Petrograd on December 29, 1917, Stuart wrote, "The future is all uncertainty and this is the hardest part of the situation. A great nation is breaking up through treason, treachery, anarchy, falsehood and everything else that is vile and it is not pleasant to be a spectator of the tragedy. I have not lost faith in Russia, however, and am looking for the time when the real Russian people will rise and take over the destinies of their own people from the gang now in control."[450] On December 20, 1918, he wrote in his Lake Forest College alma mater magazine, *The Stentor*, that "the Bolsheviks have nothing and want to share it with everybody else." Stuart continued to work for NCB and transferred to South America in 1920. Rogers called him a "funny little cuss with a mania for figures and statistics, whose idea of a good time is to read the report of the United States Steel Corporation."

[448] C.T. Swinnerton, letter, March 12, 1917, 1, File XX073-10.V. Hoover Institution Archives, Stanford University.
[449] The story of Babcock's one-month journey out of Russia is recounted in *Number Eight*, The National City Bank of New York, September 1918, 37–43.
[450] "Local Man Sees Hope for Russia if People Rise," *Grand Rapids Press*, Grand Rapids, MI, February 23, 1918, 12.

William Wilson Welsh (1889–1972) graduated from the University of Michigan before he joined National City Bank. Welsh gave his take on the events of the March Revolution: "I have come through the greatest revolution in the history of the world, well, and happy to have had the experience."[451] He returned to New York after Russia, but in June 1919, NCB sent Welsh, along with a colleague, Roger Smith, to Finland to try to re-enter Russia to "take advantage of every opportunity that presented itself to protect our Russian interests." They predicated their plan on anti-Bolshevik White Russian forces retaking Petrograd, which didn't happen, and thus returned, unsuccessful, to New York in December 1919.[452] Welsh continued with National City Bank until 1923 and was an eyewitness raconteur who contributed to the internal report NCB prepared in 1922. Welsh testified at hearings on Bolshevik propaganda held by the Subcommittee of the Committee on the Judiciary in Washington DC in February 1919. He described the disarray in Russia in 1918, stating, "A person that comes out of Russia and who has been out of Russia one month is not in a position to state what is the condition in Russia at the present time," and the state of banking in Russia as "literal chaos."[453] Rogers described Welsh as "A second Jack English, who has worked hard all his young life, a good student, and very practical."

OTHER COLLEAGUES OF LEIGHTON ROGERS

John Louis Hilton (L. H.) Fuller (1894–1962) graduated from Butler University in Indiana. A week after he left Russia, Fuller exclaimed, "It was a great relief to be finally out of Russia; a greater relief than I for one had realized would be the case before getting out."[454] Fuller then worked with the International Banking Corporation in Scandinavia and England for a year and a half.[455] Afterward, he returned to his native Indianapolis, where he continued his professional life as a businessman and insurance executive.

Henry A. Koelsch Jr. (1890–1938) graduated from Dartmouth in 1914. He married in November 1918 and on December 1, 1918, sailed with his new wife to Vladivostok, where he became the agent of NCB's short-lived Vladivostok agency. In the mid-1920s, he worked in Great Britain and became the manager of the bank's

---

451 "Revolution is Described," *The South Bend Tribune*, South Bend, IN, July 18, 1917, 8.
452 *History of the operations of the Petrograd and Moscow Branches*, June 12, 1919, 30.
453 *Hearings on Bolshevik Propaganda*, 271 and 280 (testimony of William W. Welsh, National City Bank officer).
454 *The Journal of John L. H. Fuller*, September 13, 1918, 86.
455 Ibid., Biographical Sketch.

West End London branch for six years. In June 1931, the bank promoted him to vice president, and he took charge of NCB's two branches in London. He took his own life "while of unsound mind" in London on January 18, 1938.[456]

Boies Chittenden Hart (1885–1946) graduated from the University of Michigan in 1907. He was also a Psi Upsilon fraternity brother of Rogers. After leaving Russia, Hart worked in NCB's São Paulo, Brazil, branch as a submanager, gradually rose through the ranks in the South America division, and took charge of it from 1927 to 1931. A year later, the bank appointed him to lead the Far Eastern division, which he did until 1943. Hart died in New York City in 1946.

Enevold O. Detlefsen (1882–1954) was born in Denmark. He joined the staff of NCB in the summer of 1916 as an accountant. He later worked for Chemical Bank and Trust Company in the United States.

LEIGHTON ROGERS' BOSSES

H. (Harry) Fessenden Meserve (1867–1941). The troubles that NCB underwent in Russia did not affect Meserve's later career. In 1918, he worked from his Tudor-style mansion-like home on 1825 R Street in Washington DC. In January 1919, Meserve assumed new responsibilities as vice president in Europe, based in Paris. His wife, Helen, died suddenly in Paris on April 18, 1919. In November that year, his step-daughter Lascelle married Nicolas de Basily, the councilor of the Russian Embassy in Paris representing the anti-Bolshevik Omsk government.[457] Meserve lived in Paris until 1939 but vacationed every winter in Venice, Florida, where he had a reputation as an avid hunter and fisherman. He also served as the president of the Farnsworth Woolen Mill in Maine and officer of several other woolen concerns in Maine and New Hampshire. Meserve died in Sarasota, Florida, on April 4, 1941.

Robie Reed (R.R.) Stevens (1884–1945). Stevens' obituary recounted a sad postscript to his experience in Russia: "He returned with an illness from which he never recovered," and "though under threat of death and torture and in prison for weeks, he refused to surrender to the Bolshevists the keys to the vaults of the Russian branch of the National City Bank of New York, entrusted to him; inspiring example

---

[456] "Death of Banker Termed Suicide," *Times-Union*, Albany, NY, January 21, 1938, 20.
[457] Witold S. Sworakovski, "The Authorship of the Abdication Document of Nicholas II," *The Russian Review* 30, no. 3 (July 1971): 277–86; De Basily, *Memoirs of a Lost World*, 134–35. Nicolas de Basily served at the Russian army general headquarters in Mogilev as director of the diplomatic chancellery of Tsar Nicholas II when the tsar abdicated. De Basily, not the tsar himself, drafted the tsar's abdication document.

of steadfast devotion to duty, a devotion that led to many years of ill health but that never touched his spirit ... "[458] In a signed affidavit that was part of litigation in which the bank was involved in 1923 (The National City Bank of New York vs. W.R. Grace & Co.), former NCB Petrograd branch accountant George Link declared, "During the Summer of 1919, the said Robie R. Stevens suffered a nervous breakdown. . . . His health is so precarious that he has not been able to give any continuous attention to business matters since he went to Arizona [in November 1920]. Most of his letters have not been written in his own handwriting and some of his more recent letters have not been signed by him." In 1941, his alma mater, Bowdoin College (he graduated in 1906 and was also a member of the Psi Upsilon fraternity), granted him an honorary master of arts degree. Stevens died in Altadena, California on August 2, 1945. There is no historical evidence supporting the quoted obituary's statement that Stevens was imprisoned for weeks.

NATIONAL CITY BANK LEADERSHIP IN NEW YORK

Frank A. Vanderlip (1864–1937). After he resigned from the National City Bank of New York, Frank Vanderlip remained engaged in national and international affairs. 1922, he wrote a follow-up book, *What Next in Europe?* to his earlier *What Happened in Europe?* Vanderlip promoted friendly business relations with Japan from 1919 to 1924. During the Teapot Dome scandal hearings in 1924, Vanderlip "entered upon a 'moral war' against corruption in public office"[459] and organized the Citizens Federal Research Bureau to investigate graft. In 1933, Vanderlip fought for the repeal of Prohibition and the Eighteenth Amendment. He later served as a trustee of the Carnegie Foundation, the Massachusetts Institute of Technology, and the Scarborough School, and received France's decoration of Chevalier of the Legion of Honor. Vanderlip died on June 29, 1937, at age 72. He deserves recognition as a visionary in the world of banking. Besides contributing to the founding of the Federal Reserve System and supporting the war bond savings stamp program used in both world wars, Vanderlip unceasingly argued for international engagement and "predicted and warned against a world catastrophe unless the post-war problems were solved on a basis of sound economics and American

---

[458] "Courage, Loyalty of Late Robie R. Stevens Extolled," *Metropolitan Pasadena Star-News*, Pasadena, CA, August 11, 1945, 9–10; https://library.bowdoin.edu/arch/college-history-and-archives/honors/stevens41.pdf.
[459] "Frank Vanderlip, Banker, Dies at 72," *New York Times*, June 30, 1937, 23.

participation."[460] His consummate leadership contributed to Citi becoming the global financial institution it is today.

Samuel McRoberts (1868–1947). McRoberts took a leave of absence from National City Bank on November 8, 1917, to join the Ordnance Bureau of the US Department of War. Some contend that he left the day after the Bolshevik Revolution because of his involvement in Russia. McRoberts rose to the rank of brigadier general and was sent to France. He received the United States Army Distinguished Service Medal and, like Vanderlip and Rogers, was made a Chevalier of the Legion of Honor by the French government. He returned to NCB in January 1919 and retired in January 1920. In 1921, he became president of the Metropolitan Trust Company of New York, a position he held until 1925. He then was chairman of the board of Chatham Phenix National Bank and Trust Company until 1932. McRoberts served on the boards of directors of several financial institutions and other companies, including the American Sugar Refining Company and the Chicago, Milwaukee & St. Paul Railway. He also was a trustee of Baker University, his alma mater. McRoberts resided in Mt. Kisco, New York, in his last years. He died in New York City on September 8, 1947.[461]

Charles V. Rich (1882–1951). Charles Rich met Frank Vanderlip in 1897, when he became a private secretary to Vanderlip during Vanderlip's tenure as assistant secretary of the Treasury. In World War I, Rich worked with the Liberty Loan Board. He retired from National City Bank as an executive manager in June 1921. Rich kept in close contact with his NCB colleagues in the years to follow. He sailed on a steamer from France to New York in October 1924, along with H. Fessenden Meserve. He died in New York City on January 3, 1951.

---

[460] Ibid.
[461] Sharon Tomback, "The North Castle Estate of Brigadier-General Samuel McRoberts," *The North Castle Historical Society* 40 (2013): 10-12. https://www.northcastleny.com/sites/g/files/vyhlif3581/f/file/file/north_castle_history_vol_40_-_2013_0.pdf; "Samuel M'Roberts Quits National City," *New York Times*, January 14, 1920, 20.

ABOUT THE AUTHOR

S teven Fisher is a career emerging markets finance professional and worked for thirty-five years with Citibank, including sixteen years in the former Soviet Union in senior leadership positions in Moscow and Kyiv.

Steven Fisher has spoken regularly at finance and policy forums across the world and lectured at universities in the markets which he served. He received a Master of Science degree in Foreign Service from Georgetown University and Bachelor of Arts degree from Cornell University. He speaks fluent Russian. *Into Russia's Cauldron* is his first book.

ACKNOWLEDGMENTS

I found Leighton Rogers by pure chance, and this book is the culmination of that exciting discovery. One blustery winter day in Kyiv—it was February 26, 2017—I sat down to my weekly read of the Sunday *New York Times*. Perusing the Books section, I spied a review of a new volume on Russia by Helen Rappaport, titled *Caught in the Revolution*. Anything about Russia would grab my attention, and as I read, I learned that one of the historical individuals of whom she wrote was a young American bank clerk who had worked for National City Bank in Petrograd. Fascinating! Actually, I was also a little perturbed. How could I, or any of my Citibank colleagues in Russia, never have heard of this person? That year was the centenary anniversary of Citibank in Russia, not to mention of two Russian revolutions. True, Citibank did not operate in Russia for the entire 100 years; it was absent between 1920 and 1992, except for a short-lived representative office in Moscow from 1974 to 1980. Nevertheless, the bank planned several events to celebrate this milestone, which made this discovery even more compelling to investigate. The more I learned about Leighton Rogers, the more struck I was by the many coincidences between his life and mine. I lived in Kyiv and experienced firsthand the Ukrainian Revolution of Dignity fought in the winter of 2014. My house was located only four kilometers from the center of the protests in Maidan Square and in the last, most bloody and decisive week of the revolution, every night from my bedroom window I heard the nerve-racking staccato cracking of machine guns and booming of explosives. The lyrics of the *Talking Heads'* song *Life During Wartime* suddenly felt *much* more personal. Having witnessed a revolution myself, I committed to learn about my "predecessor" and understand how he endured his.

My first stop was the Library of Congress in Washington, DC. Leighton Rogers' family had donated his papers to the library after his death in 1962. There, several dusty boxes awaited me to reveal their contents: a stack of faded, fragile, fastidiously handwritten pages. My initial goal was to harvest some choice quotes of his excitedly gushing over National City Bank's business, along with some photos of Rogers, to pass to my colleague, Ruslan Belyaev, who was Citibank's St. Petersburg branch manager. Ruslan duly incorporated my find into Citibank's centennial brochure. After I returned to the United States, Professor Michael Khodarkovsky of Loyola University Chicago invited me to lecture about Leighton Rogers' experience to his Russian history class. Afterward, over a Vietnamese lunch at Le Colonial in Chicago's Gold Coast, he suggested transcribing and annotating the entire journal, making its unique and exciting story easily accessible to the public and academic community. Perfect idea for a first-time author, I thought.

Transcribing Rogers' handwritten journal of over two hundred pages was no simple task. Covid-19 made things more difficult, if not almost impossible, because the Library of Congress closed to the public. Lara Szypszak and Matthew Young, reference librarians of the manuscript and European divisions of the library respectively, came to the rescue. Lara scanned the material in the Leighton W. Rogers collection, enabling me to proceed without undeterminable delay. I am eternally grateful to Lara and Michael for their hard work and exceptional commitment. After several months of painstaking work, I completed the transcription. Fortunately for posterity and my eyesight, Leighton Rogers had good handwriting.

I realized there was a lot more to Rogers' story after reading his journal in entirety. His experience, so well-articulated, was but part of a larger, equally interesting saga: the mission of his employer, National City Bank, to become *the* preeminent bank in Russia. I thus reoriented my research in two directions, one comparing and corroborating the diaries and memoirs of other eyewitnesses to the revolutionary events Rogers experienced, and second, mining Citibank, US government, and other archives and sources, to reconstruct the decision-making process of National City Bank in Russia and the motives of the key actors behind it.

Special thanks go to Kerri Anne Burke, the global curator of the Citi Heritage Collection in New York, and her colleague, Lyann Starkweather. I thank Citi for access to past Citi publications and the diary of Boies C. Hart. Citi was not involved in preparation or approval of the published materials.

I would like to recognize Matt Holdzkom of the Indiana Historical Society for his help with the journal of Rogers' colleague, John L. H. Fuller; Laura R. Jolley, assistant director, manuscripts, of the Center for Missouri Studies, for diplomat Fred Dearing's diary; and Megan Browndorf, the Slavic and East European studies librarian of the University of Chicago Library, who located two hard-to-find Russian journal articles containing information on H. Fessenden Meserve and National City Bank. I thank Yang Hekang, my research assistant, a PhD candidate in the Department of History at Columbia University, for his expert navigation through the Frank A. Vanderlip Papers collection in Columbia University's Rare Book & Manuscript Library. Because of Covid-19, Columbia University had restricted access to its libraries to only its students and staff. Tara Craig, head of public services at Columbia University, came to the rescue and gave Hekang access to the Vanderlip Collection. I also thank the Hoover Institution Archives at Stanford University for providing Leighton Rogers' and Chester T. Swinnerton's written accounts of Russia's March Revolution.

Noteworthy university alumni records archivists who helped me unravel the backgrounds and fates of Rogers' colleagues include John Cross of Bowdoin College Alumni Records and Roberta Schwartz, research services archivist of the George J. Mitchell Department of Special Collections & Archives, Bowdoin College Library; Amanda Ferrara, public services project archivist of the Princeton University Special Collections Seeley G. Mudd Manuscript Library; Anne Thomason, associate director of the library and head of archives and special collections of the Donnelley and Lee Library, Lake Forest College; Cinda Nofziger, lead archivist, and Caitlin Moriarty, project archivist, of the Bentley Historical Library of the University of Michigan; and Donna Muoio, director of alumni relations at Poly Prep Country Day School. A great shout out to Jan Peter Wiborg and Tore Langholm of the Norway Heritage Community, two friendly Scandinavians who invaluably assisted me in accurately plotting Rogers' itinerary across the Atlantic Ocean in September–October 1916 and providing Norwegian and Swedish press articles that authenticated his train schedules from Christiania to Petrograd.

I would like to recognize Lyubov Ginzburg, whose 2010 PhD dissertation (University of Kansas) "Confronting the Cold War Legacy: The Forgotten History of the American Colony in St. Petersburg. A Case Study of Reconciliation," was the first academic work to cite Leighton Rogers. Ginzburg's work led me to Professor Stanislav Tkachenko of St. Petersburg State University, who in 1998 published a Russian monograph about National City Bank and American capital in Russia. Professor Tkachenko's research used the National City Bank documents and business diary of H. Fessenden Meserve seized by the Bolsheviks in 1919. Less than a month after I had reached out to Professor Tkachenko, by most fortuitous coincidence, he became acquainted with Ruslan Belyaev at an American Chamber of Commerce event in St. Petersburg. The professor graciously gifted a copy of his monograph (only 250 were published) to Ruslan on behalf of Citibank. Hassan Malik, thank you for sharing your research experience in Russia. I extend my greetings to your father. I thank Professor William Whisenhunt of College of DuPage for helping resolve a mystery involving John Reed and reviewing an early version of my manuscript. Richard Conn and Raymond Benson, I appreciate your helpful advice to a first-time author. And, Helen Rappaport, thank you for *Caught in the Revolution*. Would that we could have had a beer with Leighton back in the time.

I wish to express my great appreciation to my copy editor and proofreader Barbara Frye. Barbara's deep experience, razor-sharp eyes, and, I shall add, shared interest in this revolutionary adventure, proved indispensable.

Last but not least, I am deeply grateful to Charlotte Roe, the grandniece of Leighton Rogers. Charlotte is a retired American diplomat whose entry into the foreign service was in large part inspired by Rogers' escapades. Back in 2005, the US State Department Association for Diplomatic Studies and Training, Foreign Affairs Oral History Project, interviewed her. Without her interview being lodged in the public record, I never would have found her. Charlotte and her family's unique help over the last year addressed many unanswered questions about Rogers and his journal; the delight we shared talking about her great-uncle's adventures delivered the critical fuel to finish this work.

Leighton Rogers' last home was a two-bedroom apartment in a well-maintained prewar Tudor-style building named Chateau Lafayette in Greenwich, Connecticut. I grew up in Port Chester, New York, some three miles away. What a coincidence.

I would finally like to thank the continuing encouragement of my wife, Lucille, and my two daughters to see this project to completion.

Steven Fisher
Chicago, Illinois, 2021

BIBLIOGRAPHY

BOOKS:

Allison, William T. *American Diplomats in Russia: Case Studies in Orphan Diplomacy, 1916–1919*. Westport, CT: Praeger, 1997.

Allison, William T. *Witness to Revolution: The Russian Revolution Diary and Letters of J. Butler Wright*. Westport, CT: Praeger, 2002.

Bacino, Leo J. *Reconstructing Russia: US Policy in Revolutionary Russia, 1917–1922*. Kent, OH: Kent State University Press, 1999.

Barnes, Harper. *Standing on a Volcano: The Life and Times of David Rowland Francis*. St. Louis: Missouri Historical Society Press, 2001.

Bryant, Louise. *Russia Observed: Six Months in Red Russia*. New York: Arno Press, 1970. First published 1918 by George H. Moran Company (New York).

Buchanan, Meriel. *The City of Trouble*. New York: Charles Scribner's Sons, 1918.

Cleveland, Harold van B. and Huertas, Thomas F. *Citibank: 1812–1970*. Cambridge, MA: Harvard University Press, 1985.

Crosley, Pauline S. *Intimate Letters from Petrograd*. New York: E. P. Dutton & Company, 1920.

Davies, Robert Bruce. *Peacefully Working to Conquer the World, Singer Sewing Machines in Foreign Markets, 1854-1920*. New York: Arno Press, 1976.

De Basily, Lascelle Meserve. *Memoirs of a Lost World*. Stanford, CA: Hoover Institution Press, 1975.

De Fernandez-Azabal, Lilie. *The Countess From Iowa*. New York: G.P. Putnam's Sons, 1936.

De Robien, Louis. *The Diary of a Diplomat in Russia, 1917–1918*. New York: Praeger Publishers, 1970.

Dosch-Fleurot, Arno. *Through War to Revolution, Being the Experiences of a Newspaper Correspondent in War and Revolution 1914–1920*. London: John Lane and Bodley Head Limited, 1931.

Figes, Orlando. *A People's Tragedy: The Russian Revolution 1891–1924*. New York: Penguin Books, 1997.

Filene, Peter G. *Americans and the Soviet Experiment, 1917–1933*. Cambridge, MA: Harvard University Press, 1967.

Foglesong, David S. *America's Secret War Against Bolshevism: US Intervention in the Russian Civil War, 1917–1920*. Chapel Hill: The University of North Carolina Press, 1995.

Francis, David R. *Russia from the American Embassy: April 1916–November 1918*. New York: Charles Scribner's Sons, 1921.

Hasegawa, Tsuyoshi. *The February Revolution, Petrograd, 1917*. Leiden, The Netherlands: Koninklijke Brill NV, 2018.

Heald, Edward T. *Witness to Revolution: Letters from Russia 1916–1919*. Edited by James B. Gibney. Kent, OH: Kent State University Press, 1972.

Hicks, Granville with Stuart, John. *John Reed, The Making of a Revolutionary*. New York: The MacMillan Company, 1937.

Homberger, Eric with Biggart, John. *John Reed and the Russian Revolution: Uncollected articles, letters and speeches on Russia, 1917–1920*. New York: St. Martin's Press, 1992.

Homberger, Eric. *John Reed*. Manchester, UK: Manchester University Press, 1990.

Kennan, George F. *Soviet-American Relations, 1917–1920, Volume 1, Russia Leaves the War*. Princeton, NJ: Princeton University Press, 1956.

Kennan, George F. *Soviet-American Relations, 1917–1920, Volume 2, The Decision to Intervene*. Princeton, NJ: Princeton University Press, 1958.

Lebedev, Vyacheslav Vladimirovich / Лебедев, Вячеслав Владимирович. *Russo-American Economic Relations: 1900–1917/ Русско-американские экономические отношения: 1900–1917 гг. / Russko-Amerikanskie Ekonomicheskie Otnosheniia: 1900–1917*. Moscow, Russia: Izdatel'stvo "Mezhdunarodnye Otnosheniia"/ Издательство "Международные отношения," 1964.

Lees, Lorraine M. and Rodner, William S., eds. *An American Diplomat in Bolshevik Russia: DeWitt Clinton Poole*. Madison: University of Wisconsin Press, 2014.

Mack, Vicki A. *Frank A. Vanderlip: The Banker Who Changed America*. Palo Verdes Estate, CA: Pinale Press, 2013.

Malik, Hassan. *Bankers & Bolsheviks: International Finance & The Russian Revolution*. Princeton, NJ: Princeton University Press, 2018.

Mayer, Robert Stanley. *The Influence of Frank A. Vanderlip and the National City Bank on American Commerce and Foreign Policy, 1910–1920*. New York: Garland Publishing, 1987.

McFadden, David W. *Alternative Paths: Soviets and Americans 1917–1920*. New York: Oxford University Press, 1993.

Paléologue, Maurice. *An Ambassador's Memoirs*. 3rd ed. Vol. 3, (August 19, 1916–May 17, 1917). Translated by F.A. Holt. New York: George H. Doran Company, 1924.

Pinfold, John. *Petrograd 1917: Witnesses to the Russian Revolution*. Oxford, UK: Bodleian Library, 2017.

Pipes, Richard. *The Russian Revolution*. New York: Alfred A. Knopf, 1990.

Rappaport, Helen. *Caught in the Revolution*. New York: St. Martin's Press, 2017.

Reed, John. *Ten Days that Shook the World*. London: Penguin Books, 1977. First published 1919 by Boni & Liveright (New York).

Reed, John. *Red Russia: The Triumph of the Bolsheviki*. London: Workers' Socialist Press/Warwick Digital Collections, 1919.

Rogers, Leighton. *Wine of Fury*. New York: Alfred A. Knopf, 1924.

Ruhl, Arthur. *White Nights and Other Russian Impressions*. New York: Charles Scribner's Sons, 1917.

Saul, Norman E. *War and Revolution: The United States & Russia, 1914–1921*. Kansas: University Press of Kansas, 2001.

Stopford, Albert Henry. *The Russian Diary of an Englishman Petrograd, 1915–1917*. London: William Heinemann, 1919.

Strakhovsky, Leonid Ivan. *American Opinion About Russia 1917-1920*. Toronto, ON: University of Toronto Press, 1961.

Sutton, Anthony C. *Wall Street and the Bolshevik Revolution*. Cutchogue, NY: Buccaneer Books, 1974.

Tkachenko, Stanislav L./ Ткаченко, Станислав Л. *American Bank Capital in Russia in the Years of the First World War/ Американский банковский капитал в России в годы Первой мировой войны /Amerikanskii bankovskii capital v Rossii v gody Pervoi Mirovoi voiny*. St. Petersburg, Russia/ Санкт-Петербург, Россия: VIRD/ ВИРД, 1998.

Trotsky, Leon. *History of the Russian Revolution*. Reprint, Chicago: Haymarket Books, 2008.

Vanderlip, Frank A, in collaboration with Boyden Sparkes. *From Farm Boy to Financier*. New York: D. Appleton-Century, 1935.

White, Christine A. *British & American Commercial Relations With Soviet Russia, 1918–1924*. Chapel Hill: University of North Carolina Press, 1992.

Williams, Albert Rhys. *Journey Into Revolution: Petrograd 1917–1918*. Chicago: Quadrangle Books, 1969.

Winkler, John K. *The First Billion: The Stillmans and the National City Bank*. New York: Vanguard Press, 1934.

ARTICLES, ARCHIVES, PAPERS, DIARIES AND DOCUMENT COLLECTIONS:

Dearing, Fred Morris. Unpublished papers, The State Historical Society of Missouri.

Fuller, John Lewis Hilton. *The Journal of John L. H. Fuller While in Russia 1917*, ed. Samuel A. Fuller, Indiana Historical Society, TS 1999, MO112.

Ginzburg, Lyubov. *Confronting the Cold War Legacy: The Forgotten History of the American Colony in St. Petersburg*. PhD Dissertation, 2010, University of Kansas.

Hart, Boies C. *Petrograd, Rio, Peking and Points Between. A Memoir*. New York: Citi Heritage Collection, 1946(?).

McRoberts, Samuel. *Russia*. Address before the Seventh Annual Banquet, Boston Chapter, American Institute of Banking, Boston, Massachusetts, January 16, 1917, The Library of the University of California, Los Angeles.

Roberts, Priscilla. "Frank A. Vanderlip and the National City Bank During the First World War." *Essays in Economic & Business History* 20, no. 1 (2002).

Charlotte Roe, interview by Charles Stuart Kennedy, January 10, 2005, the Association for Diplomatic Studies and Training, Foreign Affairs Oral History Project. https://www.adst.org/OH%20TOCs/Roe,%20Charlotte.toc.pdf.

Rogers, Leighton William. *An Account of the March Revolution, 1917*, Leighton W. Rogers Collection, Hoover Institution Archives, Stanford University.

Rogers, Leighton William. Unpublished journal 1916–1919, box 1; unpublished manuscript titled "Tsar, Revolution, Bolsheviks," box 3; photographs and news clippings, Leighton W. Rogers Papers, 1912–82, Library of Congress, Washington, DC. https://lccn.loc.gov/mm97083974.

Rogers, Leighton William. "Letter of Leigh Rogers, Petrograd, Russia, November 23, 1916," *Class of 1916 of Dartmouth College, First Annual Report, 1917*, Rauner Special Collections Library DC. History (1916 Class Report), Dartmouth College, Hanover, New Hampshire.

Ruhl, Arthur. *Russia Revisited*, typescript. September 1925. Hoover Institution Archives, Stanford University.

Swinnerton, Chester T. Letter from Petrograd, March 27/12, 1917. File XX073-10.V, Hoover Institution Archives, Stanford University.

Tuve, Jeanette E. "Changing Directions in Russian-American Economic Relations, 1912–1917." *Slavic Review* 31, no. 1 (March 1972).

Vanderlip, Frank A. Papers. Columbia University Rare Book and Manuscript Library, Butler Library, Columbia University, 535 West 114th St, New York, New York.

THE NATIONAL CITY BANK OF NEW YORK:

Number Eight internal employee magazines 1915–1920. The National City Bank of New York. Citi Heritage Collection, New York.

History of the operations of the Petrograd and Moscow Branches of The National City Bank of New York, compiled during January and February 1922, from material available in New York. February 20, 1922. Box RG12/Bank Histories, Citi Heritage Collection, New York.

Russia and the Imperial Russian Government. The National City Bank of New York. June 13, 1916.

Kies, William Samuel. *Opportunities for Young Men in the Foreign Field.* Address before the Senior Class of Yale University, March 1916. New York: The National City Bank of New York, 1916.

UNITED STATES CONGRESS:

US Senate Subcommittee of the Committee on the Judiciary. *Hearings on Bolshevik Propaganda.* 65th Cong., third session and thereafter. February 11, 1919, to March 10, 1919, Washington, DC: Government Printing Office, 1919.

US Senate Special Committee on Investigation of the Munitions Industry. *Report on Existing Legislation.* 74th Cong., second session, Report No. 944, Part 5. Washington, DC: Government Printing Office, 1936.

INDEX

Printed in Great Britain
by Amazon